LIVY

V

BOOKS XXI—XXII

233

LIVY

IN FOURTEEN VOLUMES

V

BOOKS XXI—XXII

WITH AN ENGLISH TRANSLATION BY

B. O. FOSTER, PH.D.
OF STANFORD UNIVERSITY

CAMBRIDGE, MASSACHUSETTS
HARVARD UNIVERSITY PRESS

LONDON
WILLIAM HEINEMANN LTD

MCMLXXXII

American ISBN 0–674–99256–3
British ISBN 0 434 99233 X

First printed 1929
Reprinted 1948, 1953, 1957, 1963, 1969, 1982

Printed in Great Britain by
Fletcher & Son Ltd, Norwich

CONTENTS

TRANSLATOR'S PREFACE

At the beginning of the Middle Ages there were extant three copies of the Third Decade, though two of these [1] contained only the second half, Books XXVI.–XXX. The incomplete manuscripts subsequently disappeared, but we still have the one that included the whole Decade, and is known as the Puteanus (= Codex Parisinus 5730 = *P*).

This famous codex was revised (in the sixth century) at Abellinum (the modern Avellino), near Naples, as appears from the subscription after several of the books: *recognobi* (for *recognovi*) *abellini*. Precisely when or where the book was originally written is not known, but it is now assigned to the fifth century. Early in the Carolingian period it came into the possession of the abbey library at Corbie in Picardy, where many copies of it were made.[2] In the second half of the sixteenth century it was acquired by Claude Dupuy (Claudius Puteanus), a jurisconsult and book-collector of Paris, whose son Jacques bequeathed it, along with the rest of his ancient manuscripts, to the King; and since 1657 it has been one of the treasures of the

[1] The Spirensis and the Turin palimpsest. Something will be said of these two MSS. in the preface to Vol. VII (Books XXVI.–XXVII.).

[2] Traube, Bamberger Fragmente, p. 16.

Bibliothèque nationale. In 1907 the Department of Manuscripts of this library issued a facsimile reproduction of the Puteanus, considerably reduced in size.[1] The manuscript is a large quarto containing 470 leaves of fine parchment, measuring 235 × 278 millimetres. The writing is in the uncial character. There are two columns to the page, of 26 lines each. Originally there were 65 gatherings of 8 leaves each, except gatherings 43 and 45, which had 6 each. Of these gatherings 1, 2, 4 and 64 have been lost, as well as leaves 2–7 of the 3rd, and the following sections of the text are consequently missing:

XXI. i. 1. (*in parte*)—xx. 8 (*auro cu-*).
xxi. 13. (*Carthagini*)—xxix. 6 (*adfirmantes in*).
xxx. 11. (*posse Poenus*)—xli. 13 (*vobis et*).
XXX. xxx. 14. (*ceteris*)—xxxvii. 3 (*haberent domitos*).
xxxviii. 2. (*-niensibus*)—xlv. 7 (*ceperunt*).

The scribe who wrote the Puteanus made a large number of corrections (distinguished in the critical notes by the symbol P^1) of his own text as he proceeded with the task of transcription. Many others are due to a second hand (P^2), and a very few to a third (P^3). From the forms of the letters employed and the colour of the ink it is almost always possible to refer these corrections to their respective scribes. The corrections were not derived from other manuscripts than *P*'s exemplar, but originated with the scribes themselves,[2] and the manuscript is not interpolated.

[1] The title-page is not dated. I am indebted to the brief introduction by H[enri] O[mont] for the description of the book.

[2] Luchs, Praef. (1888) v.–vi.

Of the other manuscripts now existing which have the text of Books XXI.–XXV. there is none which is not (directly or through one or more intermediaries) derived from *P*, and none, therefore, which possesses any value for establishing the text of these books, except for those passages at the beginning of Book XXI. where the evidence of *P* has been destroyed by the mutilation of the manuscript. To supply the place of the missing leaves editors avail themselves of two later codices, the Colbertinus and the Mediceus.

The Colbertinus (=Parisinus 5731=*C*) is a minuscule manuscript of the tenth or eleventh century, and is thought to be a direct copy of the Puteanus.

The Mediceus (=Mediceus Laurentianus LXIII. 20=*M*) is also a minuscule manuscript and was written in the eleventh century. It was formerly believed to have been copied from the Vaticanus Reginensis 762 (=*R*),[1] and inasmuch as this MS. was copied from *P*—late in the eighth century or early in the ninth[2]—it would be superfluous to cite the readings of *M*, were it not that the first and last parts of *R* are wanting and its existing text begins at XXII. vi. 5 (*veluti caeci*) and ends at XXX. v. 7 (*continua complexus*), and all that comes between is found in *P* itself. *R* is therefore of no use in constituting the text,[3] but *M*, if a copy of *R*, would

[1] Luchs, Prolegomena to edition of 1879, p. lviii.

[2] Rand and Howe argue plausibly for a date prior to the coming of Alcuin to Tours in 796.

[3] *R* is nevertheless interesting (1) as providing a means of tracing the vicissitudes of a Latin text in the process of transcription from an uncial MS. of the fifth century into the early Caroline minuscule, and (2) as being a striking

be a valuable witness (at second hand) to the text of *P* at the beginning and the end of the Third Decade, where both *P* and *R* are defective. Within recent years the statement that *R* was *M*'s exemplar has been called in question,[1] but at the same time it has been shown that the scribe of *M*—whatever his exemplar may have been—had access to the Puteanus, whose text he often reproduced, sometimes rightly, sometimes wrongly, where the scribe of *R* had departed from it.[2] Since, therefore, *M* is directly in the tradition of the Puteanus, it must continue to be given consideration—along with *C*—by the editor of Livy, whose business it is to reconstruct, as far as possible, the text which was contained on the missing leaves of *P*.

The Puteanus then and, where the Puteanus is defective, the Colbertinus and the Mediceus are the MSS. on which editors found the text of Books XXI.–XXV. The text of this volume (XXI. and XXII.) is based chiefly on the apparatus in the critical edition of August Luchs, Berlin, 1888, supplemented by the appendices to Rossbach's revision (1921[10]) of the Weissenborn-Müller edition (with

---

landmark in the history of eighth and ninth century calligraphy and the Scriptorium of Tours. In the former aspect it has been studied minutely by F. W. Shipley and in the latter by E. K. Rand and George Howe (see Bibliography).

[1] F. W. Shipley (*Studies*, p. 475) holds that Luchs's statement of the relationship between *R* and *M* needs modification; and R. S. Conway (*The Sources of the Text*, etc., p. 11) declares that evidence has been collected which shows quite certainly that *M* was not copied from *R* or *C*.

[2] Shipley p. 416 ff.; Conway, *ibid.*

German notes) of XXI., and to the Weissenborn-Müller edition of XXII. (1905 [9]), and here and there by notes and suggestions from other sources. I have aimed to inform the reader in the footnotes at every point where the reading in the text is not found either in *P* or—where *P* is wanting—in *M* or *C*, except in a few places where the correction seemed obvious and certain. The spelling conforms to that adopted (from the Oxford edition of Books I.–X. by Conway and Walters) for Volumes I.–IV. For the punctuation I must myself assume the responsibility, and hope it may prove more helpful to English and American readers than the German system, which has too often made its way into classical texts edited primarily for use elsewhere than in Germany.

In the brief Bibliography I have listed a few of the multitude of books and articles useful for the understanding of Livy. My choice has been guided by two considerations: I wished first to put the reader who is beginning the study of Livy into touch with some of the recent work on his history, and more especially the Third Decade, and the various questions as to sources, style, antiquities, etc. arising in connection with it; and secondly, to list the books that have been of most assistance to me in preparing my own text and translation. To this general acknowledgment I would add a special word of appreciation of the help I have received from the various English translations and editions, from one or another of which I have sometimes borrowed a phrase or turn of expression.

To Messrs. H. Wagner and E. Debes, of Leipzig, I am very grateful for their courteous permission to continue to adapt for the Loeb Livy the series of maps and plans in the Kromayer-Veith *Schlachten-Atlas zur antiken Kriegsgeschichte.* Thanks to the learned labours of Professor Kromayer and the generosity of his publishers, the present edition of Books XXI. and XXII. may fairly boast of being better equipped in this respect than any of its elders. It is perhaps unnecessary to remind the reader that these maps were drawn to represent the facts, so far as ascertainable by a critical study of all the ancient sources and their modern interpreters and by examination of the ground itself, and may therefore sometimes be at variance with Livy's conception of the facts. A brief summary of the evidence for the conclusions adopted will be found in the letter-press accompanying the maps in the *Schlachten-Atlas*; it is presented at greater length in the *Antike Schlachtfelder* of the same authors.

B. O. F.

Stanford University,
May 15, 1929.

The third volume of the Oxford Livy (XXI.–XXV.), edited by the late Professor Walters and Professor Conway, whose preface is dated August 13, 1928, was published in August, 1929, after this volume had been passed for the press. Professor Conway now says (p. vii.) that it can be shown that *M* was copied directly from *P*.

BIBLIOGRAPHY[1]

I. General.—A. Klotz, (9), T. Livius, in Pauly-Wissowa, Real-Encyclopädie der classischen Altertumswissenschaft, 13[1], Stuttgart, 1926, 816–852 [*compact but comprehensive discussion of the various aspects of Livy's work, with running bibliography*].

II. Sources.—H. Peter, Historicorum Romanorum Reliquiae, volumen prius,[2] Lipsiae 1914 [*contains prolegomena on the Annales Maximi, private records, and the lives and writings of the annalists* (*pp.* i–cccLXXX), *and a collection of the fragments, with full apparatus and indices* (*pp.* 1–381)]; G. De Sanctis, Storia dei Romani, Vol. III. L'età delle guerre Puniche. Parte II. Torino, 1917 [*history of the War with Hannibal, with appendices containing—inter alia—critical analyses of the several books of Livy*]; A. Klotz, op. cit., 841–843 [*cites the principal books and articles in the course of his own summary discussion of the problem. It is now generally held that Livy made direct use of Polybius in Books* XXIV.–XLV., *but scholars differ as to the precise relationship between* XXI. *and* XXII., *and Polybius* III. *Their resemblance in subject-matter—and sometimes in minute details of treatment—at very many points in the narrative is variously accounted for:* (1) *Livy used Polybius directly for this as for later parts of his history* (*so F. Lachmann, E. Wölfflin, C. Peter, H. Hesselbarth, H. A. Sanders*); (2) *Livy*

[1] See also Vol. I., Introd., p. xxxv, for a few titles not repeated here.

used Polybius here indirectly through an intermediary (Q. Claudius Quadrigarius, according to W. Soltau, A. Postumius Albinus, acc. to H. Beloch, an epitomator of Polybius, acc. to O. Hirschfeld;[1] (3) *Livy and Polybius used common sources, especially Silenus (a Sicilian Greek who accompanied Hannibal and wrote an account of the war from the Carthaginian point of view) and Fabius Pictor—Polybius drawing upon these writers directly, and Livy through the intermediation of L. Coelius Antipater (so. C. Boettcher, U. Kahrstedt, and Klotz himself)*].

III. History.—U. Kahrstedt, Geschichte der Karthager von 218–146. Berlin, 1913. [*This is Volume* III. *of O. Meltzer's Geschichte der Karthager; the war with Hannibal occupies pp.* 363–575]; G. De Sanctis [*see under* II. Sources].

IV. Manuscripts.—[*See also the prefaces to the editions of Luchs and others.*] Histoire Romaine de Tite Live. Tomes I.–IV. Reproduction du manuscrit en onciale, Latin 5730 [*P*] de la Bibliothèque Nationale. Paris, [1907]; E. Chatelain, Paléographie des classiques latins. Neuvième livraison: Tite-Live. Paris, 1895 [*gives specimen pages in facsimile of P and M*]; F. W. Shipley, Certain Sources of Corruption in Latin Manuscripts, in Amer. Journ. of Archaeology, 7 (1903) 1–25, 157–197, 405–428 [*based on the comparison of P and R*]; idem, Studies in the MSS. of the Third Decade of Livy, in Class. Philol., 4 (1909) 405–419, 5(1910) 19–27; L. Traube, Bamberger Fragmenta der vierten Dek. des Livius. Anonymus Cortesianus. Mit 7 Tafeln (= Palaeographische Forschungen, vierter Teil = Abh. der K.

[1] De Sanctis, 178–180, also thinks that the "Polybian" sections of XXI. and XXII. are taken from some unknown annalist or annalists and not directly from Polybius.

Bayer. Akad. der Wiss., III. Kl., XXIV. Bd., I. Abt.), München, 1904 [*pp.* 16–17 *deal with the MSS. of the Third Decade*]; E. K. Rand and George Howe, The Vatican Livy and the Script of Tours, in Mem. of the Amer. Acad. in Rome, 1 (1917) 19–57 and plates 1–14 [*a study of Vaticanus Reginensis* 762]; F. W. Hall, Companion to Classical Texts. Oxford, 1913 [*plates VI and VII give on opposite pp. reduced facsimiles of P and the corresponding page of R*]; R. S. Conway, The Sources of the Text of Livy's Third Decade, in Proc. of The Camb. Phil. Soc. 127–129 (1924) 11 and 12.

V. Editions.—T. Livi ab urbe condita libri a vicesimo sexto ad tricesimum. rec. Augustus Luchs. Berolini, 1879 [*with elaborate prolegomena on the text of Books* XXVI–XXX]; T. Livi a.u.c. libri, apparatu critico adiecto ed. Augustus Luchs. Vol. III. libros XXI.–XXV. continens. Berolini, 1888; Vol. IV. libros XXVI.–XXX. continens. 1889 [*best critical edition of Third Decade*]; T. Livi a.u.c. libri, erklärt von Wilhelm Weissenborn und H. J. Müller [*The Third Decade occupies volumes* 4, 5, *and* 6. *The latest revisions of the several parts are as follows*: XXI. (*by Otto Rossbach*) Berlin, 1921^{10}; XXII. 1905^{9}; XXIII. 1907^{8}; XXIV. *and* XXV. 1895^{5}; XXVI. 1911^{5}; XXVII. *and* XXVIII. 1910^{4}; XXIX. *and* XXX. 1899^{4}]; Liber XXI. erkl. von Ed. Wölfflin (Sechste Aufl. besorgt von Franz Luterbacher). Leipzig, 1914; XXII. von Wölfflin, 1905^{4} [*Preface states that Wölfflin turned over the preparation of the fourth edition to Luterbacher*]; XXIII. Luterbacher, 1906^{2}; XXIV. H. J. Müller, 1901^{2}; XXV. H. J. Müller, 1879; XXVI. F. Friedersdorff, 1880; XXVII. Friedersdorff, 1881; XXVIII. Friedersdorff, 1883; XXIX. Luterbacher, 1893; XXX. Luterbacher, 1892;

Livy, Book XXI. ed. with introd. notes and maps by L. D. Dowdall, Cambridge, 1885; Book XXII., 1888; Books XXI., XXII. and XXIII. with introd. and notes by M. T. Tatham, Oxford, 1889; Book XXI., ed. by M. S. Dimsdale, Cambridge, 1888 [*revised ed.* 1912]; Book XXII., 1889; Il libro XXI. delle storie di Tito Livio. comm. da Enrico Cocchia, seconda edizione, Torino, 1906; XXII., 1916²; Livy, Books I., XXI. and XXII. ed. with introduction, commentary and illustrations by Emory B. Lease, Boston, 1914; Hannibal's Invasion of Italy, being Livy Books XXI., XXII., partly in the original and partly in translation, ed. by John Jackson, Oxford, 1924; Book XXIII., ed. by A. G. Peskett, Cambridge, 1917. Livy, Books XXIII. and XXIV. ed. by J. C. Macaulay, London, 1885; Titi Livii a.u.c. libri XXVI.–XXX. par O. Riemann et T. Homolle, Paris, 1909⁹ [*brief notes in French, with synopsis of the language, dictionary of names, and other helps*]; Livy, Book XXVII. ed. by S. G. Campbell, Cambridge, 1913; The close of the Second Punic War, being Livy, Books XXIX., XXX., partly in the original and partly in translation, ed. by H. E. Butler, Oxford, 1925.

VI. Translations.—The Romane Historie written by T. Livius of Padua . . . Translated out of Latine into English by Philemon Holland. London, 1600; The Roman History written in Latin by Titus Livius with the supplements of the learned John Freinshemius and John Dujatius . . . Faithfully done into English. London, 1686; The History of Rome by Titus Livius, translated from the original with notes and illustrations by George Baker. 6 volumes. London, 1797 [*reprinted* 1812 *and* 1833]; The History of Rome by Titus Livius, translated with introduction by Rev. Canon [W. M.] Roberts [6 *volumes, Everyman's Library, of which* III. *and* IV. *contain the Third Decade*]. London [1912–1924]; Livy, Books XXI.–XXV. Translated into English with notes by Alfred John Church and William Jackson Brodribb. London, 1883 [*reprinted* 1890].

VII. Topography.—S. B. Platner, The Topography and Monuments of Ancient Rome. Boston, 1911²; J. Kromayer, Antike Schlachtfelder [3 *volumes*]. Dritter Band, Italien und Afrika, von J. Kromayer u. G. Veith. Erste Abt.: Italien [*with* 10 *maps and* 35 *illustrations in text*] von J. K., Berlin, 1912; Zweite Abt.: Afrika [11 *maps,* 23 *illustrations and index to whole work*] von G. V., 1912 [*searching criticism of ancient and modern authorities, with personal examination of the ground*]; J. Kromayer und G. Veith, Schlachten-Atlas zur antiken Kriegsgeschichte. 120 Karten auf 34 Tafeln mit begleitendem Text. Leipzig, 1922–1929 [*to be completed in* 6 *parts, of which* 5 *have been issued; the* 1*st and* 2*nd contain the maps and letter-press dealing with the Second Punic War*]; J. E. Marindin, Hannibal's Route over the Alps, in Class. Rev., 13 (1899) 239–249 [*seeks to reconcile the accounts in Livy and Polybius, and declares for the Genèvre*]; W. Osiander, Der Hannibalweg. Berlin, 1900 [*argues for Mont Cenis—Napoleon's choice*]; Spencer Wilkinson, Hannibal's March through the Alps. Oxford, 1911 [*Col Clapier*]; G. De Sanctis, op. cit., 64–83 [*Mont Genèvre—follows the line of argument taken by Marindin*]; O. Viedebannt, Hannibal's Alpenübergang, in Hermes, 54 (1919) 337–386 [*Little St. Bernard*]; G. Terrell, Hannibal's Pass over the Alps, in Class. Journ., 17 (1922) 446 ff., 503 ff. [*Little St. Bernard*]; Cecil Torr, Hannibal Crosses the Alps. Cambridge, 1924 [*Col de la Traversette*].

VIII. Military Antiquities.—F. Luterbacher, Die römischen Legionen und Kriegsschiffe während des zweiten punischen Krieges. Burgdorf, 1895; Eugene S. McCartney, Warfare by Land and Sea (in Our Debt to Greece and Rome). Boston, 1923; Paul Couissin, Les armes individuelles du légionaire romain. Paris, 1926; F. Lammert, Römische Kriegskunst, in Pauly-Wissowa, Real-Encyclopädie, Supplement 4 (1924) 1060–1101; J. Kromayer und G. Veith, Heerwesen und Kriegsführung der Griechen und Römer. München, 1928.

IX. Political Antiquities.—A. H. J. Greenidge, Roman Public Life. London, 1901; Frank Frost Abbott, A History and Description of Roman Political Institutions. Boston, 1901.

X. Religious Antiquities.—W. Warde Fowler, The Roman Festivals of the Period of the Republic. London, 1899; Georg Wissowa, Religion und Kultus der Römer. München, 1912 ^{2}.

XI. Hannibal.—T. A. Dodge, Hannibal; a history of the art of war among the Carthaginians and Romans down to the battle of Pydna, 168 B.C., with a detailed account of the Second Punic war. Boston, 1891; W. O'Connor Morris, Hannibal, Soldier, Statesman, Patriot (Heroes of the Nations). New York and London, 1897; J. Kromayer, Hannibal als Staatsmann, in Historische Zeitschrift, 103 (1909) 237–273; [Thomas] Lenschau, (8) Hannibal, in Pauly-Wissowa, 7^{2} (1912) 2323–2351; H. V. Canter, The Character of Hannibal, in Class. Journ. 24 (1929) 564–577.

XII. Scipio.—B. H. Liddell Hart, A Greater than Napoleon—Scipio Africanus. Boston, 1927; Werner Schur, Scipio Africanus und die Begründung der römischen Weltherrschaft. Leipzig, 1927; R. S. Conway, The Portrait of a Roman Noble, in Harvard Lectures on the Vergilian Age. Cambridge, 1928.

XIII. Style and Technique.—S. G. Stacey, Die Entwickelung des livianischen Stiles, in Archiv für lateinische Lexikographie und Grammatik, 10 (1898) 17–82 [*presents evidence to show that Books* XXI.–XLV. *differ in many points of style and diction from Books* I.–X.]; Ivo Bruns, Die Persönlichkeit in der Geschichtsschreibung der Alten. Untersuchungen zur Technik der antiken Historiographie. Berlin, 1898 [*the "indirect" mode of characterization employed by Livy, as contrasted with the "direct" mode of Polybius*]; K. Witte, Ueber die Form der Darstellung in Livius' Geschichtswerk, in Rheinisches Museum für Philologie, 65 (1910) 270–305, 369–419 [*a study of the "Einzelerzählung"—a working up of the material into vivid and dramatic episodes or "short stories"—in Livy*]; W. Kroll, Die Kunst des Livius, in Neue Jahrbücher für das klassische Altertum, 24 (1921) 97–108 [*discusses particularly Livy's art in the arrangement and presentation of his matter—largely illustrated from Book* II.]; Ragnar Ullmann, Les clausules métriques dans les discours de Salluste, Tite Live, Tacite. Symbolae Osloenses, 1925. 65–75 [*Sallust and Livy tend to prefer cadences in which the spondee is prominent, being frequently found in the next to the last foot*]; idem, La technique des discours dans Salluste, Tite Live et Tacite. La matière et la composition. Oslo, 1927 [*analysis of 141 speeches, including 90 in Livy, with a view to determining how far they are constructed in accord with ancient rhetorical theory and to showing how they are used in the portrayal of character*].

THE MANUSCRIPTS

P = Parisinus 5730 = Puteanus, 5th century.
C = Parisinus 5731 = Colbertinus, 10th century.
M = Mediceus Laurentianus LXIII. 20 = M, 11th century.
P^1, C^1, M^1 = a correction by the original scribe of *P*, *C*, or *M*.
P^2, P^3, etc. = corrections made by later hands.
ς = One or more of the inferior MSS. or early printed editions.
edd. = the early editors.
vulg. = the correction commonly adopted.

LIVY

FROM THE FOUNDING OF THE CITY

BOOK XXI

T. LIVI

AB URBE CONDITA

LIBER XXI

A.U.C. 536–553

I. In parte operis mei licet mihi praefari quod in principio summae totius professi plerique sunt rerum scriptores, bellum maxime omnium memorabile quae unquam gesta sint me scripturum, quod Hannibale duce Carthaginienses cum populo Romano gessere.
2 Nam neque validiores opibus ullae inter se civitates gentesque contulerunt arma, neque his ipsis tantum unquam virium aut roboris fuit, et haud ignotas belli artes inter sese[1] sed expertas primo Punico conferebant[2] bello, et adeo varia fortuna belli ancepsque Mars fuit ut propius periculum fuerint qui vicerunt.
3 Odiis etiam prope maioribus certarunt quam viribus, Romanis indignantibus quod victoribus victi ultro inferrent arma, Poenis quod superbe avareque crederent imperitatum victis esse.

[1] sese *C*: se (*by erasure from* sese) *M*.
[2] conferebant ς: conserebant *CM*.

---

[1] Thucydides began his history as follows: "Thucydides, an Athenian, wrote the history of the war which the Peloponnesians and Athenians waged against one another, beginning at its very outset, in the expectation that it

LIVY

FROM THE FOUNDING OF THE CITY

BOOK XXI

I. In this preface to a part of my history I may properly assert what many an historian has declared at the outset of his entire work,[1] to wit, that the war which I am going to describe was the most memorable of all wars ever waged—the war, that is, which, under the leadership of Hannibal, the Carthaginians waged with the Roman People. For neither have states or nations met in arms possessed of ampler resources, nor was their own might and power ever so great. Nor yet were they strangers to one another's modes of fighting, which the First Punic War had made them understand. And so variable were the fortunes of the war and so uncertain was its outcome that those who ultimately conquered had been nearer ruin. The animosity, too, with which they fought was almost greater than their strength: the Romans were enraged that the conquered should be actually drawing sword upon their conquerors; the Phoenicians, because they believed that the conquered had been treated with domineering arrogance and greed. B.C. 218–201

would be a great war and more worthy of relation than any that had preceded it."

A.U.C. 536–553

4 Fama est etiam Hannibalem annorum ferme novem
pueriliter blandientem patri Hamilcari ut duceretur
in Hispaniam, cum perfecto Africo bello exercitum
eo traiecturus sacrificaret, altaribus admotum tactis
sacris iure iurando adactum se cum primum posset
5 hostem fore populo Romano. Angebant ingentis
spiritus virum Sicilia Sardiniaque amissae; nam et
Siciliam nimis celeri desperatione rerum concessam
et Sardiniam inter motum Africae fraude Romanorum
stipendio etiam insuper imposito interceptam.

A.U.C. 513

II. His anxius curis ita se Africo bello, quod fuit
sub recentem Romanam pacem, per quinque annos,
ita deinde novem annis in Hispania augendo Punico
2 imperio gessit ut appareret maius eum quam quod
gereret agitare in animo bellum, et si diutius vixisset,
Hamilcare duce Poenos arma Italiae inlaturos fuisse,
quae[1] Hannibalis ductu intulerunt.

A.U.C. 517–525

3 Mors Hamilcaris peropportuna et pueritia Hannibalis distulerunt bellum. Medius Hasdrubal inter
patrem ac filium octo ferme annos imperium obtinuit,
flore aetatis, uti ferunt, primo Hamilcari conciliatus,
4 gener inde ob aliam indolem profecto animi adscitus,
et quia gener erat, factionis Barcinae[2] opibus, quae

A.U.C. 525–532

[1] quae ς: qui *CM*: cui *Heerwagen.*
[2] Barcinae *edd.*: barchinae *CM.*

---

[1] *i.e.* the western part of the island, which had been in the possession of the Carthaginians at the beginning of the First Punic War.

It is said moreover that when Hannibal, then B.C. 218-201 about nine years old, was childishly teasing his father Hamilcar to take him with him into Spain, his father, who had finished the African war and was sacrificing, before crossing over with his army, led the boy up to the altar and made him touch the offerings and bind himself with an oath that so soon as he should be able he would be the declared enemy of the Roman People. The loss of Sicily and B.C. 241 Sardinia was a continual torture to the proud spirit of Hamilcar. For he maintained that they had surrendered Sicily[1] in premature despair, and that the Romans had wrongfully appropriated Sardinia—and even imposed an indemnity on them besides—in the midst of their African disturbances.

II. Tormented by these thoughts, he so bore B.C. 237-229 himself in the African War, which followed hard upon the Roman peace and lasted for five years, and likewise afterwards, during the nine years he spent in Spain in extending the Punic empire, that it was plain to see that he meditated a more important war than the one he was engaged in, and that if his life had been prolonged, the Phoenicians would have invaded Italy under the leadership of Hamilcar, as they did in fact under that of Hannibal.

Hamilcar's very timely death and the boyhood B.C. 229-222 of Hannibal delayed the war. In the interval betwixt father and son, the supreme command devolved, for about eight years, on Hasdrubal. It was his youthful beauty, they say, that won for him in the first instance the favour of Hamilcar, who subsequently selected him, no doubt for other, that is mental, qualifications, to be his son-in-law. As such—through the influence of the Barcine

A.U.C. 525–532
apud milites plebemque plus quam modicae erant,
haud sane voluntate principum in imperio positus.
5 Is plura consilio quam vi gerens hospitiis magis
regulorum conciliandisque per amicitiam principum
novis gentibus quam bello aut armis rem Cartha-
6 giniensem auxit. Ceterum nihilo ei pax tutior fuit;
barbarus eum quidam[1] palam ob iram interfecti[2] ab
eo domini obtruncavit[3]; comprensusque ab circumstantibus haud alio quam si evasisset vultu tormentis
quoque cum laceraretur, eo fuit habitu oris ut superante laetitia dolores ridentis etiam speciem prae-
7 buerit. Cum hoc Hasdrubale, quia mirae artis in
sollicitandis gentibus imperioque suo iungendis
fuerat, foedus renovaverat populus Romanus, ut finis utriusque imperii esset amnis Hiberus Saguntinisque mediis inter imperia duorum populorum libertas servaretur.

A.U.C. 528

A.U.C. 533

III. In Hasdrubalis locum haud dubia res fuit quin praerogativa militaris, qua extemplo iuvenis Hannibal in praetorium delatus imperatorque ingenti omnium clamore atque adsensu appellatus erat, a senatu comprobaretur. Favor[4] plebis sequebatur.

[1] quidam C^2M^3: quidam quidam C^1: quidam qui M^1.
[2] interfecti M^3: interfecit *CM*.
[3] obtruncavit ς: obtruncati CM^1: obtruncat M^3.
[4] erat, a senatu comprobaretur. Favor *Rossbach*: erat favor *CM*.

---

[1] This was the war-party in Carthage, named for its leader Hamilcar Barca, which opposed the peace-at-any-price policy of the merchant-aristocracy.
[2] *i.e.* the treaty of 241 B.C. (*Per.* XX. and Chap. xix. §§ 1–5).
[3] Saguntum (Murviedro) lay about midway between the Ebro and New Carthage (Cartagena). Livy does not mean

faction,[1] which was very strong with the soldiers and the common people—he was given the command, though the leading citizens had no liking for this step. Relying more often on policy than force, Hasdrubal enlarged the sway of Carthage rather by setting up friendly relations with the petty kings and winning over new tribes through the goodwill of their leaders than by war and arms. But he was not a whit more safe for being at peace. A certain barbarian slew him openly, to avenge his master, whom Hasdrubal had put to death. On being seized by the bystanders he expressed in his countenance the cheerfulness of one who had escaped, and even as he was being tortured, joy so got the upper hand of agony that he seemed actually to smile. With this Hasdrubal, because of the marvellous skill which he had shown in tempting the native tribes to join his empire, the Roman People had renewed their covenant,[2] with the stipulation that neither side should extend its dominion beyond the Ebro, while the Saguntines, situated between the empires of the two peoples,[3] should be preserved in independence. B.C. 229–222 B.C. 226

III. For Hasdrubal's successor there could be no question but that the choice originating with the soldiers—who immediately bore young Hannibal into the praetorium and with loud and universal acclamation hailed him general—would obtain the ratification of the senate. The approval of the B.C. 221

that it lay between the two "spheres of influence"—for it must, in that case, have occupied an island in the Ebro—but, vaguely, that the Carthaginians were still far to the south of it and the Romans had not yet approached it from the north.

A.U.C. 533
2 Hunc vixdum puberem Hasdrubal litteris ad se
accersierat; actaque res etiam in senatu fuerat.
Barcinis[1] nitentibus ut adsuesceret militae Hannibal
3 atque in paternas succederet opes, Hanno, alterius
factionis princeps, "Et aequum postulare videtur"
inquit "Hasdrubal, et ego tamen non censeo quod
4 petit tribuendum." Cum admiratione tam ancipitis
sententiae in se omnes convertisset, "Florem aetatis"
inquit "Hasdrubal, quem ipse patri Hannibalis
fruendum praebuit, iusto iure eum a filio repeti[2]
censet; nos tamen minime decet iuventutem
nostram pro militari rudimento adsuefacere libidini
5 praetorum. An hoc timemus, ne Hamilcaris filius
nimis sero imperia immodica et regni paterni speciem[3]
videat, et cuius regis genero hereditarii sint relicti
exercitus nostri, eius filio parum mature serviamus?
6 Ego istum iuvenem domi tenendum, sub legibus
sub magistratibus docendum vivere aequo iure cum
ceteris censeo, ne quandoque parvus hic ignis
incendium ingens exsuscitet."

IV. Pauci ac ferme optimus quisque Hannoni
adsentiebantur; sed, ut plerumque fit, maior pars
meliorem vicit. Missus Hannibal in Hispaniam
primo statim adventu omnem exercitum in se con-
2 vertit; Hamilcarem iuvenem redditum sibi veteres

[1] Barcinis *edd.*; barchinis *CM* (*also at chap.* ix. § 4, *chap.* x. § 4 *and elsewhere*).
[2] repeti C^1M^1: repetit *CM*.
[3] speciem ς: spem *CM*.

commons followed. The new commander had been summoned to Spain by Hasdrubal when a mere lad, and the matter had even been debated in the senate. The Barcine party were urging that Hannibal should become inured to warfare and succeed to the resources of his father, when Hanno, the leader of the other faction, addressed the House. "There is reason," said he, "in Hasdrubal's request, nevertheless I am opposed to granting it." When astonishment at a speech so inconsistent had attracted everybody's attention, he continued: "The youthful charms which Hasdrubal himself permitted Hannibal's father to enjoy he considers that he has the right to require again at the hands of the son. But that we should accustom our young men, by way of military training, to gratify the concupiscence of our generals is most unseemly. Or do we fear lest Hamilcar's son may too late behold the inordinate powers and the regal pomp which his father has set up? that the son of the king who left our armies as a legacy to his son-in-law may find us too slow in accepting him for our master? For my part, I think that the young man should be kept at home and taught to live in submission to the laws and the magistrates, upon an equal footing with the others, lest one day this small fire kindle a great conflagration." B.C. 221

IV. A few, and these included nearly all the best men, supported Hanno, but, as often happens, the larger party prevailed over the better. Hannibal was sent to Spain, where he was no sooner come than he won the favour of the entire army. The old soldiers thought that Hamilcar was restored to them as he had been in his youth; they beheld

A.U.C. 533 milites credere; eundem vigorem in voltu vimque in oculis, habitum oris lineamentaque intueri. Dein brevi effecit ut pater in se minimum momentum[1] ad
3 favorem conciliandum esset; nunquam ingenium idem ad res diversissimas, parendum atque imperandum, habilius fuit. Itaque haud facile discerneres
4 utrum imperatori an exercitui carior esset; neque Hasdrubal alium quemquam praeficere malle, ubi quid fortiter ac strenue agendum esset, neque
5 milites alio duce plus confidere aut audere. Plurimum audaciae ad pericula capessenda, plurimum consilii inter ipsa pericula erat; nullo labore aut
6 corpus fatigari aut animus vinci poterat; caloris ac frigoris patientia par; cibi potionisque desiderio naturali non voluptate[2] modus finitus; vigiliarum somnique nec die nec nocte discriminata tempora;
7 id quod gerendis rebus superesset quieti datum; ea neque molli strato neque silentio accersita; multi saepe militari sagulo opertum humi iacentem inter
8 custodias stationesque militum conspexerunt. Vestitus nihil inter aequales excellens; arma atque equi conspiciebantur. Equitum peditumque idem longe primus erat; princeps in proelium ibat, ultimus
9 conserto proelio excedebat. Has tantas viri virtutes ingentia vitia aequabant: inhumana crudelitas perfidia plus quam Punica, nihil veri nihil sancti, nullus deum metus nullum ius iurandum nulla
10 religio. Cum hac indole virtutum atque vitiorum

[1] momentum ς: monumentum *CM*.

[2] non voluptate ς: non uoluntate *CM*: voluntate *H. Sauppe.*

the same lively expression and piercing eye, the B.C. 221
same cast of countenance and features. But he soon brought it to pass that his likeness to his father was the least consideration in gaining him support. Never was the same nature more adaptable to things the most diverse—obedience and command. And so one could not readily have told whether he were dearer to the general or the army. When any bold or difficult deed was to be done, there was no one whom Hasdrubal liked better to entrust with it, nor did any other leader inspire his men with greater confidence or daring. To reckless courage in incurring dangers he united the greatest judgment when in the midst of them. No toil could exhaust his body or overcome his spirit. Of heat and cold he was equally tolerant. His consumption of meat and drink was determined by natural desire, not by pleasure. His times of waking and sleeping were not marked off by day or night: what time remained when his work was done he gave to sleep, which he did not court with a soft bed or stillness, but was seen repeatedly by many lying on the ground wrapped in a common soldier's cloak amongst the sentinels and outguards. His dress was in no way superior to that of his fellows, but his arms and horses were conspicuous. Both of horsemen and of foot-soldiers he was undoubtedly the first—foremost to enter battle, and last to leave it when the fighting had begun. These admirable qualities of the man were equalled by his monstrous vices: his cruelty was inhuman, his perfidy worse than Punic; he had no regard for truth, and none for sanctity, no fear of the gods, no reverence for an oath, no religious scruple. With this endowment of

A.U.C. 533 triennio sub Hasdrubale imperatore meruit nulla re quae agenda videndaque magno futuro duci esset praetermissa.

V. Ceterum ex quo die dux est declaratus,[1] velut Italia ei provincia decreta bellumque Romanum
2 mandatum esset, nihil prolatandum ratus, ne se quoque, ut patrem Hamilcarem deinde Hasdrubalem, cunctantem casus aliquis opprimeret, Sagun-
3 tinis inferre bellum statuit. Quibus oppugnandis quia haud dubie Romana arma movebantur, in Olcadum prius fines—ultra Hiberum ea gens in parte magis quam in dicione Carthaginiensium erat —induxit exercitum, ut non petisse Saguntinos sed rerum serie finitimis domitis gentibus iungendoque
4 tractus ad id bellum videri posset. Cartalam urbem opulentam, caput gentis eius, expugnat diripitque; quo metu perculsae minores civitates stipendio imposito imperium accepere. Victor exercitus opulentusque praedā Carthaginem Novam in hiberna
5 est deductus. Ibi large partiendo praedam (stipendioque praeterito cum fide exsolvendo) cunctis civium sociorumque animis in se firmatis vere primo
6 in Vaccaeos promotum bellum. Hermandica et

[1] declaratus C^2M^4 : declaraturus C^1 : declaratis M^1.

---

[1] Up to this point it is probable that Livy has been drawing his material chiefly from Coelius Antipater. He now turns to Polybius (or an account based on Polybius), and somewhat awkwardly effects the transition by means of the sentence following, in which he tries to smooth over the contradiction between *nihil prolatandum ratus* and the two years that Hannibal now spent in wars that had nothing to do with the Saguntines. (*De Sanctis*, p. 182.)

[2] This place—unknown except for its mention in this

good and evil traits he served for the space of three years under Hasdrubal, omitting nothing that should be done or seen by one who was to become a great commander. B.C. 221

V. For the rest, from the day on which he was proclaimed commander-in-chief, as though Italy had been assigned to him for his field of operations and he had been instructed to make war on Rome, he felt that no postponement was permissible, lest he too, like his father Hamilcar, and afterwards Hasdrubal, should be overtaken, while delaying, by some accident, and resolved upon attacking the Saguntines.[1] But since an attack on them must certainly provoke the Romans to hostile action, he marched first into the territory of the Olcades—a tribe living south of the Ebro, within the limits of the Carthaginians but not under their dominion—that he might appear not to have aimed at the Saguntines but to have been drawn into that war by a chain of events, as he conquered the neighbouring nations and annexed their territories. Cartala,[2] a wealthy town, the capital of that tribe, he stormed and sacked; and this so terrified the lesser towns that they submitted and agreed to an indemnity. The victorious army, enriched with spoil, was led back to New Carthage for the winter. There, by a generous partition of the booty and the faithful discharge of all arrears of pay, he confirmed them all, both citizens and allies, in their allegiance to himself; and early in the spring pushed forward into the land of the Vaccaei. Their cities, Hermandica[3] and Arbo-

connexion—is called Althaea by Polybius (III. xiii. 5) The name is perhaps preserved in the modern Melkart.

[3] Supposed to have stood on the site of Salamanca.

A.U.C. 533 Arbocala, eorum[1] urbes, vi captae. Arbocala et
7 virtute et multitudine oppidanorum diu defensa; ab
Hermandica profugi exsulibus Olcadum, priore
aestate domitae gentis, cum se iunxissent, concitant
8 Carpetanos adortique Hannibalem regressum ex
Vaccaeis haud procul Tago flumine agmen grave
9 praeda turbavere. Hannibal proelio abstinuit castrisque super ripam positis, cum prima quies silentiumque ab hostibus fuit, amnem vado traiecit valloque
ita producto ut locum ad transgrediendum hostes
10 haberent invadere eos transeuntes statuit. Equitibus
praecepit ut cum ingressos aquam viderent, adorirentur peditum agmen; in ripa elephantos—quad-
11 raginta autem erant—disponit. Carpetanorum[2]
cum adpendicibus Olcadum Vaccaeorumque centum
milia fuere, invicta acies si aequo dimicaretur campo.
12 Itaque et ingenio feroces et multitudine freti, et
quod metu cessisse credebant hostem, id morari
victoriam rati quod interesset amnis, clamore sublato
passim sine ullius imperio qua cuique proximum est
13 in amnem ruunt. Et ex parte altera ripae vis ingens
equitum in flumen immissa, medioque alveo haud-
14 quaquam pari certamine concursum, quippe ubi pedes
instabilis ac vix vado fidens vel ab inermi equite
equo temere acto perverti posset, eques corpore

[1] eorum *Sanctius*: cartaeorum *or* castaeorum *C*: cartorum (*from* cartoerum) *M*: vaccaeorum *Sigonius*.

[2] Carpetanorum *edd.*: carpentanorum *CM*.

cala, were taken by assault. Arbocala, thanks to the bravery and numbers of its inhabitants, held out for a long time. The fugitives from Hermandica, uniting with the exiles of the Olcades—the tribe which had been subdued in the previous summer—roused up the Carpetani, and falling upon Hannibal as he was returning from the Vaccaei, not far from the river Tagus, threw his column, encumbered as it was with booty, into some disorder. Hannibal refrained from battle and encamped on the bank of the river. As soon as the enemy were settled for the night and silent, he crossed the river by a ford, and so laid out his rampart as to allow them room for crossing, resolving to attack them as they were passing over. He ordered his cavalry to charge their column of foot when they saw that it had entered the stream, and posted the elephants, of which he had forty, along the bank. The Carpetani, together with the contingents of the Olcades and Vaccaei, numbered a hundred thousand—an invincible array, had they been going to fight in a fair field. And so, inspired by a native intrepidity, confiding in their multitude, and believing—since they supposed that their enemies had retreated out of fear—that victory was delayed but till they should have passed the river, they broke into a cheer, and, staying for no man's orders, rushed into the stream wherever it happened to be nearest. From the other side a great body of cavalry was sent in against them. The meeting in mid-channel was no equal conflict, for there the footmen were unsteady, and, scarce trusting to the ford, might even have been overthrown by unarmed riders, urging their horses forward at haphazard; while the horsemen, having

B.C. 221

A.U.C. 533 armisque liber, equo vel per medios gurgites stabili,
15 comminus eminusque rem gereret. Pars magna flumine absumpta; quidam verticoso amni delati in
16 hostes ab elephantis obtriti sunt. Postremi, quibus regressus in suam ripam tutior fuit, ex varia trepidatione cum in unum colligerentur, priusquam a tanto[1] pavore reciperent animos, Hannibal agmine quadrato amnem ingressus fugam ex ripa fecit vastatisque agris intra paucos dies Carpetanos quo-
17 que in deditionem accepit. Et iam omnia trans Hiberum praeter Saguntinos Carthaginiensium erant.

A.U.C. 535 VI. Cum Saguntinis bellum nondum erat, ceterum iam belli causa certamina cum finitimis serebantur,
2 maxime Turdetanis. Quibus cum adesset idem qui litis erat sator nec certamen iuris sed vim quaeri appareret, legati a Saguntinis Romam missi auxilium
3 ad bellum iam haud dubie imminens orantes. Consules[2] tunc Romae erant P. Cornelius Scipio et Ti. Sempronius Longus.[3] Qui cum legatis in senatum introductis de re publica rettulissent placuissetque mitti legatos in Hispaniam ad res sociorum in-

[1] a tanto M^4: tanto CM^1.
[2] consules M^4 : cos̄ CM^2 : caios (?) M^1.
[3] Ti. Sempronius Longus *edd.* (*chap.* xv. § 4): titus sempronius longus *CM*.

---

[1] Not the important tribe in the S.W. part of the peninsula, but a lesser one, again mentioned as neighbour to the Saguntines at XXIV. lii. 11, and—there called Turduli—at XXVIII. xxxix. 8.

[2] These were the consuls of 218 B.C., but the siege of Saguntum took place in 219. Livy now returns to—and follows until he has finished the story of the siege in chap. xv. § 1—the source he had used for the opening chapters of this book. Coelius—if he it was—so telescoped events as to

their bodies and weapons free and horses that were B.C. 221
steady even in the deep pools, could fight either at close quarters or long range. A great part of them perished in the stream; some the eddying current carried over to their enemies, where they were trampled down by the elephants. The rearmost, who could retreat to their own bank more safely, were gathering from the various directions in which they had fled, when, before they could recover from so great a panic, Hannibal entered the stream in a fighting column, and driving them in confusion from the bank, laid waste their fields, and in a few days' time received the surrender of the Carpetani also. And now everything south of the Ebro, except Saguntum, was in the hands of the Carthaginians.

VI. With the Saguntines there was as yet no war, B.C. 219
but quarrels that might be a pretext for it were already being sown betwixt them and their neighbours, especially the Turdetani.[1] Now when the side of the Turdetani was espoused by the same man who had sowed the quarrel, and it was clearly seen that he was aiming not at arbitration but force, the Saguntines sent ambassadors to Rome, imploring help for a war that was now indubitably imminent. The Roman consuls at that time were Publius Cornelius Scipio and Tiberius Sempronius Longus.[2] After introducing the ambassadors into the senate, they had brought up the question of public policy, and the senators had voted to dispatch envoys to Spain,

make the attack on Saguntum follow immediately on the appointment of Hannibal, and the war with Rome begin in that same year. In chap. xv. Livy becomes aware of the discrepancy and endeavours to dispose of it.

A.U.C. 535 4 spiciendas, quibus si videretur digna causa, et Hannibali denuntiarent ut ab Saguntinis, sociis populi
Romani, abstineret, et Carthaginem in Africam
traicerent ac sociorum populi Romani querimonias
5 deferrent,—hac legatione[1] decreta necdum missa
omnium spe celerius Saguntum oppugnari allatum
6 est. Tunc relata de integro res ad senatum; et
alii provincias consulibus Hispaniam atque Africam
decernentes terra marique rem gerendam censebant,
alii totum in Hispaniam Hannibalemque intenderant
7 bellum; erant qui non temere movendam rem
tantam exspectandosque ex Hispania legatos cen-
8 serent. Haec sententia, quae tutissima videbatur,
vicit;[2] legatique eo maturius missi, P. Valerius
Flaccus et Q. Baebius Tamphilus,[3] Saguntum ad
Hannibalem atque inde Carthaginem, si non ab-
sisteretur bello, ad ducem ipsum in poenam foederis
rupti deposcendum.

VII. Dum ea Romani parant consultantque, iam
2 Saguntum summa vi oppugnabatur. Civitas ea
longe opulentissima ultra Hiberum fuit, sita passus
mille ferme a mari. Oriundi a Zacyntho insula
dicuntur, mixtique etiam ab Ardea Rutulorum
3 quidam generis; ceterum in tantas brevi creverant
opes seu maritimis seu terrestribus fructibus seu

[1] legatione M^2: le gecione *C*: legatio M^1.

[2] videbatur, vicit M^2C (*by erasure from* uidebantur uicit): uicit uidebatur M^1.

[3] Baebius Tamphilus *Sigonius*: fabius pamphilus *CM*.

---

[1] Saguntum is only a Latinized form of Ζάκυνθος, the name of a small island (now Zante) off the coast of Elis.

[2] Ardea (the seat of King Turnus, according to Virgil, *Aen.* VII. 409 ff.) was the chief city of the Rutuli and had been a Roman colony since 442 B.C.

to examine into the affairs of their allies, to the end B.C. 219 that, if there appeared to be just cause, they might formally warn Hannibal to keep aloof from the Saguntines, the allies of the Roman People; after which they were to cross over into Africa, to Carthage, and present the complaint of Rome's allies. This embassy had been voted but not yet sent off, when, sooner than all expectation, came the news that Saguntum was besieged. The case was then referred anew to the senate. Some were for sending the consuls into Spain and Africa respectively and waging war by land and sea; others wanted to direct their whole force against Spain and Hannibal; some there were who argued that so grave a quarrel should not be lightly entered on, and proposed to await the return of the envoys out of Spain. This last opinion, which seemed the safest, carried the day, and the envoys, Publius Valerius Flaccus and Quintus Baebius Tamphilus, were sent off with the more dispatch. They were to go to Saguntum first, to Hannibal, and thence, if he would not cease hostilities, to Carthage, to demand the surrender of the general himself in satisfaction of the broken treaty.

VII. While the Romans were thus planning and deliberating, the siege of Saguntum was already being pressed with the greatest vigour. This city was much the wealthiest of those beyond the Ebro and was situated about a mile from the sea. Its inhabitants are said to have come originally from the island of Zacynthus,[1] and to have included also a strain from the Ardeate Rutulians.[2] Be this as it may, they had attained quickly to their great prosperity, whether owing to the produce of the sea or the

A.U.C. 535
multitudinis incremento seu disciplinae sanctitate,
qua fidem socialem usque ad perniciem suam colue-
4 runt. Hannibal infesto exercitu ingressus fines
pervastatis passim agris urbem tripertito adgreditur.
5 Angulus muri erat in planiorem patentioremque
quam cetera circa vallem vergens. Adversus eum
vineas agere instituit, per quas aries moenibus
6 admoveri posset. Sed ut locus procul muro[1] satis
aequus agendis vineis fuit, ita haudquaquam prospere, postquam ad effectum operis ventum est,
7 coeptis succedebat. Et turris ingens imminebat,
et murus, ut in suspecto loco, supra ceterae modum
altitudinis emunitus erat, et iuventus delecta ubi
plurimum periculi ac timoris ostendebatur ibi vi
8 maiore obsistebant. Ac primo missilibus submovere
hostem nec quicquam satis tutum munientibus pati;
deinde iam non pro moenibus modo atque turri
tela micare, sed ad erumpendum etiam in stationes
9 operaque hostium animus erat; quibus tumultuariis
certaminibus haud ferme plures Saguntini cadebant
10 quam Poeni. Ut vero Hannibal ipse, dum murum
incautius subit, adversum femur tragulā graviter
ictus cecidit, tanta circa fuga ac trepidatio fuit
ut non multum abesset quin opera ac vineae
desererentur.

VIII. Obsidio deinde per paucos dies magis quam

[1] muro *edd.* : muros *CM.*

---

[1] Polybius, III. xviii. 3, speaks of the great fertility of their territory, and under the empire Saguntum was famous for its export of earthenware.

land,[1] to the growth of their population, or to the integrity of their discipline, which caused them to keep faith with their allies even to their own undoing. Crossing their borders with a hostile army Hannibal laid waste their country far and wide and advanced in three divisions against their city. There was an angle of the wall that gave on a valley more open and more level than the other ground about the town. Against this he determined to bring up pent-houses, that under their cover the battering-rams might be brought into contact with the walls. But though the ground at some distance from the wall was smooth enough for moving the pent-houses, the attempt succeeded very ill when it came to the final execution of it. There was a great overhanging tower, and the wall—as was natural in a suspected place—had been carried up to a greater height than elsewhere, and the pick of the fighting men having been stationed there, where the greatest danger threatened, offered a more strenuous resistance. At first they drove the assailants off with missiles and left no spot safe for their pioneers; afterwards not only did their javelins dart from wall and tower, but they even had the hardihood to sally out against the pickets and earthworks of their enemies, and in these rough and-tumble fights hardly more Saguntines fell than Phoenicians. But when Hannibal himself, who had somewhat incautiously ventured up under the wall, was severely wounded in the front of his thigh with a heavy javelin and sank to the ground, those about him fell into such confusion and dismay as almost to abandon their works and pent-houses. B.C. 219

VIII. For the next few days, while the general's

A.U.C. 535 oppugnatio fuit, dum volnus ducis curaretur. Per
quod tempus ut quies certaminum erat ita ab
apparatu operum ac munitionum nihil cessatum.
2 Itaque acrius de integro coortum est bellum, pluri-
busque partibus, vix accipientibus quibusdam opera
3 locis, vineae coeptae agi admoverique aries. Abun-
dabat multitudine hominum Poenus; ad centum
quinquaginta milia habuisse in armis satis creditur;
4 oppidani ad omnia tuenda atque obeunda multi-
5 fariam distineri coepti,[1] non sufficiebant. Itaque
iam feriebantur arietibus muri, quassataeque multae
partes erant; una continentibus ruinis nudaverat
urbem: tres deinceps turres quantumque inter eas
6 muri erat cum fragore ingenti prociderunt.[2] Captum oppidum ea ruina crediderant Poeni, qua,
velut si pariter utrosque murus[3] texisset, ita
7 utrimque in pugnam procursum est. Nihil tumul-
tuariae pugnae simile erat, quales in oppugnationibus
urbium per occasionem partis alterius conseri[4]
solent, sed iustae acies velut patenti campo inter
ruinas muri tectaque urbis modico distantia inter-
8 vallo constiterant. Hinc spes, hinc desperatio
animos inritat, Poeno cepisse iam se urbem, si
paulum adnitatur, credente, Saguntinis pro nudata
moenibus patria corpora opponentibus nec ullo
pedem referente, ne in relictum a se locum hostem
9 immitteret. Itaque quo acrius et confertim magis

[1] coepti *Weissenborn*: coepti sunt *CM*.
[2] prociderunt *CM*: prociderant ς.
[3] murus *edd.*: muros *CM*.
[4] conseri ς: consciri *CM*.

hurt was healing, there was rather a blockade than an assault; but though during this interval there was rest from combat, yet was there no slackening in the preparation of engines and defences. Accordingly the fighting broke out afresh more fiercely than before, and pent-houses began to be pushed forward and rams brought up at many points, though in some places the ground would hardly admit of them. The Phoenician was lavishly equipped with men—he is credibly supposed to have had a hundred and fifty thousand under arms—but the townsmen, who, in order to guard and defend every quarter, had been divided into numerous companies, found their strength inadequate. And so now the walls were being battered with rams and in many places had been severely shaken. One section, giving way continuously for some distance, had exposed the town: three towers in a row, together with the wall connecting them, had come down with a loud crash. The Phoenicians believed that the town was taken with that breach, through which from either side men rushed to attack, as though the wall had protected both parties alike. It was not at all like the mellays that commonly occur in sieges, where one side gets an opportunity, but regular battle lines had formed, as in an open field, between the ruins of the wall and the buildings of the city, which stood at some distance off. On this side hope, on that despair inspired courage. The Phoenicians believed the city to be theirs, if they put forth a little effort. The Saguntines opposed their bodies to defend their city, denuded of its walls, nor would one of them draw back his foot lest he admit an enemy to the spot which he had vacated. And the harder both sides fought and

B.C. 219

A.U.C. 535

utrimque pugnabant,[1] eo plures volnerabantur nullo
10 inter arma corporaque vano intercidente telo. Phalarica[2] erat Saguntinis missile telum hastili abiegno[3] et cetera[4] tereti praeterquam ad extremum unde ferrum exstabat; id, sicut in pilo, quadratum stuppa circumligabant linebantque[5] pice;
11 ferrum autem tres longum habebat pedes, ut cum armis transfigere corpus posset. Sed id maxime, etiam si haesisset in scuto nec penetrasset in corpus,
12 pavorem faciebat, quod cum medium accensum mitteretur conceptumque ipso motu multo maiorem ignem ferret, arma omitti cogebat nudumque militem ad insequentes ictus praebebat.

IX. Cum diu anceps fuisset certamen et Saguntinis, quia praeter spem resisterent, crevissent animi,
2 Poenus, quia non vicisset, pro victo esset, clamorem repente oppidani tollunt hostemque in ruinas muri expellunt, inde impeditum trepidantemque exturbant, postremo fusum fugatumque in castra redigunt.
3 Interim ab Roma legatos venisse nuntiatum est. Quibus obviam ad mare missi ab Hannibale qui dicerent nec tuto eos adituros inter tot tam effrenatarum gentium arma nec Hannibali in tanto discrimine rerum operae esse legationes audire.
4 Apparebat non admissos protinus Carthaginem ituros.

[1] pugnabant (*by erasure from* oppugnabant) *M*: pugnabantur C^1: pugnabatur C^2.

[2] phalarica C^2M^2: pharica *C*: phalaeri M^1.

[3] abiegno ς: ab ligneo *CM*.

[4] cetera *Ascensius* (1513 : cetero *CM*.

[5] timebantque ς: linebanturque (*or other corruptions*) *CM*.

the more they crowded in together, the greater was the number of those wounded, for no missile fell without taking effect on shield or body. The Saguntines had a javelin, called a *phalarica,* with a shaft of fir, which was round except at the end whence the iron projected; this part, four-sided as in the *pilum,* they wrapped with tow and smeared with pitch. Now the iron was three feet long, that it might be able to go through both shield and body. But what chiefly made it terrible, even if it stuck fast in the shield and did not penetrate the body, was this, that when it had been lighted at the middle and so hurled, the flames were fanned to a fiercer heat by its very motion, and it forced the soldier to let go his shield, and left him unprotected against the blows that followed. B.C. 219

IX. When the outcome of the struggle had long been doubtful, and the Saguntines, because they were holding out beyond their hopes, had gained new courage, while the Phoenician, because he had not conquered, was as good as beaten; suddenly the townspeople set up a shout and thrust forth their enemies amongst the ruins of the wall, and routing them out from thence, confused and frightened, drove them back at last in full flight to their camp.

In the meantime it was announced that ambassadors had come from Rome. Hannibal sent men to the shore to meet them and say that it would not be safe for them to come to him through the armed bands of so many unruly tribes, and that he had no time for listening to embassies at so critical a juncture. It was clear that, if they were denied a hearing, they would at once proceed to

A.U.C. 535 Litteras igitur nuntiosque ad principes factionis Barcinae praemittit, ut praepararent suorum animos, ne quid pars altera gratificari populo Romano[1] posset.

X. Itaque, praeterquam quod admissi auditique sunt,[2] ea quoque vana atque irrita legatio fuit.
2 Hanno unus adversus senatum[3] causam foederis
3 magno silentio propter auctoritatem suam, non cum[4] adsensu audientium egit, per deos[5] foederum arbitros ac testes senatum[6] obtestans, ne Romanum cum Saguntino suscitarent bellum: monuisse, praedixisse se ne Hamilcaris progeniem ad exercitum mitterent; non manes, non stirpem eius conquiescere viri, nec unquam, donec sanguinis nominisque Barcini quisquam supersit, quietura Romana foedera.
4 "Iuvenem flagrantem cupidine regni viamque unam ad id cernentem si ex bellis bella serendo succinctus armis legionibusque vivat, velut materiam igni praebentes ad exercitus misistis. Aluistis ergo hoc
5 incendium quo nunc ardetis. Saguntum vestri circumsedent[7] exercitus, unde arcentur foedere; mox Carthaginem[8] circumsedebunt Romanae legiones ducibus isdem dis per quos priore bello rupta
6 foedera sunt ulti. Utrum hostem an vos an fortunam utriusque populi ignoratis? Legatos ab sociis

[1] populo Romano *A. Perizonius*: pro romanis *CM*.
[2] sunt M^2: non sunt CM^1.
[3] adversus senatum *Alschefski*: aduersum senatum *C*: aduersu senatum M^1: aduerso senatu M^2.
[4] suam, non cum *Eichhof*: suam cum *CM*: quam cum *Madvig* (*reading* magis *for* magno).
[5] per deos ς: per eos *CM*?: per reos M^1 (*or M*).
[6] senatum C^3: hannonis suadentis senatum C^1: annonis suadentis senatum (*these three words were later erased*) *M*.
[7] circumsedent M^2: circumsedunt M^1: circumsident *C*.

Carthage. He therefore dispatched couriers before B.C. 219 them, with a letter for the leaders of the Barcine faction, so that they might prepare the minds of their adherents to prevent the opposing party from affording any satisfaction to the Roman People.

X. Accordingly, save for being admitted and allowed a hearing, this mission also was idle and of no effect. Hanno stood alone in pleading for the treaty against the views of the senate. There was a deep hush while he spoke, by reason of his personal authority, but he was listened to without approval. He adjured the senators in the name of the gods, vouchers for treaties and their witnesses, to provoke not a Roman along with the Saguntine war. He had advised them and forewarned them not to send the offspring of Hamilcar to the army; neither the man's ghost nor his progeny was at rest, nor ever, so long as any of the lineage and name of Barca should survive, would the treaty with the Romans rest untroubled. "You have sent to your armies," he went on, "as though heaping fuel on a fire, a youth who burns with lust for sovereign power and sees but one way to obtain it—if, by sowing seeds of war, he can raise up other wars and live girt round with arms and legions. You have therefore fed these flames with which you are now ablaze. Your armies now invest Saguntum, which the treaty forbids them to approach: ere long the Roman legions will be investing Carthage, led by those very gods who helped them in the former war to avenge the broken treaty. Is it your enemy you know not, or yourselves, or the fortunes of both peoples? When

---

[8] Carthaginem C^3M^2 : carthagine C^1M^1.

A.U.C. 535 et pro sociis venientes bonus imperator vester in castra non admisit, ius gentium[1] sustulit; hi tamen, unde ne hostium quidem legati arcentur pulsi, ad vos venerunt; res ex foedere repetunt; ut[2] publica fraus absit, auctorem culpae et reum criminis de-
7 poscunt. Quo lenius agunt segnius incipiunt, eo, cum coeperint, vereor ne perseverantius saeviant. Aegates insulas Erycemque[3] ante oculos proponite, quae terra marique per quattuor et viginti annos
8 passi sitis. Nec puer hic dux erat, sed pater ipse Hamilcar, Mars alter, ut isti volunt. Sed Tarento, id est Italia, non abstinueramus ex foedere, sicut
9 nunc Sagunto[4] non abstinemus. Vicerunt ergo di homines,[5] et id de quo verbis ambigebatur, uter populus foedus rupisset, eventus belli velut aequus
10 iudex unde ius stabat ei victoriam dedit. Carthagini nunc Hannibal vineas turresque admovet; Carthaginis moenia quatit ariete; Sagunti ruinae—falsus utinam vates sim!—nostris capitibus incident, susceptumque cum Saguntinis bellum habendum
11 cum Romanis est. 'Dedemus ergo Hannibalem?' dicet aliquis. Scio meam levem esse in eo auctori-

[1] gentium *M²C²* (*over erasure*): centium *M¹*.
[2] repetunt; ut *A. Perizonius*: repetuntur *C*: repetuntur de re repetuntur *M*.
[3] insulas Erycemque *edd.*: insulam sericemque *C*: insulam seriemque *M¹*: insulas eriemque *M²*.
[4] Sagunto *M²*: sagunti *CM*.
[5] homines *Madvig*: hominesque *CM*.

---

[1] Off these islands C. Lutatius Catulus won in 241 B.C. the naval victory which decided the First Punic War (*Per.* XIX.).

ambassadors came from allies on behalf of allies, B.C. 219 your worthy general would not admit them to his camp, but thrust aside the law of nations; nevertheless these men, being driven from a place where even an enemy's envoys are admitted, have come to you. They seek amends in accordance with a treaty. That the state may be void of offence, they demand the author of the wrong, the man on whom they charge the guilt. The more mildly they proceed, the more slowly they begin, the more obstinate, I fear, when they *have* begun, will be their rage. Set Eryx and the Aegatian islands[1] before your eyes, and all that you suffered by land and sea for four and twenty years. Nor was this boy your leader, but Hamilcar himself, the father, a second Mars, as his partisans will have it.[2] But we could not keep our hands from Tarentum, that is, from Italy, as by treaty bound, even as now we cannot keep them from Saguntum. Gods therefore vanquished men, and that which had been verbally disputed—which people of the twain had broken the treaty—the outcome of the war, like an impartial judge, decided, and to those who had the right granted the victory. It is Carthage against which Hannibal is now bringing up his pent-houses and towers; it is the walls of Carthage he is battering with his rams. Saguntum's walls—may my prophecy prove false!—will fall upon *our* heads, and the war we have entered upon with the Saguntines we must carry on against the Romans. 'Shall we then surrender Hannibal?' someone will ask. I know that my

[2] Hanno knows that most of his hearers are against him, and *isti* (literally "those men of yours") means "those who guide your opinion," *i.e.* the friends of Hannibal.

A.U.C. 535 tatem propter paternas inimicitias; sed et Hamilcarem eo perisse laetatus sum, quod si ille viveret, bellum iam haberemus cum Romanis, et hunc iuvenem tamquam furiam facemque huius belli odi
12 ac detestor; nec dedendum solum arbitror[1] ad piaculum rupti foederis, sed si nemo deposceret,[2] devehendum in ultimas maris terrarumque oras, ablegandum eo unde nec ad nos nomen famaque eius accidere[3] neque ille sollicitare quietae civitatis
13 statum posset.[4] Ego ita censeo, legatos extemplo Romam mittendos qui senatui satisfaciant, alios qui Hannibali nuntient ut exercitum ab Sagunto abducat, ipsumque Hannibalem ex foedere Romanis dedant; tertiam legationem ad res Saguntinis reddendas decerno."

XI. Cum Hanno perorasset, nemini omnium certare oratione cum eo necesse fuit, adeo prope omnis senatus Hannibalis erat; infestiusque locutum arguebant Hannonem quam Flaccum Valerium, legatum
2 Romanum. Responsum inde legatis Romanis est bellum ortum ab Saguntinis non ab Hannibale esse; populum Romanum iniuste facere si Saguntinos vetustissimae Carthaginiensium societati praeponat.
3 Dum Romani tempus terunt legationibus mittendis, Hannibal, quia fessum militem proeliis operibusque habebat, paucorum iis[5] dierum quietem dedit, stationibus ad custodiam vinearum aliorumque

[1] nec dedendum solum arbitror *Luchs*: nec dedendum solum *CM*.

[2] deposceret *Luchs*: deposcat ς: deposcit *CM*.

[3] accidere *Gronovius*: accedere *CM*.

[4] posset *Luchs*: possit *CM*.

[5] iis *edd.*: his *CM*

influence is slight, because of my quarrel with his father; but I rejoiced when Hamilcar perished, for this reason, that were he living, we should now be at war with Rome; and this young man, who, like a fury, now brandishes the torch of war, I loathe and abominate, and I hold, not only that he ought to be surrendered in expiation of the broken treaty, but that, if none demanded him, he ought to be deported to the farthest limits of land and sea—to be banished to a place whence neither name nor fame of his could reach us, nor he be able to vex the quiet of our state. My opinion is this: we should send ambassadors at once to Rome, to give satisfaction to the senate; and others to announce to Hannibal that he must withdraw his army from Saguntum, and to hand over Hannibal himself to the Romans as the treaty requires; a third embassy I would send to make restitution to the Saguntines." B.C. 219

XI. When Hanno had concluded, not a single person found it necessary to oppose his arguments, so nearly unanimous was the senate in supporting Hannibal. They declared that Hanno had spoken more bitterly than Valerius Flaccus, the Roman envoy. They then gave their answer to the envoys, to the effect that the war had been begun by the Saguntines, not by Hannibal, and that the Roman People would be doing wrong if they preferred the Saguntines to their very ancient alliance with the Carthaginians.

While the Romans were wasting time in dispatching embassies, Hannibal had allowed his soldiers, exhausted as they were with fighting and constructing works, to rest for a few days, after posting outguards to look to the pent-houses and other engines.

A.U.C. 535 operum dispositis. Interim animos eorum nunc ira in hostes stimulando, nunc spe praemiorum accendit.
4 Ut vero pro contione praedam captae urbis edixit militum fore, adeo accensi omnes sunt ut, si extemplo signum datum esset, nulla vi resisti videretur
5 posse. Saguntini, ut a proeliis quietem habuerant nec lacessentes nec lacessiti per aliquot dies, ita non nocte non die unquam cessaverant ab opere, ut novum murum ab ea parte qua patefactum oppidum ruinis erat reficerent.

6 Inde oppugnatio eos aliquanto atrocior quam ante adorta est, nec qua primum aut potissimum parte ferrent opem, cum omnia variis clamoribus stre-
7 perent, satis scire poterant. Ipse Hannibal qua turris mobilis omnia munimenta urbis superans altitudine agebatur hortator aderat. Quae cum admota catapultis ballistisque per omnia tabulata dispositis
8 muros defensoribus nudasset, tum Hannibal occasionem ratus quingentos ferme Afros cum dolabris ad subruendum ab imo murum mittit. Nec erat difficile opus, quod caementa non calce durata erant
9 sed interlita luto structurae antiquo[1] genere. Itaque latius quam qua[2] caederetur ruebat, perque patentia
10 ruinis agmina armatorum in urbem vadebant. Locum quoque editum capiunt collatisque eo catapultis ballistisque, ut castellum in ipsa urbe velut arcem imminentem haberent, muro circumdant; et Sagun-

[1] antiquo ς: antiquae *CM*.
[2] quam qua *Weissenborn*: qua qua *C*: quam qua *M*: quam ς.

---

[1] Engines for hurling darts and stones.

Meanwhile he kindled their ardour, now by inciting them to rage against their enemies, again by holding out hopes of rewards. But when he made a speech proclaiming that the spoils of the captured city should go to the soldiers, they were so excited, one and all, that if the signal had been given instantly, it seemed as if no force could have withstood them. The Saguntines, though they had had a rest from fighting, neither attacking nor being attacked for several days, had laboured incessantly, both day and night, to replace the wall where its collapse had exposed the town. B.C. 219

The assault was now resumed, with far greater fury than before, and it was hard for the inhabitants to know, when shouts and cries were resounding on every hand, to what point they should first, or preferably, bring up supports. Hannibal was present in person to urge on his men, where they were pushing up a movable tower that surpassed in height all the defences of the city. As soon as it had been brought up, and the catapults and *ballistae*[1] distributed through all its platforms had stripped the ramparts of defenders, Hannibal, believing that he now had his opportunity, sent about five hundred Africans with pickaxes to undermine the wall. This was no hard task, for the rubble had not been solidified with mortar, but filled in with mud, after an ancient mode of building. It therefore fell for wider stretches than were actually hacked away, and through the breaches bands of armed men passed into the city. They even seized an elevation, and setting up catapults and *ballistae* there, built a wall around it, so as to have within the town itself a stronghold that commanded it like a citadel. The

A.U.C. 535 tini murum interiorem ab nondum capta parte urbis
11 ducunt. Utrimque summa vi et muniunt et pugnant;
sed interiora tuendo minorem in dies[1] urbem Sagun-
12 tini faciunt. Simul crescit inopia omnium longa obsidione et minuitur exspectatio externae opis, cum tam[2]
procul Romani, unica spes, circa omnia hostium essent.
13 Paulisper tamen adfectos animos recreavit repentina
profectio Hannibalis in Oretanos Carpetanosque, qui
duo populi, dilectus acerbitate consternati, retentis
conquisitoribus metum defectionis cum praebuissent,
oppressi celeritate Hannibalis omiserunt mota arma.

XII. Nec Sagunti oppugnatio segnior erat Maharbale,[3] Himilconis[4] filio—eum praefecerat Hannibal
—ita impigre rem agente ut ducem abesse nec cives
2 nec hostes sentirent. Is et proelia aliquot secunda
fecit et tribus arietibus aliquantum muri discussit
strataque omnia recentibus ruinis advenienti Hanni-
3 bali ostendit. Itaque ad ipsam arcem extemplo
ductus exercitus, atroxque proelium cum multorum
utrimque caede initum et pars arcis capta est.

Temptata deinde per duos est exigua pacis spes,
4 Alconem Saguntinum et Alorcum Hispanum. Alco[5]

[1] dies ϛ *Valla*: diem *CM*.
[2] tam ϛ: iam *CM*.
[3] Maharbale *edd.*: mahermale C^2M: m hermale C^1.
[4] Himilconis M^2: hamilconis CM^1.
[5] Alco *edd.*: alcon *M*: alconus *C*.

Saguntines too built a wall within the old one, to protect that part of the city that was not yet taken. On both sides the soldiers worked and fought with the utmost energy; but the Saguntines, contracting their defences, were bringing their city day by day within a smaller compass. At the same time there was an increasing scarcity of everything, on account of the long blockade; and the prospect of help from without was growing less, since the Romans, their only hope, were so far away, and all the country round about was in the possession of their enemies. Yet their drooping spirits were revived for a little while by the sudden departure of Hannibal for the territories of the Oretani and the Carpetani. These two nations, exasperated by a rigorous conscription, had seized the recruiting officers and thereby given rise to fears of a revolt, but were caught unprepared by Hannibal's celerity, and laid down the arms they had taken up. B.C. 219

XII. But the siege of Saguntum did not flag. Maharbal, the son of Himilco, whom Hannibal had left in charge, so bestirred himself that the absence of the general was felt neither by his countrymen nor by the enemy. He fought a number of successful skirmishes, and with three battering-rams laid low a considerable portion of the wall, and on Hannibal's return, showed him the place all covered with the newly fallen ruins. And so the troops were led at once against the citadel itself, and a fierce battle began, in which many on both sides were killed and a part of the citadel was taken.

An all but hopeless attempt to arrange a peace was then made by two men, Alco, a Saguntine, and a Spaniard named Alorcus. Alco, thinking that some-

A.U.C. 535

insciis[1] Saguntinis precibus aliquid moturum ratus,
cum ad Hannibalem noctu transisset, postquam
nihil lacrimae movebant condicionesque tristes ut
ab irato victore[2] ferebantur, transfuga ex oratore
factus apud hostem mansit, moriturum adfirmans
5 qui sub condicionibus iis de pace ageret. Postula-
batur autem, redderent res Turdetanis[3] traditoque
omni auro atque argento egressi urbe cum singulis
vestimentis ibi habitarent ubi Poenus iussisset.
6 Has pacis leges abnuente Alcone accepturos Saguntinos, Alorcus, vinci animos ubi alia vincantur
adfirmans, se pacis eius interpretem fore pollicetur;
erat autem tum miles Hannibalis, ceterum publice
7 Saguntinis amicus atque hospes. Tradito palam telo
custodibus hostium transgressus munimenta ad
praetorem Saguntinum – et ipse ita iubebat – est
8 deductus. Quo cum extemplo concursus omnis
generis hominum esset factus, submota cetera
multitudine senatus Alorco[4] datus est, cuius talis
oratio fuit:

XIII. "Si civis vester Alco, sicut ad pacem petendam ad Hannibalem venit ita pacis condiciones[5] ab Hannibale ad vos rettulisset, supervacaneum hoc

[1] insciis ς: inconsciis *CM*.
[2] victore ς: auctore *CM*.
[3] Turdetanis *edd.*: turditanis *CM*.
[4] Alorco *C*.: alorci C^1M.
[5] condiciones C^3: condicionis C^1M.

---

[1] The stranger in an ancient city had no commercial or legal status but had to depend on the good offices of some citizen. Guest-friendship (*hospitium*) was a species of permanent (and even hereditary) alliance entered into by two citizens of different states for purposes of mutual comfort and protection in commercial and other intercourse.

thing might be effected by entreaties, went over to Hannibal in the night, without the knowledge of the Sanguntines. But finding that tears were of no avail and that the terms obtainable were such as a wrathful conqueror would impose, he changed from pleader to deserter, and remained with the enemy, declaring that anybody who should treat for peace on those conditions would be put to death. The conditions were as follows: they must make restitution to the Turdetani, and, delivering up all their gold and silver, quit their city with a single garment each and take up their abode where the Phoenician should direct them. When Alco asserted that the Saguntines would not accept such terms, Alorcus, affirming that where all else is conquered the heart is conquered too, undertook the negotiation of a peace. He was at that time a soldier in the service of Hannibal, but was officially recognized by the Saguntines as their friend and guest.[1] Openly surrendering his weapon to the sentries, he passed the enemy's lines, and was conducted—by his own command—before the Saguntine general. A crowd of all descriptions immediately flocked together there; but all save the senators were sent away, and Alorcus, being permitted to address them, spoke as follows:

B.C. 219

XIII. "If Alco, your own fellow citizen, after going to Hannibal to sue for peace, had brought back to you the terms of peace which Hannibal offers, this journey of mine would have been superfluous,

[1] When a city honoured a member of another state by formally conferring upon him the title of *hospes publicus*, it gave him the right to entertainment at the public cost, and to buy and sell and bring actions in the courts.

A.U.C. 535 mihi fuisset iter, quo nec orator Hannibalis nec
2 transfuga ad vos venissem;[1] cum ille aut vestrā aut
suā culpa manserit apud hostem—sua,[2] si metum
simulavit, vestra, si periculum est apud vos vera
referentibus—ego, ne ignoraretis esse aliquas et
salutis et pacis vobis condiciones, pro vetusto hos-
3 pitio quod mihi vobiscum est ad vos veni. Vestrā
autem causā me nec ullius alterius loqui quae loquor
apud vos vel ea fides sit quod neque dum vestris
viribus restitistis neque dum auxilia ab Romanis
sperastis, pacis unquam apud vos mentionem feci.
4 Postquam nec ab Romanis vobis ulla est spes nec
vestra vos iam aut arma aut moenia satis defendunt,
pacem adfero ad vos magis necessariam quam aequam.
5 Cuius ita aliqua spes est, si eam quem ad modum ut
victor fert Hannibal sic vos ut victi audietis[3] et[4]
non id quod amittitur in damno, cum omnia victoris
sint, sed quidquid relinquitur pro munere habituri
6 estis. Urbem vobis, quam ex magna parte dirutam,
captam fere totam habet, adimit, agros relinquit,
locum adsignaturus in quo novum oppidum aedi-
ficetis. Aurum et argentum omne, publicum priva-
7 tumque, ad se iubet deferri; corpora vestra coniugum
ac liberorum vestrorum servat inviolata, si inermes
cum binis vestimentis velitis ab Sagunto exire.

[1] venissem *CM*: veni sed *Madvig*: venissem nunc *Woelfflin*.

[2] sua C^3M^2: *omitted by* C^1M^1.

[3] audietis *Gronovius*: audiatis *CM*.

[4] et *Weissenborn*: et si ς: sed *CM*.

---

[1] Livy is not implying that Alorcus was in this detail exaggerating Hannibal's offer. The "single garment" of

for I should have come to you neither as Hannibal's spokesman nor yet as a deserter. But seeing that, whether through your fault or his own, he has stopped behind with your enemy—his own if his fears were feigned, yours if it is unsafe to bring you a true report—that you might not be ignorant that terms there are upon which you may enjoy both life and peace, I have come to you myself, having regard to the long-standing friendship which subsists between us. Moreover, that I say what I say for your sake and no other's, you may take this as proof: so long as you held your ground with your own forces, and expected to receive help from the Romans, I never mentioned peace to you; but now that you have no longer any hope from Rome, and neither your arms nor your fortifications are adequate to defend you, I bring you a peace more necessary than equitable. That this peace may be realized there is some ground for hoping only if, even as Hannibal proposes it in the spirit of a conqueror, so you shall hearken to it in the spirit of the conquered, and shall not consider as lost what is taken from you, since all things are the victor's, but consider whatever is left you as a gift. Your city, which he has in great part overthrown, and almost wholly captured, he takes from you: your lands he leaves you, and intends to designate a site whereon you may erect a new town. All your gold and silver, both public and private, he orders to be brought to him: your persons, with those of your wives and children, he preserves inviolate, if you are willing to go forth unarmed from Saguntum with two garments each.[1] These B.C. 219

chap. xii. § 5 was loosely put for "a single suit of clothes," *i.e.* the inner and outer tunic which everybody wore.

A.U.C. 535 8 Haec victor hostis imperat; haec, quamquam sunt gravia atque acerba, fortuna vestra vobis suadet. Equidem haud despero, cum omnium potestas ei
9 facta sit, aliquid ex his[1] remissurum; sed vel haec patienda censeo potius quam trucidari corpora vestra, rapi trahique ante ora vestra coniuges ac liberos belli iure sinatis."

XIV. Ad haec audienda cum circumfusa paulatim multitudine permixtum senatui esset populi concilium, repente primores secessione facta priusquam responsum daretur, argentum aurumque omne ex publico privatoque in forum conlatum in ignem ad id raptim[2] factum conicientes eodem plerique
2 semet ipsi praecipitaverunt. Cum ex eo pavor ac trepidatio totam urbem pervasisset, alius insuper tumultus ex arce auditur. Turris diu quassata prociderat, perque ruinam eius cohors Poenorum impetu facto cum signum imperatori[3] dedisset nudatam stationibus custodiisque solitis hostium esse urbem,
3 non cunctandum in tali occasione ratus Hannibal, totis viribus adgressus urbem momento cepit, signo dato ut omnes puberes interficerentur. Quod imperium crudele ceterum prope necessarium cognitum
4 ipso eventu est: cui enim parci potuit ex iis qui aut inclusi cum coniugibus ac liberis domos super se

[1] his *Woelfflin*: his (hiis *C*) rebus *CM*.
[2] raptim C^3M^2: raptum C^1M^1.
[3] imperatori ς *Valla*: imperator *CM*.

terms a victorious enemy imposes on you; these terms, albeit harsh and cruel, your fortune counsels you to accept. Indeed I am not without hope that when full control of everything shall have been granted him, he may remit somewhat of this severity; but even this you ought, I think, rather to endure than to suffer yourselves to be massacred and your wives and children to be forcibly dragged away into captivity before your eyes, in accordance with the laws of war." B.C. 219

XIV. To hear this speech the populace had little by little crowded round, and the people's council had mingled with the senate, when on a sudden the leading men, withdrawing from the throng before an answer could be given, fetched all the gold and silver, both of state and private ownership, into the market-place, and casting it into a fire which they had hurriedly made up for this purpose, many threw themselves headlong into the same flames. The resulting panic and dismay had no sooner spread to all the city, than another loud noise and outcry were heard from the citadel. A tower that had long been battered had collapsed, and through the breach a cohort of Phoenicians had rushed in and signalled to the general that the city was denuded of its customary guards and sentinels. Hannibal, deeming it no time to hesitate, when such an opportunity offered, attacked with all his strength and captured the city out of hand. He had given orders that all the grown inhabitants be put to the sword—a cruel command, but found in the upshot to have been well-nigh inevitable; for who could be spared of those who either shut themselves up with their wives and children and burned the houses over

A.U.C. 535 ipsos concremaverunt aut armati nullum ante finem pugnae quam morientes fecerunt?

XV. Captum oppidum est cum ingenti praeda. Quamquam pleraque ab dominis de industria corrupta erant et in caedibus vix ullum discrimen aetatis ira
2 fecerat et captivi militum praeda fuerant, tamen et ex pretio rerum venditarum aliquantum pecuniae redactam esse constat et multam pretiosam supellectilem [1] vestemque missam Carthaginem.

3 Octavo mense quam coeptum oppugnari captum Saguntum quidam scripsere; inde Carthaginem novam in hiberna Hannibalem concessisse; quinto deinde mense quam ab Carthagine profectus sit in
4 Italiam pervenisse. Quae si ita sunt, fieri non potuit ut P. Cornelius Ti. Sempronius consules fuerint ad quos et principio oppugnationis legati Saguntini missi sint et qui in suo magistratu cum Hannibale, alter ad Ticinum amnem, ambo aliquanto
5 post ad Trebiam, pugnaverint. Aut omnia breviora aliquanto fuere, aut Saguntum principio anni quo P. Cornelius Ti. Sempronius [2] consules fuerunt non
6 coeptum oppugnari est sed captum. Nam excessisse pugna ad Trebiam in annum Cn. Servili et C. Flamini non potest, quia C. Flaminius Arimini consulatum iniit, creatus a Ti. Sempronio consule, qui post pugnam ad Trebiam ad creandos consules Romam

their own heads, or took arms and never gave over B.C. 219
fighting till they died?

XV. The captured town yielded enormous spoils. For although much property had been destroyed on purpose by its owners, and in the carnage rage had scarce made any distinction of years, and the captives had been given as booty to the soldiers, nevertheless it is agreed that a large sum was realized from the sale of goods, and much valuable furniture and apparel sent to Carthage.

Some have recorded that Saguntum was taken in the eighth month from the beginning of the siege; that Hannibal then retired to New Carthage, into winter quarters; and then, after leaving New Carthage, arrived in the fifth month in Italy. If this is so, it cannot have been the case that Publius Cornelius and Tiberius Sempronius were the consuls to whom the Saguntine envoys were dispatched in the beginning of the siege, and who, in their own year of office, fought with Hannibal, the one at the river Ticinus, and both—a little later—at the Trebia. Either all these things took up somewhat less time, or Saguntum was not first besieged but finally captured in the outset of the year which had Cornelius and Sempronius as consuls. For the battle at the Trebia cannot have been fought as late as the consulship of Gnaeus Servilius and Gaius Flaminius; for Gaius Flaminius began his consulship at Ariminum, having been elected under the presidency of Tiberius Sempronius who was then consul, and had, after the battle at the Trebia, come to

---

[1] supellectilem *M*[2]: superlectilem *CM*[1].

[2] Ti. Sempronius ς: t. sempronius *CM*.

A.U.C. 535 cum venisset, comitiis perfectis ad exercitum in hiberna rediit.

XVI. Sub idem fere tempus et legati qui redierant ab Carthagine Romam rettulerunt omnia hostilia
2 esse et Sagunti excidium nuntiatum est; tantusque simul maeror patres misericordiaque sociorum peremptorum indigne et pudor non lati auxilii et ira in Carthaginienses metusque de summa rerum cepit, velut si iam ad portas hostis esset, ut tot uno tempore motibus animi turbati trepidarent magis
3 quam consulerent: nam neque hostem acriorem bellicosioremque secum congressum, nec rem Romanam tam desidem unquam fuisse atque imbellem.
4 Sardos Corsosque et Histros atque Illyrios lacessisse magis quam exercuisse Romana arma et cum Gallis
5 tumultuatum verius quam belligeratum: Poenum hostem veteranum, trium et viginti annorum militia durissima[1] inter Hispanas gentes semper victorem, duci acerrimo adsuetum, recentem ab excidio opu-
6 lentissimae urbis, Hiberum transire, trahere secum tot excitos Hispanorum populos, conciturum avidas

[1] durissima *CM* : durissimum *Ruehl.*

---

[1] This paragraph is a footnote, in which Livy attempts to clear up the chronological muddle which he has got himself into by disregarding the clear statements of Polybius and following an inferior authority. According to Polybius, Hannibal was made general and attacked the Olcades in 221 B.C. In 220 came the war with the Vaccaei and Carpetani. In 219 (consulship of M. Livius Salinator and L. Aemilius Paulus) came the siege of Saguntum, after which Hannibal put his army in winter quarters in New Carthage,

Rome to hold the consular elections, and then returned to the winter quarters of the army.[1] B.C. 219

XVI. At almost the same time the ambassadors who had returned from Carthage brought back word to Rome that all was hostile in that quarter, and the fall of Saguntum was announced. And so great was the grief of the senators, and their pity at the unmerited doom of their allies, and their shame at having failed to help them, and their wrath against the Carthaginians and fear for the safety of the commonwealth—as though the enemy were already at their gates—that, confounded with so many simultaneous emotions, they rather trembled than deliberated. For they felt that they had never encountered a fiercer or more warlike foe, and that Rome had never been so torpid and unwarlike. The Sardinians and Corsicans, the Histrians and Illyrians, had provoked but had hardly exercised the Roman arms; while against the Gauls there had been desultory fighting rather than real war.[2] But the Phoenician was an old and experienced enemy, who in the hardest kind of service amongst the Spanish tribes had for three and twenty years[3] invariably got the victory; he was accustomed to the keenest of commanders, was flushed with the conquest of a very wealthy city, and crossing the Ebro and drawing after him the many Spanish peoples which he

and in 218 set forth on the march to Italy (Polybius, III. xiii, xvii, xxxiii).

[2] The wars mentioned (and also a war with the Ligurians) occurred in the interval between the First and Second Punic Wars and were described in Book XX (see Summary).

[3] *i.e.* the interval between the First and Second Punic Wars, though the Carthaginian conquest of Spain had not actually begun so early as 241 B.C.

A.U.C. 535 semper armorum Gallicas gentes; cum orbe terrarum bellum gerendum in Italia ac pro moenibus Romanis esse.

XVII. Nominatae iam antea consulibus provinciae erant; tum sortiri iussi. Cornelio Hispania, Sem-
2 pronio Africa cum Sicilia evenit. Sex in eum annum decretae legiones et socium quantum ipsis videretur
3 et classis quanta parari posset. Quattuor et viginti peditum Romanorum milia scripta et mille octingenti equites, sociorum quadraginta milia peditum, quattuor milia et quadringenti equites; naves ducentae viginti
4 quinqueremes, celoces viginti[1] deducti. Latum inde ad populum, vellent iuberent populo Carthaginiensi bellum indici; eiusque belli causa supplicatio per urbem habita atque adorati di ut bene ac feliciter eveniret quod bellum populus Romanus iussisset.

5 Inter consules ita copiae divisae: Sempronio datae legiones duae—ea quaterna milia erant peditum et treceni[2] equites—et sociorum sedecim milia peditum, equites mille octingenti, naves longae centum sexa-
6 ginta, celoces duodecim. Cum his terrestribus maritimisque copiis Ti. Sempronius[3] missus in Siciliam, ita in Africam transmissurus si ad arcendum Italia
7 Poenum consul alter satis esset. Cornelio minus copiarum datum, quia L. Manlius praetor et ipse

[1] ducentae viginti quinqueremes, celoces viginti *edd.*: ccxxv remes (riemes *C*) quinque celoces xx *CM*.

[2] treceni *Crévier*: ccc *CM*: trecenti ς.

[3] Ti. Sempronius ς: t. sempronius *CM*.

had enlisted, would be rousing up the Gallic tribes— B.C. 219 always eager to unsheathe the sword—and the Romans would have to contend in war with all the world, in Italy and under the walls of Rome.

XVII. The fields of operation of the consuls had already been named: they were now commanded to draw lots for them. Cornelius obtained Spain, Sempronius Africa with Sicily. Six legions were voted for that year, with such allied contingents as the consuls themselves should approve and as large a fleet as could be got ready. There were enrolled four and twenty thousand Roman foot-soldiers and eighteen hundred horsemen, and of the allies forty thousand foot-soldiers and four thousand four hundred horsemen. Of ships there were launched two hundred and twenty quinqueremes, and twenty swift cruisers. The question was then laid before the people whether it were their will and pleasure that war be declared against the people of Carthage; and on their voting in the affirmative a supplication was held throughout the City and the gods were besought to grant a fair and prosperous outcome to the war which the Roman People had decreed.

The forces were divided between the consuls as follows: Sempronius received two legions—each numbering four thousand foot and three hundred horse—sixteen thousand foot of the allies, and eighteen hundred horse, together with a hundred and sixty warships and twelve swift cruisers. With these forces for land and sea Tiberius Sempronius was dispatched to Sicily, that he might cross by that way into Africa, if the other consul were able to keep the Phoenicians out of Italy. Cornelius was given fewer troops, since Lucius Manlius, the praetor,

A.U.C. 535 cum haud invalido praesidio in Galliam mittebatur;
8 navium maxime Cornelio numerus deminutus: sexaginta quinqueremes datae [1]—neque enim mari venturum aut ea parte belli dimicaturum hostem credebant—et duae Romanae legiones cum suo iusto equitatu et quattuordecim milibus sociorum peditum,
9 equitibus mille sescentis. Duas legiones Romanas et decem milia [2] sociorum peditum, mille equites socios, sescentos Romanos Gallia provincia eodem versa in Punicum bellum habuit.

A.U.C. 536 XVIII. His ita comparatis, ut omnia iusta ante bellum fierent, legatos maiores natu, Q. Fabium M. Livium L. Aemilium C. Licinium Q. Baebium in Africam mittunt ad percunctandos Carthaginienses publicone consilio Hannibal Saguntum oppugnasset;
2 et si, id quod facturi videbantur, faterentur ac defenderent publico consilio factum, ut indicerent
3 populo Carthaginiensi bellum. Romani postquam Carthaginem venerunt, cum senatus datus esset et Q. Fabius nihil ultra quam unum quod mandatum erat percunctatus esset, tum ex Carthaginiensibus
4 unus: "Praeceps vestra, Romani, et prior legatio fuit, cum Hannibalem tamquam suo consilio Saguntum oppugnantem deposcebatis; ceterum haec

[1] quinqueremes datae *CM*: quinqueremes datae celoces octo *Linsmayer*.

[2] decem milia *Gronovius*: cclcc C^1M: ccl (*with* x̄ Δ IIII *abov.*) C^3.

---

[1] M. Livius and L. Aemilius were consuls in 219 B.C., and since they were now available to serve on an embassy, it is a

was also being sent into Gaul with a not inconsiderable army; and of ships, in particular, he received a smaller number, namely, sixty quinqueremes, for they did not suppose that the enemy would come by sea or use that kind of warfare. He had two Roman legions with their proper complement of horse, and fourteen thousand infantry of the allies, with sixteen hundred horse. The province of Gaul received two Roman legions and ten thousand foot of the allies, with a thousand allied and six hundred Roman horse. These troops were designed for the same service—the Punic War. B.C. 219

XVIII. When these arrangements had been made, in order that, before going to war, they might observe all the formalities, they dispatched into Africa an embassy consisting of certain older men, to wit, Quintus Fabius, Marcus Livius, Lucius Aemilius,[1] Gaius Licinius, and Quintus Baebius, to demand of the Carthaginians whether Hannibal had attacked Saguntum with the sanction of the state; and if, as seemed likely to be the case, they should avow the act and stand to it as their public policy, to declare war on the Carthaginian People. As soon as the Romans had come to Carthage and the senate had granted them an audience, Quintus Fabius asked only the one question contained in his instructions. Then one of the Carthaginians replied: "There was something headlong, Romans, even in your former embassy, when you demanded that we surrender Hannibal on the ground that he was laying siege to Saguntum on his own responsibility; B.C. 218

fair inference that the embassy had not set out before the middle of March—then the beginning of the consular year—of 218 (*De Sanctis*, p. 1[1]).

A.U.C. 536

5 legatio verbis adhuc lenior est, re asperior. Tunc enim Hannibal et insimulabatur et deposcebatur; nunc ab nobis et confessio culpae exprimitur, et,
6 ut a confessis, res extemplo repetuntur. Ego autem non privato publicone consilio Saguntum oppugnatum sit quaerendum censeam, sed utrum iure an
7 iniuria; nostra enim haec quaestio atque animadversio in civem nostrum est, quid nostro aut suo fecerit arbitrio; vobiscum una disceptatio est, licue-
8 ritne per foedus fieri. Itaque quoniam discerni placet quid publico consilio quid sua sponte imperatores faciant, nobis vobiscum foedus est a C. Lutatio[1] consule ictum, in quo cum caveretur utrorumque sociis, nihil de Saguntinis—necdum enim erant socii
9 vestri—cautum est. At enim eo foedere quod cum Hasdrubale ictum est Saguntini excipiuntur. Adversus quod ego nihil dicturus sum nisi quod a vobis
10 didici. Vos enim quod C. Lutatius[2] consul primo nobiscum foedus icit,[3] quia neque auctoritate patrum nec populi iussu ictum erat, negastis vos eo teneri; itaque aliud de integro foedus publico consilio ictum
11 est. Si vos non tenent foedera vestra nisi ex auctoritate aut iussu vestro icta, ne nos quidem Hasdru-

[1] a C. Lutatio *edd.* : ac lutatio *C*: aclutacio *M*.
[2] Lutatius *edd.* : luctacius *C*: luctacios *M*.
[3] icit ς: iecit *CM*; fecit *Alschefski.*

but your present embassy, though expressed thus far more mildly, is in reality more harsh. For on that occasion Hannibal was both accused and his surrender called for; at present you are trying to wring a confession from us, and, as though we had pleaded guilty, demand instant satisfaction. But to me it would seem that you ought to ask, not whether Saguntum was besieged as the result of private or of public policy, but whether justly or unjustly. For it belongs to us to enquire what our fellow citizen has done on our authority or his own, and to punish him; with you the only question we have to discuss is this, whether what he did was permissible under the treaty. Well then, since you wish that a distinction should be drawn between the things that generals do by direction of the state and the acts for which they are themselves responsible, let me remind you that we have a treaty with you, which Gaius Lutatius, your consul, made, wherein, although the allies of both sides were protected, there was no provision made regarding the Saguntines, for as yet they were not your allies. 'But,' you will say, 'in that treaty which was made with Hasdrubal, the Saguntines are expressly cared for.' To this I shall make no other answer than the one that I have learnt from you. For you denied that you were bound by the treaty which Gaius Lutatius, the consul, originally entered into with us, because it had been made without the senate's sanction or the people's command; accordingly a new treaty, having the approval of the state, was entered into. Now, if you are not bound by your treaties, unless they are concluded at your own instance or command, no more could the B.C. 218

A.U.C. 536 balis foedus, quod nobis insciis icit, obligare potuit.
12 Proinde omittite Sagunti atque Hiberi mentionem
facere et quod diu parturit animus vester aliquando
13 pariat!" Tum Romanus sinu ex toga facto "Hic"
inquit "vobis bellum et pacem portamus: utrum
placet sumite!" Sub hanc vocem haud minus fero-
14 citer, daret utrum vellet, succlamatum est; et cum
is iterum sinu effuso bellum dare dixisset, accipere
se omnes responderunt et quibus acciperent animis
iisdem se gesturos.

XIX. Haec derecta[1] percunctatio ac denuntiatio
belli magis ex dignitate populi Romani visa est quam
de foederum iure verbis disceptare, cum ante tum
2 maxime Sagunto excisa. Nam si verborum discepta-
tionis res esset, quid foedus Hasdrubalis cum Lutati
priore foedere, quod mutatum est, comparandum
3 erat? Cum in Lutati foedere diserte additum esset
ita id ratum fore si populus censuisset, in Hasdrubalis foedere nec exceptum tale quicquam fuerit et
tot annorum silentio ita vivo eo comprobatum sit
foedus ut ne mortuo auctore quicquam mutaretur.
4 Quamquam, etsi priore foedere staretur, satis cautum
erat Saguntinis, sociis utrorumque exceptis; nam
neque additum erat "iis qui tunc essent" nec "ne

[1] derecta *Alschefski*: directa ς: decreta *CM*.

treaty of Hasdrubal, which he made without our B.C. 218
knowledge, be binding upon us. Cease then to prate of Saguntum and the Ebro, and bring forth at last the thought with which your mind has long been in travail!" Then the Roman, gathering up his toga into a fold, said, "We bring you here both war and peace; choose which you will!" When he had said these words, they cried out with no less truculence that he might give them whichever he liked; and on his shaking out the fold again, and announcing that he gave them war, they all replied that they accepted it, and in that same spirit in which they accepted it were resolved to wage it.

XIX. This straightforward demand and declaration of war seemed more in keeping with the dignity of the Roman People than to bandy words regarding the rights involved in treaties, especially at that moment, when Saguntum had been destroyed. Though for that matter, had it been proper to debate the question, what comparison could there be between Hasdrubal's treaty and the earlier treaty of Lutatius, which was altered? For in the treaty of Lutatius it had been expressly added that it should be valid only if the people ratified it; but in Hasdrubal's treaty no such proviso had been made, and by the silence of so many years the treaty had during his lifetime been so sanctioned that even on its author's death no slightest change was made in it. And yet, even if the earlier treaty were adhered to, the Saguntines had been sufficiently protected by the provision made concerning the allies of both the parties; for there had been no specification of "those who were then allies," nor exception of "such as might after-

A.U.C. 536 5 qui postea adsumerentur." Et cum adsumere novos
liceret socios, quis aequum [1] censeret aut ob nulla
quemquam merita in amicitiam recipi, aut receptos
in fidem non defendi? Tantum ne Carthaginiensium
socii aut sollicitarentur ad defectionem aut sua
sponte desciscentes reciperentur.
6 Legati Romani ab Carthagine, sicut iis Romae
imperatum erat, in Hispaniam, ut adirent civitates
et [2] in societatem perlicerent aut averterent a
7 Poenis, traiecerunt. Ad Bargusios primum venerunt; a quibus benigne excepti, quia taedebat
imperii Punici, multos trans Hiberum populos ad
8 cupidinem novae fortunae erexerunt. Ad Volcianos
inde est ventum, quorum celebre per Hispaniam
responsum ceteros populos ab societate Romana
avertit. Ita enim maximus natu ex iis in concilio
9 respondit: "Quae verecundia est, Romani, postulare
vos uti vestram Carthaginiensium amicitiae prae-
ponamus, cum qui id fecerunt [3] crudelius quam
10 Poenus hostis perdidit [4] vos socii prodideritis? Ibi
quaeratis socios, censeo, ubi Saguntina clades ignota
est; Hispanis populis sicut lugubre ita insigne
documentum Sagunti ruinae erunt, ne quis fidei
11 Romanae aut societati confidat." Inde extemplo
abire finibus Volcianorum iussi ab nullo deinde

[1] quis aequum *edd.*: quis equum C^4M^3: qui secum C^1: quis secum M^1.

[2] et ς: ut *CM*: et aut *Gronovius*.

[3] fecerunt *Madvig*: fecerunt Saguntini *CM*.

[4] perdidit *edd.*: prodidit *CM*.

---

[1] The Bargusii, N. of the Ebro, were not as yet in the power of the Carthaginians, but were growing uneasy at the prospect of annexation (cf. chap. xxiii. § 2).

wards be received." And since they were permitted B.C. 218 to take new allies, who would think it fair either that they should admit no one, however deserving, to their friendship, or that, having once taken people under their protection, they should not defend them—provided only that allies of the Carthaginians should not be tempted to desert them nor be made welcome if they left them voluntarily?

The ambassadors, conformably to the instructions given them in Rome, crossed over from Carthage into Spain for the purpose of approaching the different states and winning them to an alliance, or at least detaching them from the Phoenicians. The Bargusii were the first they visited, and being warmly welcomed by them, for men were wearying of the Punic sway,[1] they aroused in many nations south of the Ebro a desire to revolt. From there they came to the Volciani, who gave them an answer that was carried all over Spain and turned all the other states against an alliance with the Romans. For the eldest of them replied as follows in their council: "With what face, Romans, can you ask us to prefer your friendship to the Carthaginian, when those who did so have been more cruelly betrayed by you, their allies, than destroyed by their enemy, the Phoenician? You must seek allies, in my opinion, only where the disaster of Saguntum is unknown. To the Spanish peoples the ruins of Saguntum will constitute a warning, no less emphatic than deplorable, that none should trust to the honour or alliance of the Romans." Being then bidden straightway to depart out of the borders of the Volciani, they received from that day forth

A.U.C. 536 concilio Hispaniae benigniora verba tulere. Ita nequiquam peragrata Hispania in Galliam transeunt.

XX. Ibi iis[1] nova terribilisque species visa est, quod armati—ita mos gentis erat—in concilium vene-
2 runt. Cum verbis extollentes gloriam virtutemque populi Romani ac magnitudinem imperii petissent ne Poeno bellum Italiae inferenti per agros urbesque
3 suas transitum darent, tantus cum fremitu risus dicitur ortus ut vix a magistratibus maioribusque
4 natu iuventus sedaretur; adeo stolida impudensque postulatio visa est censere[2] ne in Italiam transmittant Galli bellum, ipsos id avertere[3] in se,
5 agrosque suos pro alienis populandos obicere. Sedato tandem fremitu responsum legatis est neque Romanorum in se meritum esse neque Carthaginiensium iniuriam ob quae aut pro Romanis aut adversus
6 Poenos sumant arma; contra ea audire sese gentis suae homines agro finibusque Italiae pelli a populo Romano stipendiumque pendere[4] et cetera indigna
7 pati. Eadem ferme in ceteris Galliae conciliis dicta auditaque; nec hospitale quicquam pacatumve satis
8 prius auditum quam Massiliam venere. Ibi omnia ab sociis inquisita cum cura ac fide cognita: prae-

[1] Ibi iis *C. Heraeus*: in iis *CM*.
[2] visa est censere ne *CM* : visa est ne *Gronovius*.
[3] avertere ς: aduertere *CM*.
[4] pendere ς: pendi *CM*.

---

[1] At an earlier date the Romans, too, had come armed to their assembly—the centuriate comitia (I. xliv. 1).

[2] Massilia (Marseilles), founded by Phocaeans about 600 B.C., had been, from the period of the Kings, a faithful ally of Rome.

no kinder response from any Spanish council. B.C. 218 Accordingly, having traversed that country to no purpose, they passed over into Gaul.

XX. There they beheld a strange and terrifying spectacle, for the Gauls, as was customary with the race, came armed to their assembly.[1] When the envoys, boasting of the renown and valour of the Roman People and the extent of their dominion, requested the Gauls to deny the Phoenician a passage through their lands and cities, if he should attempt to carry the war into Italy, it is said that they burst out into such peals of laughter that the magistrates and elders could scarce reduce the younger men to order—so stupid and impudent a thing it seemed, to propose that the Gauls should not suffer the invaders to pass into Italy, but bring down the war on their own heads, and offer their own fields to be pillaged in place of other men's. When at last the uproar had been quelled, the Gauls made answer to the envoys that they owed the Romans no kindness nor the Carthaginians any grudge, to induce them to draw the sword in behalf of the former or against the latter; on the contrary, they heard that men of their own race were being driven from the land and even out of the borders of Italy by the Roman People, and were paying tribute and suffering every other humiliation. In the rest of the Gallic councils their proposals and the replies they got were to substantially the same effect, nor did they hear a single word of a truly friendly or peaceable tenor until they reached Massilia.[2] Here they learned of all that had happened from their allies, who had made enquiries with faithful diligence. They reported that

A.U.C. 536 occupatos iam ante ab Hannibale Gallorum animos esse; sed ne illi quidem ipsi satis mitem gentem fore—adeo ferocia atque indomita ingenia esse—ni subinde auro, cuius avidissima gens est, principum
9 animi concilientur. Ita peragratis Hispaniae Galliaeque populis[1] legati Romam redeunt haud ita multo post quam consules in provincias profecti erant. Civitatem omnem exspectatione[2] belli erectam[3] invenerunt satis constante fama iam Hiberum Poenos tramisisse.

A.U.C. 535–536 XXI. Hannibal Sagunto capto Carthaginem novam in hiberna concesserat, ibique auditis quae Romae quaeque Carthagine acta decretaque forent seque non ducem solum sed etiam causam esse belli,
2 partitis divenditisque[4] reliquiis[5] praedae nihil ultra differendum ratus Hispani generis milites convocat.
3 "Credo ego vos," inquit "socii, et ipsos cernere[6] pacatis omnibus Hispaniae populis aut finiendam nobis militiam exercitusque dimittendos esse aut in
4 alias terras transferendum bellum; ita enim hae gentes non pacis solum sed etiam victoriae bonis florebunt, si ex aliis gentibus praedam et gloriam
5 quaeremus. Itaque cum longinqua a domo instet

[1] Hispaniae Galliaeque populis *Luchs*: hispania galliaque populisque P^2: hispaniae et galliae populis P^1.
[2] exspectatione *Heerwagen*: in expectatione *P*.
[3] erectam P^2: ereptam P^1.
[4] divenditisque ς: diuidentitisque (*from* diuidenditis) P^1: diuidendisque P^2
[5] reliquiis *edd.*: reliquis *P*.
[6] cernere P^2: gernere (*from* genere) P^1.

[1] Livy makes Hannibal speak with rhetorical exaggeration. The Spanish troops whom he is addressing have not conquered 'every tribe in Spain,' for they came themselves

Hannibal had been beforehand with the Romans in gaining the good-will of the Gauls, but that even he would find them hardly tractable—so fierce and untamed was their nature—unless from time to time he should make use of gold, of which the race is very covetous, to secure the favour of their principal men. So the envoys, having travelled through the nations of Spain and Gaul, returned to Rome, not long after the consuls had set out for their respective commands. They found the citizens all on tip-toe with expectation of the war, for the rumour persisted that the Phoenicians had already crossed the Ebro. B.C. 218

XXI. Hannibal, after the capture of Saguntum, had withdrawn his army into winter quarters at New Carthage. There he learned what had been done in Rome and Carthage and what had been decreed, and that he was not only commander in the war, but the cause of it as well. So, having divided or sold off what was left of the plunder, he thought best to defer his plans no longer, and, calling together the soldiers of Spanish blood, thus addressed them: "My allies, I doubt not that you yourselves perceive how, having conquered every tribe in Spain, we must either bring our campaigning to a close and disband our armies, or shift the seat of war to other countries.[1] For these nations here will enjoy the blessings not merely of peace, but also of victory, only if we look to other nations for spoils and glory. Since, therefore, you are on the eve of an expedition that will carry B.C. 219–218

from tribes which had been for some years friendly and subject to the Carthaginians. He had not indeed conquered all the *hostile* tribes, but only those lying south of the Ebro.

A.U.C. 535–536 militia incertumque sit quando domos vestras et quae
cuique ibi cara sunt visuri sitis, si quis vestrum suos
6 invisere volt, commeatum do. Primo vere[1] edico
adsitis, ut dis bene iuvantibus bellum ingentis gloriae
7 praedaeque futurum incipiamus." Omnibus fere
visendi domos oblata ultro potestas grata erat et iam
desiderantibus suos et longius in futurum providen-
8 tibus desiderium. Per totum tempus hiemis quies
inter labores aut iam[2] exhaustos aut mox exhauri-
endos renovavit corpora animosque ad omnia de
integro patienda. Vere primo ad edictum con-
venere.

A.U.C. 536 9 Hannibal, cum recensuisset omnium gentium
auxilia, Gades profectus Herculi vota exsolvit
novisque se obligat votis, si cetera prospera evenis-
10 sent. Inde partiens curas simul in inferendum[3]
atque arcendum bellum, ne, dum ipse terrestri per
Hispaniam Galliasque itinere Italiam peteret, nuda
apertaque Romanis Africa ab Sicilia esset, valido
11 praesidio firmare eam statuit. Pro eo supplementum
ipse ex Africa maxime iaculatorum, levium armis,
petit, ut Afri in Hispania Hispani in Africa,[4] melior
procul ab domo futurus uterque miles, velut mutuis
12 pigneribus obligati stipendia facerent. Tredecim
milia octingentos quinquaginta pedites caetratos

[1] primo vere P^2. promoueri P^1.
[2] iam ς : etiam *P*.
[3] in inferendum *Gronovius* : inferendum *P*.
[4] Hispani in Africa ς : in africa P^1 : in africa hispani P^2.

---

[1] Gades (Cadiz) was a Tyrian colony and possessed a famous temple of Melkarth (whom the Romans identified with Hercules), the tutelary god of the mother city.

[2] Like the Greek πελτασταί, these were light infantry

you far afield, and it is uncertain when you will see again your homes and what there is dear to each of you, if any of you desires to visit his friends, I grant him furlough. Be at hand, I charge you, with the first signs of spring, that with Heaven's good help we may begin a war that shall bring us vast renown and booty." There were very few who did not welcome the opportunity thus freely proffered of visiting their homes, for they were already homesick and looked forward to an even longer separation from their friends. The full winter's rest between the labours already undergone and those that were presently to come gave them new strength and courage for a fresh encounter with every hardship. Early in the spring they assembled in obedience to their orders. B.C. 219–218

When Hannibal had reviewed the contingents sent in by all the nations, he went to Gades[1] and discharged his vows to Hercules, binding himself with fresh ones, in case he should be successful in the remainder of his undertaking. Then, with equal concern for attack and defence, lest while he should be himself advancing upon Italy by an overland march through Spain and Gaul, Africa might lie exposed and open to a Roman invasion on the side of Sicily, he resolved to garrison that country with a powerful force. To supply its place he requisitioned troops for himself from Africa—light-armed slingers chiefly—so that Africans might serve in Spain and Spaniards in Africa, and both be the better soldiers for being far from home, as though mutually pledged to loyalty. Thirteen thousand eight hundred and fifty targeteers[2] and eight B.C. 218

whose defensive armour consisted of a small round shield covered with oxhide.

A.U.C. 536 misit in Africam et funditores Baliares octingentos septuaginta, equites mixtos ex multis gentibus mille
13 ducentos. Has copias partim Carthagini praesidio esse, partim distribui per Africam iubet. Simul conquisitoribus in civitates missis quattuor milia conscripta delectae iuventutis, praesidium eosdem et obsides, duci Carthaginem iubet.

XXII. Neque Hispaniam neglegendam ratus, atque id eo minus quod haud ignarus erat circumitam ab Romanis eam legatis ad sollicitandos prin-
2 cipum animos, Hasdrubali fratri, viro impigro, eam provinciam destinat firmatque[1] Africis maxime praesidiis, peditum Afrorum undecim milibus octingentis quinquaginta, Liguribus trecentis, Baliaribus
3 quingentis.[2] Ad haec peditum auxilia additi equites Libyphoenices, mixtum Punicum Afris genus, quadringenti quinquaginta et[3] Numidae Maurique, accolae Oceani, ad mille octingenti et parva Ilergetum manus ex Hispania, trecenti[4] equites, et ne quod[5] terrestris deesset auxilii genus, elephanti
4 viginti unus.[6] Classis praeterea data tuendae maritimae orae,[7] quia qua parte belli vicerant ea tum

[1] firmatque *Woelfflin*: firmatque eum *CM*²: firmatque cum M¹: firmatque eam *Linsmayer*.

[2] quingentis *added by Glareanus* (*from Polyb.* III. xxxiii. 16).

[3] quinquaginta et *added by Alschefski* (*from Polyb.* III. xxxiii. 15).

[4] trecenti *Ruperti* (*Polyb.* III. xxxiii. 16): cc *CM*.

[5] quod ς: quid *CM*.

[6] viginti unus *Sigonius* (*Polyb. ibid.*): xiiii milia (*and other corruptions*) *CM*.

[7] tuendae maritimae orae ς: ad tuende maritume ore *C*¹: ad tuendae maritumae orae *M* (*changed by original hand to* ad tuenda maritumae ora).

[1] The Baliares (Majorca and Minorca) furnished the most skilful slingers in the world. Livy says (XXVIII. xxxvii. 6)

hundred and seventy Baliaric slingers,[1] with twelve hundred horsemen drawn from many nations, he sent to Africa. A part of these troops were to be a garrison for Carthage, a part to be distributed through the country. At the same time he directed that recruiting officers be sent out into the states,[2] and that four thousand picked men be brought to Carthage, to serve at once as defenders and as hostages. B.C. 218

XXII. And considering that neither must Spain be neglected, and so much the less since he was not unaware that Roman ambassadors had journeyed through it to seek the support of its leading men, he appointed it to be the charge of his brother Hasdrubal—an active, energetic man—and secured it with troops, for the most part African. Of infantry there were eleven thousand eight hundred and fifty Africans, three hundred Ligurians, and five hundred Baliares. To these infantry forces he added the following units of cavalry: four hundred and fifty Libyphoenicians—a race of mixed Punic and African blood—and some eight hundred Numidians and Moors, who dwell near the ocean,[3] and a little company of three hundred Spanish Ilergetes. Finally, that no sort of land force might be lacking, there were twenty-one elephants. He also assigned a fleet to Spain, for the protection of its seaboard, since it might be expected that the Romans would

that no single individual of any other people was so superior in this art to his fellows as were all the Baliares to the rest of mankind. The ancients derived Baliares from *βάλλειν*, "throw."

[2] *sc.* of Africa.

[3] Mauretania corresponded to the present Fez and Morocco.

A.U.C. 536 quoque rem gesturos Romanos credi poterat, quinquaginta quinqueremes, quadriremes duae, triremes
quinque; sed aptae instructaeque remigio triginta
et duae quinqueremes erant et triremes quinque.
5 Ab Gadibus Carthaginem ad hiberna exercitus
redit; atque inde profectus praeter Onusam[1] urbem
6 ad Hiberum per maritimam oram[2] ducit. Ibi fama
est in quiete visum ab eo iuvenem divina specie, qui
se ab Iove diceret ducem in Italiam Hannibali missum: proinde sequeretur neque usquam a se deflec-
7 teret oculos. Pavidum primo nusquam circum-
spicientem aut respicientem secutum; deinde cura
ingenii humani, cum quidnam id esset quod respicere[3]
vetitus esset agitaret animo, temperare oculis nequi-
8 visse; tum[4] vidisse post sese serpentem mira magnitudine cum ingenti arborum ac virgultorum strage
ferri ac post insequi cum fragore caeli nimbum.
9 Tum quae moles ea quidve prodigii esset quaerentem
audisse vastitatem Italiae esse: pergeret porro ire
nec ultra inquireret sineretque fata in occulto esse.

XXIII. Hoc visu laetus tripertito Hiberum copias traiecit praemissis qui Gallorum animos, qua traducendus exercitus erat, donis conciliarent Alpiumque transitus specularentur. Nonaginta milia peditum,

[1] Onusam *M. Mueller*: omissam *CM.*
[2] per maritimam oram *Weissenborn*: mariti(-tu- *C*)mam oram *CM.*
[3] respicere ς: respiceret *CM.* [4] tum ς: eum *CM.*

---

[1] In this enumeration of forces Livy follows Polybius (III. xxxiii. 9), who says that he found the numbers recorded

again on this occasion employ that mode of warfare in which they had been victorious. There were fifty quinqueremes, two quadriremes, and five triremes. But only thirty-two quinqueremes and the five triremes were equipped and manned with rowers.[1] B.C. 218

From Gades Hannibal returned to New Carthage, to the winter quarters of his army. Setting out from thence, he marched along the coast, past the city of Onusa, to the Ebro. It was there, as they tell, that he saw in his sleep a youth of godlike aspect, who declared that he was sent by Jupiter to lead him into Italy: let him follow, therefore, nor anywhere turn his eyes away from his guide. At first he was afraid and followed, neither looking to the right nor to the left, nor yet behind him; but presently wondering, with that curiosity to which all of us are prone, what it could be that he had been forbidden to look back upon, he was unable to command his eyes; then he saw behind him a serpent of monstrous size, that moved along with vast destruction of trees and underbrush, and a storm-cloud coming after, with loud claps of thunder; and, on his asking what this prodigious portent was, he was told that it was the devastation of Italy: he was therefore to go on, nor enquire further, but suffer destiny to be wrapped in darkness.

XXIII. Rejoicing at this vision, he led his troops across the Ebro in three columns, after sending agents ahead, to win over with presents the Gauls who dwelt in the region which the army had to cross, and to explore the passes of the Alps. He had ninety thousand foot and twelve thousand horse

by Hannibal himself on a bronze tablet which was set up on the Lacinian Promontory (near Crotona).

A.U.C. 536 2 duodecim milia equitum Hiberum traduxit. Ilergetes
inde Bargusiosque[1] et Ausetanos et Lacetaniam,[2]
quae subiecta Pyrenaeis montibus est, subegit,
oraeque huic omni praefecit Hannonem, ut fauces
quae Hispanias Galliis iungunt in potestate essent.
3 Decem milia peditum Hannoni ad praesidium obti-
nendae regionis data et mille equites.

4 Postquam per Pyrenaeum saltum traduci exercitus
est coeptus rumorque per barbaros manavit certior
de bello Romano, tria milia inde Carpetanorum peditum iter averterunt. Constabat non tam bello motos
quam longinquitate viae insuperabilique Alpium tran-
5 situ. Hannibal, quia revocare aut vi retinere eos anceps
erat, ne ceterorum etiam feroces animi inritarentur,
6 supra septem milia hominum domos remisit, quos et
ipsos[3] gravari militia senserat, Carpetanos quoque
ab se dimissos simulans.

XXIV. Inde, ne mora atque otium animos sollici-
taret, cum reliquis copiis Pyrenaeum transgreditur
2 et ad oppidum Iliberri castra locat. Galli, quamquam
Italiae bellum inferri audiebant, tamen, quia vi
subactos trans Pyrenaeum Hispanos fama erat prae-
sidiaque valida imposita, metu servitutis ad arma
consternati Ruscinonem aliquot[4] populi conveniunt.
3 Quod ubi Hannibali nuntiatum est, moram magis

[1] Bargusiosque ς : bargutosque C^3M : barguntosque C^1.
[2] Lacetaniam *Sigonius* : aquitaniā C^3M : aquitanos C^1.
[3] ipsos *Muretus* : ipse *CM* : ipsa *Unger*.
[4] aliquot C^3 : aliquod C^1M.

---

[1] Polybius (III. xxxv. 7) says that Hannibal now had fifty thousand foot and about nine thousand horse.

[2] The modern Elne is near the site.

when he crossed the Ebro. He now subdued the Ilergetes, and the Bargusii and Ausetani, and also Lacetania, which lies at the foot of the Pyrenees. All this coast he put in charge of Hanno, that the passes connecting Spain and Gaul might be under his control. To garrison this district, he gave Hanno ten thousand foot and a thousand horse. B.C. 218

When the army had entered the defiles which lead over the Pyrenees, and more definite rumours had spread amongst the barbarians that the war was to be with Rome, three thousand of the Carpetanian foot turned back. It was understood that they were influenced not so much by the war as by the long march and the impossibility of crossing the Alps. To recall them or to detain them forcibly would have been hazardous, for it might have roused resentment in the savage bosoms of the others. And so Hannibal sent back to their homes above seven thousand more, whom he had perceived to be chafing at the service, pretending that he had also dismissed the Carpetani.

XXIV. Then, in order that his troops might not become demoralized by delay and inaction, he crossed the Pyrenees with the remainder of his forces[1] and pitched his camp by the town of Iliberri.[2] The Gauls, though they heard that the war was aimed at Italy, nevertheless, because it was said that the Spaniards beyond the Pyrenees had been forcibly subjugated and strong garrisons imposed upon them, were driven by the fear of servitude to arm themselves, and several tribes assembled at Ruscino.[3] When Hannibal was apprised of this, he was more

[3] The name is reflected in the French Tour de Roussillon, near Perpignan.

A.U.C. 536 quam bellum metuens oratores ad regulos eorum misit: conloqui semet ipsum cum iis velle; et vel illi propius Iliberrim[1] accederent, vel se Ruscinonem processurum, ut ex propinquo congressus facilior
4 esset; nam et accepturum eos in castra sua se laetum nec cunctanter se ipsum ad eos venturum. Hospitem enim se Galliae non hostem advenisse, nec stricturum ante gladium, si per Gallos liceat,
5 quam in Italiam venisset. Et per nuntios quidem haec; ut vero reguli Gallorum castris ad Iliberrim extemplo motis haud gravate[2] ad Poenum venerunt, capti donis cum bona pace exercitum per fines suos praeter Ruscinonem oppidum transmiserunt.

XXV. In Italiam interim nihil ultra quam Hiberum transisse Hannibalem a Massiliensium legatis Romam
2 perlatum erat, cum perinde ac si Alpes iam transisset, Boi sollicitatis Insubribus defecerunt nec tam ob veteres in populum Romanum iras quam quod nuper circa Padum Placentiam Cremonamque colonias in
3 agrum[3] Gallicum deductas aegre patiebantur. Itaque armis repente arreptis in eum ipsum agrum impetu facto tantum terroris ac tumultus fecerunt ut non agrestis modo multitudo sed ipsi triumviri Romani, qui ad agrum venerant adsignandum, diffisi

[1] Iliberrim *edd.*: inliberrim *C*: inliberarim *M*[1]: illiberri *M*[3].

[2] gravate ς: grauanter *CM*.

[3] agrum *C*[3]*M*[3]: agrorum *C*[1] ?*M*[1].

---

[1] Livy has said nothing of any negotiations between Hannibal and the Boi, preferring, in his love of dramatic effect, to let us see this Gallic outbreak as it appeared to the Romans—like a bolt from the blue. See chap. xxix. § 6.

afraid of delay than of fighting, and dispatched ambassadors to their chieftains to inform them that he wished to confer with them in person, and suggested that either they come nearer to Iliberri or that he would go forward to Ruscino, so that being close to one another they might meet more easily. He would be glad, he said, to receive them in his camp, nor would he hesitate to go to them. He had come into Gaul as a friend, not as an enemy, and would keep his sword sheathed, if the Gauls would let him, till he had entered Italy. Thus far his emissaries. But when the Gallic chieftains, moving up their camp at once near Iliberri, came, nothing loath, to the Phoenician, they were captivated by his gifts, and permitted the army to march unmolested through their borders and past the town of Ruscino. B.C. 218

XXV. In Italy meanwhile nothing more was known than that Hannibal had crossed the Ebro—which was the news that Massiliot envoys brought to Rome—when, as though he had already crossed the Alps, the Boi, after rousing up the Insubres, revolted.[1] To this they were incited not so much by their old animosity against the Roman People as by vexation at the recent establishment of colonies in Gallic territory, near the Po, at Placentia and Cremona.[2] Flying to arms they made an incursion into that very district, and spread such terror and confusion that not only the rural population, but the Roman commissioners themselves, who had come for the purpose of assigning lands, not trusting to the

[2] These were of the type called Latin colonies. To each of them six thousand colonists had been assigned. They had hardly got settled when the Gauls broke out (Polybius, III. xl. 3–6).

A.U.C. 536 Placentiae moenibus Mutinam confugerint, C.
4 Lutatius C. Servilius[1] M. Annius.[2] Lutati nomen
haud dubium est; pro Annio Servilioque M'.
Acilium[3] et C. Herennium habent quidam annales,
alii P. Cornelium Asinam et C. Papirium Masonem.[4]
5 Id quoque dubium est, legati ad expostulandum
missi ad Boios violati sint,[5] an in triumviros agrum
6 metantes impetus sit factus. Mutinae cum obside-
rentur et gens ad oppugnandarum urbium artes
rudis, pigerrima eadem ad militaria opera, segnis
intactis adsideret muris, simulari coeptum de pace
7 agi, evocatique ab Gallorum principibus legati ad
conloquium, non contra ius modo gentium sed
violata etiam quae data in id tempus erat fide,
comprehenduntur, negantibus Gallis nisi obsides sibi
8 redderentur eos dimissuros. Cum haec de legatis
nuntiata essent et Mutina praesidiumque in periculo
esset, L. Manlius praetor ira accensus effusum agmen
9 ad Mutinam ducit. Silvae tunc circa viam erant
plerisque incultis. Ibi inexplorato profectus in
insidias praecipitatur[6] multaque cum caede suorum
10 aegre in apertos campos emersit. Ibi castra com-

[1] C. Servilius *Sigonius*: ā seruilius *CM*.

[2] Annius ς: annilius *CM*.

[3] Annio Servilioque M'. Acilium *Weissenborn*: aulo seruilio quem acilium C^1: aulo seruilio m̄ acilium C^3: aulo seruilio quem̄ acilio (aciliū M^3)*M*.

[4] Masonem ς: nasonem *C*: nassonem *M*.

[5] sint ς: sint incertum *CM*.

[6] praecipitatur *Gronovius*: praecipitatus *CM*.

---

[1] Apparently the Gauls left hostages with the Romans when they arranged for the Romans to send representatives to talk things over with them in the Gallic camp.

[2] Neither Polybius nor Livy tells us where Manlius was when the news reached him. Weissenborn-Mueller think he

walls of Placentia, fled to Mutina. (Their names B.C. 218
were Gaius Lutatius, Gaius Servilius, and Marcus Annius. There is no question about Lutatius: for Annius and Servilius, some annals have Manius Acilius and Gaius Herennius, others Publius Cornelius Asina and Gaius Papirius Maso. This, too, is uncertain, whether envoys sent to expostulate with the Boi were maltreated, or an attack was made upon the three commissioners as they were measuring off the land.) Whilst they lay shut up in Mutina, the Gauls—who know nothing of the art of assaulting cities, and, besides, are very indolent in regard to siege-works, and were now sitting idly down before the walls without attempting them—feigned a readiness to treat for peace; and their leaders having invited the Romans to send out spokesmen to confer with them, they seized these envoys, in violation not only of the law of nations, but also of a pledge which they had given for this time, and declared that they would not let them go unless their own hostages were restored to them.[1] When word arrived of this affair of the envoys, and Mutina and its garrison were in danger, Lucius Manlius, the praetor, blazing with resentment, set out for Mutina with his army in loose marching order.[2] In those days the road led through a forest, as the country was not, for the most part, under cultivation, and Manlius, advancing without reconnaissance, plunged into an ambush, and after sustaining heavy losses, managed with difficulty to get through into the open fields. There he entrenched

was at Placentia, engaged in strengthening the new fortifications.

A.U.C. 536 munita, et quia Gallis ad temptanda ea defuit spes,
refecti sunt militum animi, quamquam ad quin-
11 gentos[1] cecidisse satis constabat. Iter deinde de
integro coeptum nec, dum per patentia[2] loca
12 ducebatur agmen, apparuit[3] hostis; ubi rursus silvae
intratae, tum postremos adorti cum magna trepidatione ac pavore omnium septingentos milites occide-
13 runt, sex signa ademere. Finis et Gallis territandi
et pavendi fuit Romanis ut e saltu[4] invio atque
impedito evasere. Inde apertis locis facile tutantes
agmen Romani Tannetum, vicum propinquum Pado,
14 contendere. Ibi se munimento ad tempus com-
meatibusque fluminis et Brixianorum etiam Gallorum
auxilio adversus crescentem in dies multitudinem
hostium tutabantur.

XXVI. Qui tumultus repens postquam est Romam
perlatus et Punicum insuper Gallico bellum auctum
2 patres acceperunt, C. Atilium praetorem cum una
legione Romana et quinque milibus sociorum dilectu
novo a consule conscriptis auxilium ferre Manlio[5]
iubent, qui sine ullo certamine—abscesserant enim
metu hostes—Tannetum pervenit.

[1] quingentos (D) *added by Gronovius.*
[2] patentia M^2: inpacientia C: inpactentia M^1.
[3] apparuit *Glareanus*: cum apparuit *CM.*
[4] e saltu M^2: e saltus M^1: exaltu C^1: ex saltu C^3.
[5] Manlio *edd.*: manilio *CM.*

---

[1] This second attack—Polybius records but the one—is suspiciously like the first. Livy, or Livy's immediate source, may unconsciously have made two episodes out of slightly different accounts of the same affair.

[2] Tannetum (now Tanneto) was really about ten miles south of the Po, on the Via Aemilia Lepida. If *commeatibus fluminis* is correctly translated, we may suppose (1) that Livy thought Tannetum was much nearer the Po, or (2) that

a camp, and since the Gauls lacked heart to assail it, B.C. 218
the soldiers recovered their spirits, though it was no secret that as many as five hundred men had fallen. Then they began their march again, nor, so long as the column advanced through open country, was the enemy to be seen; but when they had once more got into the woods, the Gauls attacked their rear, and throwing the whole column into terror and confusion, slew seven hundred soldiers and carried off six ensigns.[1] The alarming onsets of the Gauls and the panic of the Romans ended when they got clear of the trackless woods and thickets. Thereafter, marching across open ground, the Romans had no difficulty in protecting their column, and hastened to Tannetum, a village lying near the Po, where by means of temporary fortifications and supplies got in by the river, and with the help also of the Brixian Gauls, they defended themselves against the enemy, whose numbers were increasing daily.[2]

XXVI. When the news of this sudden insurrection was brought to Rome, and the Fathers learnt that the Punic War was augmented by a war with the Gauls, they commanded Gaius Atilius, the praetor, to take one Roman legion and five thousand of the allies—a force which the consul[3] had just levied—and proceed to the relief of Manlius. Atilius reached Tannetum without any fighting, for the enemy had retired in alarm.

he has confused Brixia (Brescia) with Brixellum (Bresciello), which is nearly north of Tanneto and close to the Po, and might have served as an *entrepôt* for supplies sent down from Placentia. The statement in chap. lv. § 4 that the Cenomani (whose capital was Brixia) were the only Gallic tribe that was loyal to Rome favours (1).

[3] P. Cornelius Scipio.

A.U.C. 536

3 Et P. Cornelius in locum eius quae missa cum praetore erat scripta[1] legione nova profectus ab urbe sexaginta longis navibus praeter oram Etruriae Ligurumque et inde Saluum[2] montes pervenit Mas-
4 siliam et ad proximum ostium Rhodani—pluribus enim divisus amnis in mare decurrit—castra locat vixdum satis credens Hannibalem superasse Pyre-
5 naeos montes. Quem ut de Rhodani quoque transitu agitare animadvertit, incertus quonam ei loco occurreret, necdum satis refectis ab iactatione maritima militibus, trecentos interim delectos equites ducibus Massiliensibus et auxiliaribus Gallis ad exploranda omnia visendosque ex tuto hostes praemittit.
6 Hannibal ceteris metu aut pretio pacatis iam in Volcarum[3] pervenerat agrum, gentis validae. Colunt autem circa utramque ripam Rhodani; sed diffisi citeriore agro arceri Poenum posse, ut flumen pro munimento haberent omnibus ferme suis trans Rhodanum traiectis ulteriorem ripam armis[4] obtinebant.
7 Ceteros accolas fluminis Hannibal et eorum ipsorum quos sedes suae tenuerant simul perlicit donis ad naves undique contrahendas fabricandasque, simul

[1] erat scripta *Weissenborn*: trascripta *C*: transcripta *M*.

[2] Saluum M^2 (*cf.* V. xxxiv. 7): saluium *C* (*before erasure*) M^1: saluii *C* (*after erasure*).

[3] Volcarum *edd.*: uolgarum *C*: uulgarum *M*.

[4] armis *Hearne*: amnis *C*: amnis armis *M*.

---

[1] Polybius (XXXIV. x. 5) says two, Pliny (*N.H.* III. iv. 33) three, and Strabo (IV. i. 8) cites Timaeus as authority for the number five.

[2] Polybius says that Scipio "sent out three hundred of his bravest cavalry, giving them as guides and supports certain Celts who were in the service of the Massiliots as mercenaries" (Paton's translation).

[3] It is usually held—with Napoleon—that Hannibal

Publius Cornelius, too, after enrolling a new legion B.C. 218 in place of that which had been sent with the praetor, set out from the City with sixty ships of war, and coasting Etruria and the mountainous country of Liguria and the Salui, arrived at Massilia, and went into camp at the nearest mouth of the Rhone—for the river discharges itself into the sea by several[1]—hardly believing, even then, that Hannibal could have crossed the Pyrenees. But when he found that Hannibal was actually planning how to cross the Rhone, being uncertain where he should encounter him, and his soldiers not having as yet fully recovered from the tossing of the sea, he sent out a chosen band of three hundred cavalry, with Massiliot guides and Gallic auxiliaries,[2] to make, while he was waiting, a thorough reconnaissance, and have a look at the enemy from a safe distance.

Hannibal, having pacified the others through fear or bribery, had now reached the territory of a powerful nation called the Volcae.[3] They inhabit both banks of the Rhone, but doubting their ability to keep the Phoenician from the western bank, they had brought nearly all their people over the Rhone, so as to have the river for a bulwark, and were holding the eastern bank with arms. The rest of the dwellers by the river, and such of the Volcae themselves as had clung to their homes, were enticed by Hannibal's gifts to assemble large boats from every quarter and to fashion new ones; and indeed

crossed the Rhone above the confluence with the Durance. The arguments of those who think that the crossing was just above the Delta have been recently restated by Spencer Wilkinson, *Hannibal's March Through the Alps*, pp. 14–17.

A.U.C. 536 et ipsi traici exercitum levarique quam primum regionem suam tanta[1] hominum[2] urgente turba
8 cupiebant. Itaque ingens coacta vis navium est lintriumque temere ad vicinalem usum paratarum; novasque alias primum Galli inchoantes cavabant
9 ex singulis arboribus, deinde et ipsi milites simul copia materiae simul facilitate operis inducti alveos informes, nihil, dummodo innare aquae et capere onera possent, curantes, raptim quibus se suaque transveherent, faciebant.

XXVII. Iamque omnibus satis comparatis ad traiciendum terrebant[3] ex adverso hostes omnem
2 ripam equites virique obtinentes. Quos ut averteret, Hannonem,[4] Bomilcaris[5] filium, vigilia prima noctis cum parte copiarum, maxime Hispanis, adverso
3 flumine ire iter unius diei iubet, et ubi primum possit, quam occultissime traiecto amni circumducere agmen, ut, cum opus facto sit, adoriatur ab tergo
4 hostes. Ad id dati duces Galli edocent[6] inde milia quinque et viginti ferme supra parvae insulae circumfusum amnem latiore,[7] ubi dividebatur, eoque
5 minus alto alveo transitum ostendere. Ibi raptim caesa materia ratesque fabricatae in quibus equi virique et alia onera traicerentur. Hispani sine

[1] tanta C^2M (*by erasure from* tantā): tantam C^1.
[2] hominum C^3: omnium C^1M.
[3] terrebant C^3: terrebat C^1M.
[4] Hannonem M^2: annonem C^3M^1: amonem C^1.
[5] Bomilcaris M^2: miuomilcaris CM^1.
[6] Galli edocent M^2: galliae docent CM^1.
[7] latiore *Bauer*: latiorem CM.

---

[1] The Spaniards were preferred for this duty because of their skill in swimming rivers, as we see at § 5 (*cf.* chap.

they themselves were eager to have the army set across as soon as possible and to relieve their district of the burden of so huge a horde of men. So they brought together a vast number of boats, and of canoes roughly fashioned for local traffic, and made new ones by hollowing out single trees. The Gauls took the lead in this, but the soldiers presently fell to work themselves, when they found the timber plentiful and the labour light. They were unshapely troughs, but the men could make them quickly, and their one concern was to get something that would float and hold a cargo, in which they might ferry themselves and their belongings over. B.C. 218

XXVII. Everything was now in readiness for the crossing, which, however, was menaced by the enemy on the other side, who covered the whole bank with their horse and foot. In order to draw them off, Hannibal ordered Hanno, the son of Bomilcar, to set out in the first watch of the night with a part of the troops, chiefly Spaniards,[1] and, making a march of one day up the stream, to take the first opportunity of crossing it, with the greatest secrecy, and fetch a compass with his column, so that, when the time came, he might assail the enemy in the rear. The Gauls who had been appointed to be his guides informed him that some five-and-twenty miles upstream the river flowed round a little island, and being wider where it divided, and therefore shallower, afforded a passage. There they quickly felled some trees and constructed rafts to transport the men and horses and other burdens. The Spaniards without

xlvii. § 5). The method here employed was still in vogue amongst them in Caesar's time (*Bell. Civ.* I. xlviii. 7).

A.U.C. 536

ulla mole in utres vestimentis coniectis ipsi caetris
6 superpositis incubantes flumen tranavere. Et alius exercitus ratibus iunctis traiectus, castris prope flumen positis, nocturno itinere atque operis labore fessus quiete unius diei reficitur intento duce ad
7 consilium opportune exsequendum. Postero die profecti ex loco edito[1] fumo significant transisse et haud procul abesse. Quod ubi accepit Hannibal, ne tempori deesset, dat signum ad traiciendum.
8 Iam paratas aptatasque habebat pedes lintres, eques fere propter equos naves.[2] Navium agmen ad excipiendum adversi impetum fluminis parte superiore transmittens tranquillitatem infra traicientibus lin-
9 tribus praebebat. Equorum pars magna nantes loris a puppibus trahebantur, praeter eos quos instratos frenatosque, ut extemplo egresso in ripam equiti usui essent, imposuerant in naves.

XXVIII. Galli occursant in ripa[3] cum variis ululatibus cantuque moris sui quatientes scuta super
2 capita vibrantesque dextris tela, quamquam ex adverso[4] terrebat tanta vis navium cum ingenti sono fluminis et clamore vario nautarum, militum, et qui[5] nitebantur perrumpere impetum fluminis, et qui ex

[1] edito *Clericus*: prodito *CM*: praedicto *Walch*: ex praedicto (*omitting* loco) *Weissenborn*.
[2] naves *Heerwagen*: nantes *CM*.
[3] ripa *Gronovius*: ripam *CM*.
[4] ex adverso *Crévier*: et ex aduerso *CM*.
[5] et qui M^4: equi *CM*.

---

[1] The skins of sheep and goats, such as are still used to hold wine. They could either be inflated and used merely as a kind of life-belt, or could be made to serve at the same time as kit bags.

more ado stuffed their clothes into skins,[1] and placing B.C. 218 their bucklers on top of these and supporting themselves by means of them, swam across. The rest of the force, too, got over, by means of the rafts which they had made, and went into camp near the river. They were tired by the night march and their strenuous exertions, but their commander allowed them but one day to rest, being intent on carrying out the stratagem at the proper time. Resuming their march on the following day they sent up a smoke-signal from an elevated place, to show that they had got over the river and were not far off. When Hannibal saw this, he gave the order to cross, so as not to miss the favourable moment. The infantry had their skiffs all ready and equipped, while the cavalry had large boats, for the most part, on account of their horses. The large boats were sent across higher up the stream, to take the force of the current, and provided smooth water for the skiffs that crossed below them. A good part of the horses swam and were towed by their halters from the sterns of the boats, except those which they had saddled and bridled and put on board, that their riders might have them ready for instant use on landing.

XXVIII. The Gauls rushed to meet them on the bank, with all sorts of yells and their customary songs, clashing their shields together above their heads and brandishing darts in their right hands, despite the menace of so great a multitude of vessels coming against them and the loud roaring of the river and the confused hallooing of the boatmen and the sailors, as they strove to force their way athwart the current or shouted encouragement to their fellows

A.U.C. 536 3 altera ripa traicientes suos hortabantur. Iam satis paventes adverso tumultu terribilior ab tergo adortus clamor castris ab Hannone captis. Mox et ipse aderat, ancepsque terror circumstabat et e navibus[1] tanta vi armatorum in terram[2] evadente[3] et ab tergo
4 improvisa premente acie. Galli postquam utroque[4] vim facere conati pellebantur, qua patere[5] visum maxime iter perrumpunt trepidique in vicos passim suos diffugiunt. Hannibal ceteris copiis per otium traiectis spernens iam Gallicos tumultus castra locat.
5 Elephantorum traiciendorum varia consilia fuisse credo, certe variat[6] memoria actae rei. Quidam congregatis ad ripam elephantis tradunt ferocissimum ex iis inritatum ab rectore suo, cum refugientem in aquam nantem[7] sequeretur, traxisse gregem, ut quemque timentem altitudinem destitueret vadum,[8] impetu ipso fluminis in alteram ripam rapiente.
6 Ceterum magis constat ratibus traiectos; id ut tutius consilium ante rem foret, ita acta re ad fidem
7 pronius est. Ratem unam ducentos longam pedes, quinquaginta latam a terra in amnem porrexerunt, quam, ne secundā aquā deferretur, pluribus validis retinaculis parte superiore ripae religatam pontis in

[1] e navibus *M*[2]: nauibus *CM*[1].
[2] terram *edd.*: terra *CM*.
[3] evadente *M*[2]: euadentem *CM*[1].
[4] utroque ς: ultroque *C* (*before erasure*) *M*[1]: ultro *C* (*after erasure*) *M*[2].
[5] patere ς: parte (*from* parte re) *C*: pate (*from* parte) *M*.
[6] variat *Mehler*: uariata *CM*.
[7] inde nantem *Weissenborn*: nantem *CM*.
[8] vadum *edd.*: uado *CM*.

from the further bank. But the tribesmen were already B.C. 218 somewhat daunted by the tumult which confronted them, when a still more appalling clamour arose in the rear, where Hanno had captured their camp. He was soon on the scene himself, and a twofold terror hemmed them in, as that mighty force of armed men came out upon the shore and the unlooked-for line of battle closed in from behind. When the Gauls had attempted charges in both directions and found themselves repulsed, they broke through where the way seemed least beset, and fled in confusion to their several villages. Hannibal brought over at leisure the rest of his forces, and giving himself no more concern over Gallic outbreaks, pitched his camp.

I believe that there were various plans for transporting the elephants; at all events the tradition varies as to how it was accomplished. Some say that the elephants were first assembled on the bank, and then the keeper of the fiercest of them provoked the beast and fled into the water; as he swam off, the elephant pursued him and drew the herd in his train; and though they were afraid of the deep water, yet as soon as each of them got out of his depth, the current itself swept him over to the other bank. It is, however, more generally believed that they were carried across on rafts; this method, as it would be the safer, if the thing were to be done, so, in view of its accomplishment, is more probably the one employed. A raft, two hundred feet long and fifty feet wide, was thrust out from the shore into the stream, and, after being moored to the bank above by a number of stout hawsers, so as not to be carried down the current, was covered with earth,

A.U.C. 536 modum humo iniecta constraverunt, ut beluae au-
8 dacter velut per solum ingrederentur. Altera ratis
aeque lata, longa pedes centum, ad traiciendum
flumen apta, huic copulata est; tum[1] elephanti per
stabilem ratem tamquam viam praegredientibus
feminis acti; ubi in minorem applicatam transgressi
9 sunt, extemplo resolutis quibus leviter adnexa erat
vinculis, ab actuariis aliquot navibus ad alteram
ripam pertrahitur. Ita primis expositis alii deinde
10 repetiti ac traiecti sunt. Nihil sane trepidabant,
donec continenti velut ponte agerentur; primus
erat pavor cum soluta ab ceteris rate in altum
11 raperentur. Ibi urgentes inter se cedentibus extremis ab aqua trepidationis[2] aliquantum edebant,
donec quietem ipse timor circumspectantibus aquam
12 fecisset. Excidere[3] etiam saevientes quidam in
flumen; sed pondere ipso stabiles deiectis rectoribus
quaerendis pedetemptim vadis in terram evasere.

XXIX. Dum elephanti traiciuntur, interim Hannibal Numidas equites quingentos ad castra Romana
miserat speculatum ubi et quantae copiae essent et
2 quid pararent. Huic alae equitum missi, ut ante
dictum est, ab ostio Rhodani trecenti Romanorum
equites occurrunt. Proelium atrocius quam pro
3 numero pugnantium editur; nam praeter multa

[1] tum *Madvig*: vi tum *Harant*: ut cum *CM*.
[2] trepidationis *edd.*: trepidationi *CM*.
[3] excidere M^2: excindere C^1: extendere C^3: exindere M^1.

---

[1] Polybius, who perhaps believed, as did Pliny (*N. H.* VIII. 28), that elephants could not swim, says that those that went overboard were saved by the length of their trunks, which they kept above the surface, and, breathing so, passed through the water, for the most part on their feet (III. xlvii. 12). Livy seems to have thought of them as swimming.

like a bridge, in order that the beasts might boldly B.C. 218 venture upon it, as on solid ground. A second raft, of equal width and a hundred feet long, and fit for crossing the river, was coupled to the first. Then the elephants, with the females leading, were driven out over the stationary raft, as over a road; and after they had passed on to the smaller raft adjoining it, the ropes by which this had been loosely attached were cast off and it was towed across by some row-boats to the eastern bank. After landing the first contingent in this fashion, they returned and fetched the others over. The elephants exhibited no signs of fear so long as they were being driven along as though on a connected bridge; they first became frightened when the raft was cast loose from the other and was carried out into mid-channel. The crowding together which resulted, as those on the outside shrank back from the water, gave rise to a slight panic, till terror itself, as they looked at the water all about them, made them quiet. Some, in their frenzy, even fell overboard; but, steadied by their very weight, threw off their riders, and feeling their way to the shallow places, got out upon the land.[1]

XXIX. Whilst the elephants were being got across, Hannibal had dispatched five hundred Numidian horsemen in the direction of the Roman camp, to find out where the enemy were and in what force, and what they meant to do. This body fell in with the three hundred Roman horsemen, sent out, as was mentioned before, from the mouth of the Rhone. The battle that followed was more hotly fought than the size of the contending forces would suggest, for besides the many who were

A.U.C. 536 volnera caedes etiam prope par utrimque fuit, fugaque et pavor Numidarum Romanis iam admodum fessis victoriam dedit. Victores ad centum quadraginta[1] nec omnes Romani sed pars Gallorum, victi amplius
4 ducenti ceciderunt. Hoc principium simul omenque[2] belli ut summae rerum prosperum eventum ita haud sane incruentam ancipitisque certaminis victoriam Romanis portendit.

5 Ut re ita gesta ad utrumque ducem sui redierunt, nec Scipioni stare sententia poterat, nisi ut ex con-
6 siliis coeptisque hostis[3] et ipse conatus caperet, et Hannibalem incertum utrum coeptum in Italiam intenderet iter an cum eo qui primus se optulisset Romanus exercitus manus consereret, avertit a praesenti certamine Boiorum legatorum regulique Magali adventus, qui se duces itinerum socios periculi fore adfirmantes integro bello nusquam ante libatis viri-
7 bus Italiam adgrediendam censent. Multitudo timebat quidem hostem nondum oblitterata memoria superioris belli, sed magis iter immensum Alpesque, rem fama utique inexpertis horrendam, metuebat.

XXX. Itaque Hannibal, postquam ipsi sententia stetit pergere ire atque[4] Italiam petere, advocata[5] contione varie militum versat animos castigando
2 adhortandoque: mirari se quinam pectora semper

[1] centum quadraginta *Gronovius* (*Polyb.* III. xlv. 2): clx *CM*.
[2] omenque C^3M^2: omnemque C^1M^1.
[3] hostis ς: hospiciis C^1: auspiciis C^3: hospitis *M*.
[4] atque *edd.*: adque *P*.
[5] advocata *edd.*: aduocatum *P*.

wounded, the numbers of the slain were about equal B.C. 218
on both sides, and only the dismay and panic of the Numidians gave the victory to the Romans, who were by that time fairly exhausted. The victors lost about a hundred and forty, not all Romans but some of them Gauls; the vanquished about two hundred. This was at once the beginning of the war and an omen that promised the Romans success in the final outcome, though their victory would be by no means without bloodshed and would only come after a doubtful struggle.

When the participants in this affair had returned to their respective generals, it was impossible for Scipio to adopt any settled plan, except to frame his own measures to meet the strategy and movements of the enemy; while Hannibal, uncertain whether to march on, as he had begun, to Italy, or give battle to the first Roman army that had come in his way, was diverted from an immediate trial of strength by the arrival of Boian envoys, with their chief Magalus. These assured him that they would guide his march and share its perils, and urged him to avoid a battle and to keep his forces whole and unimpaired for the invasion of Italy. The rank and file were fearful of the enemy—for their memory of the former war was not yet erased—but more fearful of the interminable march over the Alps, an undertaking which rumour made appalling, at any rate to the inexperienced.

XXX. Accordingly Hannibal, having settled in his own mind to go forward and advance on Italy, called the soldiers together and worked on their feelings with alternate chiding and encouragement. He marvelled, he said, what sudden terror had in-

A.U.C. 536 impavida repens terror invaserit. Per tot annos
vincentes eos stipendia facere neque ante Hispania
excessisse quam omnes gentesque et terrae[1] quas
duo diversa maria amplectantur Carthaginiensium
3 essent. Indignatos deinde quod quicumque Saguntum obsedissent velut ob noxam sibi dedi postu-
laret populus Romanus, Hiberum traiecisse[2] ad
delendum nomen Romanorum liberandumque orbem
4 terrarum. Tum nemini visum id longum, cum ab
5 occasu solis ad exortus intenderent iter; nunc, postquam multo maiorem partem itineris[3] emensam
cernant, Pyrenaeum saltum inter ferocissimas gentes
superatum, Rhodanum, tantum amnem, tot milibus
Gallorum prohibentibus, domita etiam ipsius fluminis
vi traiectum, in conspectu Alpes habeant, quarum
6 alterum latus Italiae sit, in ipsis portis hostium
fatigatos subsistere—quid Alpes aliud esse credentes
7 quam montium altitudines? Fingerent altiores Pyre-
naei iugis: nullas profecto terras caelum contingere
nec inexsuperabiles[4] humano generi esse. Alpes
quidem habitari coli gignere atque alere animantes;
8 pervias fauces[5] esse exercitibus. Eos ipsos quos
cernant legatos non pinnis sublime elatos Alpes
transgressos. Ne maiores quidem eorum indigenas
sed advenas Italiae cultores has ipsas Alpes in-

[1] terrae ς: terrase *P*: terras eas *P*².
[2] traiecisse *edd.*: traiecisset *P*.
[3] partem itineris *edd.*: partem in itineris *P*.
[4] inexsuperabiles *edd.*: exuperabilis *P*.
[5] fauces (faucis) *Heerwagen*: paucis *P*.

---

[1] Polybius (III. xxxix) estimates the distance covered by Hannibal as follows: New Carthage to the Ebro 2600 stades (the stade is roughly a furlong); the Ebro to Emporium 1600; Emporium to Narbo 600; Narbo to the passage of the Rhone 1600; the passage of the Rhone to the foot of the

vaded breasts that had ever been dauntless. For these many years they had been victorious in war, nor had they quitted Spain until all the tribes and territories which lay between two distant seas were in the power of the Carthaginians. Then, indignant that the Roman People should demand that whoever had laid siege to Saguntum be surrendered up to them, as though to expiate a felony, they had crossed the Ebro, in order to wipe out the Roman name and liberate the world. The march had not then seemed long to any of them, though they meant to advance from the setting to the rising sun; but now, when they could see that they had measured off the greater part of it;[1] when they had made their way, through the fiercest tribes, over the Pyrenees; when they had crossed the Rhone—that mighty river—in the teeth of so many thousand Gauls, overcoming, too, the violence of the stream itself; when the Alps, the other side of which was in Italy, were in full sight;—were they halting now, as though exhausted, at the very gates of their enemies? What else did they think that the Alps were but high mountains? They might fancy them higher than the ranges of the Pyrenees; but surely no lands touched the skies or were impassable to man. The Alps indeed were inhabited, were tilled, produced and supported living beings; their defiles were practicable for armies. Those very ambassadors whom they beheld had not crossed the Alps in the air on wings. Even the ancestors of these men had not been natives of Italy, but had lived there as foreign settlers, and had often crossed these very Alps in B.C. 218

pass over the Alps 1400; the foot of the pass to the valley of the Po 1200.

A.U.C. 536 gentibus saepe agminibus cum liberis ac coniugibus
9 migrantium modo tuto transmisisse. Militi quidem
armato nihil secum praeter instrumenta belli portanti quid invium aut inexsuperabile esse? Saguntum ut caperetur, quid per octo menses periculi,
10 quid laboris exhaustum esse? Romam, caput orbis
terrarum, petentibus quicquam adeo asperum atque
11 arduum videri, quod inceptum moretur? Cepisse
quondam Gallos ea quae adiri posse Poenus desperet?
Proinde aut cederent animo atque virtute genti per
eos dies totiens ab se victae, aut itineris finem sperent
campum interiacentem Tiberi ac moenibus Romanis.

XXXI. His adhortationibus incitatos corpora curare
2 atque ad iter se parare iubet. Postero die profectus
adversa ripa Rhodani mediterranea Galliae petit, non
quia rectior ad Alpes via esset, sed quantum a mari
recessisset minus obvium fore Romanum credens,
3 cum quo, priusquam in Italiam ventum[1] foret, non
4 erat in animo manus conserere. Quartis castris ad
Insulam pervenit. Ibi Isara[2] Rhodanusque amnes[3]
diversis ex Alpibus decurrentes agri aliquantum
amplexi confluunt in unum; mediis[4] campis Insulae
5 nomen inditum. Incolunt prope Allobroges, gens

[1] italiam ventum C^3: italia euentum C^1: italiae uentum M^1: italia uentum M^2.

[2] ibi Isara *Cluverius*: ibi arar *CM* (*corrected from* ibisarar).

[3] amnes *edd.*: amnis *CM*.

[4] mediis ς: in mediis *CM*.

---

[1] See v. xxxiv–xxxv. Livy places the earliest Gallic immigration in the reign of Tarquinius Priscus.

[2] This expression is a strange anachronism in the mouth of Hannibal; but Livy thinks of Hannibal as realizing—and so perhaps he may have done—that the struggle now be-

great companies, with their children and their wives, in the manner of emigrants.[1] For armed soldiers, taking nothing with them but the instruments of war, what could be impassable or insurmountable? To capture Saguntum, what dangers or what hardships had they not endured for eight long months? Now that Rome, the capital of the world,[2] was their objective, could anything seem so painful or so difficult as to delay their enterprise? Had Gauls once captured that which the Phoenician despaired of approaching? Then let them yield in spirit and manhood to a race which they had so often vanquished in the course of the last few days, or look to end their march in the field[3] that lay between the Tiber and the walls of Rome. B.C. 218

XXXI. After encouraging them with this exhortation, he bade them refresh themselves and make ready for the march. Setting out the following day he advanced up the Rhone towards the interior of Gaul, not that it was the more direct way to the Alps, but believing that the farther he retired from the sea, the less likely he was to fall in with the Romans, with whom he had no mind to fight a battle until he should arrive in Italy. The fourth day's march brought him to the Island. There the rivers Isara and Rhone, rushing down from different Alps, unite their waters, after enclosing a considerable territory, and the Island is the name which has been given to the plains lying between them. Near by is the country of the Allobroges, a tribe, even at

ginning would determine whether Rome or Carthage should rule the world.

[3] The Campus Martius lay outside the Servian wall, between the Capitoline, Quirinal, and Pincian Hills and the Tiber.

A.U.C. 536 iam inde nulla Gallica gente opibus aut fama inferior.
6 Tum discors erat. Regni certamine ambigebant fratres. Maior et qui prius imperitarat, Braneus nomine, a minore fratre[1] et coetu iuniorum, qui iure
7 minus vi[2] plus poterat, pellebatur. Huius seditionis peropportuna disceptatio cum ad Hannibalem reiecta esset,[3] arbiter regni factus, quod ea senatus principumque sententia fuerat,[4] imperium maiori restituit.
8 Ob id meritum[5] commeatu copiaque rerum omnium, maxime vestis, est adiutus,[6] quam infames frigoribus Alpes praeparari cogebant.

9 Sedatis Hannibal certaminibus Allobrogum cum iam Alpes peteret, non recta regione iter instituit sed ad laevam in Tricastinos flexit; inde per extremam oram Vocontiorum agri tendit in Tricorios,[7] haud usquam impedita via priusquam ad Druentiam[8]
10 flumen pervenit. Is et ipse Alpinus amnis longe omnium Galliae fluminum difficillimus transitu est;

[1] a minore fratre ς: minor erat fratre *CM*.
[2] vi ς: qui *CM*.
[3] reiecta esset ς: delecta esset C^1M^2: delectasset M^1: delata esset C^3M^3.
[4] fuerat M^2: futurum CM^1.
[5] id meritum M^2: id emeritum M^1: ide meritum C^1: idē meritum C^3.
[6] adiutus M^2: aditus CM^1.
[7] Tricorios *edd.*: trigorios *CM*.
[8] ad Druentiam M^4: adruentiam CM^1.

---

[1] The tribe in question was not the Allobroges, according to Polybius, III. xlix., but afforded the Carthaginians protection against the Allobroges.
[2] A turn to the left is unintelligible at this point in the march, and must be explained as due to a duplication of the march up the Rhone mentioned in § 2.
[3] Neither the Durance nor any of these tribes is mentioned by Polybius. But Polybius disliked to encumber his narra-

that early day, inferior to no Gallic tribe in wealth B.C. 218
or reputation. Just then it was a prey to discord.[1] Two brothers were disputing the sovereignty. The elder, Braneus by name, who had held sway before, was being driven out by a faction of juniors headed by the younger brother, whose right was less but his might greater. This quarrel having very opportunely been referred to Hannibal for settlement, who thus became arbiter of the kingdom, he espoused the sentiments of the senate and the leading men and restored the sovereign power to the elder. In requital of this service he was assisted with provisions and supplies of every sort, particularly clothing, which the notorious cold of the Alps made it necessary to provide.

Having settled the contentions of the Allobroges, Hannibal was now ready for the Alps; but instead of marching directly towards them, he turned to the left,[2] to the country of the Tricastini, and thence proceeded through the outer borders of the territory of the Vocontii to the Tricorii, by a road which nowhere presented any difficulties, until he came to the Druentia.[3] This, too, is an Alpine river and by far the most difficult of all the rivers of Gaul to

tive with outlandish geographical names that would mean nothing to his readers, and they are less likely to be arbitrary embellishments—on the part either of Livy or his source—than authentic details drawn from a source or sources common to Livy and Polybius and omitted by Polybius for the reason given. (The same may be said of the name of the Gallic prince in § 6.) If we assume that Hannibal ascended the Isère-Drac to the Druentia and thence crossed the Genèvre, he would have touched the territories of these tribes, and there would be no great difficulty in reconciling the account in Livy with that in Polybius (see *De Sanctis*, p. 69).

A.U.C. 536 nam cum aquae vim vehat ingentem, non tamen
11 navium patiens est, quia nullis coercitus ripis, pluribus simul neque iisdem alveis fluens, nova semper vada novosque gurgites gignit[1]—et ob eadem pediti quoque incerta via est—ad hoc saxa glareosa[2] volvens
12 nihil stabile nec tutum ingredienti praebet. Et tum forte imbribus auctus ingentem transgredientibus tumultum fecit, cum super cetera trepidatione ipsi sua atque incertis clamoribus turbarentur.

XXXII. P. Cornelius consul triduo fere post quam Hannibal a ripa Rhodani movit, quadrato agmine ad castra hostium venerat, nullam dimicandi
2 moram facturus. Ceterum ubi deserta munimenta nec facile se tantum praegressos[3] adsecuturum videt, ad mare ac naves rediit, tutius faciliusque ita
3 descendenti ab Alpibus Hannibali occursurus. Ne tamen nuda auxiliis Romanis Hispania esset, quam provinciam sortitus erat, Cn. Scipionem fratrem cum maxima parte copiarum adversus Hasdrubalem misit,
4 non ad tuendos tantummodo veteres socios conciliandosque novos, sed etiam ad pellendum Hispania
5 Hasdrubalem. Ipse cum admodum exiguis copiis Genuam repetit, eo qui[4] circa Padum erat exercitus Italiam defensurus.

6 Hannibal ab Druentia[5] campestri maxime itinere

[1] gurgites gignit *Kiderlin*: gurgites *CM*.

[2] glareosa *edd.*: gloriosa *CM.*: globosa ς: glareasve (*or* glareasque) *Gronovius*.

[3] praegressos ς: progressos *CM*[2]: progressus *M*[1].

[4] eo qui *M*[4]: eo *CM*[1].

[5] ab Druentia *edd.*: ab ruentia (*by erasure from* adruentia) *C*: abadruentia *M*.

---

[1] At chap. xxxix. § 3 Livy agrees with Polybius in naming Pisa as Scipio's port of debarkation, forgetting that he has here named Genoa.

cross; for, though it brings down a vast volume of water, it does not admit of navigation, since, not being confined within any banks, but flowing at once in several channels, not always the same, it is ever forming new shallows and new pools—a fact which makes it dangerous for foot-passengers as well—besides which it rolls down jagged stones and affords no sure or stable footing to one who enters it. And at that time, as it happened, it was swollen with rains, and the crossing took place amidst the wildest tumult, for the men—besides their other difficulties—were confused by their own excitement and bewildered outcries. B.C. 218

XXXII. Publius Cornelius the consul, some three days after Hannibal had left the bank of the Rhone, marched in fighting order to the enemy's camp, intending to offer battle without delay. But finding the works deserted, and perceiving that he could not readily overtake the enemy, who had got so long a start of him, he returned to the sea, where he had left his ships, thinking that he would thus be more safely and easily enabled to confront Hannibal as he descended from the Alps. Still, that he might not leave Spain stripped of Roman defenders—for the lot had assigned it to him as his province—he sent Gnaeus Scipio, his brother, with the chief part of his troops, to deal with Hasdrubal, with the object not merely of protecting the allies and of winning over new ones, but also of driving Hasdrubal out of Spain. He himself, with extremely scanty forces, sailed back to Genoa,[1] proposing to safeguard Italy with the army which lay in the valley of the Po.

Hannibal, leaving the Druentia, and advancing for the most part through a champaign country,

A.U.C. 536
ad Alpes cum bona pace incolentium ea loca
7 Gallorum pervenit. Tum, quamquam fama prius,
qua[1] incerta in maius vero ferri solent, praecepta
res erat, tamen ex propinquo visa montium altitudo
nivesque caelo prope immixtae, tecta informia
imposita rupibus, pecora iumentaque torrida frigore,
homines intonsi et inculti, animalia inanimaque[2]
omnia rigentia gelu, cetera visu quam dictu foediora,
8 terrorem renovarunt. Erigentibus in primos agmen
clivos apparuerunt imminentes tumulos insidentes
montani, qui si valles occultiores insedissent, coorti
ad pugnam repente ingentem fugam stragemque
9 dedissent. Hannibal consistere signa iussit; Gallis-
que ad visenda loca praemissis postquam comperit
transitum ea non esse, castra inter confragosa omnia
praeruptaque quam extentissima potest valle locat.
10 Tum per eosdem Gallos haud sane multum lingua
moribusque abhorrentes, cum se immiscuissent con-
loquiis montanorum, edoctus interdiu tantum ob-
sideri saltum, nocte in sua quemque dilabi tecta,
luce prima subiit tumulos, ut ex aperto atque interdiu
11 vim per angustias facturus. Die deinde simulando
aliud quam quod parabatur consumpto cum eodem
12 quo constiterant loco castra communissent, ubi
primum digressos[3] tumulis montanos laxatasque
sensit custodias, pluribus ignibus quam pro numero

[1] qua ς: quam *CM*[1].
[2] inanimaque *Valla*: inanimaliaque *CM*.
[3] digressos *CM*: degressos *Gruter*.

reached the Alps without being molested by the Gauls who inhabited those regions. Then, though report, which is wont to exaggerate uncertain dangers, had already taught them what to expect, still, the near view of the lofty mountains, with their snows almost merging in the sky; the shapeless hovels perched on crags; the frost-bitten flocks and beasts of burden; the shaggy, unkempt men; animals and inanimate objects alike stiff with cold, and all more dreadful to look upon than words can tell, renewed their consternation. As their column began to mount the first slopes, mountaineers were discovered posted on the heights above, who, had they lain concealed in hidden valleys, might have sprung out suddenly and attacked them with great rout and slaughter. Hannibal gave the command to halt, and sent forward some Gauls to reconnoitre. When informed by them that there was no getting by that way, he encamped in the most extensive valley to be found in a wilderness of rocks and precipices. He then employed these same Gauls, whose speech and customs did not differ greatly from those of the mountaineers, to mingle in their councils, and in this way learned that his enemies guarded the pass only by day, and at night dispersed, every man to his own home. As soon as it was light, he advanced up the hills, as though he hoped to rush the defile by an open attack in the daytime. Then having spent the day in feigning a purpose other than his real one, he entrenched a camp on the spot where he had halted. But no sooner did he perceive that the mountaineers had dispersed from the heights and relaxed their vigilance, than, leaving for show more fires than the B.C. 218

A.U.C. 536 manentium in speciem factis impedimentisque cum
13 equite relictis et maxima parte peditum, ipse cum expeditis, acerrimo quoque viro, raptim angustias evadit iisque ipsis tumulis quos hostes tenuerant consedit.

XXXIII. Prima deinde luce castra mota et agmen
2 reliquum incedere coepit. Iam montani signo dato ex castellis ad stationem solitam conveniebant, cum repente conspiciunt alios arce occupata sua super
3 caput imminentes, alios via transire hostes. Utraque simul obiecta res oculis animisque immobiles parumper eos defixit; deinde, ut trepidationem in angustiis suoque ipsum tumultu misceri agmen
4 videre, equis maxime consternatis, quidquid adiecissent ipsi terroris satis ad perniciem fore rati, diversis rupibus iuxta per vias[1] ac devia adsueti decurrunt.
5 Tum vero simul ab hostibus simul ab iniquitate locorum Poeni oppugnabantur, plusque inter ipsos, sibi quoque tendente[2] ut periculo prius evaderet,
6 quam cum hostibus certaminis erat. Equi maxime infestum agmen faciebant, qui et clamoribus dissonis, quos nemora etiam repercussaeque valles augebant,

[1] per vias *Widmann*: inuia *CM*.
[2] sibi quoque tendente *Freinsheim*: sibi cuique tendenti *CM*.

numbers of those who remained in camp demanded; B.C. 218
leaving, too, the baggage and the cavalry and a great part of the infantry, he put himself at the head of some light-armed soldiers—all his bravest men—and, marching swiftly to the head of the defile, occupied those very heights which the enemy had held.

XXXIII. With the ensuing dawn the Carthaginians broke camp and the remainder of their army began to move. The natives, on a signal being given, were already coming in from their fastnesses to occupy their customary post, when they suddenly perceived that some of their enemies were in possession of the heights and threatened them from above, and that others were marching through the pass. Both facts presenting themselves at the same time to their eyes and minds kept them for a moment rooted to the spot. Then, when they saw the helter-skelter in the pass and the column becoming embarrassed by its own confusion, the horses especially being frightened and unmanageable, they thought that whatever they could add themselves to the consternation of the troops would be sufficient to destroy them, and rushed down from the cliffs on either side, over trails and trackless ground alike, with all the ease of habit. Then indeed the Phoenicians had to contend at one and the same time against their foes and the difficulties of the ground, and the struggle amongst themselves, as each endeavoured to outstrip the rest in escaping from the danger, was greater than the struggle with the enemy. The horses occasioned the greatest peril to the column. Terrified by the discordant yells, which the woods and ravines redoubled with their echoes, they quaked

A.U.C. 536 territi trepidabant et icti forte aut volnerati adeo
consternabantur ut stragem ingentem simul ho-
minum ac sarcinarum omnis generis facerent;
7 multosque turba, cum praecipites deruptaeque
utrimque angustiae essent, in immensum [1] altitudinis
deiecit, quosdam et armatos; sed ruinae maxime
8 modo iumenta cum oneribus devolvebantur. Quae
quamquam foeda visu erant, stetit parumper tamen
Hannibal ac suos continuit, ne tumultum ac trepida-
9 tionem augeret. Deinde, postquam interrumpi
agmen vidit periculumque esse ne exutum impedimentis exercitum nequiquam incolumem traduxisset,
decurrit ex superiore loco et cum impetu ipso
10 fudisset hostem, suis quoque tumultum auxit. Sed
is tumultus momento temporis, postquam liberata
itinera fuga montanorum erant, sedatur; nec per
otium modo, sed prope silentio mox omnes traducti.
11 Castellum inde quod caput eius regionis erat viculos-
que circumiectos capit et captivo cibo [2] ac pecoribus
per triduum exercitum aluit; et quia nec a montanis [3]
primo perculsis nec loco magno opere impediebantur
aliquantum eo triduo viae confecit.

XXXIV. Perventum inde ad frequentem cultoribus alium ut inter montanos populum. Ibi non bello aperto sed suis artibus, fraude et insidiis, est prope

[1] in immensum ς: immensum *CM*.
[2] captivo cibo *Heusinger*: captiuo *CM*.
[3] a montanis *C. L. Bauer*: montanis *CM*.

with fear; and if they happened to be hit or wounded, were so maddened that they made enormous havoc not only of men but of every sort of baggage. Indeed the crowding in the pass, which was steep and precipitous on both sides, caused many—some of them armed men—to be flung down to a great depth; but when beasts of burden with their packs went hurtling down, it was just like the crash of falling walls. Dreadful as these sights were, still Hannibal halted for a little while and held back his men, so as not to augment the terror and confusion. Then, when he saw that the column was being broken in two, and there was danger lest he might have got his army over to no avail, if it were stripped of its baggage, he charged down from the higher ground and routed the enemy by the very impetus of the attack, though he added to the disorder amongst his own troops. But the flurry thus occasioned quickly subsided, as soon as the roads were cleared by the flight of the mountaineers; and the whole army was presently brought over the pass, not only without molestation but almost in silence. Hannibal then seized a stronghold which was the chief place in that region, together with the outlying hamlets, and with the captured food and flocks supported his troops for three days. And in those three days, being hindered neither by the natives, who had been utterly cowed at the outset, nor very greatly by the nature of the country, he covered a good deal of ground. B.C. 218

XXXIV. They came next to another canton, thickly settled for a mountain district. There, not by open fighting, but by his own devices, trickery and deception, Hannibal was all but circumvented.

A.U.C. 536

2 circumventus. Magno natu principes castellorum
oratores ad Poenum veniunt, alienis malis, utili
exemplo, doctos memorantes amicitiam malle quam
3 vim experiri Poenorum; itaque oboedienter imperata facturos; commeatum itinerisque duces et
4 ad fidem promissorum obsides acciperet. Hannibal
nec temere credendo nec aspernando,[1] ne repudiati
aperte hostes fierent, benigne cum respondisset,
obsidibus quos dabant acceptis et commeatu quem
in viam ipsi detulerant usus, nequaquam ut inter
pacatos composito agmine duces eorum sequitur.
5 Primum agmen elephanti et equites erant; ipse
post cum robore peditum circumspectans sollicitus-
6 que ad omnia[2] incedebat. Ubi in angustiorem
viam et parte altera subiectam iugo insuper imminenti ventum est, undique ex insidiis barbari a
fronte ab tergo coorti comminus eminus petunt,
7 saxa ingentia in agmen devolvunt. Maxima ab
tergo vis hominum urgebat. In eos versa peditum
acies haud dubium fecit quin, nisi firmata extrema
agminis fuissent, ingens in eo saltu accipienda clades
8 fuerit. Tunc quoque ad extremum periculi ac prope
perniciem ventum est. Nam dum cunctatur Hannibal demittere agmen in angustias, quia non, ut
ipse equitibus praesidio erat, ita peditibus quicquam

[1] credendo nec aspernando *Valla*: credendum nec aspernandos (asperandos M^1) M^2: credendum nec aspernandum *C*: credendum nec aspernandum ratus ς *Rossbach*.

[2] sollicitusque ad omnia *Luchs*: sollicitusque omnia *CM*.

The elder headmen of the strongholds waited on B.C. 218
him, as a deputation, and said that, taught by other men's misfortunes—a useful warning—they preferred to experience the friendship of the Phoenicians rather than their might; they were ready, therefore, to carry out his orders, and they requested him to accept provisions and guides and also hostages as a guarantee of good faith. Hannibal, neither blindly trusting nor yet repulsing them, lest, being spurned, they might become openly hostile, returned a friendly answer, accepted the proffered hostages, and used the supplies, which they had brought down, themselves, to the road. But he drew up his column, before following their guides, by no means as though for a march through a friendly country. The van was made up of elephants and cavalry; he himself, with the main strength of the infantry, came next, looking warily about him and watching everything. When they had got to a narrow place, which was overhung on one side by a ridge, the tribesmen rose up on every quarter from their ambush and assailed them, front and rear, fighting hand to hand and at long range, and rolling down huge boulders on the marching troops. The rear-guard bore the brunt of the attack, and as the infantry faced about to meet it, it was very evident that if the column had not been strengthened at that point, it must have suffered a great disaster in this pass. Even so, they were in the utmost peril and came near destruction. For while Hannibal was hesitating to send his division[1] down into the defile, since he had no troops left to secure the rear of the infantry, as he himself

[1] By *agmen* Livy here means the second (and larger) part of the column, under Hannibal's immediate command.

A.U.C. 536

9 ab tergo auxilii reliqui erat,[1] occursantes per obliqua montani interrupto[2] medio agmine viam insedere; noxque una Hannibali sine equitibus atque impedimentis acta est.

XXXV. Postero die iam segnius intercursantibus barbaris iunctae copiae, saltusque haud sine clade, maiore tamen iumentorum quam hominum pernicie
2 superatus. Inde montani pauciores iam et latrocinii magis quam belli more concursabant modo in primum modo in novissimum agmen, utcumque aut locus opportunitatem daret aut progressi morative aliquam
3 occasionem fecissent. Elephanti sicut per artas praecipitesque[3] vias magna mora agebantur, ita tutum ab hostibus, quacumque incederent, quia insuetis adeundi propius metus erat, agmen praebebant.[4]

4 Nono die in iugum Alpium perventum est per invia pleraque et errores, quos aut ducentium fraus aut, ubi fides iis non esset, temere initae valles a
5 coniectantibus iter faciebant. Biduum in iugo stativa habita, fessisque labore ac pugnando quies data militibus; iumentaque aliquot, quae prolapsa in rupibus erant, sequendo vestigia agminis in castra
6 pervenere. Fessis taedio tot malorum nivis etiam casus occidente iam sidere Vergiliarum ingentem

[1] reliqui erat *Luchs*: reliquum erat *Lipsius*: reliquerat *CM*.

[2] montani interrupto *Glareanus*: montani erupto *CM*²: montaniae rapto *M*¹.

[3] praecipitesque *C*³: praecipites *C*¹*M*.

[4] praebebant *ed. Moguntina*, 1518: praecedebant (— bat *C*¹) *C*³*M*.

---

[1] The morning setting of the Pleiades occurred on October 26.

secured that of the horse, the mountaineers rushed in on his flank, and breaking through the column, established themselves in the road, so that Hannibal spent one night without cavalry or baggage. B.C. 21

XXXV. On the following day, since by now the barbarians were attacking with less vigour, his forces were re-united and surmounted the pass; and though they suffered some casualties, still they lost more baggage animals than men. From this point on the mountaineers appeared in smaller numbers, and, more in the manner of brigandage than warfare, attacked sometimes the van, sometimes the rear, whenever the ground afforded an advantage, or the invaders, pushing on too far ahead or lagging behind, gave opportunity. The elephants could be induced to move but very slowly along the steep and narrow trails; but wherever they went they made the column safe from its enemies, who were unaccustomed to the beasts and afraid of venturing too near them.

On the ninth day they arrived at the summit of the Alps, having come for the most part over trackless wastes and by roundabout routes, owing either to the dishonesty of their guides, or—when they would not trust the guides—to their blindly entering some valley, guessing at the way. For two days they lay encamped on the summit. The soldiers, worn with toil and fighting, were permitted to rest; and a number of baggage animals which had fallen among the rocks made their way to the camp by following the tracks of the army. Exhausted and discouraged as the soldiers were by many hardships, a snow-storm—for the constellation of the Pleiades was now setting[1]—threw them into a great fear.

A.U.C. 536

7 terrorem adiecit. Per omnia nive oppleta cum signis
prima luce motis segniter agmen incederet pigritia-
8 que et desperatio in omnium voltu emineret, prae-
gressus signa Hannibal in promunturio quodam,
unde longe ac late prospectus erat, consistere iussis
militibus Italiam ostentat subiectosque Alpinis
9 montibus circumpadanos campos, moeniaque eos
tum transcendere non Italiae modo sed etiam urbis
Romanae; cetera plana, proclivia fore; uno aut
summum[1] altero proelio arcem et caput Italiae in
manu ac potestate habituros.

10 Procedere inde agmen coepit iam nihil ne hostibus
quidem praeter parva furta per occasionem temptan-
11 tibus. Ceterum iter multo quam in ascensu fuerat,
ut pleraque Alpium ab Italia sicut breviora ita
12 arrectiora sunt, difficilius fuit. Omnis enim ferme
via praeceps angusta lubrica erat, ut neque sustinere
se ab lapsu possent nec qui paulum titubassent
haerere adfixi vestigio suo, aliique super alios et
iumenta in homines occiderent.

XXXVI. Ventum deinde ad multo angustiorem
rupem atque ita rectis saxis ut aegre expeditus
miles temptabundus manibusque retinens virgulta
ac stirpes circa eminentes demittere sese posset.
2 Natura locus iam ante praeceps recenti lapsu terrae
in pedum mille[2] admodum altitudinem abruptus erat.

[1] summum *Gronovius*: summo *CM*: ad summum ς.
[2] in pedum mille *Valla*: impeditus dum ille *C*[1] ? *M*[1]: impeditus in mirandam ille *M*[4].

---

[1] In Polybius (III. liv. 7) the landslip carries away a stretch of road more than a stade and a half (about a thousand feet) *long*. Livy got the idea that the thousand feet represented the distance from the top to the bottom of the slip.

The ground was everywhere covered deep with snow B.C. 218 when at dawn they began to march, and as the column moved slowly on, dejection and despair were to be read in every countenance. Then Hannibal, who had gone on before the standards, made the army halt on a certain promontory which commanded an extensive prospect, and pointing out Italy to them, and just under the Alps the plains about the Po, he told them that they were now scaling the ramparts not only of Italy, but of Rome itself; the rest of the way would be level or downhill; and after one, or, at the most, two battles, they would have in their hands and in their power the citadel and capital of Italy.

The column now began to make some progress, and even the enemy had ceased to annoy them, except to make a stealthy raid, as occasion offered. But the way was much more difficult than the ascent had been, as indeed the slope of the Alps on the Italian side is in general more precipitous in proportion as it is shorter. For practically every road was steep, narrow, and treacherous, so that neither could they keep from slipping, nor could those who had been thrown a little off their balance retain their footing, but came down, one on top of the other, and the beasts on top of the men.

XXXVI. They then came to a much narrower cliff, and with rocks so perpendicular that it was difficult for an unencumbered soldier to manage the descent, though he felt his way and clung with his hands to the bushes and roots that projected here and there. The place had been precipitous before, and a recent landslip had carried it away to the depth of a good thousand feet.[1] There the cavalry

A.U.C. 536

3 Ibi cum velut ad finem viae equites constitissent, miranti Hannibali quae res moraretur agmen nun-
4 tiatur rupem inviam esse. Digressus deinde ipse ad locum visendum. Haud dubia res visa quin per invia circa nec trita antea quamvis longo ambitu
5 circumduceret agmen. Ea vero via insuperabilis fuit; nam cum super veterem nivem intactam nova modicae altitudinis esset, molli nec praealtae facile
6 pedes ingredientium insistebant; ut vero tot hominum iumentorumque incessu dilapsa est, per nudam infra glaciem fluentemque tabem liquescentis nivis
7 ingrediebantur. Taetra ibi luctatio erat via [1] lubrica non recipiente [2] vestigium et in prono citius pedes fallente, ut seu manibus in adsurgendo seu genu se adiuvissent, ipsis adminiculis prolapsis iterum corruerent; nec stirpes circa radicesve, ad quas pede aut manu quisquam eniti posset, erant; ita in levi
8 tantum glacie tabidaque nive volutabantur. Iumenta tamen etiam [3] secabant interdum infimam ingredientia nivem, et prolapsa iactandis gravius in conitendo [4] ungulis penitus perfringebant, ut pleraque velut pedica capta haererent in dura et alte concreta glacie.

XXXVII. Tandem nequiquam iumentis atque hominibus fatigatis castra in iugo posita, aegerrime

[1] via *H. Sauppe*: ut a *CM*: ita *Heerwagen*: illa *Harant*: *del. Madvig.*

[2] non recipiente *H. J. Mueller*: glacie non recipiente *CM.*

[3] tamen etiam *Rossbach*: eciam tamen *C*: etiam tam (*by erasure from* etiam tamen) *M.*

[4] conitendo *Lipsius*: continendo *CM.*

came to a halt, as though they had reached the end B.C. 218
of the road, and as Hannibal was wondering what it could be that held the column back, word was brought to him that the cliff was impassable. Going then to inspect the place himself, he thought that there was nothing for it but to lead the army round, over trackless and untrodden steeps, however circuitous the detour might be. But that way proved to be insuperable; for above the old, untouched snow lay a fresh deposit of moderate depth, through which, as it was soft and not very deep, the men in front found it easy to advance; but when it had been trampled down by the feet of so many men and beasts, the rest had to make their way over the bare ice beneath and the slush of the melting snow. Then came a terrible struggle on the slippery surface, for it afforded them no foothold, while the downward slope made their feet the more quickly slide from under them; so that whether they tried to pull themselves up with their hands, or used their knees, these supports themselves would slip, and down they would come again! Neither were there any stems or roots about, by which a man could pull himself up with foot or hand—only smooth ice and thawing snow, on which they were continually rolling. But the baggage animals, as they went over the snow, would sometimes even cut into the lowest crust, and pitching forward and striking out with their hoofs, as they struggled to rise, would break clean through it, so that numbers of them were caught fast, as if entrapped, in the hard, deep-frozen snow.

XXXVII. At last, when men and beasts had been worn out to no avail, they encamped upon the ridge,

A.U.C. 536

ad id ipsum loco purgato—tantum nivis fodiendum
2 atque egerendum fuit. Inde ad rupem muniendam,
per quam unam via esse poterat, milites ducti, cum caedendum esset saxum, arboribus circa immanibus deiectis detruncatisque struem ingentem lignorum faciunt eamque, cum et vis venti apta[1] faciendo igni coorta esset, succendunt ardentiaque saxa infuso
3 aceto putrefaciunt. Ita torridam incendio rupem ferro pandunt molliuntque anfractibus modicis clivos ut non iumenta solum, sed elephanti etiam deduci
4 possent. Quadriduum circa rupem consumptum iumentis prope fame absumptis; nuda enim fere cacumina sunt, et si quid est pabuli obruunt nives.
5 Inferiora valles et apricos quosdam[2] colles habent rivosque et[3] prope silvas et iam humano cultu
6 digniora loca. Ibi iumenta in pabulum missa, et quies muniendo fessis hominibus data. Triduo inde

[1] apta *edd.*: saepe (*by erasure from* saepte) *C*: saepta M^1: se apta M^2.

[2] et apricos quosdam ς: apricos quosdam *M*: apricos quosqam C^1: apricosque etiam *Madvig*.

[3] rivosque et *Madvig*: riuosque *CM*.

---

[1] This famous story has provoked much ridicule, but in Livy's defence may be noted, (1) the well-known disintegrating effect on certain kinds of stone of heat followed by a douche of cold water; (2) the belief entertained in ancient times, and as late as the sixteenth century, that vinegar helped to make stones friable; (3) the likelihood that Hannibal had at least a few skins of sour wine in his baggage-train (some have held that a vast quantity would have been required, but it must be remembered that Livy may have conceived of the *width* of the landslip as only a few rods; see last note). In any case those who regard the vinegar story as fiction must not fasten the fiction on Livy, if, as I think, we may discern an allusion to it in Varro's Menippean Satires (*Sesculixes*, frag. 25, p. 237, of the

after having, with the utmost difficulty, cleared B.C. 218 enough ground even for this purpose, so much snow were they obliged to dig out and remove. The soldiers were then set to work to construct a road across the cliff—their only possible way. Since they had to cut through the rock, they felled some huge trees that grew near at hand, and lopping off their branches, made an enormous pile of logs. This they set on fire, as soon as the wind blew fresh enough to make it burn, and pouring vinegar over the glowing rocks, caused them to crumble. After thus heating the crag with fire, they opened a way in it with iron tools, and relieved the steepness of the slope with zigzags of an easy gradient, so that not only the baggage animals but even the elephants could be led down.[1] Four days were consumed at the cliff, and the animals nearly perished of starvation; for the mountain tops are all practically bare, and such grass as does grow is buried under snow.[2] Lower down one comes to valleys and sunny slopes and rivulets, and near them woods, and places that begin to be fitter for man's habitation. There the beasts were turned out to graze, and the men, exhausted with toiling at the road, were allowed to rest. Thence they descended in three days' time

Buecheler-Heraeus edition: alteram viam deformasse Carneaden virtutis e cupis acris aceti), and it was probably an old and popular tradition long before the time of Varro, who died in 27 B.C. For recent discussion of the story see the article by Evan T. Sage in *C. W.* 16 (1922–1923) 73–76, and notes of modern instances by other contributors to the same volume.

[2] Polybius (III. lv. 7) says that the pack-animals and horses were sent over the road after one day's work had been done, and turned out to pasture, but that three days were employed in making it sufficiently wide for the elephants.

A.U.C. 536 ad planum descensum iam et[1] locis mollioribus et accolarum ingeniis.

XXXVIII. Hoc maxime modo in Italiam perventum est, quinto mense a Carthagine nova, ut quidam auctores sunt, quinto decimo die Alpibus superatis.
2 Quantae copiae transgresso in Italiam Hannibali fuerint nequaquam inter auctores constat. Qui plurimum, centum milia peditum viginti equitum fuisse scribunt; qui minimum, viginti milia peditum
3 sex equitum. L. Cincius Alimentus, qui captum se ab Hannibale scribit, maxime auctor moveret, nisi confunderet numerum Gallis Liguribusque additis: cum his octoginta milia peditum, decem equitum
4 adducta—in Italia magis adfluxisse veri simile est, et
5 ita quidam auctores sunt;—ex ipso autem audisse Hannibale, postquam Rhodanum transierit, triginta sex milia hominum ingentemque numerum equorum et aliorum iumentorum amisisse. Taurini Galli[2] proxima
6 gens erat in Italiam degresso. Id cum inter omnes constet, eo magis miror ambigi, quanam Alpes transierit, et volgo credere Poenino—atque inde nomen ei iugo Alpium inditum—transgressum,
7 Coelium per Cremonis iugum dicere transisse; qui

[1] iam et *Crévier*: eciam *C*: et iam *M*.

[2] Taurini Galli ς: taurinis ne galli C^1M^1: taurinis gallie C^3: taurinis quae gallis M^2.

---

[1] So Polybius (III. lvi. 4), who says that these numbers were given by Hannibal himself in an inscription at Lacinium.

[2] Praetor in Sicily, 210 B.C. He and Fabius Pictor were contemporaries and were Livy's oldest sources.

[3] Polybius (III. lv. 5) says that Hannibal left the Rhone with thirty-eight thousand infantry and eight thousand cavalry, and lost more than half his troops crossing the passes.

into the plain, through a region now that was less forbidding, as was the character of its inhabitants. B.C. 218

XXXVIII. Such were the chief features of the march to Italy, which they accomplished five months after leaving New Carthage—as certain authorities state—having crossed the Alps in fifteen days. The strength of Hannibal's forces on his entering Italy is a point on which historians are by no means agreed. Those who put the figures highest give him a hundred thousand foot and twenty thousand horse; the lowest estimate is twenty thousand foot and six thousand horse.[1] Lucius Cincius Alimentus,[2] who says that he was taken prisoner by Hannibal, would be our weightiest authority, did he not confuse the reckoning by adding in Gauls and Ligurians: including these, he says that Hannibal brought eighty thousand foot and ten thousand horse—but it is more probable, and certain historians so hold, that these people joined his standard in Italy; he says, moreover, that he had learned from Hannibal's own lips that after crossing the Rhone he lost thirty-six thousand men and a vast number of horses and other animals.[3] The Taurine Gauls were the first people he encountered on descending into Italy. Since all are agreed on this point,[4] I am the more astonished at the difference of opinion in regard to his route over the Alps, and that it should be commonly held that he crossed by the Poenine Pass[5] and that from this circumstance that ridge of the Alps derived its name—and that Coelius should state that he crossed by the ridge of Cremo;[6] for

[4] It is a moot question whether Polybius shared this view.

[5] The Great St. Bernard.

[6] Perhaps the Little St. Bernard.

A.U.C. 536 ambo saltus eum non in Taurinos sed per Salassos[1]
8 Montanos ad Libuos Gallos deduxissent.[2] Nec veri simile est ea tum ad Galliam patuisse itinera; utique quae ad Poeninum ferunt obsaepta gentibus Semi-
9 germanis fuissent. Neque hercule montibus his, si quem forte id movet, ab transitu Poenorum ullo Seduni Veragri,[3] incolae iugi eius, nomen norint[4] inditum, sed ab eo quem in summo sacratum vertice Poeninum montani appellant.

XXXIX. Peropportune ad principia rerum Taurinis, proximae genti, adversus Insubres motum bellum erat. Sed armare exercitum Hannibal, ut parti alteri auxilio esset, in reficiendo maxime sentientem
2 contracta ante mala, non poterat; otium enim[5] ex labore, copia ex inopia, cultus ex inluvie tabeque squalida et prope efferata corpora varie movebat.
3 Ea P. Cornelio consuli causa fuit, cum Pisas navibus venisset, exercitu a Manlio Atilioque accepto tirone et in novis ignominiis trepido ad Padum festinandi, ut cum hoste nondum refecto manus consereret.
4 Sed cum Placentiam consul venit, iam ex stativis

[1] Salassos (*or* Salyas) *Lipsius*: saltus C^1M^2: saltus alios (*but* alios *is erased*) C^2: saltos M^1.

[2] deduxissent ς: si duxerit (*before erasure*) C^1: duxerit (*after erasure*) C^3: deduxerint *M*.

[3] Seduni Veragri (*or* Sedunoveragri) *Gronovius*: seduno uelacri *CM*: Seduni vel Veragri *Lipsius*

[4] nomen norint *Frigell*: norint nomen ς: norint *CM*: nomen ferunt *Madvig*.

[5] enim ς: erat enim *CM*.

---

[1] Livy means Cisalpine Gaul; he is writing from Hannibal's standpoint.

both these passes would have brought him down, not amongst the Taurini but through the Salassi Montani to the Libuan Gauls. Neither is it probable that these routes to Gaul[1] were open at that time; those leading to the Poenine Pass, at any rate, would have been blocked by tribes of half-German stock. Nor for that matter—if anyone happens to consider this point of consequence—do the Seduni Veragri, who inhabit those mountains, know of their having been named from any passage of the Phoenicians (or Poeni) but from that deity whose sanctuary is established on their very summit and whom the mountaineers call Poeninus.[2] B.C. 218

XXXIX. Quite opportunely for the opening of the campaign, the Taurini, the nearest tribe, had begun a war against the Insubres. But Hannibal was unable to put an army in the field to aid the Insubres, as the soldiers while convalescing felt more keenly than ever the distress arising from the hardships they had undergone; for rest coming after toil, plenty after want, comfort after filth and wet, produced all manner of disorders in their squalid and well-nigh brutalized bodies. This was the reason why the consul Publius Cornelius, who had come by sea to Pisa, though the army which he received from Manlius and Atilius was made up of raw recruits, still quaking from their recent defeats, yet marched in all haste towards the Po, that he might join battle with an enemy not yet restored to vigour. But when the consul reached Placentia, Hannibal

[2] Coins and votive offerings have been discovered there, and the remains of the little temple of the god, who was apparently the Juppiter Poeninus of certain extant inscriptions.

A.U.C. 536 moverat Hannibal Taurinorumque unam urbem, caput gentis eius, quia volentes in amicitiam non
5 veniebant,[1] vi expugnarat; at iunxisset[2] sibi non metu solum, sed etiam voluntate Gallos accolas Padi, ni eos circumspectantes defectionis tempus subito adventu
6 consul oppressisset. Et Hannibal movit ex Taurinis, incertos quae pars sequenda esset Gallos praesentem secuturos esse ratus.

7 Iam prope in conspectu erant exercitus, conveneruntque duces, sicuti inter se nondum satis noti ita iam imbutus uterque quadam admiratione alterius.
8 Nam et Hannibalis[3] apud Romanos iam ante Sagunti excidium celeberrimum nomen erat, et Scipionem Hannibal eo ipso quod adversus se dux potissimum
9 lectus esset praestantem virum credebat; et auxerant inter se opinionem, Scipio, quod relictus in Gallia obvius fuerat in Italiam transgresso Hannibali, Hannibal[4] et conatu tam audaci traiciendarum Alpium et effectu.

10 Occupavit tamen Scipio Padum traicere, et ad Ticinum amnem motis castris, priusquam educeret in aciem, adhortandorum militum causa talem orationem est exorsus:

XL. "Si eum exercitum, milites, educerem in aciem quem in Gallia mecum habui, supersedissem

[1] volentes . . . veniebant ς: uolentis ueniebat *CM*

[2] at iunxisset *Foster*: ac iunxisset *Weissenborn*: et iunxisset *Alschefski*: iunxisset *CM*.

[3] et Hannibalis *Madvig*: Hannibalis et *CM*.

[4] Hannibali, Hannibal *Gronovius*: Hannibali (-i *erased in C*) *CM*.

had already broken camp and taken the capital city B.C. 218 of the Taurini by assault, because they would not freely come into his friendship. On the other hand, he would have brought the Gauls who dwell along the Po to join him, not alone from fear but even of their own free choice, had not the consul taken them by surprise, appearing unexpectedly whilst they were looking about them for a pretext to revolt. Hannibal, too, moved forward from the Taurini, being persuaded that the Gauls, uncertain which side they had best adhere to, would attach themselves to those who were on the spot.

The armies were now almost within sight of each other, and the opposing generals, though as yet they did not know one another well, had yet each been imbued with a kind of admiration for his antagonist. For Hannibal's name had been very renowned amongst the Romans, even before the destruction of Saguntum, and Scipio was a man of mark in the eyes of Hannibal, from the mere fact of his having been selected, in preference to any other, to command against himself. Each had increased the other's good opinion—Scipio, because, though left behind in Gaul, he had confronted Hannibal at his crossing over into Italy; Hannibal by the audacity with which he had conceived and executed his passage of the Alps.

Scipio, however, was the first to cross the Po. He brought his army up to the river Ticinus, and in order to put heart into the men before leading them out to fight, harangued them after the following fashion:

XL. "Soldiers, if I were leading into battle the army that I had under me in Gaul, I should have

A.U.C. 536
2 loqui apud vos; quid enim adhortari referret aut
eos equites, qui equitatum hostium ad Rhodanum
flumen egregie vicissent,[1] aut eas legiones cum
quibus fugientem hunc ipsum hostem secutus
confessionem cedentis ac detractantis certamen pro
3 victoria habui? Nunc, quia ille exercitus, Hispaniae
provinciae scriptus, ibi cum fratre Cn. Scipione meis
auspiciis rem gerit, ubi eum gerere senatus populus-
4 que Romanus voluit, ego, ut consulem ducem adversus Hannibalem ac Poenos haberetis, ipse me huic
voluntario certamini obtuli, novo imperatori apud
novos milites pauca verba facienda sunt.

5 "Ne genus belli neve hostem ignoretis, cum iis est
vobis, milites, pugnandum quos terra marique priore
bello vicistis, a quibus stipendium per viginti annos
exegistis, a quibus capta[2] belli praemia Siciliam ac
6 Sardiniam habetis. Erit igitur in hoc certamine is
vobis illisque animus qui victoribus et victis esse
solet. Nec nunc illi quia audent sed quia necesse
7 est pugnaturi sunt; nisi creditis qui exercitu
incolumi pugnam detractavere, eos duabus partibus
peditum equitumque in transitu Alpium amissis[3]
8 plus spei nactos esse. At enim pauci quidem sunt,
sed vigentes animis corporibusque, quorum robora
9 ac vires vix sustinere vis ulla possit. Effigies immo,

[1] egregie vicissent *edd.* : aegre evicissent *CM.*
[2] a quibus capta *edd.* : quibus capta *CM.*
[3] amissis *Gruter* : amissis qui plures paene perierint quam supersunt *CM.*

deemed it unnecessary to address you. For what B.C. 218
point would there have been in exhorting either those horsemen who at the river Rhone had signally defeated the horsemen of the enemy, or those legions with which I pursued this very enemy in his flight, and by the confession implied in his withdrawal and avoidance of a battle, gained a virtual victory? As it is, since that army, enrolled for service in Spain, is campaigning there under my auspices with my brother Gnaeus Scipio, where the senate and the Roman People desired that it should serve, and I myself, that you might have a consul for your leader against Hannibal and the Phoenicians, have of my own choice undertaken the present conflict, it is right that your new commander should say a word or two to his new soldiers.

"That you may not be ignorant what manner of war it is, or what your enemies are, you are to fight, my men, with those whom you defeated in the former war, on land and sea; with those from whom you exacted tribute for twenty years; with those from whom you wrested Sicily and Sardinia, which you now hold as the spoils of war. You and they will therefore enter the present struggle with such spirits as usually attend the victors and the vanquished. Nor are they now going to fight because they dare, but because they must; unless you think that those who avoided battle when their strength was unimpaired would, now that they have lost two-thirds of their infantry and cavalry in the passage of the Alps, have become more hopeful! But, you will say, their numbers indeed are small, but their courage and vigour are so great that scarce any force could withstand their might and power. Nay, not so! They

A.U.C. 536 umbrae hominum, fame frigore, inluvie squalore enecti, contusi ac debilitati inter saxa rupesque; ad hoc praeusti artus, nive rigentes nervi, membra torpida[1] gelu, quassata fractaque arma, claudi ac
10 debiles equi. Cum hoc equite, cum hoc pedite pugnaturi estis; reliquias extremas hostis, non hostem habetis. Ac nihil magis vereor quam ne, cum vos[2] pugnaveritis, Alpes vicisse Hannibalem
11 videantur. Sed ita forsitan decuit, cum foederum ruptore duce ac populo deos ipsos sine ulla humana ope committere ac profligare bellum, nos, qui secundum deos violati sumus, commissum ac profligatum conficere.

XLI. "Non vereor ne quis me haec vestri adhortandi causa magnifice loqui existimet, ipsum aliter
2 animo adfectum esse. Licuit in Hispaniam, provinciam meam, quo iam profectus eram, cum exercitu ire meo, ubi et fratrem consilii participem ac periculi socium haberem et Hasdrubalem potius quam Hannibalem hostem et minorem haud dubie molem
3 belli; tamen, cum praeterveherer navibus Galliae oram, ad famam huius hostis in terram egressus praemisso equitatu ad Rhodanum movi castra.
4 Equestri proelio, qua parte copiarum conserendi manum fortuna data est, hostem fudi: peditum agmen, quod in modum fugientium raptim agebatur, quia adsequi terra non poteram, regressus ad naves,[3] quanta maxime potui celeritate tanto maris terra-

[1] torpida *Lipsius*: torrida *CM*.

[2] quam ne, cum vos *Madvig*: nec umquam uos cum *CM*.

[3] regressus ad naves (navis) *Luchs* (ς): neque regressus ad navis erat *CM*.

are but the semblance, the shadows of men, wasted B.C. 218 away with hunger and cold, with filth and squalor; bruised and crippled amongst the rocks and cliffs; moreover, their limbs are frost-bitten, their muscles stiffened by the snow, their bodies numb with cold, their arms shattered and broken, their horses lame and feeble. That is the cavalry, that the infantry with which you are to fight; you have no enemy—only the last relics of an enemy! And I fear nothing more than this, that when you have fought, it may seem to have been the Alps that conquered Hannibal. But perhaps it was right that the gods themselves, without any human aid, should begin and decide a war with a general and a people who break their treaties; and that we, whose injury was second to that of the gods, should add the finishing stroke to a war already so begun and so decided.

XLI. "I am not afraid that anyone may suppose that I am using these brave words to encourage you, but that in my heart I think otherwise. It was open to me to proceed with my army to my own province, Spain, for which I had already started; I might there have had a brother to share my counsels and my dangers, and Hasdrubal instead of Hannibal for my enemy, and a war undoubtedly less difficult to conduct; nevertheless, when rumours of this enemy reached me, as I sailed along by the coast of Gaul, I landed, and sending my cavalry ahead, moved my camp up to the Rhone. In a cavalry engagement—for this was the arm with which I was given the opportunity of fighting—I put the enemy to rout: his infantry column, marching hastily off as if in flight, I could not overtake by land; returning therefore to my ships I accomplished with all

A.U.C. 536 rumque circuitu, in radicibus prope Alpium huic
5 timendo hosti obvius fui. Utrum, cum declinarem
certamen, improvidus [1] incidisse videor an occurrere
in vestigiis eius, lacessere ac trahere ad decernen-
6 dum? Experiri iuvat utrum alios repente Carthaginienses per viginti annos terra ediderit, an idem
sint qui ad Aegates pugnaverunt insulas et quos ab
7 Eryce duodevicenis denariis aestimatos emisistis, et
utrum Hannibal hic sit aemulus itinerum Herculis,
ut ipse fert, an vectigalis stipendiariusque et servus
8 populi Romani a patre relictus. Quem nisi Saguntinum scelus agitaret, respiceret profecto si
non patriam victam domum certe patremque et
9 foedera Hamilcaris scripta manu, qui iussus ab
consule nostro praesidium deduxit ab Eryce, qui
graves impositas victis Carthaginiensibus leges
fremens maerensque accepit, qui decedens Sicilia
10 stipendium populo Romano dare pactus est. Itaque
vos ego, milites, non eo solum animo quo adversus
alios hostes soletis pugnare velim, sed cum indigna-
tione quadam atque ira, velut si servos videatis
11 vestros arma repente contra vos ferentes. Licuit ad
Erycem clausos ultimo supplicio humanorum,[2] fame
interficere; licuit victricem classem in Africam traicere

[1] improvidus *Thomann*: inprouisus *CM*.
[2] humanorum *CM*: humano (*or* suppliciorum humanorum) *Gustafsson*.

---

[1] The First Punic War had ended in 241 B.C.
[2] Hercules was fabled to have crossed the Alps on his return from the island Erythea with the cattle of Geryon. Livy has alluded to this story before (I. vii. 3 and V. xxxiv. 6).

possible expedition so circuitous a voyage and march, and am come to confront this redoubtable enemy almost at the very foot of the Alps. Does it look as though I were avoiding battle and had blundered upon him unawares? or, rather, as though I were in hot haste to encounter him and to provoke and bait him into fighting? I would willingly make trial whether the earth has suddenly produced in the last twenty years[1] another breed of Carthaginians, or whether they are the same who fought at the Aegatian islands and whom you suffered to depart from Eryx at a rating of eighteen denarii a head; and whether our friend Hannibal is a rival, as he himself would have it, of the wandering Hercules,[2] or has been left to the Roman People by his father to be their tributary, tax-payer, and slave. Were he not maddened by the crime he committed at Saguntum, he would surely have regard, if not for his conquered country, yet at least for his house and his father and the treaties written by the hand of Hamilcar, who, under the orders of our consul, withdrew his garrison from Eryx; who submitted with rage and anguish to the heavy terms imposed upon the beaten Carthaginians; who agreed, on withdrawing from Sicily, to pay tribute to the Roman People. And so I could wish you, soldiers, to fight not only with that courage with which you are wont to fight against other enemies, but with a kind of resentful rage, as if you saw your slaves all at once take up arms against you. When we had shut them up at Eryx, we might have killed them by starvation, the worst torment that man can know; we might have dispatched our victorious fleet to Africa, and in a few days' time, without

B.C. 218

A.U.C. 536 atque intra paucos dies sine ullo certamine Carthagi-
12 nem delere :—veniam dedimus precantibus, emisimus
ex obsidione, pacem cum victis fecimus, tutelae
deinde nostrae duximus, cum Africo bello urgerentur.
13 Pro his impertitis furiosum iuvenem sequentes oppugnatum patriam nostram veniunt! Atque utinam
pro decore tantum hoc vobis et non pro salute esset
14 certamen: non de possessione Siciliae ac Sardiniae,
de quibus quondam agebatur, sed pro Italia vobis
15 est pugnandum. Nec est alius ab tergo exercitus,
qui nisi nos vincimus hosti obsistat, nec Alpes aliae
sunt, quas dum superant comparari nova possint
praesidia. Hic est obstandum, milites, velut si ante
16 Romana moenia pugnemus. Unus quisque se non
corpus suum, sed coniugem ac liberos parvos armis
protegere putet; nec domesticas solum agitet curas,
sed identidem hoc animo reputet, nostras nunc
intueri manus senatum populumque Romanum;
17 qualis nostra vis virtusque fuerit, talem deinde
fortunam illius urbis[1] ac Romani imperii fore."
Haec apud Romanos consul.

XLII. Hannibal rebus prius quam verbis adhortandos milites ratus, circumdato ad spectaculum exercitu captivos montanos vinctos in medio statuit armisque Gallicis ante pedes eorum proiectis interrogare interpretem iussit, ecquis, si vinculis levaretur

[1] illius verbis *CM*: ipsius urbis *Gronovius*: urbis *T. Faber*.

the slightest struggle, have annihilated Carthage. B.C. 218
But we gave them the quarter they besought of us; we lifted the siege and let them go; we made peace with them when we had conquered them; and thereafter, when they were hard pressed by the war in Africa, we regarded them as under our protection. In requital of these benefits they are coming in the train of a crazy youth to assail our country! And I would that your honour only and not your very existence were in jeopardy: you have got to fight not for the ownership of Sicily and Sardinia, which were formerly in dispute, but for Italy. There is no second army at our back to stop the enemy, in case we fail to beat him, nor are there other Alps to obstruct his advance while we make ready new defences. Here, soldiers, is the spot where we must make our stand, as though we were fighting before the walls of Rome. Let each and every one of you consider that his arms protect, not his own person, but his wife and little children; nor let him be concerned for his family alone, but remember that ours are the hands to which the senate and the Roman People are now looking, and that even as our might and valour shall prove to be, such henceforward will be the fortune of that City and the Roman empire." So spoke the consul to the Romans.

XLII. Hannibal thought it well to encourage his soldiers by an object lesson before haranguing them. He therefore caused the army to gather in a circle for the spectacle, and setting in the midst some captive mountaineers with fetters on them, gave the order to throw some Gallic weapons down at their feet, and bade an interpreter enquire if any were willing to fight for life or death, on condition of

A.U.C. 536 armaque et equum victor acciperet, decertare ferro
2 vellet. Cum ad unum omnes ferrum pugnamque poscerent et deiecta in id sors esset, se quisque eum
3 optabat quem fortuna in id certamen legeret; cuiusque sors exciderat alacer inter gratulantes gaudio exsultans cum sui moris tripudiis arma raptim capie-
4 bat. Ubi vero dimicarent, is habitus animorum non inter eiusdem modo condicionis homines erat, sed etiam inter spectantes volgo, ut non vincentium magis quam bene morientium fortuna laudaretur.

XLIII. Cum sic aliquot spectatis paribus adfectos dimisisset, contione inde advocata ita apud eos
2 locutus fertur: "Si, quem animum in alienae sortis exemplo paulo ante habuistis, eundem mox in aestimanda fortuna vestra habueritis, vicimus, milites; neque enim spectaculum modo illud sed quaedam
3 veluti imago vestrae condicionis erat. Ac nescio an maiora vincula maioresque necessitates vobis quam
4 captivis vestris Fortuna circumdederit: dextra laevaque duo maria claudunt nullam ne ad effugium quidem navem habentes;[1] circa Padus amnis—maior Padus ac violentior Rhodano; ab tergo Alpes urgent,
5 vix integris vobis ac vigentibus transitae. Hic vincendum aut moriendum, milites, est, ubi primum hosti occurristis. Et eadem Fortuna quae necessita-

[1] habentes *Doujat*: habentibus *P.*

---

[1] Polybius gives substantially the same account of the episode (III. lv. 2), except that he speaks of only one pair of combatants.

being granted freedom, if victorious, and presented with a horse and arms. When the captives, to the last man, called for sword and combat, and lots were being cast to decide amongst them, each hoped that he should be the one whom fortune selected for that contest; and he who had drawn the lot would leap for joy, and dancing about—as their custom is—while the others showered congratulations on him, would eagerly snatch up his weapons. But when they fought, the feeling, not only in the bosoms of the other captives but even amongst the onlookers in general, was such that the fortune of those who conquered was not more praised than that of those who met an honourable death.[1] B.C. 218

XLIII. Having thus, by the exhibition of several pairs, worked on the passions of his troops, he dismissed them. Then, convening an assembly, he addressed them—so it is said—in the following strain: "If that spirit which but now was roused in you by the example of the plight of others shall presently be yours, when you consider your own prospects, then, soldiers, the victory is ours. For that was no mere spectacle, but a kind of picture, as it were, of your own condition. And I incline to think that Fortune has laid you under stronger bonds and heavier necessities than your captives. On the right and on the left two seas encompass you, and you have not a single ship, even to flee in; round you is the river Po—the Po, a greater and more turbulent river than the Rhone; behind you tower the Alps, which you hardly scaled when you were fresh and vigorous. Here, soldiers, you must conquer or die, where for the first time you have faced the enemy. And the same Fortune which has laid upon you the

A.U.C. 536

tem pugnandi imposuit praemia vobis ea victoribus
proponit, quibus ampliora homines ne ab dis quidem
6 immortalibus optare solent. Si Siciliam tantum ac
Sardiniam parentibus nostris ereptas nostra virtute
reciperaturi essemus, satis tamen ampla pretia essent;
nunc quidquid[1] Romani tot triumphis partum
congestumque possident, id omne vestrum cum ipsis
7 dominis futurum est. In hanc tam opimam mercedem
8 agitedum,[2] dis bene iuvantibus arma capite! Satis
adhuc in vastis Lusitaniae Celtiberiaeque montibus
pecora consectando nullum emolumentum tot
9 laborum periculorumque vestrorum vidistis; tempus
est iam opulenta vos ac ditia stipendia facere et
magna operae pretia mereri tantum itineris per tot
montes fluminaque et tot armatas gentes emensos.
10 Hic vobis terminum laborum Fortuna dedit; hic
dignam mercedem emeritis stipendiis dabit.

11 "Nec quam magni nominis bellum est tam difficilem
existimaritis victoriam fore: saepe et contemptus
hostis cruentum certamen edidit et incliti populi
12 regesque perlevi momento victi sunt. Nam dempto
hoc uno[3] fulgore nominis Romani quid est cur illi
13 vobis comparandi sint? Ut viginti annorum militiam
vestram cum illa virtute cum illa fortuna taceam,
ab Herculis columnis ab Oceano terminisque ultimis
terrarum per tot ferocissimos Hispaniae et Galliae
populos vincentes huc pervenistis; pugnabitis cum

[1] nunc quidquid *Woelfflin*: quidquid *P.*
[2] agitedum *Koch*: agite cū *P.*
[3] uno *P*: vano *Luchs.*

necessity of fighting holds forth the promise of such B.C. 218 prizes, in the event of victory, that men are wont to ask not even the immortal gods for greater. If it were only Sicily and Sardinia, wrested from our fathers, that we were going to recover by our valour, these would still be great enough rewards. As it is, whatever the Romans have won and heaped up in the course of all their triumphs, whatever they possess, is all destined—and its owners with it—to be yours. Come then! Arm yourselves, with Heaven helping you, to earn this splendid wage! Long enough have you been chasing flocks on the barren mountains of Lusitania and Celtiberia, without seeing any recompense for all your toil and dangers. It is now time for you to make rich and lucrative campaigns, and reap the large rewards of so long a march over so many mountains and rivers and through so many warlike tribes. Here Fortune has fixed the final goal of your labours; here, when your wars are ended, she will worthily requite you.

"Nor must you think that in proportion to the great name of the war will be the difficulty you will have in winning it. It has often happened that even an enemy held cheap has caused a bloody battle, and that nations and princes of renown have been very lightly overcome. Take from your enemies this one glory of the Roman name, and in what particular can they bear comparison with you? To say nothing of your twenty years of service and your far-famed courage and good fortune, you have come from the Pillars of Hercules, from the Ocean and the uttermost limits of the world, and through so many of the fiercest tribes of Spain and Gaul have fought your way victoriously to this field. You will be

A.U.C. 536 14 exercitu tirone, hac ipsa aestate caeso victo circumsesso a Gallis, ignoto adhuc duci suo ignorantique
15 ducem. An me in praetorio patris, clarissimi imperatoris, prope natum,[1] certe eductum, domitorem Hispaniae Galliaeque, victorem eundem non Alpinarum modo gentium, sed ipsarum, quod multo maius est, Alpium, cum semenstri hoc conferam
16 duce, desertore exercitus sui? Cui si quis demptis signis Poenos Romanosque hodie ostendat, ignoraturum certum habeo utrius exercitus sit consul.
17 Non ego illud parvi aestimo, milites, quod nemo est vestrum cuius non ante oculos ipse saepe militare aliquod ediderim facinus, cui non idem ego virtutis spectator ac testis notata temporibus locisque referre
18 sua possim decora. Cum laudatis a me[2] miliens donatisque, alumnus prius omnium vestrum quam imperator, procedam in aciem adversus ignotos inter se ignorantesque.

XLIV. "Quocumque circumtuli oculos, plena omnia video animorum ac roboris, veteranum peditem, generosissimarum gentium equites frenatos
2 infrenatosque,[1] vos socios fidelissimos fortissimosque, vos, Carthaginienses, cum pro patria[3] tum ob iram
3 iustissimam pugnaturos. Inferimus bellum infestisque signis descendimus in Italiam tanto audacius

[1] natum *Valla*: notum *P*.
[2] cum laudatis a me ς: tum laudatis me *P*.
[3] pro patria *Weissenborn*: patriam *P*: ob patriam ς.

[1] The Numidians used no bridles: the cavalry using them were Spaniards.

pitted against an army of recruits, who have been this very summer cut to pieces, routed, and besieged by Gauls—an army as yet unknown to its general and one that knows not him. Or am I, who if not actually born in the headquarters of my father—most illustrious of commanders—was at least brought up there, am I, the subjugator of Spain and Gaul and conqueror not only of the Alpine tribes, but—what is much more—of the Alps themselves, am I, I ask you, to compare myself to this six-months general, who has deserted his own army? Why, if one were to show him to-day the Phoenicians and Romans without their standards, I am certain he would not know which army he was consul of. For my part, soldiers, I regard it as no slight advantage that there is not one of you in whose sight I have not often myself performed some soldierly feat; not one of whose courage I have not in my turn been a spectator and eye-witness—whose deeds of prowess, noted, together with their times and circumstances, I am not able to rehearse. I shall enter the battle in company with men whom I have praised and decorated a thousand times, and to all of whom I was a foster-son before I was their general. Opposed to me will be men who do not even know each other. B.C. 218

XLIV. "Wherever I turn my eyes I see nothing but eagerness and strength, a veteran infantry, cavalry from the noblest tribes, riding with bridles or without,[1] here the trustiest and most valiant of allies, there Carthaginians, prepared to fight not only in defence of their native land, but in satisfaction of a most righteous indignation. We are the assailants, and are descending with hostile standards into Italy,

A.U.C. 536 fortiusque pugnaturi quam hostis quanto maior spes, maior est animus inferentis vim quam arcentis.
4 Accendit praeterea et stimulat animos dolor iniuria indignitas. Ad supplicium depoposcerunt me ducem primum, deinde vos omnes qui Saguntum oppugnassetis; deditos ultimis cruciatibus adfecturi fuerunt.
5 Crudelissima ac superbissima gens sua omnia suique arbitrii facit. Cum quibus bellum, cum[1] quibus pacem habeamus, se modum imponere aequum censet. Circumscribit includitque nos terminis montium fluminumque quos non excedamus; neque eos quos
6 statuit terminos observat. 'Ne transieris Hiberum! Ne quid rei tibi sit cum Saguntinis!' At liberum est Saguntum.[2] 'Nusquam te vestigio moveris!'
7 Parum est quod veterrimas provincias meas Siciliam ac Sardiniam ademisti?[3] Adimis etiam Hispanias? Et inde si decessero,[4] in Africam transcendes? Transcendes dico?[5] Duos consules huius anni, unum in Africam, alterum in Hispaniam miserunt. Nihil usquam[6] nobis relictum est, nisi quod armis
8 vindicarimus. Illis timidis et ignavis esse licet qui respectum habent, quos sua terra suus ager per tuta ac pacata itinera fugientes accipient: vobis necesse est fortibus viris esse et omnibus inter victoriam mortemve[7] certa desperatione abruptis aut

[1] bellum, cum ς: bellum *P.*

[2] at liberum est Saguntum *Krauss* (*chap.* ii. § 7): ad Hiberum est Saguntum *P.*

[3] Sardiniam ademisti? *Heerwagen*: Sardiniam *P.*

[4] Et inde si decessero *H. J. Mueller*: et si inde cessero ς: inde cessero *P.*

[5] Transcendes dico? *Luchs*: transcendisse autem dico *P.*

[6] usquam *edd.*: umquam *P.*

where we shall fight with more boldness and courage than our foes in proportion as our hopes are higher and the gallantry of the assailant greater than his who but defends himself. Moreover, our hearts are kindled and pricked by rancour, wrongs, and insults. They called for the punishment of myself first, as your leader, then of all of you who had borne a part in the assault upon Saguntum; had we been given up, they meant to have inflicted upon us the worst of tortures. Most inhuman and most arrogant of nations, they reckon the world as theirs and subject to their pleasure. With whom we are to be at war, with whom at peace, they think it right that they should determine. They circumscribe and hem us in with boundaries of mountains and rivers which we may not cross; yet they do not observe those boundaries which they have set. 'Do not cross the Ebro! Have naught to do with the Saguntines!' But Saguntum is free. 'Do not budge from where you are in any direction!' Is it not enough that you have taken away my ancient provinces of Sicily and Sardinia? Are you taking away Spain as well? If I withdraw from these, shall you cross over into Africa? *Shall*, do I say? They *have* dispatched the two consuls of this year, the one into Africa, and the other into Spain! Nothing is left us anywhere, except what we shall defend by force of arms. They can afford to be timid and unenterprising who have something to fall back upon; whom their own country and their own fields will receive as they flee over safe and peaceful roads. As for you, you must be stout-hearted men, and discarding, without vain regrets, all hopes of anything but B.C. 218

[7] mortemve *Wesenberg* (*Madvig*): mortemque *P.*

A.U.C. 536 vincere aut, si Fortuna dubitabit, in proelio potius
9 quam in fuga mortem oppetere. Si hoc bene fixum
omnibus, si destinatum[1] animo est, iterum dicam,
vicistis; nullum contemptu mortis telum[2] ad vincendum
homini ab dis immortalibus acrius datum
est."

XLV. His adhortationibus cum utrimque ad
certamen accensi militum animi essent, Romani ponte
Ticinum iungunt tutandique pontis causa castellum
2 insuper imponunt; Poenus hostibus opere occupatis
Maharbalem cum ala Numidarum, equitibus quingentis,
ad depopulandos sociorum populi Romani
3 agros mittit; Gallis parci quam maxime iubet principumque
animos ad defectionem sollicitari. Ponte
perfecto traductus Romanus exercitus in agrum
Insubrium quinque milia passuum a Victumulis con-
4 sedit. Ibi Hannibal castra habebat; revocatoque
propere Maharbale atque equitibus, cum instare
certamen cerneret, nihil unquam satis dictum praemonitumque
ad cohortandos milites ratus, vocatis ad
contionem certa praemia pronuntiat in quorum spem
5 pugnarent: agrum sese daturum esse in Italia Africa
Hispania, ubi quisque velit,[3] immunem ipsi qui accepisset
liberisque; qui pecuniam quam agrum maluisset,
6 ei se argento satis facturum; qui sociorum cives
Carthaginienses fieri vellent, potestatem facturum;
qui domos redire mallent, daturum se operam ne
cuius suorum popularium mutatam secum fortunam

[1] si destinatum animo *Heerwagen*: destinatum in animo *P*.
[2] contemptu mortis telum *Stroth*: contemptum *P*.
[3] velit *P*: vellet *Wesenberg* (*Madvig*).

victory or death, either conquer or, if Fortune falters, B.C. 218 sooner perish in battle than in flight. If this idea has been firmly fixed and implanted in your hearts, let me say once more: the victory is already yours. The immortal gods have bestowed on man no sharper weapon for winning victories than contempt of death."

XLV. When the spirits of the soldiers on both sides had been whetted for the struggle by these speeches, the Romans threw a bridge over the Ticinus and erected a fort besides for its protection; and the Phoenician, whilst his enemies were engaged in fortification, sent Maharbal with a squadron of Numidians, numbering five hundred horse, to ravage the fields belonging to the allies of the Roman People, with orders to spare the Gauls as much as possible and tempt their leaders to desert. On the completion of the bridge, the Roman army marched over into the country of the Insubres, and took up a position five miles from Victumulae. It was there that Hannibal had his camp, who, quickly recalling Maharbal and his cavalry, when he saw that a battle was imminent, called his troops together—for he never felt that he had done enough in the way of preparing and cheering the men—and held out definite rewards to them to fight for; he would give them land, he said, in Italy, Africa, or Spain, as each might choose, tax-free to the recipient and to his children; those who had rather have money than land he would content with silver; if any of the allies desired to become citizens of Carthage, he would give them the opportunity; as for such as preferred to go back to their homes, he would see to it that they should feel no inclination to change

A.U.C. 536

7 esse vellent; servis quoque dominos prosecutis libertatem proponit binaque pro iis mancipia dominis
8 se redditurum. Eaque ut rata scirent fore, agnum laeva manu dextra silicem retinens, si falleret, Iovem ceterosque precatus deos, ita se mactarent quem ad modum ipse agnum mactasset,[1] secundum pre-
9 cationem caput pecudis saxo elisit. Tum vero omnes, velut dis auctoribus in spem suam quisque acceptis, id morae quod nondum pugnarent ad potienda sperata rati proelium uno animo et voce una poscunt.

XLVI. Apud Romanos haudquaquam tanta alacritas erat super cetera recentibus etiam territos
2 prodigiis; nam et lupus intraverat castra laniatisque obviis ipse intactus evaserat, et examen[2] apum in
3 arbore praetorio imminente consederat. Quibus procuratis Scipio cum equitatu iaculatoribusque expeditis profectus ad castra hostium ex propinquo copiasque,[3] quantae et cuius generis essent, speculandas, obvius fit Hannibali, et ipsi cum equitibus ad
4 exploranda circa loca progresso. Neutri alteros primo cernebant; densior deinde incessu tot hominum equorum oriens pulvis signum propinquantium hostium fuit. Consistit utrumque agmen et ad proelium[4]

[1] mactasset *ed. Frob.* 1531: mactasset et *P.*
[2] et examen ϛ: examen *P.*
[3] ex propinquo copiasque *Gronovius*: ex quo propinquo copias *P.*
[4] ad proelium ϛ: proelium *P.*

---

[1] In this ceremony the flint symbolizes the thunderbolt of Jupiter. The rite was characteristic of the Roman fetials (I. xxiv. 9), and Livy here ascribes it to Hannibal, to add to the dramatic effect of the scene.

places with any of their countrymen; besides this he promised freedom to the slaves who had come with their masters, and declared that he would make restitution to the latter, at the rate of two for one. And that they might know that these promises would be kept, he held a lamb with his left hand, and with his right a flint, and praying that if he should deceive them, then Jupiter and the other gods might slay him, even as he had slain the lamb, he thereupon smote the lamb's head with the stone.[1] Then indeed they all, as though each had received the blessing of the gods on his own particular hopes, and thought that their fulfilment was being delayed only because they were not yet fighting, cried out with one accord and one voice for battle. B.C. 218

XLVI. On the Roman side there was far less alacrity, for, besides other things, they were also frightened by some recent portents: a wolf had entered the camp and after rending those whom it met, had itself escaped unharmed; and a swarm of bees had settled in a tree that hung over the consul's tent. After averting these omens,[2] Scipio set out with his cavalry and light-armed darters to reconnoitre at close hand the enemy's camp and the size and character of his forces, and encountered Hannibal, who had likewise come out with his cavalry to explore the surrounding country. Neither party descried the other at first; afterwards an increasingly thick cloud of dust, that rose with the advance of so many men and horses, gave them notice that their enemies were approaching. Both bodies halted and began to make ready for battle.

[2] *i.e.* having by sacrifice to the gods averted the evil portended by these omens.

A.U.C. 536

5 sese expediebant. Scipio iaculatores et Gallos
equites in fronte locat, Romanos sociorumque quod
roboris fuit in subsidiis; Hannibal frenatos equites
6 in medium accipit, cornua Numidis firmat. Vixdum
clamore sublato iaculatores fugerunt inter subsidia
ad secundam aciem. Inde equitum certamen erat
aliquamdiu anceps, dein quia turbabant equos pedites
intermixti, multis labentibus ex equis aut desilienti-
bus, ubi suos premi circumventos vidissent, iam
magna ex parte ad pedes pugna venerat,[1] donec
7 Numidae, qui in cornibus erant, circumvecti paulum
ab tergo se ostenderunt. Is pavor perculit Romanos
auxitque pavorem consulis volnus periculumque
intercursu tum primum pubescentis filii propulsa-
8 tum.[2] Hic erit iuvenis penes quem perfecti huiusce
belli laus est, Africanus ob egregiam victoriam de
9 Hannibale Poenisque appellatus. Fuga tamen
effusa iaculatorum maxime fuit, quos primos Numidae
invaserunt; alius confertus equitatus consulem in
medium acceptum non armis modo sed etiam
corporibus suis protegens in castra nusquam trepide
10 neque effuse cedendo reduxit. Servati consulis decus
Coelius ad servum natione Ligurem delegat. Malim
equidem de filio verum esse, quod et plures tradidere
auctores et fama obtinuit.

[1] ad pedes pugna venerat *Gronovius*: ad | despugnavierat P^1: anceps pugna erat P^2.

[2] propulsatum ς: pulsatum *P*.

---

[1] Polybius, who had the story from Laelius, the bosom friend of the younger Africanus, is among those who make Scipio the hero of this anecdote (x. iii. 2). Coelius dedicated his work to L. Aelius (Peter, *Rell.* I. ccxv.), not, as formerly thought, to Laelius, which would have made his rejection of the version honouring Scipio strange.

Scipio stationed his darters and Gallic horse in front, B.C. 218
holding in reserve the Romans and the best of the allies; Hannibal put the cavalry who rode with bridles in the centre, and made his wings strong with Numidians. Hardly had the battle-cry been raised, when the darters fled through their supports to the second line. Then followed a cavalry fight of which the issue was for a time in doubt; but by and by the horses became excited by the presence of the foot-soldiers who were mingled with them, and many riders lost their seats or dismounted on seeing their fellows in distress, and the battle was now fought chiefly on foot; until the Numidians, who were posted on the flanks, rode round in a little circuit and showed themselves on the rear. So alarming a sight filled the Romans with dismay, and, to add to their fear, the consul was wounded and was only saved from danger by the intervention of his son, who was just reaching manhood. This is the youth who will have the glory of finishing this war, and be surnamed Africanus, from his famous victory over Hannibal and the Phoenicians. However, the rout was chiefly amongst the darters, the first to be charged by the Numidians: the cavalry rallied, and receiving the consul into their midst, and shielding him not only with their arms but with their persons also, brought him back to camp without panic or confusion at any point in their retreat. (The credit for saving the consul's life is given by Coelius to a Ligurian slave. I should prefer, for my own part, that the story about his son were the true one, and this is the version which most authorities have handed down and tradition has established.[1])

A.U.C. 536 XLVII. Hoc primum cum Hannibale proelium fuit, quo facile apparuit et equitatu meliorem Poenum esse et ob id campos patentes, quales sunt inter Padum Alpesque, bello gerendo Romanis aptos non
2 esse. Itaque proxima nocte iussis militibus vasa silentio colligere castra ab Ticino mota festinatumque ad Padum est, ut ratibus quibus iunxerat flumen nondum resolutis sine tumultu atque insectatione
3 hostis copias traiceret. Prius Placentiam pervenere quam satis sciret Hannibal ab Ticino profectos; tamen ad sescentos[1] moratorum in citeriore ripa Padi segniter ratem solventes cepit. Transire pontem[2] non potuit, ut extrema resoluta erant tota rate in secundam aquam labente.

4 Coelius auctor est Magonem cum equitatu et Hispanis peditibus flumen extemplo tranasse, ipsum Hannibalem per superiora Padi vada exercitum traduxisse elephantis in ordinem ad sustinendum
5 impetum fluminis oppositis. Ea peritis amnis eius vix fidem fecerint; nam neque[3] equites armis equisque salvis tantam vim fluminis superasse veri simile est, ut iam Hispanos omnes inflati travexerint utres, et multorum dierum circuitu Padi vada petenda fuerunt, qua exercitus gravis impedimentis traduci posset.

[1] ad sescentos *Gronovius* (*Polyb.* III. lxvi. 4): ad haec P.
[2] pontem *P*: ponte *H. J. Mueller.*
[3] nam neque ς: namque *P.*

---

[1] Polybius (III. lxvi) makes Hannibal pursue Scipio only as far as the Ticinus (where Polybius places the episode of the six hundred), then turn back and march W. along the Po two days, till he found a place where he could bridge it. See Map 2, *Operations on the Po.*

[2] One of the very few places where Livy implies a first-hand acquaintance with the scene of events described.

XLVII. Such was the first battle fought with Hannibal, in which it was clearly seen that the Phoenician was superior in cavalry and that consequently open plains, like those between the Po and the Alps, were ill-suited to the Romans for campaigning. Accordingly, the next night Scipio gave his men the order to pack up without making any noise, and quitting his camp on the Ticinus, marched swiftly to the Po, intending to use the bridge of boats which he had thrown across the river and had not yet broken up, in order to set his army over without confusion or interruption by the enemy. They were at Placentia before Hannibal was well aware that they were gone from the Ticinus; nevertheless some six hundred men, who were lingering on the northern bank and taking their time about casting off the raft, fell into Hannibal's hands. He was not able to cross the bridge, for when the end was cast off, the whole raft swung down stream with the current.[1] B.C. 218

Coelius states that Mago with the cavalry and the Spanish foot immediately swam the river, and that Hannibal himself led his army across the Po by an upper ford, after placing the elephants in a line to break the current of the river. Those who are acquainted with the Po will hardly credit this account;[2] for, in the first place, it is unlikely that the horsemen could have breasted so strong a current without the loss of arms or horses, even if all the Spaniards had swum over on inflated skins, and in the second place it would have needed a circuitous march of many days to reach fords on the Po by which an army encumbered with baggage could get across.

A.U.C. 536

6 Potiores apud me auctores sunt qui biduo vix locum rate iungendo flumini inventum tradunt; ea cum Magone equites et Hispanorum[1] expeditos
7 praemissos. Dum Hannibal citra[2] flumen legationibus Gallorum audiendis moratus traicit gravius peditum agmen, interim Mago equitesque ab transitu fluminis diei unius itinere Placentiam ad hostes
8 contendunt. Hannibal paucis post diebus sex milia a Placentia castra communivit et postero die in conspectu hostium acie derecta potestatem pugnae fecit.

XLVIII. Insequenti nocte caedes in castris Romanis, tumultu tamen quam re maior, ab auxiliari-
2 bus Gallis facta est. Ad duo milia peditum et ducenti equites vigilibus ad portas trucidatis ad Hannibalem transfugiunt, quos Poenus benigne adlocutus et spe ingentium donorum accensos in civitates quemque suas ad sollicitandos popularium
3 animos dimisit. Scipio caedem eam signum defectionis omnium Gallorum esse ratus contactosque
4 eo scelere velut iniecta rabie ad arma ituros, quamquam gravis adhuc volnere erat, tamen quarta vigilia noctis insequentis tacito agmine profectus ad Trebiam fluvium iam in[3] loca altiora collesque
5 impeditiores equiti[4] castra movet. Minus quam ad Ticinum fefellit; missisque Hannibal primum Nu-

[1] et Hispanorum *Weissenborn*: hispanorum *P.*
[2] citra ς (*Madvig*, *cf.* § 3; *chap.* xlviii. § 6; *chap.* liv. § 4): circa *P.*
[3] iam in ς: iam *P.*
[4] equiti ς (*Valla*): equites *P.*

Those writers seem to me more worthy of belief B.C. 218 who relate that in two days' search a place was scarcely found where the river could be spanned by a bridge of boats; by this the cavalry and light Spanish infantry were sent forward under Mago. While Hannibal, who had lingered on the northern bank to give a hearing to some Gallic embassies, was bringing over the heavy infantry, Mago and his horsemen advanced a day's march from the crossing of the river towards Placentia and the enemy. A few days later, Hannibal went into camp behind entrenchments, six miles from the town, and on the following day drew up his troops in sight of the enemy and offered battle.

XLVIII. The next night there was a bloody affray in the Roman camp, occasioned by some Gallic auxiliaries, though the confusion was greater than the loss of life. Some two thousand foot-soldiers and two hundred horsemen cut down the guards doing duty at the gates and fled to Hannibal, who received them with fair words, and after encouraging them to hope for great rewards, sent them off to their several states to solicit the support of their countrymen. Scipio apprehended that this bloodshed would prove to be a signal for the defection of all the Gauls, and that they would fly to arms, as if maddened by the contagion of this crime. Accordingly, though still troubled with his wound, he marched silently away in the fourth watch of the next night to the river Trebia, and encamped on higher ground, where hills made it more difficult for cavalry to operate. He was less successful than he had been on the Ticinus in eluding the observation of Hannibal, who sent after him first the Numidians and then all his

A.U.C. 536 midis deinde omni equitatu turbasset utique novissimum agmen, ni aviditate praedae in vacua Romana
6 castra Numidae devertissent. Ibi dum perscrutantes loca omnia castrorum nullo satis digno morae pretio tempus terunt, emissus hostis est de manibus et cum iam transgressos Trebiam Romanos metantesque castra conspexissent, paucos moratorum occiderunt
7 citra flumen interceptos. Scipio nec vexationem volneris in via iactati[1] ultra patiens et collegam—iam enim et revocatum ex Sicilia audierat—ratus exspectandum, locum qui prope flumen tutissimus stativis est visus delectum communiit.

8 Nec procul inde Hannibal cum consedisset, quantum victoria equestri elatus, tantum anxius inopia, quae per hostium agros euntem nusquam praeparatis
9 commeatibus maior in dies excipiebat, ad Clastidium vicum, quo magnum frumenti numerum congesserant Romani, mittit. Ibi cum vim pararent, spes facta proditionis; nec sane magno pretio, nummis aureis quadringentis, Dasio[2] Brundisino, praefecto praesidii, corrupto traditur Hannibali Clastidium. Id horreum

[1] iactati *Doujat*: iactanti *P*.
[2] Dasio *Gronovius*: dasiro P^1: dati pro P^2.

cavalry, and would have thrown the rearguard at least into disorder, had not the Numidians, in their greed for booty, turned aside to plunder the camp which the Romans had abandoned. Whilst they frittered away the time there, rummaging in every nook and cranny without finding anything that really repaid them for the loss of time, they let their enemies slip through their fingers. The Romans had already passed the Trebia and were marking out their camp, when the Numidians caught sight of them and cut down a few loiterers whom they intercepted on the hither side of the stream. Scipio could no longer bear the pain occasioned by the jolting of his wound in travelling, and besides he judged it best to wait for the arrival of his colleague, who was already recalled—so he had heard—from Sicily. He therefore chose what seemed to be the safest place near the river for a permanent camp, and proceeded to entrench it. B.C. 218

Hannibal, too, went into camp not far away. Elated as he was at the victory of his horse, he was no less worried by the dearth of food, which increased from day to day, as he advanced through hostile territory without having anywhere arranged beforehand for supplies. In the village of Clastidium the Romans had got together a great quantity of corn. Thither Hannibal dispatched some soldiers, who were making preparations to assault the place, when hopes were held out of its betrayal. The price was not a large one: Dasius of Brundisium, who was in command of the garrison, accepted a bribe of four hundred gold pieces, and turned Clastidium over to Hannibal. This served the Phoenicians as a granary, while they lay encamped on

A.U.C. 536 10 fuit Poenis sedentibus ad Trebiam. In captivos ex
tradito praesidio, ut fama clementiae in principio
rerum colligeretur, nihil saevitum est.

XLIX. Cum ad Trebiam terrestre constitisset
bellum, interim circa Siciliam insulasque Italiae
imminentes et a Sempronio consule et ante adven-
2 tum eius terra marique res gestae. Viginti quinqueremes cum mille armatis ad depopulandam oram
Italiae a Carthaginiensibus missae, novem Liparas,
octo ad insulam Volcani tenuerunt, tres in fretum
3 avertit[1] aestus. Ad eas conspectas Messana duodecim naves ab Hierone rege Syracusanorum missae,
qui tum forte Messanae erat consulem Romanum
opperiens, nullo repugnante captas naves Messanam
4 in portum deduxerunt. Cognitum ex captivis
praeter viginti naves cuius ipsi classis essent in
Italiam missas quinque et triginta alias quinqueremes
5 Siciliam petere ad sollicitandos veteres socios; Lilybaei occupandi praecipuam curam esse; credere
eadem tempestate qua ipsi disiecti forent eam
6 quoque classem ad Aegates insulas deiectam. Haec,
sicut audita erant, rex M. Aemilio praetori cuius
Sicilia provincia erat perscribit[2] monetque[3] Lily-
7 baeum firmo teneret praesidio. Extemplo et a
praetore circa civitates[4] missi legati tribunique suos
ad curam custodiae intendere, et[5] ante omnia Lily-

[1] avertit ς: aduertit *P*. [2] perscribit ς: praescribit *P*.

[3] monetque ς: (*Woelfflin*): monetque ut ς: monetque et *P*.

[4] et a praetore circa civitates *Madvig*: et circa praetore a ciuitate *P*: et circa civitates a praetore *Frigell*.

[5] intendere, et *Madvig*: intenderent *P*.

---

[1] This island, south of Lipara, and known also as Thermissa, Ἡφαίστου νῆσος, and Hiera, is now called Volcano.

the Trebia. The surrendered garrison were spared, B.C 218 as Hannibal wished to gain at the very outset a reputation for clemency.

XLIX. Though the war on land had come to a standstill at the Trebia, engagements had in the meantime been fought by land and sea off Sicily and the islands near the Italian coast, not only by Sempronius the consul, but even before his coming thither. Twenty quinqueremes with a thousand men at arms had been sent by the Carthaginians to lay waste the coast of Italy; nine of them reached Liparae and eight the Isle of Vulcan;[1] three the current diverted from their course into the Straits. These last were sighted by the people of Messana, and Hiero, king of the Syracusans, who happened to be in Messana at the time, waiting for the Roman consul, dispatched twelve ships, which captured the enemy's ships without a struggle and brought them into the harbour of Messana. It was learned from the prisoners that, besides the fleet of twenty galleys to which they themselves belonged—which had sailed for Italy—five and thirty other quinqueremes were on the way to Sicily to rouse up the old allies; the seizure of Lilybaeum was their prime object; but they supposed that the same storm by which they had themselves been scattered had struck this fleet as well and had driven it out of its course to the Aegatian Islands. The king wrote a full account of these rumours, just as they had come to him, to Marcus Aemilius, the praetor, who was in command in Sicily, and warned him to garrison Lilybaeum strongly. The praetor at once sent out his lieutenants and tribunes to the cities round about, and urged his people to be on their guard. Above all, Lilybaeum

A.U.C. 536 baeum teneri apparatu instructum[1] belli, edicto
proposito ut socii navales decem dierum cocta
8 cibaria ad naves deferrent, ut[2] ubi signum datum
esset ne quid[3] moram conscendendi faceret, perque
omnem oram qui ex speculis prospicerent adventan-
9 tem hostium classem missi.[4] Itaque, quamquam
de industria morati cursum navium erant Carthaginienses ut ante lucem accederent Lilybaeum,
praesensum tamen est, quia et luna pernox erat et
10 sublatis armamentis veniebant; extemplo datum
signum[5] ex speculis et in oppido ad arma conclama-
tum est et in naves conscensum; pars militum in
muris portarumque stationibus,[6] pars in navibus
11 erant. Et Carthaginienses, quia rem fore haud cum
imparatis cernebant, usque ad lucem portu se
abstinuerunt demendis armamentis eo tempore
12 aptandaque ad pugnam classe absumpto. Ubi inluxit, recepere classem in altum ut spatium pugnae
esset exitumque liberum e portu naves hostium
13 haberent. Nec Romani detrectavere pugnam et
memoria circa ea ipsa loca gestarum rerum freti et
militum multitudine ac virtute. (L.) Ubi in altum
evecti sunt, Romanus conserere pugnam et ex pro-
2 pinquo vires conferre velle; contra eludere Poenus
et arte non vi rem gerere naviumque quam virorum

[1] teneri apparatu instructum *Foster*: teneri instructum apparatu *Weissenborn*: instructum teneri apparatu *Riemann*: teneri apparatum *P*.

[2] deferrent, ut *Heerwagen*: deferrent et *P*.

[3] quid ς: quis *P*.

[4] missi *Weissenborn*: simi P^1: simili P^2.

was kept in a state of readiness for war, an edict having been published directing the naval allies to bring to their ships cooked rations for ten days, so that, on the signal being given, there might be nothing to delay their embarkation. All along the coast men were sent to keep a look-out from the watch-towers for the coming of the enemy's fleet. And so, notwithstanding that the Carthaginians had delayed their sailing on purpose that they might come up to Lilybaeum in the dark, they were nevertheless perceived, because there was a moon all night and they bore down under a spread of canvas. The signal was at once displayed from the watch-towers, and in the town the call to arms was sounded and the ships were manned; some of the troops were at once on the walls or guarding the gates, some on the ships. And the Carthaginians, seeing that they should have to do with men who were not unprepared, stood off from the harbour until dawn and employed the time in taking down their masts and sails and putting the fleet in fighting trim. When the day broke, they withdrew into the open sea, to give room for the battle and to allow their enemy's ships a ready egress from the harbour. Nor did the Romans shun the encounter. They remembered the victories that had been won in that same vicinity, and relied on the numbers and the bravery of their men. (L.) Once at sea, the Romans wanted to join battle and match their strength against the enemy's at close quarters. The Phoenicians, on the contrary, preferred to manœuvre; to conduct the affair by strategy, not by force, and to make it a contest B.C. 218

[5] datum signum ς: datum *P.*
[6] stationibus ς: in stationibus *P.*

A.U.C. 536

3 aut armorum malle certamen facere. Nam ut sociis
navalibus adfatim[1] instructam classem, ita inopem
milite habebant; et sicubi concerta navis esset,
haudquaquam par numerus armatorum ex ea pug-
4 nabat. Quod ubi animadversum est, et Romanis
multitudo sua auxit animum et paucitas illis minuit.
5 Extemplo septem naves Punicae circumventae;
fugam ceterae ceperunt. Mille et septingenti fuere
in navibus captis milites nautaeque, in his tres
6 nobiles Carthaginiensium. Classis Romana in-
columis, una tantum perforata navi sed ea quoque
ipsa reduce, in portum rediit.

7 Secundum hanc pugnam, nondum gnaris eius qui
Messanae erant, Ti. Sempronius consul Messanam
venit. Ei fretum intranti rex Hiero classem ornatam
8 armatamque[2] obviam duxit transgressusque ex regia
in praetoriam navem, gratulatus sospitem cum exercitu et navibus advenisse precatusque prosperum
9 ac felicem in Siciliam transitum, statum deinde
insulae et Carthaginiensium conata exposuit polli-
citusque est, quo animo priore bello populum
Romanum iuvenis adiuvisset, eo senem adiuturum;
10 frumentum vestimentaque sese legionibus consulis
sociisque navalibus gratis praebiturum; grande periculum Lilybaeo maritimisque civitatibus esse, et
11 quibusdam volentibus novas res fore. Ob haec
consuli nihil cunctandum visum quin Lilybaeum

[1] adfatim ς: adfatim minus *P*.

[2] ornatam armatamque *Hertz*: armatam ornatamque *Alschefski*: ornatamque *P*.

---

[1] So the flagship was called, from the old use of *praetor* in the sense of "commander"; cf. praetorian camp, praetorian guard. The consuls were at first called praetors (III. lv. 12).

rather of ships than of men or arms. For although B.C. 218
their fleet was well equipped with rowers, they were short of fighting men; and when a ship was grappled, the men-at-arms in her were greatly outnumbered by their enemies. Perceiving this, the Romans derived a fresh access of courage from their numbers, and the other side were correspondingly disheartened by their fewness. Seven Punic ships were instantly cut out and captured, and the rest took to flight. There were seventeen hundred soldiers and sailors on the captured ships, including three Carthaginian nobles. The Roman fleet returned intact into the harbour: one ship only had been rammed, and even this was brought safely in.

After this engagement, but before the people in Messana had got wind of it, the consul Tiberius Sempronius came to that city. As he was entering the straits, King Hiero put out to meet him, with his fleet in fighting order, and passing over from the royal galley to the praetorian,[1] congratulated Sempronius on having arrived in safety with his army and his ships, and prayed that he might have a safe and successful passage to Sicily. He then described conditions in the island and the attempts made by the Carthaginians, and promised that with the same spirit with which, in his youth, he had helped the Roman People in the former war he would help them now, as an old man, and would furnish corn and clothing gratis to the legions of the consul and the naval allies. He added that Lilybaeum and the cities of the coast were in great danger, and that some of them would welcome a revolution. In view of these things, the consul saw fit to sail without delay for Lilybaeum, and the king attended him with

A.U.C. 536 classe peteret. Et rex regiaque classis una profecti. Navigantes inde pugnatum ad Lilybaeum fusasque et captas hostium naves accepere.

LI. A Lilybaeo consul Hierone cum classe regia dimisso relictoque praetore ad tuendam Siciliae oram ipse in insulam Melitam, quae a Carthaginiensibus
2 tenebatur, traiecit. Advenienti Hamilcar, Gisgonis filius, praefectus praesidii, cum paulo minus duobus[1] milibus militum oppidumque cum insula traditur. Inde post paucos dies reditum Lilybaeum, captivique et a consule et a praetore praeter insignes nobilitate
3 viros sub corona venierunt. Postquam ab ea parte satis tutam Siciliam censebat consul, ad insulas Volcani, quia fama erat stare ibi Punicam classem, traiecit; nec quisquam hostium circa eas insulas
4 inventus. Iam forte transmiserant ad vastandam Italiae oram depopulatoque Viboniensi agro urbem
5 etiam terrebant. Repetenti Siciliam consuli escensio hostium in agrum Viboniensem facta nuntiatur, litteraeque ab senatu de transitu in Italiam Hannibalis, et ut primo quoque tempore collegae ferret auxilium,
6 missae traduntur. Multis simul anxius curis exercitum extemplo in naves impositum Ariminum mari supero misit, Sex. Pomponio legato cum viginti quinque longis navibus Viboniensem agrum mariti-
7 mamque oram Italiae tuendam adtribuit, M. Aemilio praetori quinquaginta navium classem explevit. Ipse

[1] duobus milibus ς: duo millibus *P.*

---

[1] Malta.

[2] *i.e.* Africa. Livy has omitted to mention the fact, recorded by Coelius (quoted by the grammarian Charisius, II. p. 203 K), that Sempronius even sent a swift galley to spy out a good landing-place for a Roman army on the coast of Africa.

the royal fleet. On the voyage they learned of the action that had been fought near that city, and the defeat and capture of the enemy's ships. B.C. 218

LI. From Lilybaeum the consul dismissed King Hiero and his fleet, and leaving the praetor to protect the coast of Sicily, set sail for the island of Melita,[1] which was held by the Carthaginians. On his arrival, Hamilcar, Gisgo's son, the commandant of the garrison, surrendered himself and nearly two thousand soldiers, together with the town and island. From Melita Sempronius returned in a few days to Lilybaeum, and consul and praetor sold into slavery the prisoners they had made, with the exception of those who were distinguished by noble birth. When the consul judged that Sicily was in no danger from that quarter,[2] he crossed over to the Isles of Vulcan, where it was rumoured that a Punic fleet was lying; but no single enemy was discovered near those islands. They had already, as it happened, sailed across to ravage the Italian coast, and after pillaging the country about Vibo, were even threatening the town. The consul was returning again to Sicily when tidings reached him of the enemy's raid on the lands of Vibo, and a letter was delivered to him from the senate, apprising him of Hannibal's descent into Italy and bidding him go to the assistance of his colleague at the earliest possible moment. Beset with many cares at once, he immediately embarked his army and dispatched it through the Adriatic to Ariminum; to Sextus Pomponius, his lieutenant, he assigned five and twenty ships of war, with the task of defending the territory of Vibo and the coast of Italy; the fleet under Marcus Aemilius the praetor he increased to fifty sail. He himself,

A.U.C. 536 compositis Siciliae rebus decem navibus oram Italiae legens Ariminum pervenit. Inde cum exercitu suo profectus ad Trebiam flumen conlegae coniungitur.

LII. Iam ambo consules et quidquid Romanarum virium erat Hannibali oppositum aut illis copiis defendi posse Romanum imperium aut spem nullam
2 aliam esse satis declarabat. Tamen consul alter, equestri proelio uno et volnere suo aeger et minutus,[1] trahi rem malebat: recentis animi alter eoque ferocior nullam dilationem patiebatur.
3 Quod inter Trebiam Padumque agri est Galli tum incolebant, in duorum praepotentium populorum certamine per ambiguum favorem haud dubie gratiam
4 victoris[2] spectantes. Id Romani, modo ne quid moverent, aequo satis, Poenus periniquo animo ferebat, ab Gallis accitum se venisse ad liberandos
5 eos dictitans. Ob eam iram, simul ut praeda militem aleret, duo milia peditum et mille equites, Numidas plerosque, mixtos quosdam et Gallos, populari omnem
6 deinceps agrum usque ad Padi ripas iussit. Egentes ope Galli, cum ad id dubios servassent animos, coacti ab auctoribus iniuriae ad vindices futuros

[1] aeger et minutus *Heerwagen*: et minutus P^1: eminutus P^2.

[2] victoris *edd.*: uictor *P*.

---

[1] This important sketch of affairs in Sicily (chapters xlix–li) is drawn from a source which cannot be identified. De Sanctis (p 186) thinks that the condensed and unrhetorical character of the style excludes its attribution to Coelius: neither Fabius nor Cincius is likely to have been so impartial in giving credit to the allies, like Hiero, and we know of no Greek writer who would have treated minor incidents with such particularity. He conjectures that the unknown writer may have been Eumachus of Naples (who wrote in Greek of

after settling the affairs of Sicily, took ten ships, and skirting the Italian coast, arrived at Ariminum. Thence he marched with his army to the Trebia and effected a junction with his colleague.[1] B.C. 218

LII. Now that both the consuls and all the forces which the Romans could muster were opposing Hannibal, it was obvious enough either that the troops there under arms were able to defend Rome's empire or that her case was hopeless. Nevertheless one of the consuls, disheartened by a single cavalry engagement and weak from his wound, preferred to postpone the decision. The other, unwearied and therefore the more impetuous, would put up with no delay.

The country between the Trebia and the Po was in those days inhabited by Gauls, who in this struggle of two mighty peoples maintained a neutral attitude and plainly intended to court the good-will of the victor. This policy was agreeable enough to the Romans, if only the Gauls made no disturbance, but was far from acceptable to Hannibal, who declared repeatedly that he had come on the invitation of the Gauls, to set them free. In his resentment at this state of affairs, and in order at the same time to sustain his troops with plunder, he ordered two thousand foot and a thousand horse—chiefly Numidians but with a sprinkling of Gauls—to waste the entire country-side, field after field, right up to the banks of the Po. The helpless Gauls, who had been undecided until then, were compelled to turn from the authors of their wrongs to those who might avenge them; and, sending envoys

the war with Hannibal) or some other Italian or Sicilian historian.

A.U.C. 536 declinant legatisque ad consules missis auxilium
Romanorum terrae ob nimiam cultorum fidem in
7 Romanos laboranti orant. Cornelio nec causa nec
tempus agendae rei placebat, suspectaque ei gens
erat cum ob infida multa facinora tum, ut illa[1]
vetustate obsolevissent, ob recentem Boiorum per-
8 fidiam; Sempronius contra continendis in fide sociis
maximum vinculum esse primos qui eguissent[2] ope
9 defensos censebat. Is tum collega cunctante[3] equitatum suum mille peditum iaculatoribus ferme admixtis ad defendendum Gallicum agrum trans Tre-
10 biam mittit. Sparsos et incompositos, ad hoc graves
praeda plerosque cum inopinato[4] invasissent, ingentem terrorem caedemque ac fugam usque ad
castra stationesque hostium fecere; unde multitudine effusa pulsi rursus subsidio suorum proelium
11 restituere. Varia inde pugna sequentes inter cedentesque; cumque[5] ad extremum aequassent certamen,
maior tamen hostium numerus cecidisset, penes Romanos[6] fama victoriae fuit.

LIII. Ceterum nemini omnium maior ea[7] iusti-
orque quam ipsi consuli videri; gaudio efferri, qua
parte copiarum alter consul victus foret, ea se vi-
2 cisse, restitutos ac refectos militibus animos, nec
quemquam esse praeter collegam qui dilatam dimi-

[1] ut illa *Weissenborn*: ut alia ς: ob iutilia P^1: ob utilia P^2.

[2] primos qui eguissent *Gronovius*: primosque qui coissent *P*.

[3] Is tum collega cunctante *Luchs*: tum collega cunctante ς: cum collegam cunctantem *P*.

[4] inopinato *Madvig*: inopinatos *P*.

[5] sequentes inter cedentesque; cumque *Madvig*: sequentes cumque *P*: sequentes cedentesque cum *Heusinger*.

[6] hostium numerus cecidisset, penes Romanos *Rossbach*: hostium Romanos *P*.

[7] maior ea *Dederich*: maiora P^1: maior P^2.

to the consuls, besought the Romans to come to the B.C. 218
aid of a land that was suffering for its inhabitants' too great loyalty to Rome. Cornelius liked neither the occasion nor the time for fighting, and regarded the Gauls with suspicion, both because of many acts of perfidy, and especially—even though time had obliterated those ancient grievances—because of the recent treachery of the Boi. Sempronius, on the contrary, held that the strongest bond for keeping the allies to their obligations was the defence of those who should first stand in need of help. On the present occasion, while his colleague hesitated, Sempronius sent his cavalry, interspersed with about a thousand foot-soldiers, armed with darts, to protect the Gallic lands beyond the Trebia. Falling unexpectedly upon the enemy, who were scattered and disorganized—most of them laden too with spoils—they drove them with great slaughter in a terror-stricken rout to the very outposts of the Carthaginian camp. Thence the enemy poured out in numbers and repulsed the Romans, in their turn; but reserves came up and restored the day. Thereafter the fortune of the battle shifted, as pursuit was followed by retreat; and though in the end the opposing armies were on even terms, still the enemy had lost more men and the Romans got the credit of a victory.

LIII. But to no one did the victory seem greater or more unequivocal than to Sempronius the consul; he was beside himself with joy that with that arm of the service with which the other consul had been beaten, he himself had been successful. He declared that the spirits of the men were restored and renewed, and that no one but his colleague desired

A.U.C. 536 cationem vellet; eum animo magis quam corpore
aegrum memoria volneris aciem ac tela horrere. Sed
3 non esse cum aegro senescendum. Quid enim ultra
differri aut teri tempus? Quem tertium consulem,
4 quem alium exercitum exspectari? Castra Carthaginiensium in Italia ac prope in conspectu urbis esse.
Non Siciliam ac Sardiniam victis ademptas nec cis Hiberum Hispaniam peti, sed solo patrio terraque in qua
5 geniti forent pelli Romanos. "Quantum ingemes-
cant" inquit "patres nostri circa moenia Carthaginis
bellare soliti, si videant nos, progeniem suam, duos
consules consularesque exercitus, in media Italia
paventes intra castra, Poenum quod inter Alpes
6 Appenninumque agri sit suae dicionis fecisse." Haec
adsidens aegro collegae, haec in praetorio prope con-
tionabundus agere. Stimulabat et tempus propinquum comitiorum, ne in novos consules bellum differ-
retur, et occasio in se unum vertendae gloriae, dum
7 aeger collega erat. Itaque nequiquam dissentiente
Cornelio parari ad propinquum certamen milites
iubet.

Hannibal cum quid optimum foret hosti cerneret,
vix ullam spem habebat temere atque improvide
8 quicquam consules acturos; cum alterius ingenium,
fama prius deinde re cognitum, percitum ac ferox

---

[1] *praetorium* here means the open space in front of the general's tent, not (as often) the tent itself. Sempronius meant that the soldiers should know his sentiments, but did not quite go the length of declaring them in a formal harangue.

to put off the struggle; Cornelius, he said, was sick B.C. 218
in spirit rather than in body, and the recollection of his wound made him dread a battle and its missiles. But they must not droop and languish along with a sick man. Why indeed should they further postpone the conflict, or waste time? What third consul, what other army were they waiting for? The Carthaginians were encamped in Italy and almost within sight of Rome. Their object was, not to get back Sicily and Sardinia, taken from them after their defeat, nor to cross the Ebro and occupy northern Spain, but to expel the Romans from the land of their fathers and from their native soil. "How would our fathers groan," he cried, "that were wont to wage war about the walls of Carthage, could they see us, their offspring, two consuls and two consular armies, cowering within our camp in the heart of Italy; and the Phoenician in full sway over all the territory between the Alps and the Apennines!" Thus he ran on, as he sat by the bed of his sick colleague; thus he argued in the praetorium,[1] almost as if haranguing the troops. His impatience was increased, too, by the near approach of the elections, lest the war go over to the term of the new consuls and he lose the opportunity of gaining all the glory for himself, while his colleague was laid up. Accordingly, despite the unavailing protests of Cornelius, he commanded the soldiers to make ready for an early battle.

Hannibal, since he saw what was best for the enemy, hardly dared to hope that the consuls would take any rash or ill-considered step; but knowing, as he did—by hearsay first and afterwards by experience—that one of them was of a fiery and reck-

A.U.C. 536 sciret esse ferociusque factum prospero cum praedatoribus suis certamine crederet, adesse gerendae
9 rei fortunam haud diffidebat. Cuius ne quod praetermitteret tempus sollicitus intentusque erat, dum tiro hostium miles esset, dum meliorem ex ducibus inutilem volnus faceret, dum Gallorum animi vigerent,
10 quorum ingentem multitudinem sciebat segnius secu-
11 turam quanto longius ab domo traherentur. Cum ob haec taliaque speraret propinquum certamen et facere, si cessaretur, cuperet, speculatoresque Galli, ad ea exploranda quae vellet tutiores quia in utrisque castris militabant, paratos pugnae esse Romanos rettulissent, locum insidiis circumspectare Poenus coepit.

LIV. Erat in medio rivus praealtis utrimque clausus ripis et circa obsitus palustribus herbis, et quibus inculta ferme vestiuntur, virgultis vepribusque. Quem ubi equites[1] quoque tegendo satis latebrosum locum circumvectus ipse oculis perlustravit, "Hic erit locus" Magoni fratri ait, "quem teneas.
2 Delige centenos viros ex omni pedite atque equite, cum quibus ad me vigilia prima venias; nunc corpora
3 curare tempus est." Ita praetorium missum. Mox cum delectis Mago aderat. "Robora virorum cerno"

[1] equites *P*: equiti ς (*Madvig*).

less disposition, and believing that the late successful brush with the Carthaginian raiders would have made him still more headstrong, he was fairly confident that the good fortune of a general engagement was at hand. It was therefore his one concern to let slip no opportunity for bringing this about, while the soldiers of the enemy still lacked experience, while the abler of their generals was incapacitated by his wound, while the courage of the Gauls was up—since he knew that their vast multitude would follow the less willingly, the farther they were drawn from home. For these and similar reasons he hoped that a battle would soon be fought, and was eager, should there be any hesitation, to force it on. And so, when his Gallic scouts—who were safer for gathering the information that he wanted because there were men of that nation in both camps—had reported that the Romans were prepared to fight, the Phoenician began to look about for a place in which to lay an ambush. B.C. 218

LIV. Between the two camps was a water-course, shut in by very high banks on either side and overgrown all round with marsh-grass and the underbrush and brambles with which uncultivated land is usually clothed. When Hannibal, riding over the ground himself, saw that this place afforded sufficient cover even for cavalry, he said to his brother Mago, "This will be the place for you to hold. Choose out a hundred men from all the infantry and a hundred from the cavalry, and come with them to my quarters at the first watch. It is time now to sup and rest." With that he broke up the council. In a little while Mago presented himself with his picked men. "I see the stoutest of my men," said Hanni-

A.U.C. 536 inquit Hannibal; "sed uti numero etiam non animis modo valeatis, singuli[1] vobis novenos ex turmis manipulisque vestri similes eligite. Mago locum monstrabit quem insideatis; hostem caecum ad has
4 belli artes habetis." Ita cum mille equitibus Magone, mille peditibus dimisso,[2] Hannibal prima luce Numidas equites transgressos Trebiam flumen obequitare iubet hostium portis iaculandoque in stationes[3] elicere ad pugnam hostem, iniecto deinde certamine cedendo
5 sensim citra flumen pertrahere. Haec mandata Numidis. Ceteris ducibus peditum equitumque praeceptum ut prandere omnes iuberent, armatos deinde instratisque equis signum exspectare.

6 Sempronius ad tumultum Numidarum primum omnem equitatum, ferox ea parte virium, deinde sex milia peditum, postremo omnes copias ad destinatum iam ante consilio avidus certaminis eduxit.
7 Erat forte brumae tempus et nivalis dies in locis Alpibus Appenninoque interiectis, propinquitate
8 etiam fluminum ac paludum praegelidis. Ad hoc raptim eductis hominibus atque equis, non capto ante cibo, non ope ulla ad arcendum frigus adhibita, nihil caloris inerat, et quidquid aurae fluminis ad-
9 propinquabant, adflabat acrior frigoris vis. Ut vero refugientes Numidas insequentes aquam ingressi sunt—et erat pectoribus tenus aucta nocturno

[1] singuli *Forchhammer*: singulis *P*.
[2] ita cum mille equitibus Magone . . . dimisso *Madvig*: ita mille equitibus magoni . . . dimissis *P*.
[3] in stationes ς: stationes *P*.

bal, "but that your numbers too may be strong to match your bravery, choose, each of you, from the squadrons and the maniples, nine others like yourselves. Mago will point out to you the spot where you are to lie in ambush; you have an enemy who is blind to these stratagems." Mago and his thousand horse and thousand foot being thus dispatched, Hannibal ordered the Numidian cavalry to cross the Trebia at dawn, and riding up to the enemy's gates and discharging missiles against his outposts, to lure him into battle; and then, when the fight was on, to give ground insensibly and draw him across the river. Such were the orders of the Numidians. The other officers, both of cavalry and of infantry, were instructed to make their men have breakfast, and then, armed and with horses saddled, to await the signal. B.C. 218

On the flurry caused by the Numidians, Sempronius, confident where cavalry was concerned, first led out all of this part of his forces; then six thousand of the infantry; and finally all the rest of his troops. He had fully made up his mind beforehand and was eager for the battle. It chanced to be the time of year when the days are shortest, and it was snowing in the region between the Alps and the Apennines, and the proximity of rivers and marshes intensified the bitter cold. Moreover, men and horses had been turned out in haste, without stopping for food or doing anything to guard against becoming chilled; there was no warmth in them, and the nearer they approached the atmosphere of the river the sharper grew the cold wind in their faces. But when, in pursuit of the fleeing Numidians, they entered the water—swollen breast-high with the

A.U.C. 536

imbri,—tum utique egressis rigere omnibus corpora, ut vix armorum tenendorum potentia essent,[1] et simul lassitudine[2] et procedente iam die fame etiam deficere.

LV. Hannibalis interim miles ignibus ante tentoria factis oleoque per manipulos, ut mollirent artus, misso et cibo per otium capto, ubi transgressos flumen hostes nuntiatum est, alacer animis corpori-
2 busque arma capit atque in aciem procedit. Baliares locat ante signa, levem armaturam, octo ferme milia hominum, dein graviorem armis peditem, quod virium quod roboris erat; in cornibus circumfudit decem milia equitum et ab cornibus in utramque partem
3 divisos elephantos statuit. Consul effuse sequentes equites, cum ab resistentibus[3] subito Numidis incauti exciperentur, signo receptui dato revocatos
4 circumdedit peditibus. Duodeviginti milia Romana erant, socium nominis Latini viginti, auxilia praeterea Cenomanorum; ea sola in fide manserat Gallica gens. Iis copiis concursum est.

5 Proelium a Baliaribus ortum est; quibus cum maiore robore legiones obsisterent, diducta propere in cornua levis armatura est,[4] quae res effecit ut
6 equitatus Romanus extemplo urgeretur; nam cum vix iam per se resisterent decem milibus equitum

[1] essent ς: esset *P.*
[2] simul lassitudine ς: similitudine *P.*
[3] ab resistentibus *P*: ab refugientibus et resistentibus *Weissenborn.*
[4] diducta . . . armatura est *Madvig*: deductae . . . armaturae sunt *P.*

rain that had fallen in the night—or at any rate B.C. 218 when they got out upon the further bank, then indeed their bodies were all so benumbed that they could hardly hold their weapons; and at the same time they were fainting with fatigue, and, as the day wore on, with hunger as well.

LV. Hannibal's soldiers had in the meantime made fires before their tents; in each company they had been served with oil to supple their joints, and had breakfasted at leisure. When, therefore, they were told that the enemy had crossed the river, they were eager both in mind and body, as they armed and went out to battle. In front of the standards Hannibal placed the Baliares, light-armed troops numbering about eight thousand, and behind these his heavy infantry, the strength and flower of his army; the wings he formed of ten thousand horse, and, dividing the elephants, stationed them outside the wings. The consul's troopers were scattered in pursuit of the Numidians, when suddenly the latter made a stand and took them unawares; whereupon he called them back and posted them on either flank of the infantry. There were eighteen thousand Romans and twenty thousand allies of the Latin name, besides the auxiliaries of the Cenomani, the only Gallic tribe that continued loyal. These were the contending forces.

The Baliares began the battle, but those light-armed troops, finding the legions too strong to cope with, were quickly withdrawn and sent to the wings. This manœuvre at once caused the Roman cavalry acute distress; for they numbered but four thousand, and, tired as they were, would scarce have been able to hold out any longer against the enemy's ten

A.U.C. 536 quattuor milia et fessi integris plerisque, obruti sunt
insuper velut nube iaculorum a Baliaribus coniecta.
7 Ad hoc elephanti eminentes ab extremis cornibus,
equis maxime non visu modo, sed odore insolito
8 territis, fugam late faciebant. Pedestris pugna par
animis magis quam viribus erat, quas recentes Poenus
paulo ante curatis corporibus in proelium attulerat;
contra ieiuna fessaque corpora Romanis et rigentia
gelu torpebant. Restitissent tamen animis, si cum
9 pedite solum foret pugnatum; sed et Baliares pulso
equite iaculabantur in latera et elephanti iam in
mediam peditum aciem sese tulerant et Mago
Numidaeque, simul latebras eorum improvida prae-
terlata acies est, exorti ab tergo ingentem tumultum
10 ac terrorem fecere. Tamen in tot circumstantibus
malis mansit aliquamdiu immota acies, maxime
11 praeter spem omnium adversus elephantos. Eos
velites ad id ipsum locati verutis coniectis et avertere
et insecuti aversos sub caudis, qua maxime molli cute
volnera accipiunt, fodiebant.

LVI. Trepidantesque et prope[1] iam in suos consternatos e media[2] acie in extremam ad sinistrum cornu adversus Gallos auxiliares agi iussit Hannibal. Ibi[3] extemplo haud dubiam fecere fugam. Quo

[1] et prope *Rost*: in prope *P*.
[2] e media *Gronovius*: media *P*.
[3] Hannibal. Ibi *Weissenborn*: hannibali *P*.

thousand cavalry alone, who were most of them fresh; and now they were overwhelmed, as it were with a cloud of missiles, by the Baliares. Besides this, the elephants, looming large on the outer extremities of the wings, gave rise to such a panic, particularly among the horses, not only by their strange appearance, but also by their unfamiliar smell, as to bring about a general flight. As for the infantry, they were fairly matched in courage, but not in strength, which was unimpaired in the case of the Phoenicians, who had refreshed themselves shortly before entering the battle, while the Romans were faint with fasting and fatigue, and were stiff and numb with cold. Yet their courage would have enabled them to resist, had they fought against infantry alone. But the Baliares, having put the cavalry to flight, were raining missiles on their flanks; the elephants had now charged the centre of the line; and Mago and his Numidians, as soon as the Roman army had passed their ambuscade without observing it, started up in their rear, and caused the wildest panic and confusion. Nevertheless, amidst all these evils, the line held for a time unshaken, and even—what no one had dared to hope for—against the elephants. Skirmishers, expressly posted to deal with the beasts, would throw darts at them and make them turn away, and then pursuing them would strike them under the tail, where the skin is softest and it is possible to wound them. B.C. 218

LVI. In their terror they were now on the point of charging their own people, when Hannibal gave orders to drive them from the centre to the extreme left wing, against the Gallic auxiliaries. Here they immediately caused a decided stampede, and the

A.U.C. 536 novus[1] terror additus Romanis, ut fusa auxilia sua
2 viderunt. Itaque cum iam in orbem pugnarent,
decem milia ferme hominum, cum alibi[2] evadere
nequissent, media Afrorum acie, qua Gallicis auxiliis
firmata erat, cum ingenti caede hostium perrupere,
3 et cum neque in castra reditus esset flumine inter-
clusis neque prae imbri satis discernere[3] possent,
qua suis opem ferrent, Placentiam recto itinere
4 perrexere. Plures deinde in omnes partes eruptiones
factae; et qui flumen petiere aut gurgitibus absumpti sunt aut inter cunctationem ingrediendi ab
5 hostibus oppressi; qui passim per agros fuga sparsi
erant vestigia cedentis sequentes agminis Placentiam
contendere; aliis timor hostium audaciam ingrediendi
flumen fecit, transgressique in castra pervenerunt.
6 Imber nive mixtus et intoleranda vis frigoris et
homines multos et iumenta et elephantos prope
7 omnes absumpsit. Finis insequendi hostes Poenis
flumen Trebia fuit, et ita torpentes gelu in castra
8 rediere ut vix laetitiam victoriae sentirent. Itaque
nocte insequenti, cum praesidium castrorum et quod
reliquum ex fuga inermium[4] ex magna parte militum
erat ratibus Trebiam traicerent, aut nihil sensere
obstrepente pluvia aut, quia iam moveri nequibant
prae lassitudine ac volneribus, sentire sese dissimu-

[1] quo novus *Frigell*: quoque nouus *P*.
[2] alibi *Weissenborn*: alii *P*.
[3] discernere ς: decernere *P*.
[4] reliquum ex fuga inermium *Luchs*: relicum *P*.

---

[1] Livy appears to have thought of Placentia as west of the Trebia, which the ten thousand were therefore not now obliged to cross, though Scipio and the garrison were (§ 8).

[2] At chap. lviii. § 11 Livy speaks of the loss of *seven* of the elephants which survived the Trebia. According to

Romans experienced a fresh alarm when they saw their auxiliaries routed. And so, hemmed in as they now were on every side, about ten thousand men, when they found it impossible to escape at any other point, forced a passage, with great slaughter of their enemies, through the Carthaginian centre, which was composed of Gallic auxiliaries, and being cut off by the river from returning to their camp and so blinded by the rain that they could not well discern where to help their comrades, took the shortest way to Placentia.[1] After that sundry groups broke out at various points. Those who headed for the river were either drowned in its eddies, or, while they hesitated to enter it, were overtaken by the enemy; but those who scattered over the countryside in flight made their way by following the tracks of the retreating column, to Placentia; others, venturing, in their terror of the enemy, to attempt the river, got across, and reached the camp. The mingled rain and snow and the intolerable sharpness of the cold brought death to many men and beasts of burden and to almost all the elephants.[2] The Phoenicians pursued their enemies no further than to the river Trebia, and got back to camp so benumbed and chilled as hardly to feel the joy of victory. Consequently, when, in the night that followed, the garrison of the camp, and such soldiers—without arms for the most part—as had survived the rout, were crossing the Trebia on rafts, they either heard nothing, owing to the noise made by the rain, or being unable, for weariness and wounds, to bestir themselves, pretended not to hear; and unmolested B.C. 218

Polybius (III. lxxiv. 11), all but *one* perished from the effects of the rain and snow that followed the battle.

A.U.C. 536 larunt; quietisque Poenis tacito agmine ab Scipione consule exercitus Placentiam est perductus, inde Pado traiecto[1] Cremonam, ne duorum exercituum hibernis una colonia premeretur.

LVII. Romam tantus terror ex hac clade perlatus est ut iam ad urbem Romanam crederent infestis signis hostem venturum, nec quicquam spei aut auxilii esse quo a portis[2] moenibusque vim arcerent:
2 uno consule ad Ticinum victo alterum ex Sicilia revocatum[3]; duobus consulibus, duobus consularibus exercitibus victis quos alios duces, quas alias legiones
3 esse quae arcessantur? Ita territis Sempronius consul advenit, ingenti periculo per effusos passim ad praedandum hostium equites audacia magis quam consilio aut spe fallendi resistendive, si non
4 falleret, transgressus, id quod unum maxime in praesentia desiderabatur, comitiis consularibus habitis, in hiberna rediit. Creati consules Cn. Servilius et C. Flaminius iterum.[4]

5 Ceterum ne hiberna quidem Romanis quieta erant vagantibus passim Numidis equitibus et, ut quaeque[5] iis impeditiora erant, Celtiberis Lusitanisque. Omnes igitur undique clausi commeatus
6 erant, nisi quos Pado naves subveherent. Emporium prope Placentiam fuit et opere magno munitum et

[1] Pado traiecto ς: pado traiectus *P*.
[2] quo a portis *Heerwagen*: qua portis *P*.
[3] alterum ex Sicilia revocatum *Madvig*: altero ex Sicilia reuocato *P*.
[4] C. Flaminius iterum *Glareanus*: C. Flaminius *P*.
[5] ut quaeque *Fabri*: quaeque *P*.

---

[1] The descriptions of the terror occasioned in Rome by news of the defeat and of the journey of Sempronius are not found in Polybius and are very likely drawn from Coelius Antipater.

by the enemy Scipio led his army in silence to Placentia, and thence—after crossing the Po—to Cremona, so that that one town might not be overburdened with furnishing winter quarters for two armies. B.C. 218

LVII. To Rome the news of this disaster brought such consternation that people looked for the immediate appearance of the hostile army before their very City, and knew not which way to turn for any hope or help in defending their gates and walls against its onset.[1] When one consul had been defeated on the Ticinus, the other had been summoned back from Sicily; but now that two consuls and two consular armies had been beaten, what other generals, what other legions had they to call upon? In the midst of this alarm the consul Sempronius arrived. He had made his way, taking tremendous risks, through the enemy's cavalry—which was widely dispersed in quest of booty—relying more on audacity than calculation or the prospect of eluding his enemies, or of resisting, should he be unable to elude them. The election of consuls was the one crying need of the hour. This Sempronius accomplished and returned forthwith to his winter quarters. The choice had fallen on Gnaeus Servilius and—for the second time—on Gaius Flaminius.

For the rest, the Romans were given no peace even in their winter quarters. The Numidian cavalry ranged far and wide, and any ground that was too rough for them was covered by the Celtiberians and Lusitani. The result was the cutting off of all supplies from every quarter, save such as were brought up the Po in ships. Their magazine, which was near Placentia, was elaborately fortified

A.U.C. 536 valido firmatum praesidio. Eius castelli expugnandi[1]
spe cum equitibus ac levi armatura profectus Hannibal, cum plurimum in celando incepto ad effectum
spei habuisset, nocte adortus non fefellit vigiles.
7 Tantus repente clamor est sublatus ut Placentiae
quoque audiretur. Itaque sub lucem cum equitatu
consul aderat iussis quadrato agmine legionibus
8 sequi. Equestre interim proelium commissum, in
quo quia saucius Hannibal pugna excessit, pavore
hostibus iniecto defensum egregie praesidium est.
9 Paucorum inde[2] dierum quiete sumpta et vixdum
satis percurato volnere ad Victumulas[3] oppugnandas
10 ire pergit. Id emporium Romanis Gallico bello
fuerat; munitum inde locum frequentaverant ad-
colae mixti undique ex finitimis populis, et tum
terror populationum eo plerosque ex agris com-
11 pulerat. Huius generis multitudo, fama impigre
defensi ad Placentiam praesidii accensa, armis
12 arreptis obviam Hannibali procedit. Magis agmina
quam acies in via concurrerunt, et cum ex altera
parte nihil praeter inconditam turbam esset, in
altera et dux militi et miles duci[4] fidens, ad triginta
13 quinque milia hominum a paucis fusa. Postero die
deditione facta praesidium intra moenia accepere;
iussique arma tradere cum dicto paruissent, signum

[1] expugnandi *Perizonius*: oppugnandi *P.*
[2] inde ς: in *P.*
[3] Victumulas *Mommsen*: uictumuias *P.*
[4] miles duci ς: duci miles *P.*

and strongly garrisoned. This place Hannibal hoped B.C. 218
to capture by assault, and set out thither with his cavalry and light infantry. He had counted mainly on the concealment of his movements for their effectiveness; but his night attack failed to catch the sentries off their guard, and the defenders at once set up so loud an outcry that it was heard even in Placentia. And so at break of day the consul was on the spot with his cavalry, having ordered the legions to follow him in fighting column. Meanwhile, a cavalry engagement took place, in which Hannibal was wounded and withdrew from the fight, and the enemy were so alarmed by this that the post was successfully defended. After this Hannibal, when he had rested only a few days and his wound was scarce healed over, set out to attack Victumulae. This had been a Roman magazine in the Gallic war, and having then been fortified had since attracted numerous settlers from the various peoples dwelling in the neighbourhood; and just then the fear of raids had caused large numbers to flock in from the countryside. Such was the character of the population, which, fired by the story of the stout defence of the fortress near Placentia, flew to arms and went out to meet Hannibal. More like marching columns than embattled armies they encountered each other in the road; and since on one side there was only an undisciplined rabble, and on the other a general who relied upon his soldiers, and soldiers who confided in their general, some thirty-five thousand men were routed by a very few. The next day they surrendered and received a garrison within their walls. Being commanded to give up their weapons they complied: whereupon a

A.U.C. 536 repente victoribus datur ut tamquam vi captam
14 urbem diriperent. Neque ulla quae in tali re
memorabilis scribentibus videri solet praetermissa
clades est: adeo omne[1] libidinis crudelitatisque et
inhumanae superbiae editum in miseros exemplum
est. Hae fuere hibernae expeditiones Hannibalis.

A.U.C. 537 LVIII. Haud longi inde temporis,[2] dum intolera-
2 bilia frigora erant, quies militi data est, et ad prima
ac dubia signa veris profectus ex hibernis in Etruriam
ducit, eam quoque gentem, sicut Gallos Liguresque,
3 aut vi aut voluntate adiuncturus. Transeuntem
Appenninum adeo atrox adorta tempestas est ut
Alpium prope foeditatem superaverit. Vento
mixtus imber cum ferretur in ipsa ora, primo, quia
aut arma omittenda erant, aut contra enitentes
4 vertice intorti adfligebantur, constitere; dein, cum
iam spiritum includeret nec reciprocare animam
5 sineret, aversi a vento parumper consedere. Tum
vero ingenti sono caelum strepere et inter horrendos
fragores micare ignes; capti[3] auribus et oculis metu
6 omnes torpere; tandem effuso imbre, cum eo magis
accensa vis venti esset, ipso illo quo deprensi erant
7 loco castra ponere necessarium visum est. Id vero
laboris velut de integro initium fuit: nam nec
explicare quicquam nec statuere poterant, nec quod
statutum esset manebat, omnia perscindente vento

[1] omne *Luchs*: omnes *P*: omnis ς.

[2] longi inde temporis *Gronovius*: longis inde temporibus *P*

[3] capti ς: captis *P*.

signal was suddenly given to the victors to sack the town, as if they had taken it by storm. Nor was any cruelty omitted which historians generally deem worth noting on such an occasion; but every species of lust and outrage and inhuman insolence was visited upon the wretched inhabitants. Such were Hannibal's winter expeditions. B.C. 218

LVIII. For no long time thereafter, while the cold was still unbearable, he allowed his men to rest, and on the first doubtful signs of spring broke up his winter quarters and marched towards Etruria, with the object of drawing that nation also to his standards, either by force or with their own consent, as he had done with the Gauls and the Ligurians. In attempting to cross the Apennines he was assailed by a storm so terrible as almost to surpass the horrors of the Alps. With the wind and rain blowing full in their faces, at first—because they must either have dropped their arms or else, if they struggled against it, be caught by the hurricane and hurled to the ground—they halted; then, when it actually stopped their breath and would not allow them to respire, they turned their backs on the gale and for a time huddled together on the ground. And now the heavens resounded with a frightful tumult, and between the terrific crashes the lightning flashed. Deafened and blinded, they were all stunned with fear. At length the downpour ceased, but the wind only blew the more furiously, and there seemed to be nothing to do but to pitch camp on the very spot where they had been caught. This, however, was but a fresh beginning of their troubles, for they could neither spread nor set up a tent, nor, once set up, would it stay in place, for the wind rent B.C. 217

A.U.C. 537 8 et rapiente; et mox aqua levata vento cum super
gelida montium iuga concreta esset, tantum nivosae
grandinis deiecit ut omnibus omissis procumberent
homines tegminibus suis magis obruti quam tecti;
9 tantaque vis frigoris insecuta est ut ex illa miserabili
hominum iumentorumque strage cum se quisque
attollere ac levare vellet, diu nequiret, quia tor-
pentibus rigore nervis vix[1] flectere artus poterant.
10 Deinde, ut tandem agitando sese movere ac recepere[2] animos et raris locis ignis fieri est coeptus, ad
alienam opem quisque inops tendere. Biduum eo
11 loco velut obsessi mansere. Multi homines, multa
iumenta, elephanti quoque ex iis qui proelio ad
Trebiam facto superfuerant septem absumpti.

LIX. Degressus[3] Appennino retro ad Placentiam
castra movit et ad decem milia progressus consedit.
Postero die duodecim milia peditum quinque equitum
2 adversus hostem ducit; nec Sempronius consul—
iam enim redierat ab Roma—detrectavit certamen.
Atque eo die tria milia passuum inter bina castra
3 fuere; postero die ingentibus animis vario eventu
pugnatum est. Primo concursu adeo res Romana
superior fuit ut non acie vincerent solum sed pulsos
hostes in castra persequerentur, mox castra quoque
4 oppugnarent. Hannibal paucis propugnatoribus in

[1] vix ς: suis *P*. [2] recepere ς (*Rossbach*): recipere *P*.
[3] degressus ς: digressus *P*.

everything to shreds and swept it away; and when B.C. 217
presently the moisture taken up by the wind had been congealed over the cold mountain ridges, it descended in such a storm of sleet that the men let go of everything and threw themselves on their faces on the ground, overwhelmed by their shelters rather than protected by them; and the cold that ensued was so severe that when anyone sought to rise and lift himself from out that pitiful heap of men and beasts, for a long time he would be unable, because his sinews were so stiff and tense that he could hardly bend his joints. Afterwards, when at last by exerting themselves they had recovered the power of motion and regained their courage, and had begun here and there to kindle fires, each, in his helplessness, applied to someone else for help. For two days they remained on that spot as if beleaguered. Many men and many horses perished, and seven of the elephants that had survived the battle on the Trebia.

LIX. Descending from the Apennines, Hannibal turned back once more towards Placentia, and after marching about ten miles went into camp. The next day he advanced against the enemy with twelve thousand foot and five thousand horse. Nor did the consul Sempronius, who had now returned from Rome, decline the combat. That day there were only three miles between the two encampments. On the following day they fought, with great spirit and with shifting fortunes. At the first encounter the Romans had so far the best of it that not only were they victorious in the battle, but they pursued the beaten enemy to his camp, and were soon attacking the camp itself. Hannibal stationed

A.U.C. 537 vallo portisque positis ceteros confertos in media castra recepit intentosque signum ad erumpendum
5 exspectare iubet. Iam nona ferme diei hora erat, cum Romanus nequiquam fatigato milite, postquam nulla spes erat potiundi castris, signum receptui
6 dedit. Quod ubi Hannibal accepit laxatamque pugnam et recessum a castris vidit, extemplo equitibus dextra laevaque emissis in hostem ipse
7 cum peditum robore mediis[1] castris erupit. Pugna raro magis ulla saeva aut[2] utriusque partis pernicie clarior fuisset, si extendi eam dies in longum
8 spatium sivisset;[3] nox accensum ingentibus animis proelium diremit. Itaque acrior concursus fuit quam caedes, et sicut aequata ferme pugna erat, ita clade pari discessum est. Ab neutra parte sescentis plus
9 peditibus et dimidium eius equitum cecidit; sed maior Romanis quam pro numero iactura fuit, quia equestris ordinis aliquot et tribuni militum quinque
10 et praefecti sociorum tres sunt interfecti. Secundum eam pugnam Hannibal in Ligures, Sempronius Lucam concessit. Venienti in Ligures Hannibali per insidias intercepti duo quaestores Romani, C. Fulvius et L. Lucretius, cum duobus tribunis militum et quinque equestris ordinis, senatorum

[1] robore mediis *Lipsius*: roborē | diis P^1: roborē | de his P^2.
[2] saeva aut *Hertz*: aeaut *P*: saeva et *Valla*.
[3] sivisset ς: uisset P^1: quiuisset P^2: sisset *Gronovius*.

---

[1] Approximately three o'clock in the afternoon.

a few defenders on the rampart and at the gates B.C. 217 and received the rest in a crowded throng within the enclosure, where he bade them watch intently for the signal to sally forth. It was now about the ninth hour of the day,[1] when the Roman general, who had worn out his men to no avail and saw no prospect of capturing the camp, bade sound the recall. When Hannibal heard this and perceived that the fighting had grown lax and that the enemy had retired from his rampart, he suddenly sent his cavalry against them from the right and left and rushed out himself with the strength of his infantry from the centre of the camp. Seldom has there been a fiercer battle or one more notable for the losses on both sides than this would have been, had the light permitted it to be prolonged; but darkness put an end to a conflict which had been begun with the greatest ardour. The fury of the combatants was consequently greater than the carnage, and as the battle was practically a drawn one, so were the losses equal when the opposing forces separated. On neither side had more than six hundred of the infantry fallen or half as many of the cavalry; but the loss of the Romans was out of proportion to the number slain, for it included several knights, five tribunes of the soldiers, and three praefects of the allies. After this engagement Hannibal retired into Liguria and Sempronius to Luca. The Ligurians had ambushed and made prisoners of two Roman quaestors, Gaius Fulvius and Lucius Lucretius, with two tribunes of the soldiers and five members of the equestrian order—mostly sons of senators. These men they handed over to Hannibal on his coming among them, as a

A.U.C. 537 ferme liberis, quo magis ratam fore cum iis pacem societatemque crederet, traduntur.

A.U.C. 536 LX. Dum haec in Italia geruntur, Cn. Cornelius
2 Scipio in Hispaniam cum classe et exercitu missus cum ab ostio Rhodani profectus Pyrenaeosque montes circumvectus Emporias[1] adpulisset classem,
3 exposito ibi exercitu orsus a Laeetanis[2] omnem oram usque ad Hiberum flumen partim renovandis societatibus, partim novis instituendis, Romanae
4 dicionis fecit. Inde conciliata clementiae iustitiaeque[3] fama non ad maritimos modo populos sed in mediterraneis quoque ac montanis ad ferociores iam gentes valuit; nec pax modo apud eos sed societas etiam armorum parta[4] est, validaeque aliquot auxiliorum cohortes ex iis conscriptae sunt.

5 Hannonis cis Hiberum provincia erat; eum reliquerat Hannibal ad regionis eius praesidium. Itaque, priusquam alienarentur omnia, obviam eundum ratus castris in conspectu hostium positis in aciem
6 eduxit. Nec Romano differendum certamen visum, quippe qui sciret cum Hannone et Hasdrubale sibi dimicandum esse malletque adversus singulos separatim quam adversus duos simul rem gerere.
7 Nec magni certaminis ea dimicatio fuit. Sex milia

[1] Emporias *Luchs*: temporis *P*: emporiis ς.
[2] Laeetanis *Huebner*: lacetanis *P*.
[3] clementiae iustitiaeque *Weissenborn*: clementiaeque *P*: clementiae *Madvig*.
[4] parta ς: parata *P*.

[1] For the events recorded in this chapter Livy is thought to have drawn upon some late and worthless annalist. That the Romans should have been able, so soon after their discomfiture on the Trebia, to hold their own in open battle—and a battle too where cavalry cut so large a figure—is improbable, to say the least. Polybius says nothing of any

further earnest of their peaceful and friendly disposition towards him.[1] B.C. 217

LX. Whilst these things were going on in Italy, Gnaeus Cornelius Scipio, who had been sent out to Spain with a fleet and an army, had set sail from the mouth of the Rhone and passing the Pyrenees had put into Emporiae. Landing his army there and beginning with the Laeetani, he had brought all that coast, as far as the river Ebro, under Roman sway, partly by renewing old alliances and partly by forming new ones. The reputation which he there acquired for clemency and justice availed not only with the maritime tribes, but also with the more warlike clans inhabiting the interior and the mountainous parts; so that he was able not only to establish peaceful relations but even to conclude a military alliance with them, and several strong cohorts of auxiliaries were raised there. B.C. 218

North of the Ebro Hanno was the Carthaginian commander, for Hannibal had left him there to defend that region. Feeling, therefore, that something ought to be done, before everything was lost to Carthage, he pitched his camp in sight of the enemy and offered battle. The Roman general saw no reason to put off the engagement; he knew that he must fight with Hanno and Hasdrubal, and chose rather to deal with them separately than both at once. Neither was the battle very difficult to win. Six thousand of the enemy were killed and

such operations, nor of the march to Luca, which contradicts Livy's own statement, at chap. lxiii. § 1, that the army of Sempronius wintered at Placentia (see also chap. lxiii. § 15). The whole question is discussed by De Sanctis, pp. 186 f. Cf. too the notes in Weissenborn–Mueller–Rossbach.

A.U.C. 536 hostium caesa, duo capta cum praesidio castrorum; nam et castra expugnata sunt atque ipse dux cum
8 aliquot principibus capiuntur, et Cissis,[1] propinquum castris oppidum, expugnatur. Ceterum praeda oppidi parvi pretii rerum fuit, supellex barbarica
9 ac vilium mancipiorum; castra militem ditavere non eius modo exercitus qui victus erat sed et eius qui cum Hannibale in Italia militabat omnibus fere caris rebus, ne gravia impedimenta ferentibus essent, citra Pyrenaeum relictis.

LXI. Priusquam certa huius cladis fama accideret, transgressus Hiberum Hasdrubal cum octo milibus peditum, mille equitum, tamquam ad primum adventum Romanorum occursurus, postquam perditas res ad Cissim amissaque castra accepit, iter
2 ad mare convertit. Haud procul Tarracone classicos milites navalesque socios vagos palantesque per agros, quod ferme fit ut secundae res neglegentiam creent, equite passim dimisso cum magna caede,
3 maiore fuga ad naves compellit. Nec diutius circa ea loca morari ausus, ne ab Scipione opprimeretur,
4 trans Hiberum sese recepit. Et Scipio raptim ad famam novorum hostium agmine acto, cum in paucos praefectos navium [2] animadvertisset, praesidio Tarracone modico relicto Emporias cum classe rediit.

[1] Cissis *Alschefski*: scissis *P*.
[2] navium *Gronovius*: pauiu *P*[1]: paulum *P*[2]: palam *Lipsius*.

---

[1] Later (under Augustus) made the capital of the Roman province of Tarraconensis. There are still in existence remains of Iberian walls and of the Roman citadel, circus, amphitheatre, and water-system.

two thousand captured, together with the garrison B.C. 218 of the camp—for this too was attacked and taken. The general himself and several chieftains were made prisoners, and Cissis, a town which stood near the camp, was carried by assault. The plunder of the town yielded objects of little worth—household belongings of barbarians and slaves of no great price—but the camp made the soldiers rich; for in it they found not only the valuables of the army that they had just defeated, but also those of the army that was now serving under Hannibal in Italy, for the men had left nearly all their treasures behind when they crossed the Pyrenees, so as not to burden themselves with heavy baggage on the march.

LXI. Hasdrubal had not yet received definite tidings of this disaster when he crossed the Ebro with eight thousand infantry and a thousand cavalry, as though to confront the Romans at their first arrival; but on learning of the catastrophe at Cissis and the loss of the camp, he turned and marched in the direction of the sea. Not far from Tarraco[1] he came upon the soldiers of the fleet and the naval allies, who were dispersed and wandering over the country-side, with the carelessness which usually attends success; and sending out his cavalry in all directions he drove them, with much slaughter and more confusion, to their ships. But not venturing to tarry longer in that region, lest Scipio should be down upon him, he retreated across the Ebro. Scipio, hearing of these new enemies, did indeed march thither with all speed; but after punishing a few of the ships' captains, he left a garrison of moderate size in Tarraco and returned with the

A.U.C. 536

5 Vixdum digresso eo Hasdrubal aderat et Ilergetum
populo, qui obsides Scipioni dederat, ad defectionem
impulso cum eorum ipsorum iuventute agros fidelium
6 Romanis sociorum vastat. Excito deinde Scipione
hibernis toto cis[1] Hiberum rursus cedit agro. Scipio
relictam ab auctore defectionis Ilergetum gentem
cum infesto exercitu invasisset, compulsis omnibus
Atanagrum urbem, quae caput eius populi erat,
7 circumsedit intraque dies paucos pluribus quam
ante obsidibus imperatis Ilergetes pecunia etiam
8 multatos in ius dicionemque recepit. Inde in
Ausetanos prope Hiberum, socios et ipsos Poenorum,
procedit atque urbe eorum obsessa Lacetanos
auxilium finitimis ferentes nocte haud procul iam
9 urbe, cum intrare vellent, excepit insidiis; caesa
ad duodecim milia.[2] Exuti prope omnes armis
domos passim palantes per agros diffugere. Nec
obsessos alia ulla res quam iniqua oppugnantibus
10 hiems tutabatur. Triginta dies obsidio fuit, per
quos raro unquam nix minus quattuor pedes alta
iacuit; adeoque pluteos ac vineas Romanorum
operuerat ut ea sola ignibus aliquotiens coniectis
11 ab hoste etiam tutamentum fuerit. Postremo, cum
Amusicus princeps eorum ad Hasdrubalem pro-

[1] toto cis ς: stoi/cosis *P*: hostico cis *Sabellicus and Stroth.*

[2] ad duodecim milia ς: ad XII. P^1: anxii P^2.

---

[1] Site unknown: perhaps not far from Ilerda (Lerida) on the Sicoris.

fleet to Emporiae. No sooner was he gone than B.C. 218 Hasdrubal appeared, and inciting the Ilergetes, who had given Scipio hostages, to revolt, he used the young men of this very tribe to lay waste the fields of the allies who were faithful to the Romans. But this having roused Scipio from his winter quarters, he retreated again and abandoned all the territory north of the Ebro. Scipio invaded the country of the Ilergetes—left thus in the lurch by the instigator of their revolt—with fire and sword, and driving them all into the city of Atanagrus,[1] the capital of that nation, laid siege to them. Within a few days he had exacted more hostages of them than before, and mulcting them also in a sum of money, had received them under his authority and rule. Thence he marched against the Ausetani, near the Ebro, who were likewise allies of the Phoenicians; and besieging their city, laid an ambush for the Lacetani, as they were bringing assistance to their neighbours, and fell upon them in the night, not far from the city, when they would have entered it. The slain amounted to about twelve thousand; almost all the others lost their arms, and scattering over the fields in all directions, fled to their homes. As for the besieged, nothing could have saved them but a winter that was most unfavourable to the besiegers. The blockade lasted thirty days, during which time the snow rarely lay less than four feet deep, and so completely had it covered the mantlets and pent-houses of the Romans that this alone was sufficient to protect them from the firebrands that were several times discharged upon them by the enemy. Finally, when their chief Amusicus had fled and taken refuge with Hasdrubal,

A.U.C. 536 fugisset, viginti argenti talentis pacti deduntur. Tarraconem in hiberna reditum est.

LXII. Romae aut circa urbem multa ea hieme prodigia facta aut, quod evenire solet motis semel in religionem[1] animis, multa nuntiata et temere credita
2 sunt; in quis ingenuum infantem semestrem in
3 foro olitorio triumphum clamasse, et in foro[2] boario bovem in tertiam contignationem sua sponte escendisse atque inde tumultu habitatorum territum
4 sese deiecisse, et navium speciem de caelo adfulsisse, et aedem Spei, quae est in foro olitorio, fulmine ictam, et Lanuvi hostiam[3] se commovisse et corvum in aedem Iunonis devolasse atque in ipso pulvinario
5 consedisse, et in agro Amiternino multis locis hominum species procul candida veste visas nec cum ullo congressas,[4] et in Piceno lapidibus pluvisse, et Caere sortes extenuatas, et in Gallia lupum vigili
6 gladium ex vagina raptum abstulisse. Ob cetera prodigia libros adire decemviri iussi; quod autem

[1] religionem *edd.*: regionem *P.*

[2] in foro ς: e (ex *H. J. Mueller*) foro *Luterbacher*: foro *P.*

[3] hostiam *P* (*Rossbach's note*): hastam *Sabellicus.*

[4] species . . . visas nec cum ullo congressas *Ruperti*: species . . . uisas nec cum ullo congressos ς: specie . . . uisos nec cum illis congressos *P.*

---

[1] Polybius knows nothing of the events recounted in §§ 5–11, but makes Scipio retire for the winter to Emporiae and Hasdrubal to Tarraco, at the conclusion of the campaign described by Livy in §§ 1–4. The source which Livy used for the latter part of the chapter was perhaps a Greek writer whose account of Hasdrubal's offensive was so different from that of Polybius that Livy thought that they related to two distinct campaigns. It is possible that Livy's immediate source in §§ 5–11 was Coelius and that the dis-

they made terms and surrendered, agreeing to pay twenty talents of silver. The Romans returned to Tarraco and went into winter quarters.[1] B.C. 218

LXII. In Rome or near it many prodigies occurred that winter, or—as often happens when men's thoughts are once turned upon religion—many were reported and too easily credited. Some of these portents were: that a free-born infant of six months had cried "Triumph!" in the provision market; that in the cattle market an ox had climbed, of its own accord, to the third storey of a house and then, alarmed by the outcry of the occupants, had thrown itself down; that phantom ships had been seen gleaming in the sky; that the temple of Hope, in the provision market, had been struck by lightning; that in Lanuvium a slain victim had stirred, and a raven had flown down into Juno's temple and alighted on her very couch; that in the district of Amiternum, in many places, apparitions of men in shining raiment had appeared in the distance, but had not drawn near to anyone; that in the Picentian country there had been a shower of pebbles; that at Caere the lots had shrunk;[2] that in Gaul a wolf had snatched a sentry's sword from its scabbard and run off with it. For the other prodigies the decemviri were commanded to consult the Books,[3] but for

comfiture of the Lacetani is an embellishment of the story due to the latter's patriotic inventiveness. See De Sanctis, pp. 184, 185.

[2] The lots were inscribed on little wooden or bronze tablets; they are also associated with Praeneste, Falerii, and Patavium.

[3] The Sibylline Books were wont to be consulted (but only on the express command of the senate) as to the meaning and proper expiation of portents.

A.U.C. 536 lapidibus pluvisset in Piceno, novemdiale sacrum edictum; et subinde aliis procurandis prope tota
7 civitas operata fuit. Iam primum omnium urbs lustrata est, hostiaeque maiores quibus editum est
8 dis caesae, et donum ex auri pondo quadraginta Lanuvium Iunoni[1] portatum est, et signum aeneum matronae Iunoni in Aventino dedicaverunt, et lectisternium Caere, ubi sortes adtenuatae erant, imperatum, et supplicatio Fortunae in Algido;
9 Romae quoque et lectisternium Iuventati[2] et supplicatio ad aedem Herculis nominatim, deinde universo populo circa omnia pulvinaria indicta, et
10 Genio maiores hostiae caesae quinque, et C. Atilius Serranus praetor vota suscipere iussus, si in decem
11 annos res publica eodem stetisset statu. Haec procurata votaque ex libris Sibyllinis magna ex parte levaverant religione animos.

A.U.C. 537 LXIII. Consulum designatorum alter Flaminius, cui eae legiones quae Placentiae hibernabant sorte evenerant, edictum et litteras ad consulem misit, ut is exercitus idibus Martiis Arimini adesset in castris.
2 Hic in provincia consulatum inire consilium erat memori veterum certaminum cum patribus, quae tribunus plebis et quae postea consul, prius de con-

[1] Iunoni ς: et iuononi *P*: ad Iunonis *Gronovius.*
[2] Iuventati *P*: iuuentuti ς (*Madvig*).

---

[1] A *lectisternium* (for the first one in 399 B.C. see I. xiii. 6) was a banquet tendered to the gods, at which their images were placed on couches (*pulvinaria*). Juventas is here associated with Hercules, as was Hebe in Greece.

[2] In the year 232 B.C. he had carried a law in the Comitia Tributa providing that certain Picentine and Gallic lands should be divided among the poorer citizens.

the shower of pebbles in the Picentian country a nine days' sacrifice was proclaimed. They then set about the expiation of the other portents, and in this virtually all the citizens bore a part. First of all, the city was purified, and major victims were offered up to the designated gods; a gift of gold weighing forty pounds was carried to Lanuvium for Juno, and a bronze statue was dedicated to Juno, by the matrons, on the Aventine; a *lectisternium* was ordered at Caere, where the lots had shrunk; and a supplication was ordered to be made to Fortune on Mount Algidus; in Rome, too, a *lectisternium* was specially appointed for Juventas, and a supplication at the temple of Hercules, and later the entire people was commanded to observe this rite at all the *pulvinaria*;[1] also five major victims were slain in honour of the Genius of the Roman People; and Gaius Atilius Serranus the praetor was ordered to make a vow, "if the commonwealth should abide for ten years in its present state." The making of these vows and expiations, as prescribed by the Sibylline Books, went far to alleviate men's anxiety concerning their relations with the gods. B.C. 218

LXIII. Of the consuls designate, Flaminius, to whom the legions wintering at Placentia had been assigned by lot, dispatched an edict and a letter to the consul, commanding that these troops should be ready in the camp at Ariminum on the Ides of March. It was here, in his province, that he designed to enter on the consulship, for he remembered his former controversies with the senators, which he had waged when a tribune of the plebs,[2] and later as consul—in the first place about his B.C. 217

A.U.C. 537 sulatu, qui abrogabatur, dein de triumpho habuerat.
3 Invisus etiam patribus[1] ob novam legem, quam Q. Claudius tribunus plebis adversus senatum[2] atque uno patrum adiuvante C. Flaminio tulerat, ne quis senator cuive senator pater fuisset maritimam navem quae plus quam trecentarum amphorarum esset
4 haberet—id satis habitum ad fructus ex agris vectandos, quaestus omnis patribus indecorus visus. Res per summam contentionem acta invidiam apud nobilitatem suasori legis Flaminio, favorem apud
5 plebem alterumque inde consulatum peperit. Ob haec ratus auspiciis ementiendis Latinarumque feriarum mora et consularibus aliis impedimentis retenturos se in urbe, simulato itinere privatus clam
6 in provinciam abiit. Ea res ubi palam facta est, novam insuper iram infestis iam ante patribus movit: non cum senatu modo, sed iam cum dis immortalibus
7 C. Flaminium bellum gerere. Consulem ante inauspicato factum revocantibus ex ipsa acie dis atque

[1] patribus *P*: patribus erat (*or* erat patribus) *H. J. Mueller*.

[2] adversus senatum P: aduerso senatu *Gronovius*.

---

[1] In 223 B.C. the senate commanded the consuls Furius and Flaminius, who had marched against the Insubrian Gauls, to return to Rome and resign their magistracies, on the ground that unfavourable auguries had been reported. But Flaminius refused to return, fought and won a battle, and triumphed in the face of senatorial opposition—by virtue of a decree of the people.

[2] The amphora—a wine-jar with two handles—was standardized as a liquid measure roughly equal to six gallons. In our terminology such a vessel would be described as of about seven tons burden.

[3] The new consuls were required to fix the date of the Feriae Latinae, at the first session of the senate after their

consulship, which they tried to annul, and again concerning his triumph.[1] He was also hated by the senators on account of an unprecedented law which Quintus Claudius the tribune of the plebs had introduced, despite the opposition of the senate, with the backing of Gaius Flaminius alone of all that body, providing that no senator or senator's son should own a sea-going ship of more than three hundred amphoras burden[2]—this was reckoned to be sufficient to transport the crops from one's fields, and all money-making was held unseemly in a senator. The measure, which was vehemently opposed, had been productive of great resentment on the part of the nobles against Flaminius, who had advocated its enactment; but had procured for him the favour of the plebs and afterwards a second consulship. Believing, therefore, that his enemies would falsify the auspices and make use of the Latin Festival[3] and other means of hindering a consul, to detain him in the City, he pretended that he had to take a journey, and departing, as a private citizen, slipped away secretly to his province. This behaviour, when the truth came out, aroused fresh indignation in the breasts of the already hostile senators: Gaius Flaminius, they said, was waging war not only with the senate, but this time with the immortal gods. He had formerly been made consul without the confirmation of the auspices, and, though both gods and men had sought to recall him from the very battle-line, he B.C. 217

entering upon office, and they might not take the field for the summer's campaign before they had duly presided over the sacrifice to Jupiter Latiaris, which was the essential feature of the celebration.

A.U.C. 537 hominibus non paruisse; nunc conscientia spretorum
et Capitolium et sollemnem votorum nuncupationem
8 fugisse, ne die initi magistratus Iovis optimi maximi
templum adiret, ne senatum invisus ipse[1] et sibi uni
invisum videret consuleretque, ne Latinas indiceret
Iovique Latiari sollemne sacrum in monte faceret,
9 ne auspicato profectus in Capitolium ad vota nuncu-
panda paludatus[2] inde cum lictoribus in provinciam
iret; lixae modo sine insignibus, sine lictoribus profectum clam, furtim, haud aliter quam si exsilii causa
10 solum vertisset; magis pro maiestate videlicet imperii Arimini quam Romae magistratum initurum et
in deversorio hospitali quam apud penates suos
11 praetextam sumpturum. Revocandum universi re-
trahendumque censuerunt et cogendum omnibus
prius praesentem in deos hominesque fungi officiis,
12 quam ad exercitum et in provinciam iret. In eam
legationem—legatos enim mitti placuit—Q. Terentius et M. Antistius profecti nihilo magis eum
moverunt quam priore consulatu litterae moverant
13 ab senatu missae. Paucos post dies magistratum
iniit, immolantique ei vitulus iam ictus e manibus
sacrificantium sese cum proripuisset, multos circum-
14 stantes cruore respersit; fuga procul etiam maior

[1] ipse ς: ipsi *P*.
[2] paludatus ς: paludatis *P*.

---

[1] The *paludamentum*, typifying military imperium, might be assumed by the consul on leaving the City, the *toga praetexta*, white with a purple border, was worn by the consul while in Rome.

had not obeyed; now, conscious of having spurned B.C. 217
them, he had fled the Capitol and the vows that were regularly undertaken, that he might not, on the day of entering upon his office, approach the temple of Jupiter Optimus Maximus; that he might not see and consult the senate, which hated him and which he alone of all men hated; that he might not proclaim the Latin Festival and offer the accustomed sacrifice to Jupiter Latiaris on the Alban Mount; that he might not, after receiving auspices, go up to the Capitol to make his vows, and thence proceed, in the general's cloak[1] and accompanied by lictors, to his province; like some camp-follower, without insignia and without lictors, he had set out in secret and by stealth, precisely as though going into exile; he thought, forsooth, that it was more in keeping with the dignity of his high command to begin his magistracy in Ariminum than in Rome—to assume the purple-bordered toga[1] in an inn than in the presence of his household gods! With one accord they voted to recall him and drag him back and compel him to discharge in person all his obligations to gods and men, before he went to his army and his province. On this commission—for commissioners they resolved to dispatch—Quintus Terentius and Marcus Antistius set forth, but moved Flaminius no more than the letter sent him by the senate had moved him in his former consulship. A few days later he entered on his magistracy, and as he was offering up a calf, it escaped—after being struck—out of the hands of those who would have sacrificed it, and spattered many of the bystanders with its blood. The dismay and confusion

A.U.C. 537 apud ignaros quid trepidaretur et concursatio fuit. Id a plerisque in omen magni terroris acceptum. Legionibus inde duabus a Sempronio, prioris anni consule, duabus a C. Atilio praetore acceptis in Etruriam per Appennini tramites exercitus duci est coeptus.

---

[1] This dreadful omen is not mentioned by Polybius and looks like an invention of the aristocratic opponents of Flaminius. Livy perhaps found the story in Coelius.

were even greater among those who stood farther B.C. 217
off and knew not what was occasioning the panic. By most people it was regarded as an omen of great terror.[1] After this the army comprising the two legions received from Sempronius, the consul of the year before, and the two taken over from Gaius Atilius the praetor, began its march into Etruria through the passes of the Apennines.

LIBRI XXI PERIOCHA

Belli Punici secundi ortum[1] narrat et Hannibalis, ducis Poenorum, contra foedus per Hiberum flumen transitum. A quo Saguntini, sociorum populi Romani,[2] civitas obsessa, octavo mense capta est. De quibus iniuriis missi legati ad Carthaginienses, qui quererentur. Cum satisfacere nollent, bellum his indictum est. Hannibal superato Pyrenaeo saltu per Gallias fusis Volcis,[3] qui obsistere conati erant ei, ad Alpes venit et laborioso per eas transitu, cum montanos quoque Gallos obvios aliquot proeliis reppulisset, descendit in Italiam et ad Ticinum flumen Romanos equestri proelio fudit. In quo vulneratum P. Cornelium Scipionem protexit filius, qui Africani postea nomen accepit. Iterumque exercitu Romano ad flumen Trebiam fuso Hannibal Appenninum quoque permagna vexatione[4] militum propter vim tempestatium transiit. Cn. Cornelius Scipio[5] in Hispania contra Poenos prospere pugnavit duce hostium Magone capto.

[1] ortum ς: actum *MSS.*

[2] sociorum populi Romani *ed. prin.* (*Liv.* xxi. vi. 4): populi Romani *MSS.*

[3] Volcis *Sigonius*: uulscis *MSS.*

[4] permagna vexatione *O. Jahn*: per magnam uexationem *MSS.*

[5] Cn. Cornelius Scipio ς: c. cornelius scipio *MSS.*

SUMMARY OF BOOK XXI

In this book is described the beginning of the Second Punic War, and how Hannibal, the general of the Phoenicians, crossed the river Ebro in violation of the treaty. Besieging Saguntum, a city belonging to allies of the Roman People, he captured it in the eighth month. These injuries led to the dispatch of ambassadors to the Carthaginians, to complain. On their refusing satisfaction, war was declared against Carthage. Hannibal, after surmounting the passes of the Pyrenees, traversed Gaul—having routed the Volcae, who had attempted to stop him—and arrived at the Alps. After a troublesome passage of these mountains, in the course of which he also defeated in several battles the Gallic mountaineers, when they blocked his way, he descended into Italy and routed the Romans in a cavalry battle near the river Ticinus. In this battle Publius Cornelius Scipio was wounded and was saved by his son, who later received the name of Africanus. Again a Roman army was routed near the river Trebia. After this Hannibal crossed the Apennines, with great distress to his soldiers, because of violent storms. In Spain Gnaeus Cornelius Scipio fought successfully against the Phoenicians and captured the enemy's general, Mago.[1]

[1] This name is a mistake (found also in Orosius, IV. xiv, 9) for Hanno (chap. lx. § 4).

BOOK XXII

LIBER XXII

A.U.C. 537

I. Iam ver adpetebat; itaque[1] Hannibal ex
hibernis movit, et nequiquam[2] ante conatus transcendere Appenninum intolerandis frigoribus et cum
2 ingenti periculo moratus ac metu. Galli, quos
praedae populationumque conciverat spes, postquam
pro eo ut ipsi ex alieno agro raperent agerentque,
suas terras sedem belli esse premique utriusque
partis exercituum hibernis videre,[3] verterunt retro
3 in Hannibalem[4] ab Romanis odia; petitusque saepe
principum insidiis, ipsorum inter se fraude eadem
levitate qua consenserant consensum indicantium
servatus erat, et mutando nunc vestem nunc tegu-
menta capitis errore etiam sese ab insidiis munierat.
4 Ceterum hic quoque ei timor causa fuit maturius
movendi ex hibernis.

Per idem tempus Cn. Servilius consul Romae
5 idibus Martiis magistratum iniit. Ibi cum de re
publica rettulisset, redintegrata in C. Flaminium

[1] adpetebat; itaque *Woelfflin*: adpetebatque *P*.
[2] nequiquam (nequicquam) *Valla*: neque eo qui iam *P*.
[3] videre *Alschefski*: uiderent *P*.
[4] in Hannibalem ς: hannibalem *P*.

[1] Polybius says that "he had a number of wigs made, dyed to suit the appearance of persons differing widely in age, and kept constantly changing them, and at the same time also dressing in a style suited to the wig, so that not only those who had seen him but for a moment, but even his familiars, found difficulty in recognizing him" (III.

BOOK XXII

I. SPRING was now drawing on, and accordingly Hannibal moved out of his winter encampment. He had tried before this to cross the Apennines, but had failed because of the intolerable cold. And the delay had been attended with the greatest danger and anxiety; for when the Gauls, whom the hope of spoil and pillage had excited to revolt, perceived that instead of harrying and plundering the fields of others, their own lands were the seat of war and were burdened with the winter quarters of both armies, they turned their hatred back again from the Romans upon Hannibal. But though their leaders laid many a plot against him, their treachery to one another saved him, for they gave him information of these conspiracies with the same inconstancy with which they had conspired. Moreover, changing now his dress and now his head-gear,[1] he protected himself against their plots by the uncertainty which this gave rise to. Still, the fear of such plots was another reason for quitting his winter quarters early. B.C. 217

About the same time, on the Ides of March, Gnaeus Servilius entered on his consulship at Rome. On his then referring the state of the nation to the senate for discussion, their anger at Gaius Flaminius

xxxviii, Paton's Trans.). Livy prefers ambiguity to the use of a technical or undignified word.

A.U.C. 537 invidia est: duos se consules creasse, unum habere;
quod enim illi iustum imperium, quod auspicium
6 esse?[1] Magistratus id a domo, publicis privatisque
penatibus, Latinis feriis actis, sacrificio in monte
perfecto, votis rite in Capitolio nuncupatis secum
7 ferre; nec privatum auspicia sequi, nec sine auspiciis
profectum in externo ea solo nova atque integra
concipere posse.

8 Augebant metum prodigia ex pluribus simul locis
nuntiata: in Sicilia militibus aliquot spicula, in
Sardinia autem in muro circumeunti vigilias equiti
scipionem quem manu tenuerat[2] arsisse, et litora
crebris ignibus fulsisse, et scuta duo sanguine sudasse,
9 et milites quosdam ictos fulminibus, et solis orbem
minui visum, et Praeneste ardentes lapides caelo
cecidisse, et Arpis parmas in caelo visas pugnan-
10 temque cum luna solem, et Capenae duas interdiu
lunas ortas, et aquas Caeretes sanguine mixtas
fluxisse fontemque ipsum Herculis cruentis manasse
respersum maculis, et Antii[3] metentibus cruentas
11 in corbem spicas cecidisse, et Faleriis caelum findi
velut magno hiatu visum, quaque patuerit ingens
lumen effulsisse; sortes adtenuatas unamque sua

[1] esse ς: esset *P*. [2] tenuerat *P*: tenuerit *Ruperti*.
[3] Antii ς: in Antii *P*: in Antiati (-te) *Gronovius*.

[1] The enemies of Flaminius argued that he was not, in fact, a consul, for, though elected to that office he had not been duly inaugurated in Rome, but had left the City before taking the auspices. It would not be possible for him to repair the omission in camp, since even a consul who had set out after receiving the auspices was required, in case it was afterwards discovered that there had been some flaw in them, to return to Rome and renew them there, and it followed, *a fortiori*, that no one could take them in the first instance—*nova atque integra*—anywhere else.

was renewed. They had chosen two consuls, they said, but had only one; for what proper authority or right of auspices did Flaminius possess? Magistrates, they urged, carried with them this prerogative when they set out from home—from their own and the nation's hearth—after celebrating the Latin Festival, sacrificing on the Alban Mount and duly offering up their vows on the Capitol; but a private citizen could neither take the auspices with him, nor, if he had left Rome without them, receive them new from the beginning on foreign soil.[1] B.C. 217

Men's fears were augmented by the prodigies reported simultaneously from many places: that in Sicily the javelins of several soldiers had taken fire, and that in Sardinia, as a horseman was making the round of the night-watch, the same thing had happened to the truncheon which he held in his hand; that many fires had blazed up on the shore; that two shields had sweated blood; that certain soldiers had been struck with lightning; that the sun's disk had seemed to be contracted; that glowing stones had fallen from the sky at Praeneste; that at Arpi bucklers had appeared in the sky and the sun had seemed to be fighting with the moon; that at Capena two moons had risen in the daytime; that the waters of Caere had flowed mixed with blood, and that bloodstains had appeared in the water that trickled from the spring of Hercules itself; that at Antium, when some men were reaping, bloody ears of corn had fallen into their basket; that at Falerii the sky had seemed to be rent as it were with a great fissure, and through the opening a bright light had shone; and that lots[2] had shrunk

[2] See note on p. 185.

A.U.C. 537 sponte excidisse[1] ita scriptam: "Mavors telum suum
12 concutit;" et per idem tempus Romae signum
Martis Appia via ac simulacra luporum sudasse, et
Capuae speciem caeli ardentis fuisse lunaeque[2] inter
13 imbrem cadentis. Inde minoribus etiam dictu prodigiis fides habita: capras lanatas quibusdam factas, et
gallinam in marem, gallum in feminam sese vertisse.
14 His sicut erant nuntiata expositis auctoribusque
in curiam introductis consul de religione patres con-
15 suluit. Decretum ut ea prodigia partim maioribus
hostiis, partim lactentibus procurarentur, et uti supplicatio per triduum ad omnia pulvinaria haberetur;
16 cetera, cum decemviri libros inspexissent, ut ita
fierent quem ad modum cordi esse divis[3] e car-
17 minibus[4] praefarentur. Decemvirorum monitu decretum est Iovi primum donum fulmen aureum
pondo quinquaginta fieret et Iunoni[5] Minervaeque
ex argento dona darentur et Iunoni reginae in
Aventino Iunonique Sospitae Lanuvii maioribus
18 hostiis sacrificaretur matronaeque pecunia conlata,
quantum conferre cuique commodum esset, donum
Iunoni reginae in Aventinum ferrent lectisterniumque fieret,[6] et ut libertinae et ipsae, unde Feroniae

[1] sortes adtenuatas unamque sua sponte excidisse *Fleckeisen*: sortes sua sponte adtenuatas, etc., *P*.
[2] lunaeque *P*: lanaeque *Drakenborch*.
[3] esse divis ς: esset diuinis *P*.
[4] e carminibus *Madvig*: carminibus *P*.
[5] et Iunoni *Woelfflin*: iunoni *P*.
[6] fieret C^2: fieretque PC^1.

---

[1] The archaic form of Mars.
[2] *i.e.* the Greek hexameters of the Sibylline Books, of which the *decemviri sacris faciundis* were custodians and interpreters.
[3] See note on p. 186.

and that one had fallen out without being touched, B.C. 217
on which was written, "Mavors[1] brandishes his spear;" that in Rome, about the same time, the statue of Mars on the Appian Way and the images of the wolves had sweated; that at Capua there had been the appearance of a sky on fire and of a moon that fell in the midst of a shower of rain. Afterwards less memorable prodigies were also given credence: that certain folk had found their goats to have got woolly fleeces; that a hen had changed into a cock and a cock into a hen.

When the consul had laid these reports before the senate exactly as they had come to him and had introduced into the House the men who vouched for their truth, he consulted the Fathers regarding their religious import. It was voted that these prodigies should be expiated, in part with greater, in part with lesser victims, and that a supplication should be held for three days at all the couches of the gods; as for the rest, when the decemvirs should have inspected the Books, such rites were to be observed as they should declare, in accordance with the sacred verses,[2] to be pleasing to the gods. Being so admonished by the decemvirs, they decreed that the first gift should be made to Jupiter, a golden thunderbolt weighing fifty pounds; and that Juno and Minerva should be given offerings of silver; that Juno Regina on the Aventine and Juno Sospita at Lanuvium should receive a sacrifice of greater victims, and that the matrons, each contributing as much as she could afford, should make up a sum of money and carry it as a gift to Juno Regina on the Aventine and there celebrate a *lectisternium*[3]; and that even the very freed-women

A.U.C. 537 donum daretur, pecuniam pro facultatibus suis conferrent.

19 Haec ubi facta, decemviri Ardeae in foro maioribus hostiis sacrificarunt. Postremo Decembri iam mense ad aedem Saturni Romae immolatum est lectisterniumque imperatum—eum[1] lectum senatores
20 straverunt—et convivium publicum, ac per urbem Saturnalia diem ac noctem clamata,[2] populusque eum diem festum habere ac servare in perpetuum iussus.

II. Dum consul placandis Romae dis habendoque[3] dilectu dat operam, Hannibal profectus ex hibernis, quia iam Flaminium consulem Arretium pervenisse[4]
2 fama erat, cum aliud longius ceterum commodius ostenderetur iter, propiorem viam per paludes petit, qua fluvius Arnus per eos dies solito magis inun-
3 daverat. Hispanos[5] et Afros et omne veterani robur exercitus[6] admixtis ipsorum impedimentis, necubi consistere coactis necessaria ad usus deessent, primos ire iussit, sequi Gallos, ut id agminis medium esset,
4 novissimos ire equites, Magonem inde cum expeditis Numidis cogere agmen, maxime Gallos, si taedio

[1] eum *Madvig*: et eum *P*.
[2] clamata *Gronovius*: clamatam *P*.
[3] dis habendoque ϛ: distrahendoque *P*.
[4] pervenisse ϛ: praeuenisse *P*.
[5] Hispanos *Drakenborch*: at spanos *P*.
[6] robur exercitus *C*: exercitus robur *M*: erat robur exercitus *P*.

---

[1] Feronia was an old Etruscan deity, whose cult was brought to Rome from Capena. A goddess of springs and groves, she was also the traditional patroness of freedwomen.

[2] It was usually carried out by the decemvirs mentioned in § 7.

[3] The Saturnalia had been established as an annual

should contribute money, in proportion to their abilities, for an offering to Feronia.[1] B.C. 217

These measures being taken, the decemvirs sacrificed at Ardea in the market-place with the greater victims. Finally—the month was now December—victims were slain at the temple of Saturn in Rome and a *lectisternium* was ordered—this time senators administered the rite[2]—and a public feast, and throughout the City for a day and a night "Saturnalia" was cried, and the people were bidden to keep that day as a holiday and observe it in perpetuity.[3]

II. While the consul was occupied at Rome in appeasing the gods and levying troops, Hannibal, who had left his winter quarters, heard that Flaminius, the other consul, had already arrived at Arretium; and so, though another route, longer, to be sure, but less difficult, was pointed out to him, he took the shorter, through the marshes, which the river Arno had lately flooded to an unusual extent. He ordered the Spaniards and the Africans and all the flower of his veteran army, taking their own baggage with them so as not to want the necessities of life wherever they might be forced to halt, to march in the van; the Gauls to follow them and form the centre of the column; and the cavalry to fall in behind. Mago and the Numidian light horse were to bring up the rear, their principal duty being to keep the Gauls in order, in case they should weary of the long and

festival in connexion with the dedication of the temple of Saturn on December 19th, 497 B.C. (I. xxi 2). Now the public feast was added to the former rites, and in course of time the festival was prolonged for several days.

A.U.C. 537 laboris longaeque viae, ut est mollis ad talia gens,
dilaberentur aut subsisterent, cohibentem.
5 Primi, qua modo praeirent duces, per praealtas
fluvii ac profundas voragines, hausti paene limo
6 immergentesque se, tamen signa sequebantur. Galli
neque sustinere se prolapsi neque adsurgere ex
voraginibus poterant neque aut[1] corpora animis aut
7 animos spe sustinebant; alii fessa aegre trahentes
membra, alii, ubi semel victis taedio animis pro-
cubuissent, inter iumenta et ipsa iacentia passim
morientes; maximeque omnium vigiliae conficiebant
8 per quadriduum iam et tres noctes toleratae. Cum
omnia obtinentibus aquis nihil ubi in sicco fessa
sternerent corpora inveniri posset, cumulatis in aqua[2]
9 sarcinis insuper incumbebant, aut iumentorum[3]
itinere toto prostratorum passim acervi, tantum quod
exstaret aqua quaerentibus ad quietem parvi temporis, necessarium cubile dabant.
10 Ipse Hannibal, aeger oculis ex verna primum
intemperie variante calores frigoraque, elephanto
qui unus superfuerat quo altius ab aqua exstaret
11 vectus, vigiliis tamen et nocturno umore palustrique
caelo gravante caput, et quia medendi nec locus nec
tempus erat, altero oculo capitur.

[1] neque aut *A. Perizonius* : aut *P.*
[2] aqua ς: aquas *P.*
[3] aut iumentorum *Hertz*: iumentorum *P.*

painful march—for the race is ill adapted to such hardships—and attempt to steal away or refuse to go forward. B.C. 217

Those in front only asked that their guides lead on before. Through deep and well-nigh bottomless quagmires left by the flood, almost engulfed in the mud into which they plunged, they nevertheless followed on after their standards. But the Gauls could neither keep from falling when they slipped, nor regain their footing, once they had plunged into a hole; the flesh was neither sustained by the spirit nor the spirit by hope. Some could hardly drag their tired limbs along; others, their courage yielding once for all to their weariness, dropped down and died amongst the baggage-animals, for these too were lying all about. What distressed them most of all was the want of sleep, which they had now endured for four days and three nights. And since everything was under water and they could find no dry spot on which to stretch their weary bodies, they would pile their packs in the flood and lie down on these; or the heaps of sumpter-animals that were everywhere strewn about along the line of march would afford a makeshift bed—for all they asked was a place that stood out above the water, where they could snatch a little sleep.

Hannibal himself, whose eyes were suffering in the first place from the trying spring weather, alternating betwixt hot and cold, rode upon the sole surviving elephant, that he might be higher above the water. But lack of sleep, damp nights, and the air of the marshes affected his head, and since he had neither place nor time for employing remedies, he lost the sight of one of his eyes.

A.U.C. 537

III. Multis hominibus iumentisque foede amissis cum tandem de paludibus emersisset, ubi primum in sicco potuit, castra locat; certumque per praemissos exploratores habuit exercitum Romanum
2 circa[1] Arreti moenia esse. Consulis deinde consilia atque animum et situm regionum itineraque et copias ad commeatus expediendos et cetera quae cognosse in rem erat summa omnia cum cura inquirendo exsequebatur.
3 Regio erat in primis Italiae fertilis, Etrusci campi, qui Faesulas inter Arretiumque iacent, frumenti ac
4 pecoris et omnium copia rerum opulenti; consul ferox ab consulatu priore et non modo legum aut patrum maiestatis sed ne deorum quidem satis metuens. Hanc insitam ingenio eius temeritatem fortuna prospero civilibus bellicisque rebus successu
5 aluerat. Itaque satis apparebat nec deos nec homines consulentem ferociter omnia ac praepropere acturum; quoque pronior esset in vitia sua, agitare eum atque
6 inritare Poenus parat, et laeva relicto hoste insidias[2] petens medio Etruriae agro praedatum profectus quantam maximam vastitatem potest caedibus incendiisque consuli procul ostendit.
7 Flaminius, qui ne quieto quidem hoste ipse

[1] circa ς: in circa *P*: in stativis circa *Luchs*.
[2] insidias *Luterbacher*: Faesulas *P*: a Faesulis petens medios Etruriae agros *Voss*.

---

[1] When, in defiance of the senate, he had refused to abdicate his command because of an alleged flaw in his election, and had conquered the Insubres and triumphed in virtue of a popular decree (223 B.C.). See Summary of Book XIX, and XXI. lxiii. 2.

[2] Livy has in mind the passage of an agrarian law in 232 B.C., the continuation of the Via Flaminia to Ariminum,

III. Many men and beasts had perished miserably, when at last he got out from the marshes, and pitching his camp on the first dry ground available, ascertained from scouts whom he had sent on ahead that the Roman army lay around the walls of Arretium. He then went to work with all possible diligence to learn the plans and temper of the consul, the lie of the land and the roads, his resources for provisioning the army—everything, in short, which it was important to find out. B.C. 217

The district was one of the most fertile in Italy, for the Etruscan plains between Faesulae and Arretium abound in corn and flocks and all sorts of provisions. The consul had been proud and headstrong since his former consulship,[1] and lacked all proper reverence, not only for the laws and for the senate's majesty, but even for the gods. This native rashness had been nourished by the success which Fortune had bestowed on him in political and military enterprises.[2] It was therefore sufficiently apparent that, seeking no counsel, either divine or human, he would manage everything with recklessness and headlong haste; but to make him incline the more towards his characteristic faults, the Phoenician planned to provoke and exasperate him. Leaving the enemy therefore on his left,[3] and looking out for an opportunity to ambush him, he proceeded to lay waste the heart of Etruria and exhibited to the consul from afar all the havoc that fire and sword could possibly effect.

Flaminius, even had his enemy sat still, was not

the erection of the Circus Flaminius, and the victory over the Insubres.

[3] See Map 4.

A.U.C. 537 quieturus erat, tum vero, postquam res sociorum
ante oculos prope suos ferri agique vidit, suum id
dedecus ratus, per mediam iam Italiam vagari
Poenum atque obsistente nullo ad ipsa Romana
8 moenia ire oppugnanda, ceteris omnibus in consilio
salutaria magis quam speciosa suadentibus—collegam
exspectandum, ut coniunctis exercitibus communi
9 animo consilioque rem gererent, interim equitatu
auxiliisque levium armorum ab effusa praedandi
licentia hostem cohibendum—iratus se ex consilio
proripuit signumque simul itineris pugnaeque cum
10 dedisset,[1] "Immo Arreti ante moenia sedeamus"
inquit; "hic enim patria et penates sunt. Hannibal
emissus e manibus perpopuletur Italiam vastandoque
et urendo omnia ad Romana moenia perveniat, nec
ante nos hinc moverimus quam, sicut olim Camillum
a Veis,[2] C. Flaminium ab Arretio patres acciverint."
11 Haec simul increpans cum ocius signa convelli
iuberet et ipse in equum insiluisset, equus repente
corruit consulemque lapsum super caput effudit.
12 Territis omnibus qui circa erant velut foedo omine
incipiendae rei insuper nuntiatur signum omni vi
13 moliente signifero convelli nequire. Conversus ad

[1] cum dedisset ς: cum *P*.
[2] a Veis (Veiis) *Fuegner*: abuelis P^1: abueios P^2.

the man to have sat still himself; but now, when B.C. 217 he saw the farms of the allies being harried and pillaged almost under his own eyes, he felt it as a personal disgrace that the Phoenician should be roaming through the midst of Italy, and marching, with no one to dispute his passage, to assault the very walls of Rome. In the council of war the rest were all for safe in preference to showy measures: he should wait, they said, for his colleague to come up, in order that they might unite their forces and conduct the war with a common policy and resolution; meantime, he should employ his cavalry and skirmishers to check the enemy's widespread, unrestricted pillaging. Enraged by this advice, Flaminius flung out of the council, and having given the signal at once for marching and for fighting, exclaimed, "Ay, truly! Let us sit still under the walls of Arretium, for here are our native city and our household gods; let Hannibal slip through our fingers and ravage Italy, and, laying waste and burning everything, march clear to Rome; and let us not move from this spot, till the Fathers, as once they summoned Camillus from Veii, shall summon Gaius Flaminius from Arretium."

Uttering these scornful words he bade pluck up the standards quickly, and vaulted upon his horse, when suddenly the charger stumbled, and unseating the consul threw him over his head. The dismay which this occasioned in all who were present, as an evil omen for beginning the campaign, was intensified on its being reported that, although the standard-bearer was exerting all his might, the standard could not be pulled up. Rounding upon

A.U.C. 537 nuntium "Num litteras quoque" inquit "ab senatu adfers quae me rem gerere vetent?[1] Abi, nuntia effodiant signum, si ad convellendum manus prae metu obtorpuerunt."[2]

14 Incedere inde agmen coepit primoribus, superquam quod dissenserant ab consilio, territis etiam duplici prodigio, milite in volgus laeto ferocia ducis, cum spem magis ipsam quam causam spei intueretur.

IV. Hannibal quod agri est inter Cortonam urbem Trasumennumque[3] lacum omni clade belli pervastat, quo magis iram hosti ad vindicandas sociorum iniurias
2 acuat. Et iam pervenerat[4] ad loca nata insidiis, ubi maxime montes Cortonenses Trasumennus subit. Via tantum interest perangusta, velut ad id[5] ipsum de industria relicto spatio; deinde paulo latior
3 patescit campus; inde colles insurgunt.[6] Ibi castra in aperto locat, ubi ipse cum Afris modo Hispanisque consideret; Baliares ceteramque levem armaturam post montes circumducit; equites ad ipsas fauces saltus tumulis apte tegentibus locat, ut ubi intrassent Romani obiecto equitatu clausa omnia lacu ac montibus essent.

4 Flaminius cum pridie solis occasu ad lacum pervenisset, inexplorato postero die vixdum satis certa

[1] vetent ς: uetant *P*.

[2] obtorpuerunt *Madvig*: obtorpuerit *P*: obtorpuerint ς.

[3] *Here and elsewhere the word is printed with the spelling approved by Ritschl, Rhein. Mus.* 22 (1867) 603: *the MSS. display various corruptions.*

[4] pervenerat *Stroth*: peruenerant *P*.

[5] velut ad id ς: uel ad *P*.

[6] insurgunt *Madvig*: adinsurgunt *P*: adsurgunt ς.

the messenger the consul cried, "Do you bring me a dispatch too from the senate, forbidding me to fight? Go, tell them to *dig* the standard out, if their hands are too numb with fear to *pull* it up!" B.C. 217

The column then began to advance, though the higher officers, besides disapproving of the consul's plan, were terrified by the double prodigy. The soldiers, most of them, rejoiced in the temerity of their commander: their hopes ran high: the grounds for hoping they did not scrutinize.

IV. Hannibal laid waste the land between the city of Cortona and Lake Trasumennus with every circumstance of cruelty known to war, in order the more to whet his enemy's anger and prompt him to avenge the sufferings of his allies. And now he had reached a spot designed by nature for an ambuscade, where Trasumennus approaches closest to the mountains of Cortona. Between them is nothing but a very narrow track, as though room had been left expressly for this purpose; the ground then widens into a little plain; beyond this the hills rise steeply. At this point he laid out a camp in the open, for himself and his African and Spanish troops only; the Baliares and the rest of his light-armed forces he led round behind the mountains; the cavalry he stationed near the entrance to the defile, where some hillocks formed a convenient screen for them, so that when the Romans should have entered the pass, they might block the road, and trap the entire army between the lake and the mountains.

Flaminius had reached the lake at sunset; the next morning, without reconnoitring, and scarcely waiting for broad daylight, he passed through the

A.U.C. 537 luce angustiis superatis, postquam in patentiorem
campum pandi agmen coepit, id tantum hostium
quod ex adverso erat conspexit; ab tergo ac super
5 caput non detectae[1] insidiae. Poenus ubi, id quod
petierat, clausum lacu ac montibus et circumfusum
suis copiis habuit hostem, signum omnibus dat simul
6 invadendi. Qui ubi qua cuique[2] proximum fuit
decucurrerunt, eo magis Romanis subita atque improvisa res fuit, quod orta ex lacu nebula campo
quam montibus densior sederat agminaque hostium
ex pluribus collibus[3] ipsa inter se satis conspecta
7 eoque magis pariter decucurrerant. Romanus clamore prius undique orto quam satis cerneret, se
circumventum esse sensit, et ante in frontem latera-
que pugnari coeptum est quam satis instrueretur
acies aut expediri arma stringique gladii possent.

V. Consul perculsis omnibus ipse satis, ut in re
trepida,[4] impavidus turbatos ordines vertente se quoque ad dissonos clamores instruit, ut tempus locusque
patitur, et quacumque adire[5] audirique potest ad-
2 hortatur ac stare ac pugnare iubet: nec enim inde
votis aut imploratione deum, sed vi ac virtute
evadendum esse; per medias acies ferro viam fieri,
et quo timoris minus sit eo minus ferme periculi

[1] non detectae *Novák*: deceptae *P*.
[2] qua cuique *Priscian* x. xliii: quaque *P*.
[3] collibus *Lipsius*: uallibus *P*: callibus *Rossbach* (*Praef. Per p* xxvi.[1]).
[4] re trepida ς: trepida *P*.
[5] adire *Gebhard*: adiri *P*.

---

[1] Polybius (III. lxxxiv. 6) says that Flaminius was in "the utmost dismay and dejection" (δυσχρηστούμενον καὶ περικακοῦντα). Livy's description of the battle agrees in the main with that of Polybius; the praise of Flaminius may perhaps be derived from Coelius Antipater. See J. Janssen in *Mnemosyne*, 54 (1926), 189–194.

defile. As the column began to spread out on the more open ground, they caught sight of those enemies only who were right in front of them; the ambush in their rear and that above them they failed to perceive. The Phoenician had now gained his object, the Romans were hemmed in between the mountains and the lake and their escape cut off by his own troops, when he made the signal for all his forces to attack at once. As they charged down, each at the nearest point, their onset was all the more sudden and unforeseen inasmuch as the mist from the lake lay less thickly on the heights than on the plain, and the attacking columns had been clearly visible to one another from the various hills and had therefore delivered their charge at more nearly the same instant. From the shouting that arose on every side the Romans learned, before they could clearly see, that they were surrounded; and they were already engaged on their front and flank before they could properly form up or get out their arms and draw their swords. B.C. 217

V. Amidst the general consternation the consul himself displayed—if allowance be made for the terrifying circumstances—considerable coolness.[1] He brought such order as time and place permitted out of the confusion in the ranks, where the men were all turning different ways to face the various shouts; and wherever he could go and make himself heard, he tried to encourage them and bade them stand and fight. Their position, he said, was one from which vows and supplications to the gods could not extricate them, but only their own brave exertions: it was the sword that opened a way through embattled enemies, and the less men

A.U.C. 537

3 esse. Ceterum prae strepitu ac tumultu nec consilium nec imperium accipi poterat, tantumque aberat ut sua signa atque ordines et[1] locum noscerent[2] ut vix ad arma capienda aptandaque pugnae competeret animus opprimerenturque quidam onerati magis iis quam tecti. Et erat in tanta caligine maior
4 usus aurium quam oculorum. Ad gemitus volnerum[3] ictusque corporum aut armorum et mixtos terrentium paventiumque clamores circumferebant ora oculosque.
5 Alii fugientes pugnantium globo inlati haerebant, alios redeuntes in pugnam avertebat fugientium
6 agmen. Deinde, ubi in omnes partes nequiquam impetus capti et ab lateribus montes ac lacus, a fronte et ab tergo hostium acies claudebant, apparuitque nullam nisi in dextera ferroque salutis
7 spem esse, tum sibi quisque dux adhortatorque factus ad rem gerendam, et nova de integro exorta pugna est, non illa ordinata per principes hastatosque ac triarios, nec ut pro signis antesignani post signa alia pugnaret acies, nec ut in sua legione miles aut
8 cohorte aut manipulo esset: fors conglobabat,[4] et animus suus cuique ante aut post pugnandi ordinem dabat; tantusque fuit ardor animorum, adeo intentus pugnae animus,[5] ut eum motum terrae qui multarum

[1] ordines et *Hertz*: ordinemsed *P*.
[2] noscerent ς: nosceret *P*.
[3] vol(uul-)nerum *P*: vulneratorum *Ruperti*.
[4] conglobabat ς: conglobat *P* (*Gronovius*).
[5] adeo intentus pugnae animus *P*: adeoque intentus pugnae *Riemann* (*but cf. Weissenborn-Mueller on* IV. lxi. 8).

feared, the less, in general, was their danger. But B.C. 217
the din and confusion were so great that neither advice nor orders could be heard, and so far were the men from knowing their proper standards companies and places, that they had hardly enough spirit to arm and prepare themselves to fight, and some were borne down while more encumbered than protected by their armour. Indeed the fog was so thick that ears were of more use than eyes, and the groans of the wounded, the sound of blows on body or armour and the mingled shouts and screams of assailants and assailed made them turn and gaze, now this way and now that. Some, as they sought to escape, were swept into a crowd of combatants and held there; others, trying to get back into the fight, were turned aside by a throng of fugitives. When attempts to break through had resulted everywhere in failure and they found themselves shut in on the flanks by the mountains and the lake, and in front and rear by the enemy; when it became apparent that their only hope of safety lay in their right arms and their swords; then every man became his own commander and urged himself to action, and the battle began all over again. It was no ordered battle, with the troops marshalled in triple line, nor did the vanguard fight before the standards and the rest of the army behind them, neither did each soldier keep to his proper legion cohort and maniple: it was chance that grouped them, and every man's own valour assigned him his post in van or rear; and such was the frenzy of their eagerness and so absorbed were they in fighting, that an earthquake, violent enough to overthrow large portions of many of the towns of

A.U.C. 537 urbium Italiae magnas partes prostravit avertitque cursu rapidos amnes, mare fluminibus invexit, montes lapsu ingenti proruit, nemo pugnantium senserit.

VI. Tres ferme horas pugnatum est et ubique atrociter; circa consulem tamen acrior infestiorque
2 pugna.[1] Eum et robora virorum sequebantur, et ipse, quacumque in parte premi ac laborare senserat
3 suos, impigre ferebat opem; insignemque armis et hostes summa vi petebant et tuebantur cives, donec Insuber eques—Ducario nomen erat—facie quoque noscitans consulem, "En" inquit "hic est,"[2] popularibus suis, "qui legiones nostras cecidit agrosque
4 et urbem est depopulatus; iam ego hanc victimam manibus peremptorum foede civium dabo;" subditisque calcaribus equo per confertissimam hostium turbam impetum facit obtruncatoque prius armigero, qui se infesto venienti obviam obiecerat, consulem lancea transfixit; spoliare cupientem triarii obiectis scutis arcuere.

5 Magnae partis fuga inde primum coepit; et iam nec lacus nec montes pavori obstabant; per omnia arta praeruptaque velut caeci evadunt, armaque et
6 viri super alios alii[3] praecipitantur. Pars magna, ubi locus fugae deest, per prima vada paludis in aquam progressi, quoad capitibus umerisque[4] exstare

[1] pugna *H. J. Mueller*: pugna est *P*: pugna erat ς.

[2] "En" inquit "hic est" *Weissenborn*: inquit hic est *P*.

[3] super alios alii *H. J. Mueller*: super alium alii *P*: super alium alius *Riemann*.

[4] umerisque (hu-) ς: umeris *P*: umerisve *Weissenborn*

---

[1] The *triarii* were, properly speaking, the soldiers of the third line. These would be veterans, and Livy uses the word in that general sense here. As he has told us

Italy, turn swift streams from their courses, carry B.C. 217
the sea up into rivers, and bring down mountains with great landslides, was not even felt by any of the combatants.

VI. The conflict lasted for about three hours, and was bitterly contested at every point; but nowhere did it rage so fiercely as about the consul. He was attended by the bravest of his soldiers and stoutly lent a hand himself, wherever he saw the Romans hard pressed and in dire straits. His arms made him conspicuous, and the enemy attacked and his own people defended him with the greatest fury, until an Insubrian horseman, named Ducarius, who recognized the consul also by his face, cried out to his countrymen, "Behold the man who massacred our legions and laid waste our fields and our city! Now will I offer him up as a sacrifice to the shades of our fellow citizens so foully slain!" Then clapping spurs to his horse, he dashed through the very thick of his enemies, and first cutting down the armour-bearer, who had thrown himself in the way of his onset, transfixed the consul with his spear, but could not despoil him, for the veterans[1] interposed their shields and kept him off.

A great part of the Romans now began to run; neither lake nor mountains could any longer check the panic; defiles and precipices were all alike to them, as they rushed blindly to escape, and arms and men came down pell-mell together. Many, having no room to flee, waded out into the shallow water at the margin of the lake, and kept on till only their heads and shoulders were above the

(chap. v. § 7), the army had no time to form into the usual three lines (*hastati, principes, triarii*).

A.U.C. possunt sese immergunt. Fuere quos inconsultus
537 7 pavor nando etiam capessere fugam impulerit, quae
ubi immensa ac sine spe erat, aut deficientibus
animis hauriebantur gurgitibus aut nequiquam fessi
vada retro[1] aegerrime repetebant atque ibi ab in-
gressis aquam hostium equitibus passim trucida-
bantur.

8 Sex milia ferme primi agminis per adversos hostes
eruptione impigre facta, ignari omnium quae post
se agerentur, ex saltu evasere; et cum in tumulo
quodam constitissent, clamorem modo ac sonum
armorum audientes, quae fortuna pugnae esset neque
9 scire nec perspicere prae caligine poterant. In-
clinata denique re cum incalescente sole dispulsa
nebula aperuisset diem, tum liquida iam luce montes
campique perditas res stratamque ostendere foede
10 Romanam aciem. Itaque, ne in conspectos procul
immitteretur eques, sublatis raptim signis quam
11 citatissimo poterant agmine sese abripuerunt. Postero
die cum super cetera extrema fames etiam instaret,
fidem dante Maharbale, qui cum omnibus equestribus
copiis nocte consecutus erat, si arma tradidissent,
abire cum singulis vestimentis passurum, sese de-
12 diderunt; quae Punica religione servata fides ab
Hannibale est, atque in vincula omnes coniecti.

VII. Haec est nobilis ad Trasumennum pugna

[1] fessi vada retro *Gronovius*: festiua/darentro P^1: festina·uerant retro P^2.

surface. Some were driven by their unreasoning B.C. 217 panic even to attempt escape by swimming; but this was an endless, desperate undertaking, and either their hearts failed them and they sank in the deep water, or else, exhausted to no purpose, they struggled back with difficulty to the shoals, and were cut down on every hand by the horsemen, who rode into the water after them.

Some six thousand of those in the van made a valiant thrust through the enemy that barred their way, and got out of the defile without knowing anything of what was going on behind them. Taking up their stand on some rising ground, whence they could only hear the shouting and the clash of arms, they could neither know nor make out, for the murk, which way the victory was going. It was not until the battle was decided, that the mist dissolved with the growing heat of the sun and revealed the day, when the clear light on hill and plain showed that all was lost and the Roman army shamefully discomfited. And so, lest they should be seen afar and the enemy's cavalry be sent against them, they hurriedly pulled up their standards and marched off as fast as they could go. On the following day, when besides their other misfortunes they were threatened also with the extremity of hunger, Maharbal—who with all the cavalry had overtaken them in the night—pledged his word that if they delivered up their arms, he would let them go, with a single garment each, and they surrendered. This pledge Hannibal observed with true Punic reverence and threw them all into chains.

VII. Such was the famous battle of Trasumennus,

A.U.C. 537 atque inter paucas memorata populi Romani clades.
2 Quindecim milia Romanorum in acie caesa; decem
milia sparsa fuga per omnem Etruriam diversis iti-
3 neribus urbem petiere; duo milia quingenti hostium
in acie, multi postea[1] ex volneribus periere. Multi-
4 plex caedes utrimque facta traditur ab aliis; ego,
praeterquam quod nihil auctum ex vano velim, quo
nimis inclinant ferme scribentium animi, Fabium
aequalem temporibus huiusce belli potissimum auc-
5 torem habui. Hannibal captivorum qui Latini nominis essent sine pretio dimissis, Romanis in vincula
datis, segregata ex hostium coacervatorum cumulis
corpora suorum cum sepeliri iussisset, Flamini quoque corpus funeris causa magna cum cura inquisitum
non invenit.

6 Romae ad primum nuntium cladis eius cum ingenti
terrore ac tumultu concursus in forum populi est factus.
7 Matronae vagae per vias, quae repens clades adlata
quaeve fortuna exercitus esset, obvios pecunctantur.
Et cum frequentis contionis modo turba in comitium
8 et curiam versa magistratus vocaret, tandem haud
multo ante solis occasum M. Pomponius praetor
9 "Pugna," inquit "magna victi sumus"; et quamquam nihil certius ex eo auditum est, tamen alius ab
alio impleti rumoribus domos referunt consulem cum

[1] postea *Perizonius*: postea utrimque *P.*

---

[1] Fabius Pictor, who wrote annals in Greek, was used by Polybius, as well as by Livy.

a disaster memorable as few others have been in Roman history. Fifteen thousand Romans were killed on the field; ten thousand, scattered in flight over all Etruria, made their way by different roads to the City. Two thousand five hundred of the enemy fell in the battle and many perished subsequently of their wounds. Some writers multiply the losses on both sides: I myself, besides that I would not idly exaggerate anything—a vice to which historians are in general all too prone—have taken Fabius,[1] who lived at the time of this war, as my authority, in preference to any other. Hannibal dismissed scot-free the prisoners of the Latin name and gave the Romans into captivity. Having issued orders that the bodies of his own dead should be sorted out from the heaps of their enemies and buried, he would have given the body of Flaminius burial also, but though he caused it to be searched for with great diligence, he could not find it. B.C. 217

At Rome the first tidings of this defeat brought the citizens into the Forum in a frightened and tumultuous throng, while the matrons wandered about the streets and demanded of all they met what sudden disaster had been reported and how it was going with the army. And when the crowd, like some vast public assembly, turned to the Comitium and the senate-house and called for the magistrates, at last, as the sun was almost going down, Marcus Pomponius, the praetor, said, "A great battle has been fought, and we were beaten." And although they learned nothing more definite from him, still they picked up a rumour here and a rumour there, and returning to their homes brought word that the

A.U.C. 537 magna parte copiarum caesum, superesse paucos aut
fuga passim per Etruriam sparsos aut captos ab
hoste.

10 Quot casus exercitus victi fuerant, tot in curas
distracti [1] animi eorum erant quorum propinqui sub
C. Flaminio consule meruerant, ignorantium quae
cuiusque suorum fortuna esset; nec quisquam satis
11 certum habet, quid aut speret aut timeat. Postero
ac deinceps aliquot diebus ad portas maior prope
mulierum quam virorum multitudo stetit aut suorum
aliquem aut nuntios de iis opperiens; circumfunde-
banturque obviis sciscitantes neque avelli, utique ab
notis, priusquam ordine omnia inquisissent, poterant.
12 Inde varios voltus digredientium ab nuntiis cerneres,
ut cuique laeta aut tristia nuntiabantur, gratulantes-
que aut consolantes redeuntibus domos circumfusos.
Feminarum praecipue et gaudia insignia erant et
13 luctus. Unam in ipsa porta sospiti filio repente
oblatam in complexu [2] eius exspirasse ferunt; alteram,
cui mors filii falso nuntiata erat, maestam sedentem
domi ad primum conspectum redeuntis [3] gaudio
14 nimio exanimatam. Senatum praetores per dies
aliquot ab orto usque ad occidentem solem in curia
retinent, consultantes quonam duce aut quibus copiis
resisti victoribus Poenis posset.

[1] distracti *Weissenborn*: dispraeti *P*.

[2] com(con-)plexu *Alschefski* (*cf. Val. Max.* IX. xii. 2): conspexu *P*¹: conspectu *P*².

[3] redeuntis *H. J. Mueller* (*Val. Max. l.l.*): redeuntis fili *P*.

consul and a great part of his soldiers had been slain: that only a few survived, either dispersed as fugitives throughout Etruria or taken prisoners by the enemy. B.C. 217

The vicissitudes of the defeated army were no more various than the apprehensions which preyed upon the minds of those whose relatives had served under Gaius Flaminius, the consul. They were ignorant of how those dear to each of them were faring, nor did anyone really know what to hope or fear. On the next and on several succeeding days the City gates were thronged with a crowd in which the women almost outnumbered the men, waiting for some kinsman, or for news of him. Surrounding anybody who came along, they plied him with questions, nor could they tear themselves away—especially from those they were acquainted with—until they had enquired into every detail. Very different were the expressions you would have noted in their countenances, according as the tidings they received were glad or sorrowful, when they moved away from their informants and returned to their homes, surrounded by friends, congratulating or consoling them. The women especially exhibited extremes of joy and grief; one, on suddenly meeting her son safe and sound at the very gate, expired, they say, in his embrace; another, whose son had been falsely reported dead, sat sorrowing at home, and no sooner beheld him entering the house, than she died of excessive joy. For some days the praetors kept the senate in session in the Curia, from sunrise until sunset, deliberating with what possible commander or what forces they could withstand the victorious Phoenicians.

A.U.C. 537

VIII. Priusquam satis certa consilia essent, repens
alia nuntiatur clades, quattuor milia equitum cum C.
Centenio[1] propraetore missa ad collegam ab Servilio
consule in Umbria, quo post pugnam ad Trasumennum auditam averterant iter, ab Hannibale circum-
2 venta. Eius rei fama varie homines adfecit: pars
occupatis maiore aegritudine animis levem ex com-
paratione priorum ducere recentem equitum iacturam;
3 pars non id quod acciderat per se aestimare, sed, ut
in adfecto corpore quamvis levis causa magis quam
4 in valido[2] gravior sentiretur, ita tum aegrae et
adfectae civitati quodcumque adversi incideret non
rerum magnitudine sed viribus extenuatis, quae
nihil quod adgravaret pati possent, aestimandum
5 esse. Itaque ad remedium iam diu neque desidera-
tum nec adhibitum, dictatorem dicendum, civitas
confugit. Et quia et consul aberat, a quo uno dici
posse videbatur, nec per occupatam armis Punicis
6 Italiam facile erat aut nuntium aut litteras mitti,[3]
quod nunquam ante eam diem factum erat, dictatorem populus creavit Q. Fabium Maximum et
7 magistrum equitum M. Minucium Rufum; iisque
negotium ab senatu datum ut muros turresque urbis
firmarent et praesidia disponerent, quibus locis

[1] Centenio *Sigonius*: centonio *P*.
[2] in valido *Drakenborch*: ualido *P*: ualitudo *P*².
[3] mitti *Mommsen*: mitti nec dictatorem populo creare poterat *P*: mitti, nec dictatorem praetor creare poterat *Weissenborn*.

VIII. They had not yet fully determined what to do, when, lo! another disaster was reported, for which they were quite unprepared. Four thousand horse under the propraetor Gaius Centenius had been sent by the Consul Servilius to join his colleague; but on hearing of the battle at Trasumennus they had turned aside into Umbria, and had there fallen into the hands of Hannibal. The news of this affair affected people variously: some, whose thoughts were taken up with a greater sorrow, regarded this fresh loss of the cavalry as trivial in comparison with their former losses; others refused to judge of the misfortune as an isolated fact, but held that, just as when a man was sick, any disorder, however slight, was felt more than a worse one would be by a healthy man, so now, when the state was sick and suffering, any untoward occurrence should be gauged not by its intrinsic importance but by the enfeebled condition of the commonwealth, which could endure no aggravation. And so the citizens had recourse to a remedy that had now for a long time neither been employed nor needed—the creation of a dictator. And because the consul, who alone was supposed to possess the power to nominate one, was absent, and because it was no easy matter, when Italy was beset with Punic arms, to get a courier or a letter through to him, they did what had never been done until that day, and created a dictator by popular election. Their choice fell on Quintus Fabius Maximus, and Marcus Minucius Rufus they made master of the horse. To them the senate entrusted the task of strengthening the walls and towers of the City, of disposing its defences as to them seemed good, and B.C. 217

A.U.C. 537 videretur, pontesque rescinderent fluminum: pro urbe ac penatibus dimicandum esse, quando Italiam tueri nequissent.

IX. Hannibal recto itinere per Umbriam usque
2 ad Spoletium venit. Inde cum perpopulato agro urbem oppugnare adortus esset, cum magna caede suorum repulsus, coniectans ex unius coloniae haud[1] prospere temptatae viribus quanta moles Romanae
3 urbis esset, in agrum Picenum avertit iter non copia solum omnis generis frugum abundantem, sed refertum praeda, quam effuse avidi atque egentes rapie-
4 bant. Ibi per dies aliquot stativa habita refectusque miles hibernis itineribus ac palustri via proelioque magis ad eventum secundo quam levi aut facili
5 adfectus. Ubi satis quietis datum praeda ac populationibus magis quam otio aut requie gaudentibus, profectus Praetutianum Hadrianumque agrum, Marsos inde Marrucinosque et Paelignos devastat circaque Arpos et Luceriam proximam Apuliae regionem.

6 Cn. Servilius consul levibus proeliis cum Gallis factis[2] et uno oppido ignobili expugnato postquam de collegae exercitusque caede audivit, iam moenibus patriae metuens, ne abesset in discrimine extremo, ad urbem iter intendit.

7 Q. Fabius Maximus dictator iterum quo die magis-

[1] haud ς: haud minue *P*: haud maximae minime *Madvig*.
[2] factis *Gronovius*: actis *P*.

---

[1] The Anio and the Tiber.
[2] Servilius, on marching south with his consular army, left in northern Italy the forces originally destined to hold the Gauls in check.

of breaking down the bridges over the rivers:[1] B.C. 217 they would have to fight for their City and their homes, since they had not been able to save Italy.

IX. Hannibal marched straight on through Umbria as far as Spoletium. But when, after systematically ravaging the country, he attempted to storm the town, he was repulsed with heavy losses; and conjecturing from the strength of a single colony which he had unsuccessfully attacked how vast an undertaking the City of Rome would be, he turned aside into the Picentine territory, a land not only abounding in all kinds of produce, but filled with livestock, which his greedy and impoverished men gathered in from far and wide. He remained in camp there for some days, while his soldiers recovered from the marches they had made in wintry weather and through swamps, and from the battle, which, however successful its outcome, had been no light or easy adventure. After allowing sufficient rest to his soldiers, who delighted more in booty and rapine than in quiet and repose, he resumed his march and laid waste the Praetutian and Hadrian fields, and after these the lands of the Marsi, Marrucini and Paeligni, and the nearest part of Apulia, in the vicinity of Arpi and Luceria.

Gnaeus Servilius, the consul, had engaged in skirmishes with the Gauls and had taken one insignificant town by assault, when he learned of the destruction of his colleague and the army, and being now alarmed for the safety of the capital, lest he should be absent in the very crisis of its peril, set out for Rome.[2]

Quintus Fabius Maximus, dictator now for the

A.U.C. 537 tratum iniit vocato senatu, ab dis orsus cum edocuisset
patres plus neglegentia caerimoniarum auspiciorum-
que quam[1] temeritate atque inscitia peccatum a C.
Flaminio consule esse, quaeque piacula irae deum
8 essent ipsos deos consulendos esse, pervicit ut, quod
non ferme decernitur, nisi cum taetra prodigia
nuntiata sunt, decemviri libros Sibyllinos adire
9 iuberentur. Qui inspectis fatalibus libris rettulerunt patribus, quod eius belli causa votum Marti
foret, id non rite factum de integro atque amplius
10 faciundum esse, et Iovi ludos magnos et aedes
Veneri Erycinae ac Menti vovendas esse et supplica-
tionem lectisterniumque habendum et ver sacrum
vovendum, si bellatum prospere esset resque publica
in eodem quo ante bellum fuisset statu permansis-
11 set. Senatus, quoniam Fabium belli cura occupatura
esset, M. Aemilium praetorem, ex collegii pontificum
sententia, omnia ea ut mature fiant curare iubet.

X. His senatus consultis perfectis L. Cornelius Lentulus pontifex maximus consulente collegium praetore[2] omnium primum populum consulendum de

[1] auspiciorumque quam ς (*Sigonius*): auspiciorum *P.*
[2] collegium praetore *Lipsius*: collegio praetorum *P.*

---

[1] Fabius had been named dictator (probably in one of the years 221 to 219), to preside over the elections, but there had been no military dictator since Aulus Atilius Calatinus in 249.

[2] This vow is not mentioned at XXI. xvii. 4 or lxii. 10.

[3] The Romans prayed to Mens (or Mens Bona) for good sense and modesty (σωφροσύνη), qualities which had been conspicuously lacking in the conduct of Flaminius. The context here (Venus of Eryx, Sibylline books), together with coins of Paestum representing a goddess shown by the legend to be Bona Mens, and many inscriptions from Magna Graecia attesting the existence of priestly officials called *magistri Mentis Bonae*, points clearly to a Greek origin for the cult, which is several times alluded to by Roman authors

second time,[1] convened the senate on the day he entered upon his office. Taking up first the question of religion, he convinced the Fathers that the consul Flaminius had erred more through his neglect of the ceremonies and the auspices than through his recklessness and ignorance; and asserting that they ought to enquire of the gods themselves how the displeasure of the gods might be appeased, prevailed with them to do what is rarely done except when dreadful prodigies have been announced, and order the decemvirs to consult the Sibylline books. When the decemvirs had inspected the Books of Fate, they reported to the Fathers that the vow which had been made to Mars on account of this war[2] had not been duly performed, and must be performed afresh and on an ampler scale; that great games must be vowed to Jupiter, and temples to Venus Erycina and to Mens[3]; and finally that a supplication and *lectisternium* must be celebrated in honour of the gods, and a Sacred Spring be vowed, if they proved victorious and the state remained as it had been before the outbreak of hostilities. The senate, seeing that Fabius would be occupied with the conduct of the war, commanded Marcus Aemilius the praetor, as the college of pontifices had recommended, to see that all these measures were promptly put into effect. B.C. 217

X. When the senate had passed these resolutions, the praetor consulted the college, and Lucius Cornelius Lentulus, the Pontifex Maximus, gave his opinion that first of all a popular vote must

(Cicero, Propertius, Ovid, Persius). The two shrines stood close together on the Capitol (XXX. XXX. 16). See Wissowa, p. 313 f.

A.U.C. 537 vere sacro censet: iniussu populi voveri non posse.
2 Rogatus in haec verba populus: "Velitis iubeatisne haec sic fieri? Si res publica populi Romani Quiritium ad quinquennium proximum, sicut[1] velim eam[2] salvam, servata erit[3] hisce duellis, quod duellum populo Romano cum Carthaginiensi est, quaeque
3 duella cum Gallis sunt qui cis Alpes sunt, ratum[4] donum duit populus Romanus Quiritium,[5] quod ver attulerit ex suillo ovillo caprino bovillo grege, quaeque profana erunt, Iovi fieri, ex qua die senatus
4 populusque iusserit. Qui faciet, quando volet quaque lege volet facito; quo modo faxit, probe factum esto.
5 Si id moritur quod fieri oportebit, profanum esto neque scelus esto; si quis rumpet occidetve insciens, ne fraus esto; si quis clepsit,[6] ne populo scelus esto
6 neve cui cleptum erit; si atro die faxit insciens, probe factum esto; si nocte sive luce, si servus sive liber faxit, probe factum esto; si antidea quam[7]

[1] sicut *Ursinus*: sic *P*.

[2] eam *Ursinus*: eamque *P*: eam esse *Haupt*: voveamque *Madvig*: olim *Hasenmueller*.

[3] servata erit *Ursinus*: seruaverit *P*.

[4] ratum *Rossbach*: datum *P*: tum *Madvig*.

[5] *The words* datum donum duit populus Romanus Quiritium *stand in P before* quod duellum populo. *Lipsius transposed them*.

[6] clepsit *vulg.*: clepset *P* (*and below* cleptum *vulg.*: coeptum *PM*: ceptum *C*).

[7] antidea quam *Luchs*: antidea ac *Stroth*: anteidea *P*.

---

[1] The *ver sacrum* was not actually celebrated until 195 B.C., and a flaw in the ceremonies necessitated a repetition in the following year (XXXIV. lxiv. 1–3).

[2] The period appointed was March 1st to April 30th (*ibid.*).

be taken about the Sacred Spring; for it could B.C. 217 not be vowed without the authorization of the people. The question was put to them in this form: "Do you will and so order that these things be done in the manner following? If the Republic of the Roman People, the Quirites, shall be preserved for the next five years[1]—as I would wish it preserved—in these wars, to wit, the war of the Roman People with the People of Carthage and the wars with the Gauls on this side of the Alps, let the Roman People, the Quirites, offer up in indefeasible sacrifice to Jupiter what the spring shall have produced of swine, sheep, goats and cattle—which shall not have been consecrated to some other deity—beginning with the day which the senate and the People shall have designated.[2] Let him who shall make a sacrifice do so at such time and by such rite as shall seem good to him; in what manner soever he does it, let it be accounted duly done. If the animal which he ought to sacrifice dies, let it be deemed unconsecrate and let no guilt attach to him; if any shall hurt it or slay it unawares, let it be no sin; if any shall steal it, let no guilt attach to the People nor to him from whom it shall have been stolen; if he shall sacrifice unwittingly on a black day,[3] let the sacrifice be deemed to have been duly made; by night or by day, if slave or freeman perform the sacrifice, let it be deemed to have been duly made; if sacrifice shall be performed before the senate and the People

[3] *Dies atri*—called also *nefasti* and *religiosi*—were the days following the Calends, Nones and Ides, and the anniversaries of certain national disasters, like the defeat on the Allia. On such days no public business might be transacted.

A.U.C. 537 senatus populusque iusserit fieri[1] faxitur, eo populus solutus liber esto."

7 Eiusdem rei causa ludi magni voti aeris trecentis[2] tringinta tribus milibus trecentis triginta tribus[3] triente, praeterea bubus Iovi trecentis, multis aliis divis
8 bubus albis atque ceteris hostiis. Votis rite nuncupatis supplicatio edicta; supplicatumque iere cum[4] coniugibus ac liberis non urbana multitudo tantum sed agrestium etiam quos in aliqua sua fortuna
9 publica quoque contingebat cura. Tum lectisternium per triduum habitum[5] decemviris sacrorum curantibus. Sex pulvinaria in conspectu fuerunt: Iovi ac Iunoni unum, alterum Neptuno ac Minervae, tertium Marti ac Veneri, quartum Apollini ac Dianae, quintum Volcano ac Vestae, sextum Mercurio et Cereri.
10 Tum aedes votae: Veneri Erycinae aedem Q. Fabius Maximus dictator vovit, quia ita ex fatalibus libris editum[6] erat, ut is voveret cuius maximum imperium in civitate esset; Menti aedem T. Otacilius praetor vovit.

XI. Ita rebus divinis peractis tum de bello deque

[1] fieri *Stroth*: fieri ac *P.*
[2] trecentis triginta tribus *Budaeus* (*Plut.*, *Fab.* 4): CCXXXIII *P.*
[3] trecentis triginta tribus *inserted by Budaeus* (*Plut.*, ibid.).
[4] supplicatumque iere cum *Gronovius*: supplicatumquiregum *P.*
[5] habitum ς: habitum per *P.*
[6] editum ς: edictum *P.*

---

[1] These were probably libral *asses* (of a pound each) and not the reduced *asses* of one *uncia* (ounce) each which Pliny says were coined this year (*Q. Fabio Maximo dictatore*) and were reckoned at sixteen to the *denarius* (*Nat. Hist.*, XXXIII, xlv.). With this use of the number three editors cp. Aen. I, 265ff., where Jupiter foretells that Aeneas shall reign *three*

shall have ordered it to be performed, let the People be absolved therefrom and free of obligation." B.C. 217

For the same cause great games were vowed, to cost three hundred and thirty-three thousand, three hundred and thirty-three and a third bronze *asses*,[1] and, besides, a sacrifice to Jupiter of three hundred oxen, and of white oxen and the other customary victims to many other gods. When the vows had been duly pronounced, a supplication was decreed, and was performed not only by the urban population, with their wives and children, but by such country folk besides, as, having some fortune of their own, were beginning to feel concern for the Commonwealth. A *lectisternium* was then celebrated during three days under the supervision of the decemvirs who had charge of sacrifices. Six couches were displayed: one for Jupiter and Juno, a second for Neptune and Minerva, a third for Mars and Venus, a fourth for Apollo and Diana, a fifth for Vulcan and Vesta, a sixth for Mercury and Ceres.[2] The temples were then vowed—that to Venus Erycina by Quintus Fabius Maximus the dictator, because the Books of Fate had given out that he whose authority in the state was paramount should make the vow; and the temple to Mens by the praetor Titus Otacilius.

XI. Religious duties being thus acquitted, the

years, Ascanius *thirty*, and the Alban kings *three hundred*. H. Usener, *Dreiheit* (Rheinisches Museum für Philologie 58 (1903) *pp*. 1ff., 161ff, 321ff.), discusses with a wealth of illustration, the significance in ancient folk-lore and religion of the number three.

[2] The twelve great Olympian gods, arranged in pairs as with the Greeks, here make their appearance together for the first time in Roman history.

A.U.C. 537 re publica[1] dictator rettulit, quibus quotve legionibus victori hosti obviam eundum esse patres censerent.
2 Decretum ut ab Cn. Servilio consule exercitum acciperet; scriberet praeterea ex civibus sociisque quantum equitum ac peditum videretur; cetera omnia ageret faceretque ut e re publica duceret.
3 Fabius duas legiones se adiecturum ad Servilianum exercitum dixit. Iis per magistrum equitum scriptis
4 Tibur diem ad conveniendum edixit. Edictoque proposito ut quibus oppida castellaque immunita essent, uti commigrarent in loca tuta, ex agris quoque demigrarent omnes regionis eius qua iturus
5 Hannibal esset, tectis prius incensis ac frugibus corruptis, ne cuius rei copia esset, ipse via Flaminia profectus obviam consuli exercituque, cum ad Tiberim circa Ocriculum prospexissit agmen consulemque cum equitibus ad se progredientem, viatorem misit[2] qui consuli nuntiaret ut sine lictoribus
6 ad dictatorem veniret. Qui cum dicto paruisset congressusque eorum ingentem speciem dictaturae apud cives sociosque vetustate iam prope oblitos eius imperii fecisset, litterae ab urbe allatae sunt naves onerarias commeatum ab Ostia in Hispaniam ad exercitum portantes a classe Punica circa portum

[1] deque re publica ς: reque de publica *PM*: reque publica *C*.

[2] viatorem misit ς: uiatore misso *P*: substitit viatore misso *Weissenborn*.

dictator turned to affairs of war and state, and called upon the senate to decide with what and how many legions the victorious enemy should be faced. It was voted that he should take over the army of Gnaeus Servilius, the consul; that he should enroll, besides, from the citizens and the allies, as many horsemen and foot-soldiers as seemed good to him; and with regard to all other questions should act as he deemed conducive to the welfare of the state. Fabius announced that he should add two legions to the army that Servilius had commanded. These legions he enlisted, through his master of the horse, and commanded them to assemble at Tibur on a given day. He also issued an edict that those who dwelt in unfortified towns and hamlets should remove to places of safety; and that all the inhabitants of that district where Hannibal was likely to be marching should abandon their farms, first burning the buildings and destroying the crops, that there might be no supplies for him of any kind. He himself went out by the Flaminian way to meet the consul and his army, and when, close to the Tiber near Ocriculum, he came in sight of the column and saw the consul riding towards him at the head of his cavalry, he dispatched an orderly to bid the consul appear before the dictator without lictors. The consul obeyed, and their meeting vividly impressed the greatness of the dictatorship on citizens and allies, who had now, with the lapse of years, almost forgotten that supreme authority. Just then a dispatch was delivered from the City, announcing that ships of burden with supplies from Ostia for the army in Spain had been captured by the Punic B.C. 217

A.U.C. 537 7 Cosanum captas esse. Itaque extemplo consul Ostiam proficisci iussus navibusque quae ad urbem Romanam aut Ostiae essent completis milite ac navalibus sociis persequi hostium classem ac litora
8 Italiae tutari. Magna vis hominum conscripta Romae erat; libertini etiam quibus liberi essent et[1]
9 aetas militaris in verba iuraverant. Ex hoc urbano exercitu qui minores quinque et triginta annis erant in naves impositi, alii ut urbi praesiderent relicti.

XII. Dictator exercitu consulis accepto a Fulvio Flacco legato per agrum Sabinum Tibur, quo diem[2] ad conveniendum edixerat novis militibus, venit
2 Inde Praeneste ac transversis limitibus in viam Latinam est egressus, unde itineribus summa cum cura exploratis ad hostem ducit, nullo loco, nisi quantum necessitas cogeret, fortunae se commissurus.

3 Quo primum die haud procul Arpis in conspectu hostium posuit castra, nulla mora facta quin Poenus educeret in aciem copiamque pugnandi faceret.
4 Sed ubi quieta omnia apud hostes nec castra ullo tumultu mota videt, increpans quidem, victos tandem illos[3] Martios animos Romanis debellatumque et concessum propalam de virtute ac gloria esse, in
5 castra rediit; ceterum tacita cura animum incessit,[4]

[1] et ϛ: ita *P.* [2] diem *vulg.*: die *P.*
[3] illos *Haupt*: quos *P.*
[4] incessit ϛ (*Muretus*): incensum *P.*

---

[1] The *socii navales* served as rowers.

fleet off the port of Cosa. Accordingly, the consul was ordered to set out at once for Ostia and, manning such ships as were at Rome or Ostia with soldiers and naval allies,[1] to pursue the enemy's fleet and protect the coasts of Italy. A vast number of men had been enrolled in Rome; even freedmen who had children and were of military age had taken the oath. Of this urban levy those who were less than thirty-five years old were sent on board the ships; the others were left to garrison the City. B.C. 217

XII. The dictator, after taking over the consul's army from Fulvius Flaccus, his lieutenant, marched through the Sabine country to Tibur, where he had given the new levies notice to assemble on a certain day. From Tibur he marched to Praeneste, and striking across the country came out into the Latin Way, and then, reconnoitring the roads with the utmost circumspection, advanced in the direction of the enemy, though resolved nowhere to commit himself to fortune, except in so far as necessity might compel him.

On the day when Fabius first encamped in sight of the enemy, not far from Arpi, the Phoenician promptly led out his forces into line and offered battle. But when he perceived that all was quiet on the other side, and could hear no sounds of commotion in their camp, he went back to his quarters, exclaiming scornfully that the boasted martial spirit of the Romans was broken at last, that the war was fought and won, that they had openly bade valour and renown farewell; but in the silence of his heart he was troubled by the thought that he would have a general to deal with by no means

A.U.C. 537 quod cum duce haudquaquam Flamini Semproniique[1]
simili futura sibi res esset ac tum demum edocti
malis Romani parem Hannibali ducem quaesissent.
6 Et prudentiam quidem novi[2] dictatoris extemplo
timuit: constantiam hauddum expertus agitare ac
temptare animum movendo crebro castra populan-
7 doque in oculis eius agros sociorum coepit; et modo
citato agmine ex conspectu abibat, modo repente
in aliquo flexu viae, si excipere degressum in aequum
posset, occultus subsistebat.

8 Fabius per loca alta agmen ducebat modico ab
hoste intervallo, ut neque omitteret eum neque
congrederetur. Castris, nisi quantum usus necessarii
cogerent,[3] tenebatur miles; pabulum et ligna nec
pauci petebant nec passim; equitum levisque arma-
9 turae statio, composita instructaque in subitos
tumultus, et suo militi tuta omnia et infesta effusis
10 hostium populatoribus praebebat; neque universo
periculo summa rerum committebatur et parva
momenta levium certaminum ex tuto coeptorum
finitimoque receptu[4] adsuefaciebant territum pris-
tinis cladibus militem minus iam tandem aut
virtutis aut fortunae paenitere suae.

11 Sed non Hannibalem magis infestum tam sanis
consiliis habebat quam magistrum equitum, qui nihil
aliud quam quod impar erat[5] imperio morae ad rem
12 publicam praecipitandam habebat. Ferox rapidus-

[1] Flamini Semproniique *Alschefski*: flaminis sempronio-que *P*.

[2] novi (*and* ductoris *for* dictatoris) *Gronovius*: non uim *P*.

[3] necessarii cogerent *Weissenborn*: necessari cogeret P^1: necessario cogeret P^2.

[4] finitimoque receptu (finitimo receptu *Lipsius*) *Luchs*: finitimorum receptum quae *P*.

[5] impar erat *Jac. Gronovius*: imperabat *P*.

like Flaminius or Sempronius, since the Romans, schooled by their misfortunes, had now at last sought out a leader to match Hannibal. The prudence of the dictator was indeed an immediate source of worry to him, but, possessing as yet no experience of his firmness, he began to provoke and try his temper by frequent shifting of his camp and by pillaging the lands of the allies before his very eyes. Now he would march off rapidly and disappear; and now would lie in wait at some turn of the road, in hopes to cut the Romans off when they had descended on to level ground. B.C. 217

Fabius kept leading his troops along the heights, at a moderate distance from the enemy, so as neither to lose touch nor yet come to blows with him. He would keep his men in camp, except for such necessary duties as obliged their leaving it; when they went out for wood and fodder, they were neither few in number nor dispersed; a corps of cavalry and skirmishers drawn up and ready for sudden onsets made everything safe for his own men and dangerous for the scattered pillagers of the enemy. He refused to stake all on a general engagement, and yet by means of little skirmishes, undertaken from a safe position and with a place of refuge close at hand, he at length accustomed his soldiers, disheartened by their former defeats, to be less diffident of their own courage and good fortune.

But even Hannibal was not more vexed by these prudent measures than was the master of the horse, who was only withheld from plunging the nation into ruin by his subordinate authority. Violent and hasty in his opinions and of unbridled tongue, he

A.U.C. 537 que in consiliis[1] ac lingua immodicus primo inter paucos, dein propalam in volgus pro cunctatore segnem pro cauto timidum, adfingens vicina virtutibus vitia, compellabat premendoque superiorem, quae pessima ars nimis prosperis multorum successibus crevit, sese extollebat.

XIII. Hannibal ex Hirpinis in Samnium transit, Beneventanum depopulatur agrum, Telesiam urbem capit; inritat etiam de industria ducem Romanum,[2] si forte accensum tot indignitatibus cladibusque sociorum detrahere ad aequum certamen possit.
2 Inter multitudinem sociorum Italici generis qui ad Trasumennum capti ab Hannibale dimissique fuerant tres Campani equites erant, multis iam tum inlecti donis promissisque Hannibalis ad conciliandos popu-
3 larium animos. Hi nuntiantes, si in Campaniam exercitum admovisset, Capuae potiendae copiam fore, cum res maior quam auctores esset, dubium Hannibalem alternisque fidentem ac diffidentem tamen
4 ut Campanos ex Samnio peteret moverunt. Monitos etiam atque etiam ut[3] promissa rebus adfirmarent, iussosque cum pluribus et aliquibus principum redire
5 ad se dimisit. Ipse imperat duci ut se in agrum Casinatem ducat, edoctus a peritis regionum, si eum saltum occupasset, exitum Romano ad opem feren-

[1] rapidusque in consiliis ς: rapidusquem consiliis *P*: rapidusque consiliis ς.

[2] ducem Romanum *Pauly*: ducem *P*: dictatorem *Woelfflin*.

[3] etiam atque etiam ut *Gron.* (*Madvig in later edd.*): ut etiam etque (atque *P*[2]) etiam *P*: etiam atque etiam *Madvig* (1*st ed.*): ut etiam atque etiam viderent (*or* curarent) ut *Novák*.

---

[1] By Samnium Livy here means the territory of the Caudini lying to the north of the Hirpini. Both tribes, as well as the Frentani and the Pentri, had belonged to the old Samnite League.

spoke of Fabius—at first in the hearing of a few, but after a time quite openly to everybody—not as deliberate but as slothful, not as cautious but as timid, inventing faults that neighboured on his virtues; and exalted himself by disparaging his superior—an infamous practice, which has grown in favour from the all too great prosperity of many who have followed it. B.C. 217

XIII. Hannibal, leaving the Hirpini, crossed over into Samnium,[1] laid waste the lands of Beneventum, and captured the city of Telesia. He even deliberately sought to vex the Roman general, for he hoped that by so often insulting and distressing his allies he might anger him and induce him to come down and fight on equal terms. Amongst the numerous allies of Italian stock who had been made prisoners by Hannibal at Trasumennus and afterwards released were three Campanian knights, whom he had even then enticed with gifts and promises to procure for him the goodwill of their countrymen. These men now informed him that if he would bring his army into Campania the opportunity would be afforded him of taking Capua. It was a weighty undertaking for such men to enter into, and Hannibal hesitated, now trusting and again distrusting them, but in the end they persuaded him to march from Samnium into Campania. He warned them again and again to confirm their words with deeds, and dismissed them with orders to come back to him with more people, including some of their leading men. He then ordered his guide to conduct him to the territory of Casinum, for he had been told by those who knew the country that if he occupied that pass he could keep the Romans from marching to the aid of their

A.U.C. 537 6 dam sociis interclusurum. Sed Punicum abhorrens
ab Latinorum nominum pronuntiatione os, Casilinum
pro[1] Casino dux ut acciperet fecit; aversusque ab
suo itinere per Allifanum Caiatinumque[2] et Calenum
7 agrum in campum Stellatem descendit. Ubi cum
montibus fluminibusque clausam regionem circum-
spexisset, vocatum ducem percunctatur ubi terrarum
8 esset. Cum is Casilini eo die[3] mansurum eum
dixisset, tum demum cognitus est error, et Casinum
9 longe inde alia regione esse; virgisque caeso duce
et ad reliquorum terrorem in crucem sublato, castris
communitis, Maharbalem cum equitibus in agrum
10 Falernum praedatum dimisit. Usque ad aquas
Sinuessanas populatio ea pervenit. Ingentem
cladem, fugam tamen terroremque latius Numidae
11 fecerunt; nec tamen is terror, cum omnia bello
flagrarent, fide socios dimovit, videlicet quia iusto et
moderato regebantur imperio nec abnuebant, quod
unum vinculum fidei est, melioribus parere.

XIV. Ut vero, postquam[4] ad Volturnum flumen
castra sunt posita, exurebatur amoenissimus Italiae
ager villaeque passim incendiis fumabant, per iuga
Massici montis Fabio ducente, tum prope de integro
2 seditio accensa;[5] quieverant[6] enim per paucos dies,
quia cum celerius solito ductum agmen esset, festinari
ad prohibendam populationibus Campaniam credide-

[1] nominum pronuntiatione os, Casilinum pro *Weissenborn*: nominum pro *P*.

[2] Allifanum Caiatinumque *Kiehl and Stier*: alifanum calatinumque *P*: Callifanum Allifanumque *Madvig*.

[3] eo die ς: eodem *P*: eodem die ς.

[4] postquam *Alschefski*: quam *P*.

[5] seditio accensa *Lipsius*: seditio ac de seditione accensi *P*.

[6] quieverant *Gronovius*: quidam fuerant *P*: quieti fuerant *Lipsius*.

allies. But the difficulty experienced by Carthaginians in pronouncing Latin names caused the guide to understand *Casilinum* instead of *Casinum*; and quitting the proper road he led him down through the districts of Allifae, Caiatia and Cales into the Plain of Stella. There Hannibal, looking round on the mountains and rivers that enclosed the plain, called up the guide and asked him where in the world he was. And only when the guide had answered that he should lodge that night in Casilinum, did he perceive at last how the man had blundered, and that Casinum lay far off in another direction. Whereupon he scourged the guide, and, to terrify the others, crucified him, and going into camp behind entrenchments, dispatched Maharbal with the cavalry to ravage the Falernian countryside. The devastation extended even to the Baths of Sinuessa. The Numidians wrought great havoc and spread dismay and terror more widely still; yet this terror, even though all the country blazed with war, did not cause the allies to waver in their loyalty, assuredly because the rule under which they were governed was just and temperate, nor did they refuse—and that is the only guarantee of loyalty—to yield obedience to their betters. B.C. 217

XIV. But when Hannibal had encamped by the river Volturnus, and the fairest district in all Italy was in flames, and the smoke went curling up from burning farm-houses, while Fabius continued to march along the ridges of Mount Massicus, there was almost a new outburst of sedition. For the disaffected had kept quiet for several days, believing that the army, which had been moving more rapidly than usual, was hastening to preserve Campania

A.U.C. 537

3 rant. Ut vero in extrema iuga Massici montis ventum
est et[1] hostes sub oculis erant Falerni agri colonorum-
que Sinuessae tecta urentes nec ulla erat mentio
4 pugnae, "Spectatum huc"[2] inquit Minucius, "ut
ad[3] rem fruendam oculis, sociorum caedes et in-
cendia, venimus? Nec, si nullius alterius nos, ne
civium quidem horum pudet quos Sinuessam colonos
patres nostri miserunt ut ab Samnite hoste tuta haec
ora esset, quam nunc non vicinus Samnis urit sed
5 Poenus advena, ab extremis orbis terrarum terminis
nostra cunctatione et socordia iam huc progressus?
6 Tantum pro degeneramus a patribus nostris ut
praeter quam oram illi[4] Punicas vagari classes
dedecus esse imperii sui duxerint, eam nunc plenam
hostium Numidarumque ac Maurorum iam factam
7 videamus? Qui modo Saguntum oppugnari indig-
nando non homines tantum sed foedera et deos
ciebamus, scandentem moenia Romanae coloniae
8 Hannibalem[5] lenti[6] spectamus. Fumus ex incendiis villarum agrorumque in oculos atque ora venit;
strepunt aures clamoribus plorantium sociorum,
saepius nostram quam[7] deorum invocantium opem;
nos hic pecorum modo per aestivos saltus deviasque
calles exercitum ducimus conditi nubibus silvisque.
9 Si hoc modo peragrando cacumina saltusque M. Furius

[1] est et *Weissenborn*: est *P*: et *Gronovius*.
[2] spectatum huc ς: spectatum est hoc *P*.
[3] ut ad *Madvig*: ad *P*.
[4] oram illi ς: per oram illi suam *P*.
[5] Hannibalem ς: et hannibalem *P*.
[6] lenti ς: laetis *P*: taciti *Novák*.
[7] nostram quam ς: nos quamquam *P*.

---

[1] *i.e.* the western extremity.

from devastation. But when they reached the farthest extremity[1] of the range, and saw the enemy down below them setting fire to the farms of the Falernian district and the colony of Sinuessa, and yet no word was uttered about fighting, Minucius cried, "Are we come here as to a spectacle, that we may gratify our eyes with the slaughter of our friends and the burning of their homes? If nothing else can awaken us to a sense of shame, do we feel none when we behold these fellow citizens of ours whom our fathers sent as colonists to Sinuessa to secure this frontier from the Samnite enemy? It is not our Samnite neighbours who are wasting it now, but Phoenician invaders, who have been suffered to come all this way, from the farthest, limits of the world, by our delays and slothfulness. So greatly, alas! do we degenerate from our fathers that we behold overrun with enemies and in the possession of Numidians and Moors that coast past which *they* could not see the Punic navies cruising without feeling that their empire was disgraced. When, a little while ago, Saguntum was besieged, we appealed indignantly, not to men only, but to treaties and to the gods; but now that Hannibal is scaling the walls of a Roman colony, we look on with indifference. The smoke from burning farm-houses and fields comes into our eyes and mouths; our ears are ringing with the lamentations of our allies, who invoke our aid more often than that of Heaven; and here we are, leading our army—like a flock of sheep—through summer pastures and by devious mountain trails, and hiding ourselves in clouds and forests. If Marcus Furius had tried to recover Rome from the Gauls by wandering thus over

B.C. 217

A.U.C. 537 recipere a Gallis urbem voluisset quo hic novus
Camillus, nobis dictator unicus in rebus adfectis
quaesitus, Italiam ab Hannibale reciperare parat,
10 Gallorum Roma esset, quam vereor ne sic cunctanti-
bus nobis Hannibali ac Poenis totiens servaverint
11 maiores nostri. Sed vir ac vere Romanus, quo die
dictatorem eum ex auctoritate patrum iussuque
populi dictum Veios allatum est, cum esset satis
altum Ianiculum ubi sedens prospectaret hostem,
descendit in aequum atque illo ipso die media in urbe,
qua[1] nunc busta Gallica sunt, et postero die citra
12 Gabios cecidit Gallorum legiones. Quid? Post
multos annos cum ad furculas Caudinas ab Samnite
hoste sub iugum missi sumus, utrum tandem L.
Papirius Cursor iuga Samnii perlustrando an Luceriam
premendo obsidendoque et lacessendo victorem
hostem depulsum ab Romanis cervicibus iugum
13 superbo Samniti imposuit? Modo C. Lutatio quae
alia res quam celeritas victoriam dedit, quod postero
die quam hostem vidit classem gravem commeatibus,
impeditam suomet ipsam instrumento atque ad-
14 paratu, oppressit? Stultitia est sedendo aut votis
debellari credere posse; arma[2] capias oportet et
descendas[3] in aequum et vir cum viro congrediaris.
Audendo atque agendo res Romana crevit, non his

[1] qua ς : q. *P* : quae ς (*Luchs*).
[2] arma *Madvig* armari *P*.
[3] descendas *Heerwagen* : deducendas *P*.

---

[1] A place in Rome where the Gauls—so tradition said—had piled up and burned the bodies of those who died of a pestilence which had broken out among them while they were beleaguering the Capitol (v. xlviii. 3).

[2] For the story of this famous episode see IX. i–xv.

mountain heights and passes, even as this new Camillus, this wonderful dictator to whom we have turned in our distress, is planning to recover Italy from Hannibal, the Gauls would be in Rome to-day; and I fear that if we linger thus, our fathers will so often have preserved it only for Hannibal and the Phoenicians. But that brave man and true Roman, on the day that the news was brought to Veii of his being appointed dictator, by command of the people in pursuance of a senatorial resolution—though Janiculum was high enough for him to have sat there and enjoyed a prospect of the enemy—came down into the plain, and on that very day, in the midst of the City—where now the Gallic Pyres[1] are—and again on the following day, this side of Gabii, cut the legions of the Gauls to pieces. What! When, many years later, at the Caudine Forks, our Samnite foe had sent us under the yoke,[2] was it, pray, by scouring the heights of Samnium, or by pressing Luceria hard and laying siege to it, and by challenging the victorious enemy, that Lucius Papirius Cursor struck off the yoke from Roman necks and imposed it on the haughty Samnite? What else was it than swiftness that gave the victory, not long since,[3] to Gaius Lutatius, who bore down upon the enemy's fleet, laden deep with stores and hampered with its own munitions and equipment, on the day after he sighted it? It is folly to think that a war can be won by sitting still or making vows; you must arm and go down into the field, and do battle, man to man! Rome's greatness has come from daring and B.C. 217

[3] The victory of Lutatius off the Aegatian Islands had been won twenty-four years before (Summary of Book xx).

A.U.C. 537 15 segnibus[1] consiliis quae timidi cauta vocant." Haec
velut contionanti Minucio circumfundebatur tribunorum equitumque Romanorum multitudo, et ad aures quoque militum dicta ferocia evolvebantur; ac, si militaris suffragii res esset, haud dubie ferebant Minucium Fabio ducem[2] praelaturos.

XV. Fabius, pariter in suos haud minus quam in
hostes intentus, prius ab illis[3] invictum animum
praestat. Quamquam probe scit non in castris modo
suis sed iam etiam Romae infamem suam cunctationem esse, obstinatus tamen tenore eodem con-
2 siliorum aestatis reliquum extraxit, ut Hannibal
destitutus ab spe summa ope petiti[4] certaminis iam
hibernis locum circumspectaret, quia ea regio prae-
sentis erat copiae, non perpetuae, arbusta vineaeque
et consita omnia magis amoenis quam necessariis
3 fructibus. Haec per exploratores relata Fabio.
Cum satis sciret per easdem angustias quibus intraverat Falernum agrum rediturum, Calliculam[5] mon-
4 tem et Casilinum occupat modicis praesidiis, quae
urbs Volturno flumine dirempta Falernum a Campano
agro dividit; ipse iugis iisdem exercitum reducit
misso exploratum cum quadringentis equitibus

[1] his segnibus ς: iis sensibus *P*.
[2] ducem *Gronovius*: duci *P*.
[3] illis ς: aliis *P*.
[4] ope petiti *Alschefski*: oppetiti *P*.
[5] Calliculam ς (*chap.* xvi. § 5): gallicanum *P*.

from doing; not from these sluggish policies that timid folk term cautious." When Minucius held forth in this fashion, like a general encouraging his troops, a crowd of tribunes and Roman knights would gather round him, and his fiery words even reached the ears of the common soldiers; and if the election of their general had rested with the men, they showed unmistakably that Minucius would have been preferred to Fabius. B.C. 217

XV. But Fabius, watching his own men no less carefully than the enemy, proved first that it was not in *them* to overcome his resolution. Though he knew full well that his policy of waiting was in bad repute, not only in his camp but by this time in Rome as well, he held doggedly to the same line of conduct and dragged out the remainder of the summer; so that Hannibal, disappointed in his hopes of the battle which he had made every effort to bring on, was now looking round for a place to winter in; for the country where he was, though a land of plenty for the time being, could not support him permanently, being taken up with orchards and vineyards, and planted everywhere with agreeable rather than necessary fruits. Fabius was informed of this by his scouts. Feeling certain that Hannibal would leave the Falernian district, by the same passes through which he had entered it, he posted a fair-sized garrison on Mount Callicula and another in Casilinum. (The river Volturnus runs through this town, which marks the boundary between the Falernian district and Campania). The main army he led back by the same ridges, after sending on Lucius Hostilius Mancinus with four hundred cavalry of the allies to reconnoitre.

A.U.C. 537 5 sociorum L. Hostilio Mancino. Qui ex turba iuvenum audientium saepe ferociter contionantem magistrum equitum progressus primo exploratoris modo, ut ex tuto specularetur hostem, ubi[1] vagos passim per vicos[2] Numidas prospexit[3] ac per[4]
6 occasionem etiam paucos occidit, extemplo occupatus certamine est animus excideruntque praecepta dictatoris, qui, quantum[5] tuto posset progressum, prius recipere sese iusserat quam in conspectum hostium
7 veniret. Numidae alii atque alii occursantes refugientesque ad castra prope ipsa eum[6] cum fatigatione equorum atque hominum pertraxere.[7]
8 Inde Carthalo, penes quem summa equestris imperii erat, concitatis equis invectus, cum prius quam ad coniectum teli veniret avertisset hostes, quinque ferme milia continenti cursu secutus est fugientes.
9 Mancinus, postquam nec hostem desistere sequi nec spem vidit effugiendi esse, cohortatus suos in proe-
10 lium rediit omni parte virium impar. Itaque ipse et delecti equitum circumventi occiduntur; ceteri effuso cursu[8] Cales primum, inde prope inviis callibus ad dictatorem perfugerunt.

11 Eo forte die Minucius se coniunxerat Fabio, missus ad firmandum praesidio saltum qui super Tarracinam in artas coactus fauces imminet mari, ne ab Sinuessa[9]

[1] ubi ς: urbis *P*.
[2] per vicos *P*²: uicos *P*.
[3] prospexit *Heraeus*: *omitted by P*.
[4] ac per *Wesenberg*: per *P*.
[5] quantum ς: quem *P*.
[6] ipsa eum *Weissenborn*: ipsum *P*.
[7] pertraxere ς: pertrahere *P*.
[8] cursu *Voss*: rursus cursu *P*.
[9] ab Sinuessa *Gronovius*: adminuissea *P*¹: adminuessa *C*: adminuisse *P*²*M*.

Mancinus was one of the crowd of young officers B.C. 217 who often listened to the blustering speeches of the master of the horse. He advanced at first as if making a reconnaissance, with the object of observing the enemy from a safe distance. But when he saw the Numidians roaming about through the villages, and had even seized the opportunity to cut off a few of them, his heart was suddenly filled with the lust of combat, and he forgot the instructions of the dictator, who had bade him proceed as far as was compatible with safety, and retire before the enemy should see him. The Numidians, first one troop and then another, by charging and then retreating, drew him on almost to their very camp and wore out his horses and his men. Then Carthalo, the commander of all the enemy's cavalry, swooped down upon the Romans at a gallop, and routing them before he had got within a javelin-throw, pursued them as they fled for nearly five miles at one stretch. As soon as Mancinus perceived that the enemy would not give over the pursuit, and that he could not hope to get away, he rallied his men and led them back into the fight, though overmatched in every particular. Accordingly, he himself and the best of his troopers were surrounded and slain, and the rest in a scattered flight made their way first to Cales, and thence, by well-nigh impassable trails, to the dictator.

It happened that on that day Minucius had joined Fabius. He had been sent to secure the pass which contracts above Tarracina into a narrow gorge close to the sea,[1] to prevent the Phoenician from taking

[1] This was the pass of Lautulae, mentioned at VII. xxxix. 7.

A.U.C. 537 Poenus Appiae limite pervenire in agrum Romanum
12 posset. Coniunctis exercitibus dictator ac magister equitum castra in viam deferunt qua Hannibal ducturus erat.

XVI. Duo inde milia hostes aberant. Postero die Poeni quod viae inter bina castra erat agmine com-
2 plevere. Cum Romani sub ipso constitissent vallo haud dubie aequiore loco, successit tamen Poenus cum expeditis equitibusque ad lacessendum hostem. Carptim Poeni et procursando recipiendoque sese
3 pugnavere; restitit suo loco Romana acies. Lenta pugna et ex dictatoris magis quam Hannibalis fuit voluntate. Ducenti ab Romanis, octingenti hostium cecidere.

4 Inclusus inde videri Hannibal via[1] ad Casilinum obsessa, cum Capua et Samnium et tantum ab tergo divitum sociorum Romanis commeatus subveheret, Poenus inter Formiana[2] saxa ac Literni[3] arenas stagnaque et per horridas silvas[4] hibernaturus esset.
5 Nec Hannibalem fefellit suis se artibus peti. Itaque cum per Casilinum evadere non posset petendique montes et iugum Calliculae superandum esset, necubi Romanus inclusum vallibus agmen adgrederetur,
6 ludibrium oculorum specie terribile ad frustrandum

[1] via *Gronovius*: ut *P*.

[2] Formiana *Sabellicus*: fortunā/minas *P*[1]: fortunae minas *P*[2].

[3] Literni *Sabellicus*: literne *P*.

[4] per horridas silvas *Madvig*: perhorridas situas *P*[1]: perhorridas situ *P*[2]: horridas silvas *Luterbacher*.

---

[1] Polybius (III. xcii. 11) says that Fabius had encamped "on a hill, in front of the pass and overlooking it."

[2] Weissenborn understands the reference to be to the Silva Gallinaria, now Pineta di Castel Volturno, in the neighbourhood of Liternum.

the Appian Way from Sinuessa into Roman territory. B.C. 217
Combining their forces, the dictator and the master of the horse camped on the road where Hannibal was going to march.

XVI. The enemy was two miles away. Next day the Phoenicians were on the march, filling the road which lay between the two camps. The Romans had formed up just under their rampart and had clearly the advantage of position.[1] None the less did Hannibal advance with his light infantry and cavalry, to provoke them into fighting. At one point after another the Phoenicians attacked, dashing up and then retreating. The Roman line stood firm. The battle was long drawn out and was more to the liking of the dictator than of Hannibal. Two hundred fell on the Roman side, and eight hundred of the enemy.

Hannibal now seemed to be hemmed in, the road to Casilinum being blocked. The Romans had Capua and Samnium at their backs and all their wealthy allies to furnish them with provisions; but the Phoenicians faced the prospect of passing the winter between the cliffs of Formiae and the sands and marshes of Liternum, and amid tangled forests.[2] Hannibal did not fail to perceive that his own strategy was being turned against him. Accordingly, since he could not get out by way of Casilinum, but must take to the mountains and cross the ridge of Callicula, fearing lest the Romans should assail his troops as they were marching through the gorges, he resolved to approach the mountains under cover of darkness in the forepart of the night, after first contriving a terrifying exhibition, to cheat the enemy's eyes. Preparations

A.U.C. 537 hostem commentus, principio noctis furtim succedere
ad montes statuit. Fallacis consilii talis apparatus
7 fuit: faces undique ex agris collectae fascesque
virgarum atque aridi sarmenti praeligantur [1] cornibus
boum, quos domitos indomitosque multos inter
8 ceteram agrestem praedam agebat. Ad duo milia
ferme boum effecta, Hasdrubalique negotium datum
ut nocte [2] id armentum accensis cornibus [3] ad montes
ageret, maxime, si posset, super saltus ab hoste
insessos.

XVII. Primis tenebris silentio mota castra; boves
2 aliquanto ante signa acti. Ubi ad radices montium
viasque angustas ventum est, signum extemplo datur
ut accensis cornibus armenta in adversos concitentur
montes. Et metus ipse relucentis flammae extemplo
a capite [4] calorque iam ad vivum ad imaque [5] cornua
veniens [6] velut stimulatos furore agebat boves.
3 Quo repente discursu haud secus quam silvis monti-
busque accensis omnia circa [7] virgulta ardere visa; [8]
capitumque irrita quassatio [9] excitans flammam
hominum passim discurrentium speciem praebebat.
4 Qui ad transitum saltus insidendum locati erant, ubi
in summis montibus ac super se quosdam ignes con-
spexere, circumventos se esse rati praesidio exces-

[1] praeligantur ς: praeliganturque *P*.

[2] nocte *Weissenborn*: primis tenebris noctem (noctes P^2)*P*: primis tenebris nocte *C*: primis tenebris ortis *Reuss*.

[3] armentum accensis cornibus *P*: armentum *H. J. Mueller*: accensis in cornibus sarmentis *Weissenborn*.

[4] extemplo a capite *Greenough*: ex campie a capite P^1: ex capite a capite P^2: a capite ς.

[5] ad imaque ς: diuatimaque *P*.

[6] cornua veniens *Luchs*: cornuumaueniens *P*.

[7] circa *Woelfflin*: circuma *P*.

[8] ardere visa *Perizonius*: ardere *P*.

for the ruse were made as follows. Pine-knots, B.C. 217 collected from all the country round, and bundles of twigs and dry branches were tied to the horns of cattle, of which—counting those that were broken in and those that were not—they possessed, among their other rustic spoils, a considerable number. Of these they got together about two thousand head, and Hasdrubal was commissioned to drive this herd in the night, with their horns ablaze, on to the mountains, and particularly—if it should be feasible—above the pass held by the enemy.

XVII. In the dusk of evening the Carthaginians broke camp in silence, driving on the cattle a little way before the standards. When they reached the foothills and the narrow roads, the signal was immediately given to set fire to the horns and drive the herd up the mountain. And their very fear, as the flames at once shot up from their heads, and the heat, that soon penetrated to the quick at the base of their horns, made the cattle as wild as though they had gone crazy. As they suddenly rushed this way and that, all the bushes far and near seemed to be burning, as if the woods and mountains had been set on fire; and when they shook their heads, they only fanned the blaze and made it look as if men were running about in all directions. When the troops who had been posted to hold the pass caught sight of certain fires on the mountain-tops above them, they thought that they were surrounded and forsook their station. Where the fewest flames were

---

[9] capitumque irrita quassatio *Gronovius*: captumque rita quaesatio *P*[1]: captumque rita quae ratio *P*[2].

A.U.C. 537
sere; qua minime[1] densae micabant flammae, velut
tutissimum iter, petentes summa montium iuga,
tamen in quosdam boves palatos a suis gregibus in-
5 ciderunt. Et primo, cum procul cernerent veluti
6 flammas spirantium, miraculo attoniti constiterunt;
deinde ut humana apparuit fraus, tum vero insidias
rati esse cum maiore tumultu[2] concitant se in fugam.
Levi quoque armaturae hostium incurrere; ceterum
nox aequato timore neutros pugnam incipientes ad
7 lucem tenuit. Interea toto agmine Hannibal trans-
ducto per saltum et quibusdam in ipso saltu hostium
oppressis in agro Allifano[3] posuit castra.

XVIII. Hunc tumultum sensit Fabius; ceterum
et insidias esse ratus et ab nocturno utique abhorrens
2 certamine suos munimentis tenuit. Luce prima sub
iugo montis proelium fuit, quo interclusam ab suis
levem armaturam facile—etenim numero aliquantum
praestabant—Romani superassent, nisi Hispanorum
cohors ad id ipsum remissa ab Hannibale supervenis-
3 set.[4] Ea adsuetior montibus et ad concursandum
inter saxa rupesque aptior ac levior[5] cum velocitate
corporum tum armorum habitu campestrem hostem,
gravem armis statariumque, pugnae genere facile
4 elusit. Ita haudquaquam pari certamine digressi,

[1] qua minime *Gronovius*: quamnim *P*.
[2] tumultu ς (*Lipsius*): multo *P*.
[3] Allifano ς: albano *P*.
[4] supervenisset *Gronovius*: peruenisset *P*.
[5] levior ς: leuiorque *P*.

flashing—for this seemed the safest way—they made B.C. 217 for the summits of the ridges, but nevertheless fell in with some of the cattle which had strayed from their herds. And at first, when they saw them afar, breathing fire, as they supposed, they were dazed by the wonder of it, and stood stock still; but afterwards, perceiving it to be a trick devised by men, they concluded that it was an ambush and took to their heels in greater confusion than before. They also ran into some light-armed soldiers of the enemy; the darkness, however, by equalizing their fears, kept both sides there till daylight without either beginning the battle. In the meanwhile Hannibal had conveyed his entire army through the pass—surprising some of his enemies in the pass itself—and had pitched his camp in the district of Allifae.

XVIII. Fabius heard the din, but believing it to be an ambush, and disliking, in any case, to fight at night, kept his men within their works. At break of day there was a battle under the ridge. The Romans had cut off the light-armed troops of the enemy from the others, and possessing some superiority in numbers, would easily have overpowered them, had it not been for the arrival of a cohort of Spaniards, which Hannibal had sent back expressly to forestall them. These troops were more used to mountains, and better suited to skirmishing amid rocks and crags, and being more agile and more lightly armed, they had no difficulty—thanks to the nature of the fighting—in getting the better of an enemy whose heavy armour and stationary tactics were adapted to level ground. Thus the struggle had been far from equal, when they parted and made off for their respective camps. Hardly any

A.U.C. 537 Hispani fere omnes incolumes, Romani aliquot suis
amissis in castra contenderunt.

5 Fabius quoque movit castra transgressusque saltum
6 super Allifas loco alto ac munito consedit. Tum per
Samnium Romam se petere simulans Hannibal usque
in Paelignos populabundus rediit: Fabius medius
inter hostium agmen urbemque Romam iugis duce-
7 bat nec absistens nec congrediens. Ex Paelignis
Poenus flexit iter retroque Apuliam repetens
Gereonium[1] pervenit, urbem metu, quia conlapsa
8 ruinis pars moenium erat, ab suis desertam; dictator
in Larinati[2] agro castra communiit. Inde sacrorum
causa Romam revocatus, non imperio modo, sed consilio
etiam ac prope precibus agens cum magistro equitum
ut plus consilio quam fortunae confidat et se potius
9 ducem quam Sempronium Flaminiumque imitetur;
ne nihil actum censeret extracta prope aestate per
ludificationem hostis; medicos quoque plus interdum quiete[3] quam movendo atque agendo proficere;
10 haud parvam rem esse ab totiens victore hoste vinci
desisse ac respirasse ab continuis cladibus[4]—haec
nequiquam praemonito magistro equitum Romam est
profectus.

XIX. Principio aestatis qua haec gerebantur in Hispania quoque terra marique coeptum bellum est.

[1] Gereonium *Alschefski*: gleronum *P*.
[2] Larinati ς (XXII. xxiv. 1 *and* XLV. ii. 11): larinate *P*.
[3] medicos . . . quiete *Valla*: medico . . . quippe *P*.
[4] ac respirasse ab continuis cladibus *Luchs*: ab continuis cladibus ac respirasse *P*: et ab continuis cladibus respirasse ς (*Madvig*).

---

[1] Polybius (III. c.) knows nothing of this story, but says that Hannibal took the place, which he calls Γερούνιον, by

of the Spaniards had been hurt, but the Romans had lost a considerable number of their men. B.C. 217

Fabius, too, broke camp, and marching through the pass established himself in a lofty and naturally strong position above Allifae. Hannibal now feigned a movement upon Rome by way of Samnium, and marched back right to the land of the Paeligni, pillaging as he went. Fabius led his troops along the ridges between the enemy's army and the City, neither shunning his foe nor coming to grips with him. From the Paelignian country the Phoenician turned, and marched back towards Apulia till he came to Gereonium, a town which its own inhabitants had abandoned in their alarm at the collapse of a part of its walls.[1] The dictator encamped in the country about Larinum, and being summoned thence to Rome on religious business, commanded, counselled, and all but entreated the master of the horse to put more trust in prudence than in fortune, and rather to imitate his strategy than that of Sempronius and Flaminius. He was not to suppose, said Fabius, that nothing had been accomplished, because almost the whole summer had been tediously spent in baffling the enemy; physicians too sometimes found rest more efficacious than motion and activity; it was no small matter to have ceased to be defeated by an enemy who had so often been victorious, and to have breathed again after a series of disasters. When he had thus fore-warned the master of the horse—but all in vain—he set out for Rome.

XIX. At the beginning of the summer in which these operations were carried on, war was also begun

siege, and Livy himself, in chap. xxiii. § 9, is inconsistent with his statement here.

A.U.C. 537
2 Hasdrubal ad eum navium numerum quem a fratre
3 instructum paratumque acceperat decem adiectis,[1]
quadraginta navium classem Himilconi tradit atque
ita Carthagine profectus naves[2] prope terram, exercitum in litore ducebat, paratus confligere quacumque
4 parte copiarum hostis occurrisset. Cn. Scipio postquam movisse ex hibernis hostem audivit, primo idem
consilii fuit; deinde minus terra propter ingentem
famam novorum auxiliorum concurrere ausus, delecto
milite ad naves imposito quinque et triginta navium
classe ire obviam hosti pergit.
5 Altero ab Tarracone die ad stationem[3] decem
milia passuum distantem ab ostio Hiberi amnis pervenit. Inde duae Massiliensium speculatoriae prae-
missae rettulere classem Punicam[4] stare in ostio
6 fluminis castraque in ripa posita. Itaque ut impro-
vidos incautosque universo simul effuso terrore
opprimeret, sublatis ancoris ad hostem vadit. Multas
et locis altis positas turres Hispania habet, quibus et
speculis et propugnaculis adversus latrones utuntur.
7 Inde primo conspectis hostium navibus datum signum
Hasdrubali est, tumultusque prius in terra et castris
quam ad mare et ad naves[5] est ortus, nondum aut
pulsu remorum strepituque alio nautico exaudito aut
8 aperientibus classem promunturiis, cum repente

[1] adiectis *Luchs*: adiecit *P* (*Madvig*).
[2] naves *Ruperti*: nauibus *P*.
[3] ad stationem ς: stationem *P*.
[4] Punicam ς: in publicam *P*.
[5] et ad naves *P*: ac naves *Luchs*.

---

[1] These numbers do not exactly agree with those given at XXI. xxii. 4.
[2] *i.e.* New Carthage, the modern Cartagena.

in Spain by land and sea. To the number of ships, B.C. 217 all rigged and fitted out, which Hasdrubal had taken over from his brother he added ten, and entrusted the fleet of forty sail to Himilco;[1] and then, setting out from Carthage,[2] he made his ships keep near the land and led his army along the shore, prepared to do battle with whatever part of their forces the Romans might bring against him. When Gnaeus Scipio learned that the enemy had left his winter quarters, he was minded at first to do the same; but on second thoughts concluded not to risk a battle on land, in view of the enormous number of auxiliaries with which rumour credited the Carthaginian, and embarking some of his best troops, went out to meet the enemy with a fleet of five and thirty ships.

On the second day out of Tarraco he came to an anchorage ten miles from the mouth of the river Ebro. Thence he dispatched two Massiliot scouting vessels, who reported that the Punic fleet was lying in the mouth of the river and their camp established on the bank. Accordingly, in order to take them off their guard and unprepared, while at the same time spreading a universal panic, he weighed anchor and proceeded towards the enemy. The Spaniards have numerous towers built on heights, which they use both as watch-towers and also for protection against pirates. From one of these the hostile ships were first descried, and on a signal being made to Hasdrubal, the alarm broke out on land and in the camp before it reached the sea and the ships; for no one had yet heard the beat of the oars or other nautical sounds, nor had the promontories yet disclosed the fleet to view, when suddenly

A.U.C. 537 eques alius super alium ab Hasdrubale missus vagos
in litore quietosque in tentoriis suis, nihil minus
quam hostem aut proelium eo die exspectantes, con-
scendere naves propere atque arma capere iubet;
classem Romanam iam haud procul portu esse.
9 Haec equites dimissi passim imperabant; mox
Hasdrubal ipse cum omni exercitu aderat, varioque
omnia tumultu strepunt ruentibus in naves simul
remigibus militibusque fugientium magis e terra[1]
10 quam in pugnam euntium modo. Vixdum omnes
conscenderant, cum alii resolutis oris in ancoras
evehuntur,[2] alii, ne quid teneat, ancoralia incidunt,
raptimque omnia ac[3] praepropere agendo militum
apparatu nautica ministeria impediuntur, trepidatione nautarum capere et aptare arma miles prohibetur.[4]
11 Et iam Romanus non adpropinquabat modo, sed
derexerat etiam in pugnam naves. Itaque non ab
hoste et proelio magis Poeni quam suomet ipsi
tumultu turbati et temptata verius pugna quam inita
12 in fugam averterunt classem. Et cum adversi amnis
os[5] lato agmini et tum[6] multis simul venientibus
haud sane intrabile esset, in litus passim naves
egerunt, atque alii vadis alii sicco litore excepti, partim

[1] e terra ς: e terrarum *P*: *deleted by Bisschop.*
[2] evehuntur *Gronovius*: eueherentur *P*.
[3] omnia ac *Gronovius and Drakenborch*: omnia *P*.
[4] prohibetur ς: prohibebatur *P*.
[5] amnis os *Gronovius*: adnisos *P*.
[6] tum *Luchs*: tam *P*.

---

[1] The *orae* were cables by which the stern of the vessel was made fast to the shore while the prow was held in position by anchors.

one galloper after another, sent off by Hasdrubal, B.C. 217 dashed up to the sailors, who were strolling about the beach or resting in their tents and thinking of nothing so little as of the enemy or of fighting on that day, and bade them board their ships in haste and arm themselves, for the Roman fleet was even then close to the harbour. These orders the gallopers who had been sent out carried far and wide, and presently Hasdrubal himself appeared on the scene with his entire army, and all was noise and confusion as the rowers and soldiers rushed down together to their ships, as though their object were rather to flee the shore than to enter battle. Hardly were they all on board, when some cast off the hawsers[1] and swung out on to their anchors, and others—that nothing might detain them—cut the anchor cables, and, in the hurry and excessive haste with which everything was done, the soldiers' gear interfered with the sailors in the performance of their tasks, and the confusion of the sailors kept the soldiers from taking and fitting on their armour.

By this time the Romans were not only drawing near, but had already formed their ships in order of battle. The result was that the Phoenicians were dismayed alike by the enemy's attack and by their own confusion, and after making rather a pretence of fighting than actually engaging, turned about and ran for it. With a line so extended—and many ships came up at the same time—they were quite unable to get into the river's mouth against the current, but rowed in anywhere to the land; and getting ashore, some through shoals and others on a dry beach, some with their arms and some with-

A.U.C. 537 armati partim inermes, ad instructam per litus aciem suorum perfugere; duae tamen primo concursu captae erant Punicae naves, quattuor suppressae.

XX. Romani, quamquam terra hostium erat armatamque aciem toto praetentam litore[1] cernebant, haud cunctanter insecuti trepidam hostium classem,
2 naves omnes, quae non aut perfregerant proras litori[2] inlisas aut carinas fixerant vadis religatas puppibus in altum extraxere, ad quinque et viginti naves e
3 quadraginta cepere. Neque id pulcherrimum eius victoriae fuit, sed quod una levi pugna toto eius orae mari potiti erant.

4 Itaque ad Onusam classe provecti; escensio ab navibus in terram facta. Cum urbem vi cepissent
5 captamque diripuissent, Carthaginem inde petunt, atque omnem agrum circa depopulati postremo tecta
6 quoque iniuncta[3] muro portisque incenderunt. Inde iam praeda gravis ad Longunticam pervenit classis, ubi vis magna sparti erat,[4] ad rem nauticam congesta ab Hasdrubale. Quod satis in usum fuit sublato
7 ceterum omne incensum est. Nec continentis modo praelecta est ora[5] sed in Ebusum insulam trans-

[1] litore *Madvig*: in litore *P*.
[2] litori ς: litoreis *P*.
[3] iniuncta *edd.*: incuncta P^1: incomta P^2.
[4] sparti erat *Madvig*: spartis *P*: sparti fuit ς.
[5] praelecta est ora *Weissenborn and Madvig*: periectas oras *P*: perlecta est ora *Frigell*.

---

[1] Polybius says that they lost two ships with their crews, and the oars and marines of four others (III. xcvi. 4).

[2] Longuntica, otherwise unknown, was probably not far from New Carthage, for the Spartarius Campus (so named from a kind of rush-grass, still called esparto, which was

out, they fled to the battle-line of their friends, which was drawn up along the shore. Two, however, of the Punic ships had been taken in the first attack and four had been sunk.[1] B.C. 217

XX. The Romans, although the land was in the possession of the enemy, whose line of battle could be seen extending all along the shore, continued without the slightest hesitation to press their pursuit of the terror-stricken fleet, and, attaching cables to the stern of every vessel which had neither broken its prow on the beach nor grounded its keel in the shoals, they towed it out to sea, until they had captured some twenty-five of the forty ships. Nor was this the most brilliant feature of the victory, but the fact that the Romans in one easy battle had made themselves the masters of all that coast.

So they spread their sails for Onusa, where they disembarked and stormed and sacked the city, and thence laid a course for Carthage, and after devastating all the country round about, ended by setting fire even to the buildings that adjoined the walls and gates. Then the fleet—heavy-laden now with plunder—sailed to Longuntica,[2] where they found a great quantity of esparto-grass, which Hasdrubal had got together for the use of his ships. Of this they took what they needed and burned all the rest. And they not only cruised along the mainland, but crossed over to the island of Ebusus.[3]

used for twisting into rope) lay inland from the latter town (see Strabo, III iv. 9, p. 160; and Pliny, *N.H.* XIX. XXX.).

[3] Ebusus is the Phoenician name for either of the two islands usually known by their Greek name Pityusae—both names signifying pine-clad. Here the larger of the two is meant.

A.U.C. 537 missum. Ibi[1] urbe, quae caput insulae est, biduum
8 nequiquam summo labore oppugnata, ubi in spem
9 inritam frustra teri tempus animadversum est, ad
populationem agri versi, direptis aliquot incensisque
vicis, maiore quam ex continenti praeda parta cum
in naves se recepissent, ex Baliaribus insulis legati
pacem petentes ad Scipionem venerunt.
10 Inde flexa retro classis reditumque in citeriora
11 provinciae, quo omnium populorum, qui cis Hiberum
incolunt,[2] multorum et ultimae Hispaniae legati concurrerunt; sed qui vere dicionis imperiique Romani
facti sint obsidibus datis populi amplius fuere[3]
12 centum viginti.[4] Igitur terrestribus quoque copiis
satis fidens Romanus usque ad saltum[5] Castulonensem
est progressus. Hasdrubal in Lusitaniam ac propius
Oceanum concessit.

XXI. Quietum inde fore videbatur reliquum
aestatis tempus fuissetque per Poenum hostem;
2 sed praeterquam quod ipsorum Hispanorum inquieta
avidaque in novas res sunt ingenia, Mandonius In-
3 dibilisque,[6] qui antea Ilergetum regulus fuerat, postquam Romani ab saltu recessere ad maritimam oram,
concitis popularibus in agrum pacatum sociorum
4 Romanorum ad populandum venerunt. Adversus

[1] ibi ς: ubi *P.*
[2] cis Hiberum incolunt *Gronovius*: hiberum incolunt *P.*
[3] fuere *edd.*: fuerent *P*: fuerunt ς.
[4] centum viginti ς: centu uiginti milia *P.*
[5] saltum ς: factum *P.*
[6] Indibilisque ς: indebilisque *P* (*for the evidence see Weissenborn-Mueller, Anhang p.* 154).

[1] Now Cazlona. The pass led through the Sierra Morena, north of the city, which was famous for the silver and lead mines in its neighbourhood. Castulo enjoyed a close alliance

There they endeavoured strenuously for two days, B.C. 217
but without success, to capture the chief city of the island. And when they saw that their hopes were vain and their time was being wasted, they betook themselves to pillaging the country-side, and after sacking and burning several villages, returned to their ships with more booty than they had collected from the mainland. Here envoys from the Baliaric islands came to Scipio to sue for peace.

The fleet now put about and returned to the northern part of the province, and thither flocked ambassadors from all the communities on this side of the Ebro and even from many places in farthest Spain; but the communities that gave hostages and really came under the rule and government of Rome were more than a hundred and twenty. Feeling, therefore, sufficiently strong on land, as well as on the sea, the Roman general advanced as far as the pass of Castulo.[1] Hasdrubal retired into Lusitania, nearer the ocean.

XXI. It looked as if the rest of the summer would be undisturbed, and so it would have been as far as the Phoenicians were concerned. But, besides that the Spaniards themselves are constitutionally restless and eager for change, no sooner had the Romans withdrawn from the pass to the sea-coast, than Mandonius and Indibilis—the latter had formerly been a chieftain of the Ilergetes—roused up their countrymen and invaded the peaceful territories of Rome's allies, on a marauding expedition.

with the Carthaginians and one of its daughters became the wife of Hannibal. In 214 B.C. it revolted to the Romans, but by 211 was again in the hands of the Carthaginians (XXIV. xii. 7; XXVI. xx. 6).

A.U.C. 537 eos tribunus militum[1] cum expeditis auxiliis a Scipione missi levi certamine ut tumultuariam manum fudere, mille hominibus[2] occisis quibusdam captis[3]
5 magnaque parte armis exuta. Hic tamen tumultus cedentem ad Oceanum Hasdrubalem cis Hiberum
6 ad socios tutandos retraxit. Castra Punica in agro Ilergavonensium,[4] castra Romana ad Novam Classem
7 erant, cum fama repens alio avertit bellum. Celtiberi, qui principes regionis suae legatos miserant[5] obsidesque dederant Romanis, nuntio misso a Scipione exciti arma capiunt provinciamque Carthaginiensium
8 valido exercitu invadunt. Tria oppida vi expugnant; inde cum ipso Hasdrubale duobus proeliis egregie pugnant; ad quindecim milia hostium occiderunt, quattuor milia cum multis militaribus signis capiunt.

XXII. Hoc statu rerum in Hispania P. Scipio in provinciam venit prorogato post consulatum imperio ab senatu missus cum triginta longis navibus et octo
2 milibus militum magnoque commeatu advecto. Ea classis ingens agmine onerariarum procul visa cum magna laetitia civium sociorumque portum Tarra-
3 conis ex alto tenuit. Ibi milite exposito profectus

[1] tribunus militum *Gronovius*: tribus mili//bus (ti *stood where erasure is*) *P*.
[2] mille hominibus *Madvig*: momnis P^1: omnibus P^2.
[3] captis ς: captisque *P*.
[4] Ilergavonensium *Alschefski*: lergavonensium *P*.
[5] legatos miserant *Gronovius*: legatos *P*.

---

[1] Perhaps identical with *ad Novas* mentioned in the *Itinerarium Antonini* as between Ilerda and Tarraco.

[2] The mention of captured standards points to Valerius Antias as Livy's source, for similar references occur in no less than five of the extant fragments.

To oppose them Scipio dispatched a tribune of the soldiers with light-armed auxiliaries. They easily routed the enemy—a mere hastily-organized militia—slaying a thousand of them, making some prisoners, and disarming the greater part. Nevertheless, this outbreak induced Hasdrubal, who was retreating towards the ocean, to turn back and cross the Ebro, for the purpose of protecting his allies. The Phoenicians were in camp in the country of the Ilergavonenses, the Romans near Nova Classis,[1] when tidings came which gave at once a new turn to the campaign. The Celtiberians, who had sent their leading men to treat with the Romans and had given hostages, incited by a message from Scipio, rose up in arms and invaded the Carthaginian province with a powerful army. They captured three towns by assault, and afterwards twice engaged successfully in battle with Hasdrubal himself, slaying some fifteen thousand of their enemies, and taking four thousand prisoners, with many military standards.[2] B.C. 217

XXII. Such was the position of affairs in Spain when Publius Scipio came into the province.[3] The senate had prolonged his command after the consulship and had sent him out with thirty[4] men-of-war and eight thousand soldiers and a great convoy of supplies. This fleet, which the number of cargo-vessels swelled to an enormous size, caused great rejoicing amongst the Romans and their allies, when it was made out in the offing and standing in dropped anchor in the harbour of Tarraco. There

[3] Scipio had been appointed when consul (218 B.C.) to take command of the Roman forces destined for Spain (xxi. lx. 1 and Polyb. iii. xcvii. 2).

[4] Polybius says twenty (*ibid.*).

A.U.C. 537 Scipio fratri se[1] coniungit, ac deinde communi animo consilioque gerebant bellum.

4 Occupatis igitur Carthaginiensibus Celtiberico bello haud cunctanter Hiberum transgrediuntur nec ullo viso hoste Saguntum pergunt ire, quod ibi obsides totius Hispaniae traditos ab Hannibale fama
5 erat modico in arce custodiri praesidio. Id unum pignus inclinatos ad Romanam societatem omnium Hispaniae populorum animos morabatur, ne sanguine
6 liberum suorum culpa defectionis lueretur. Eo vinculo Hispaniam vir unus sollerti[2] magis quam fideli consilio exsolvit. Abelux[3] erat Sagunti nobilis Hispanus, fidus ante Poenis, tum, qualia plerumque sunt barbarorum ingenia, cum fortuna mutaverat
7 fidem. Ceterum transfugam sine magnae rei proditione venientem ad hostes nihil aliud quam unum vile atque infame corpus esse ratus id agebat ut quam maximum emolumentum novis sociis esset.
8 Circumspectis igitur omnibus, quae fortuna potestatis eius poterat facere, obsidibus potissimum tradendis animum adiecit, eam unam rem maxime ratus conciliaturam Romanis principum Hispaniae amicitiam.
9 Sed cum iniussu Bostaris praefecti satis sciret nihil obsidum custodes facturos esse, Bostarem ipsum

[1] fratri se ς: fratris *P.*
[2] sollerti (solerti) ς: sollertia *P.*
[3] exsolvit. Abelux (abelox) ς: exsollicitatelux *P.*

[1] The town had not, apparently, been completely razed, as Alorcus had informed the Saguntines that it would be (XXI. xiii. 6).

Scipio disembarked his troops and set out to join B.C. 217
his brother; and from that time forward they carried on the war with perfect harmony of temper and of purpose.

Accordingly, while the Carthaginians were taken up with the Celtiberian campaign, they lost no time in crossing the Ebro, and seeing nothing of any enemy, marched directly on Saguntum,[1] where it was said that hostages from all over Spain were being guarded in the citadel by a small garrison, to whose keeping they had been consigned by Hannibal. It was this pledge alone that checked the inclination of all the Spanish states to ally themselves with Rome, for fear that the blood of their own children might expiate the guilt of their defection. From this constraint Spain was released by the machinations—more clever than honest—of one man. Abelux was his name, and he was a noble Spaniard of Saguntum. Loyal hitherto to the Phoenicians, he had now—as barbarians are for the most part prone to do—altered his allegiance with the alteration in their fortunes. But reflecting that a deserter who went over to the enemy without betraying to them something of great moment was but a single worthless and dishonoured individual, he proposed to benefit his new allies to the utmost extent of his ability. And considering everything that fortune could put into his power, he inclined for choice to deliver up the hostages, believing that this was the one thing that would most effectively secure for the Romans the friendship of the Spanish leaders.

But since he knew that the men guarding the hostages would do nothing without the orders of

A.U.C. 537 10 arte adgreditur. Castra extra urbem in ipso litore
habebat Bostar, ut aditum ea parte[1] intercluderet
Romanis. Ibi eum in secretum abductum velut
11 ignorantem monet quo statu sit res: metum con-
tinuisse ad eam diem Hispanorum animos, quia
procul Romani abessent; nunc cis Hiberum castra
Romana esse, arcem tutam perfugiumque novas
volentibus res; itaque quos metus non teneat bene-
12 ficio et gratia devinciendos esse. Miranti Bostari
percunctantique quodnam id subitum tantae rei
donum posset esse, "Obsides" inquit "in civitates
13 remitte. Id et privatim[2] parentibus, quorum maximum nomen in civitatibus est suis, et publice populis
14 gratum erit. Volt sibi quisque credi, et habita fides
ipsam plerumque obligat fidem. Ministerium resti-
tuendorum domos obsidum mihimet deposco ipse, ut
opera quoque impensa consilium adiuvem meum et
rei suapte natura gratae quantam insuper gratiam
possim adiciam."

15 Homini non ad cetera Punica ingenia callido ut
persuasit, nocte clam progressus ad hostium stationes,
conventis quibusdam auxiliaribus Hispanis et ab his
16 ad Scipionem perductus, quid adferret expromit et
fide accepta dataque ac loco et tempore constituto
ad obsides tradendos Saguntum redit. Diem insequentem absumpsit cum Bostare mandatis ad rem

[1] ea parte ς: ex parte *P*.
[2] id et privatim ς: de priuatim *P*: inde priuatim P^{2}.

Bostar, the governor, he artfully approached Bostar B.C. 217
himself, who was encamped outside the city, on the very shore, to preclude the approach of the Romans from that quarter. Taking him on one side, he explained the situation, as though the other had no knowledge of it. Fear, he said, had until then kept the Spaniards down, because the Romans were a long way off; now the Roman camp was on this side of the Ebro, a sure stronghold and asylum for any who wished a change; those, accordingly, who were not bound by fear must be secured by kindness and generosity. When Bostar asked in amazement what this gift could be that should suddenly be of so great value, "Send back the hostages to their homes," said Abelux. "That will at once be grateful personally to their parents, who are the people of most consequence in their own states, and to their tribes in general. Everyone wishes to be trusted: confide in people, and almost always you confirm their confidence in you. The task of restoring the hostages to their homes I request for myself, that I may work, as well as counsel, for the furtherance of my plan, and to an act that is gracious in itself lend such added grace as I am able."

Once he had brought Bostar round—for his wits were not as sharp as those of most Phoenicians—he departed secretly by night for the enemy's outposts, and encountering certain Spanish auxiliaries, who conducted him to Scipio, disclosed his plan, and when he had given pledges and received them, and had agreed upon a time and place for turning over the hostages, returned to Saguntum. The following day he spent with Bostar, receiving

A.U.C. 537 17 agendam accipiendis. Dimissus cum se nocte iturum,
ut custodias hostium falleret, constituisset, ad com-
positam cum iis horam excitatis custodibus puerorum
profectus, veluti ignarus in praeparatas sua fraude
18 insidias ducit. In castra Romana perducti; cetera
omnia de reddendis obsidibus sicut cum Bostare
constitutum erat acta per eum eodem[1] ordine, quo
si Carthaginiensium nomine sic ageretur.

19 Maior aliquanto Romanorum gratia fuit in re pari
quam quanta futura Carthaginiensium fuerat. Illos
enim graves superbosque in rebus secundis expertos
20 fortuna et timor mitigasse videri poterat: Romanus
primo adventu, incognitus ante, ab re clementi
liberalique initium fecerat; et Abelux, vir prudens,
21 haud frustra videbatur socios mutasse. Itaque ingenti consensu defectionem omnes spectare; armaque extemplo mota forent, ni hiems, quae Romanos
quoque et Carthaginienses concedere[2] in tecta coegit,
intervenisset.

XXIII. Haec in Hispania[3] secunda aestate Punici
belli gesta, cum in Italia paulum intervalli cladibus
2 Romanis sollers cunctatio Fabi fecisset; quae ut

[1] eum eodem *Weissenborn*: eundem eodem: *Heerwagen*: eundem *P*.

[2] concedere P^2: quoque concedere P^1.

[3] in Hispania *Koch*: in hispania quoque *P*.

instructions how to carry out the enterprise, and B.C. 217 left him with the understanding that he was to go at night, in order to elude the enemy's sentinels. At the hour agreed on with the Romans he wakened the boys' custodians, and led them all, as if unwittingly, into the trap prepared by his own treachery. They were then conducted to the Roman camp. The remainder of the plan for the restoration of the hostages to their friends was carried out, through the agency of Abelux, exactly as he and Bostar had agreed, and everything was done as it would have been if he had been acting in the name of the Carthaginians.

The gratitude which the Romans won under such circumstances was much greater than the Carthaginians would have enjoyed. For the Carthaginians had been found to be harsh and arrogant in the hour of their prosperity, and their gentleness might have appeared as the result of misfortune and timidity; but the Romans on first coming thither —and till then they were unknown—had begun with an act of clemency and liberality, and Abelux was held to have shown discernment, and not without reason to have changed his friends. The Spaniards were therefore all with one accord intending to revolt, and would have drawn the sword at once, if winter had not intervened and compelled both Romans and Carthaginians to retire to their quarters.

XXIII. Such was the course of events in Spain in the second summer of the Punic war. In Italy meanwhile the defeated Romans had been afforded a little breathing space by Fabius's wise policy of holding back. This policy, though it occasioned

A.U.C. 537 Hannibalem non mediocri sollicitum cura habebat,
tandem eum militiae magistrum delegisse Romanos
3 cernentem, qui bellum ratione non fortuna gereret,
ita contempta erat inter cives armatos pariter toga-
tosque, utique postquam absente eo temeritate
magistri equitum laeto verius[1] dixerim quam pros-
4 pero eventu pugnatum fuerat. Accesserant duae
res ad augendam invidiam dictatoris, una fraude ac
dolo Hannibalis, quod, cum a perfugis ei monstratus
ager dictatoris esset, omnibus circa solo aequatis ab
uno eo ferrum ignemque et vim omnem hostilem[2]
abstineri iussit, ut occulti alicuius pacti ea merces
5 videri posset, altera ipsius facto, primo forsitan
dubio, quia non exspectata in eo senatus auctoritas
est, ad extremum haud ambigue in maximam laudem
6 verso. In permutandis captivis, quod sic primo
Punico bello factum erat, convenerat inter duces
Romanum Poenumque ut quae pars plures[3] reciperet
quam daret argenti pondo bina et selibras in militem
7 praestaret. Ducentis[4] quadraginta septem cum plures
Romanus quam Poenus recepisset argentumque pro
eis debitum saepe iactata in senatu re, quoniam non
8 consuluisset patres, tardius erogaretur, inviolatum

[1] verius *Gronovius*: ueprius *P*: ut uerius ς.
[2] hostilem *Crévier*: hostium *P* (*Madvig*).
[3] plures *Valla*: prius *P*: plus ς (*Madvig*).
[4] ducentis *Madvig*: CC *P*: ducentos *edd. before Madvig.*

---

[1] So Coriolanus had spared the farms of the patricians in order to make bad blood between them and the plebeians (II. xxxix. 6).

Hannibal no small anxiety—for he saw that the B.C. 217
Romans had finally chosen a military leader who waged war as reason and not as blind chance dictated—yet incurred the scorn of Fabius's fellow citizens, both soldiers and civilians, especially when his absence had been followed, thanks to the rashness of the master of the horse, by a battle which may truthfully be characterized as having ended with more rejoicing than success. Two things, moreover, increased the dictator's unpopularity. One was a crafty ruse of Hannibal's. Some deserters having pointed out to him the dictator's farm, he razed to the ground all the buildings in its neighbourhood, but ordered that this one place should be preserved from fire and sword and every kind of hostile violence, in order that it might appear that Fabius was in this way being rewarded for some secret compact.[1] The other was something that he did himself, which, though perhaps open to criticism in the first place—because he had not waited for the authorization of the senate—redounded in the upshot, and in no uncertain manner, greatly to his fame. In exchanging prisoners the Roman and Phoenician generals had followed the example set in the first Punic war and had agreed that the side which recovered more men than it restored should pay for each two pounds and a half of silver. The Romans recovered two hundred and forty-seven more than the Phoenicians, but the senate, though the matter was often discussed, was slow in voting the money owing for them, on the ground that the dictator had not consulted them; till finally Fabius sent his son Quintus to Rome to sell the farm which the enemy had spared,

A.U.C. 537 ab hoste agrum misso Romam Quinto filio[1] vendidit
fidemque publicam impendio privato exsolvit.
9 Hannibal pro Gereoni moenibus, cuius urbis captae
atque incensae ab se in usum horreorum pauca re-
10 liquerat tecta, in stativis erat. Inde frumentatum
duas exercitus partes mittebat; cum tertia ipse ex-
pedita in statione erat simul castris praesidio et
circumspectans necunde impetus in frumentatores
fieret.

XXIV. Romanus tunc exercitus in agro Larinati
erat. Praeerat Minucius magister equitum, profecto, sicut ante dictum est, ad urbem dictatore.
2 Ceterum castra, quae in monte alto ac tuto loco
posita fuerant, iam in planum deferuntur; agita-
banturque pro ingenio ducis consilia calidiora, ut
impetus aut in frumentatores palatos aut in castra
relicta cum levi praesidio fieret.
3 Nec Hannibalem fefellit cum duce mutatam esse
belli rationem et ferocius quam consultius rem hostes
4 gesturos. Ipse autem—quod minime quis crederet
—cum hostis propius esset, tertiam partem militum
frumentatum duabus in castris retentis dimisit;
5 dein castra ipsa propius hostem movit duo ferme
a Gereonio milia in tumulum hosti conspectum, ut
intentum se[2] sciret esse ad frumentatores, si qua
6 vis fieret, tutandos. Propior inde ei atque ipsis

[1] Quinto filio *Gronovius*: qui filio P^1: filio P^2.
[2] intentum se *Geist*: intentum *P*.

and discharged the nation's obligation at his own expense. B.C. 217

Hannibal lay encamped under the walls of Gereonium, where he had left a few buildings standing, to serve as granaries, when he captured and burned the city. From there he would send two-thirds of his army to gather corn; the other third, ready to march, he kept at the post under his own command, with the twofold object of protecting the camp and of guarding lest any attack be made upon his foragers.

XXIV. The Roman army was at that time in the neighbourhood of Larinum. Minucius, the master of the horse, was in command, for the dictator, as has been said before, had departed for the City. The camp had been established on a high hill in a position of security, but was now brought down to level ground; and more vigorous measures were being discussed—in keeping with the temper of the general—for attacking the enemy's scattered foragers, or his camp, which was left but lightly garrisoned.

Hannibal saw well enough that the change in leaders had brought a change in strategy, and that the Romans were likely to be more bold than prudent. But though the enemy was close at hand, he himself did something that would almost seem incredible, and sent out a third part of his troops to forage, retaining two-thirds in his camp; then he brought the camp itself up nearer the enemy, about two miles away from Gereonium, to a hill in full sight of the Romans, that they might know that he was watching to protect his foragers, if they should be at all molested. He then observed

A.U.C. 537 imminens Romanorum castris tumulus apparuit; ad quem capiendum si luce palam iretur, quia haud[1] dubie hostis breviore via praeventurus erat, nocte
7 clam missi Numidae ceperunt. Quos tenentes locum contempta paucitate Romani postero die cum deiecissent,[2] ipsi eo transferunt castra. Tum utique[3]
8 exiguum spatii vallum a vallo aberat, et id ipsum totum[4] prope compleverat Romana acies. Simul et per aversa castra[5] equitatus cum levi armatura emissus in frumentatores late caedem fugamque
9 hostium palatorum fecit. Nec acie certare Hannibal ausus, quia tanta paucitate vix castra, si oppugna-
10 rentur, tutari poterat. Iamque artibus Fabi,[6] sedendo et cunctando, bellum gerebat receperatque suos in priora castra, quae pro Gereoni moenibus erant.
11 Iusta quoque acie et conlatis signis dimicatum quidam auctores sunt: primo concursu Poenum usque ad castra fusum, inde eruptione facta repente versum terrorem in Romanos, Numeri Decimi[7] Samnitis
12 deinde interventu[8] proelium restitutum. Hunc, principem genere ac divitiis non Boviani modo, unde erat, sed toto Samnio, iussu dictatoris octo milia

[1] quia haud ς: haud quia *P*.
[2] deiecissent *Gronovius*: iecissent *P*.
[3] tum utique *Weissenborn*: tumutitaque *P*: itaque *Madvig*.
[4] totum ς: tota *P*.
[5] per aversa castra *Gronovius*: per auersa castra e castris hannibalis *P*: per aversa a castris Hannibalis *Madvig*.
[6] *After* Fabi *P has* pars exercitus aberat iam fame *which Hertz deleted*.
[7] Numeri (Num.) Decimi ς: numeris deciri *P*.
[8] interventu ς: uentu *P*: aduentu ς.

---

[1] By the *Porta Decumana*.

a hill even nearer the Romans and threatening their very camp; but since, if he should attempt to take it openly by daylight, the Romans, who had a shorter way to go, would doubtless get ahead of him, he sent some Numidians secretly in the night, and they seized the hill. They were holding the place next day, when the Romans, despising their scanty numbers, dislodged them and transferred their own camp thither. There was now, at all events, but a very little space between rampart and rampart, and this the Romans had pretty well covered with their troops, which they had drawn up in line of battle. At the same time they had sent out their cavalry and skirmishers from the side of the camp which was farthest from the enemy,[1] and these had fallen upon the scattered foragers, whom they routed with great slaughter. Still, Hannibal did not dare to fight a battle, for his forces were so small that he was hardly able to defend his camp, if the Romans should assault it, and he now began to wage war by the arts of Fabius, inaction and delay, and had withdrawn his troops to their former camp, which lay under the walls of Gereonium. B.C. 217

Some writers relate that there was even a regular pitched battle, in which the Phoenicians were driven from the field at the first encounter and pursued all the way to their camp, from which they sallied and quickly dismayed the Romans in their turn; but that Numerius Decimius the Samnite then came up and restored the day. They say that Decimius, who was the person of most consequence both for family and fortune, not only in his own town of Bovianum but in all Samnium, was on his way to

A.U.C. 537 peditum et equites quingentos ducentem[1] in castra, ab tergo cum apparuisset Hannibali, speciem parti utrique praebuisse[2] novi praesidii cum Q. Fabio ab
13 Roma venientis. Hannibalem insidiarum quoque aliquid timentem recepisse suos, Romanum insecutum adiuvante Samnite duo castella eo die expugnasse.
14 Sex milia hostium caesa, quinque admodum Romanorum; tamen in tam pari prope clade vanam famam[3] egregiae victoriae cum vanioribus litteris magistri equitum Romam perlatam.

XXV. De iis rebus persaepe et in senatu et in
2 contione actum est. Cum laeta civitate dictator unus nihil nec famae nec litteris crederet, et ut vera omnia essent, secunda se magis quam adversa
3 timere diceret, tum M. Metilius[4] tribunus plebis id
4 enim vero[5] ferendum esse negat: non praesentem solum dictatorem obstitisse rei bene gerendae, sed absentem etiam gestae obstare et in ducendo bello sedulo[6] tempus terere, quo diutius in magistratu sit solusque et Romae et in exercitu imperium habeat;
5 quippe consulum alterum in acie cecidisse, alterum specie classis Punicae persequendae procul ab Italia
6 ablegatum; duos praetores Sicilia atque Sardinia occupatos, quarum[7] neutra hoc tempore provincia praetore egeat; M. Minucium magistrum equitum,

[1] quingentos ducentem *Gronovius*: adducentem *P.*
[2] utrique praebuisse ς: utriusque praebuisset *P.*
[3] vanam famam *Woelfflin*: famam *P.*
[4] Metilius *Sigonius* (Plut. *Fab.* 7, 8, 9): metellus *P.*
[5] id enim vero ς: id enim *P.*
[6] sedulo ς: ac sedulo *P.*
[7] quarum ς: quorum *P.*

the camp, by the dictator's order, at the head of eight thousand foot and five hundred horse, when, appearing on Hannibal's rear, he was mistaken by both armies for reinforcements coming up with Quintus Fabius from Rome. Hannibal, fearing some trap as well, drew back his men, and the Romans, pressing forward and assisted by the Samnites, carried, that same day, two redoubts. Six thousand of the enemy were slain and fully five thousand Romans. Nevertheless, though the losses had been so nearly equal, a foolish tale was carried to Rome of an extraordinary victory, with a letter from the master of the horse that was more foolish still. B.C. 217

XXV. These events were the occasion of many speeches both in the senate and in the popular assembly. The citizens rejoiced, and only the dictator refused to credit either rumour or dispatch, and declared that even though the story were all true, he feared success more than adversity. Then Marcus Metilius, tribune of the plebs, cried out that this was past all bearing: not only had the dictator prevented a successful engagement being fought while he was present, but he even objected now that the victory was won, and persisted in drawing out the war and wasting time, in order the longer to remain in office, and to continue, both at Rome and in the army, in sole possession of authority; for one of the consuls had fallen in battle, and the other—under the pretext of pursuing the Punic fleet—had been sent a great way off from Italy; the two praetors were employed in Sicily and Sardinia, neither of which required a praetor at this time; and Marcus Minucius, the master of the horse, that he might not see the enemy or

A.U.C. 537 ne hostem videret, ne quid rei bellicae gereret,
7 prope in custodia habitum. Itaque hercule non
Samnium modo, quo iam tamquam trans Hiberum
agro Poenis concessum sit, sed[1] Campanum Cale-
numque et Falernum agrum pervastatos esse, sedente
Casilini dictatore et legionibus populi Romani agrum
8 suum tutante. Exercitum cupientem pugnare et
magistrum equitum clausos prope intra vallum re-
tentos, tamquam hostibus captivis arma adempta.
9 Tandem, ut abscesserit inde dictator, ut obsidione
liberatos extra vallum egressos fudisse ac fugasse
10 hostes. Quas ob res, si antiquus animus plebei
Romanae esset, audaciter se laturum fuisse de[2]
abrogando Q. Fabi imperio; nunc modicam rogationem promulgaturum de aequando magistri equitum
11 et dictatoris iure. Nec tamen ne ita quidem prius
mittendum ad exercitum Q. Fabium quam consulem
in locum C. Flamini suffecisset.
12 Dictator contionibus se abstinuit in actione minime
populari.[3] Ne in senatu quidem satis aequis auribus
audiebatur, cum[4] hostem verbis extolleret biennique
clades per temeritatem atque inscitiam ducum ac-
13 ceptas referret et magistro[5] equitum quod contra
dictum suum pugnasset rationem diceret reddendam
14 esse. Si penes se summa imperii consiliique sit,

[1] sit, sed C^2: sititet *P*: sitit sed C^1: sit sed et ς.
[2] de ς: deinde *P*. [3] populari ς (*Madvig*): popularis *P*.
[4] cum *Hertz*: huncum P^1: hunc cum P^2.
[5] et magistro *Madvig*: magister *P*: magistroque ς: magistro *Frigell*.

---

[1] Livy appears not to have believed that Minucius was made a dictator. But *C.I.L.*, I. 1503 = Dessau, *Inscriptiones Latinae Selectae*, 11 (Hercolei | sacrum | M. Minuci. C. f. | dictator vov|| it), is ascribed by Mommsen to our Minucius, and Polybius (III. ciii. 4) says unequivocally that "two dictators were actually appointed for the same field of action."

carry out any military operation, had been kept almost a prisoner. Thus it had actually come to pass that not only Samnium—whose territories, as though they lay beyond the Ebro, had already been surrendered to the Phoenicians—but Campania, and the districts both of Cales and Falerii had been utterly laid waste; while the dictator sat still at Casilinum and used the legions of the Roman People to protect his own estate. The army—eager as it was to fight—and the master of the horse had virtually been cooped up and confined within the rampart; and their swords, as though they had been captured enemies, had been taken from them. At last, when the dictator had gone away, they had come out from behind their works, as if released from a blockade, and had routed and put to flight their enemies. For all these reasons, if their ancient spirit had still animated the Roman plebs, he would boldly have proposed the abrogation of Quintus Fabius's command; as it was, he should move the adoption of a moderate measure, to wit, the elevation of the master of the horse to a footing of equality with the dictator.[1] Yet, even so, they must not let Fabius rejoin his army till he had first installed a consul in the place of Gaius Flaminius. B.C. 217

The dictator refrained from making speeches to the people, in a cause that was far from popular. Even the senate listened coldly when he spoke in high terms of the enemy, and charging the reverses of the past two years to the rashness and ignorance of the Roman generals, declared that the master of the horse must answer to him for having fought against his orders. If his authority and

A.U.C. 537 prope diem effecturum ut sciant homines bono imperatore haud magni fortunam momenti esse, mentem
15 rationemque dominari, et in tempore et sine igno-
minia servasse exercitum quam multa milia hostium
16 occidisse maiorem gloriam esse. Huius generis
orationibus frustra habitis et consule creato M. Atilio
Regulo, ne praesens de iure imperii dimicaret, pridie
quam rogationis ferendae dies adesset, nocte ad exercitum abiit.

17 Luce orta cum plebis concilium esset, magis tacita
invidia dictatoris favorque magistri equitum animos
versabat quam satis audebant homines ad suadendum
quod volgo placebat prodire, et favore superante
18 auctoritas tamen rogationi deerat. Unus inventus
est suasor legis C. Terentius Varro, qui priore anno
praetor fuerat, loco non humili solum sed etiam
19 sordido ortus. Patrem lanium fuisse ferunt, ipsum
institorem mercis, filioque hoc ipso in servilia eius
artis ministeria usum.

XXVI. Is iuvenis, ut primum[1] ex eo genere
quaestus pecunia a patre relicta animos ad spem
liberalioris fortunae fecit togaque et forum placuere
2 proclamando pro sordidis hominibus causisque adversus rem et famam bonorum primum in notitiam

[1] ut primum *Perizonius*: utrum *P*: ut iam *Luterbacher*.

---

[1] This is possibly a sneer at Scipio, who after the Trebia took refuge with his beaten army behind the walls of Placentia and Cremona. In 205 B.C., Fabius's distrust of the Scipios was to take the form of bitter opposition to the son's project for invading Africa (XXVIII. xl.–xliii. and XXIX. xix.).

[2] He had been consul before, in 227 B.C.

strategy should be paramount, he would soon let B.C. 217
people know that with a good commander fortune was of little moment; that mind and reason were in control; and that to have preserved the army in its hour of danger, yet without disgrace,[1] was more glorious than to have slain many thousands of the enemy. After making several speeches to this purport, yet without effect, and presiding over the election of Marcus Atilius Regulus[2] to the consulship, that he might not take a personal part in the dispute about the command, on the day preceding the bringing forward of the resolution he left by night for the army.

When at break of day the plebs assembled in their council, though at heart they were inclined to dislike the dictator and to favour the master of the horse, yet they wanted sufficient courage to come forward and advocate a course which most of them approved, so that the motion, despite its exceeding popularity, lacked support. One man alone was found to urge the passage of the bill. This was Gaius Terentius Varro, praetor of the year before, whose antecedents were not merely base but even sordid. It is said that his father had been a butcher, who peddled his wares himself, and that he had employed this very son about the menial tasks associated with that calling.

XXVI. The young man had no sooner inherited from his father the money gained in this kind of occupation than he felt encouraged to hope for a more liberal career, and resolved to enter public life; and by declaiming on behalf of ignoble men and causes against the property and reputation of persons of the better sort achieved first notoriety

A.U.C. 537 3 populi, deinde ad honores pervenit, quaesturaque[1] et duabus aedilitatibus, plebeia et curuli, postremo et praetura perfunctus iam ad consulatus spem cum
4 adtolleret animos, haud parum callide auram favoris popularis ex dictatoria[2] invidia petit scitique plebis unus gratiam tulit.

5 Omnes eam rogationem, quique Romae quique in exercitu erant, aequi atque iniqui, praeter ipsum dictatorem in contumeliam eius latam acceperunt;
6 ipse qua gravitate animi criminantes se ad multitudinem inimicos tulerat eadem et populi in se
7 saevientis[3] iniuriam tulit; acceptisque in ipso itinere litteris senatus[4] de aequato imperio, satis fidens haudquaquam cum imperii iure artem imperandi aequatam, cum invicto[5] a civibus hostibusque animo ad exercitum rediit.

XXVII. Minucius vero, cum iam ante vix tolera-
2 bilis fuisset rebus secundis ac favore volgi, tum utique immodice immodesteque non Hannibale
3 magis victo ab se quam Q. Fabio gloriari: illum in rebus asperis unicum ducem ac parem quaesitum Hannibali, maiorem minori, dictatorem magistro equitum, quod nulla memoria habeat annalium, iussu populi aequatum in eadem civitate, in qua magistri

[1] quaesturaque ς (*Gronovius*): quaestura quoque *P*.
[2] dictatoria *P*: dictatoris ς (*Madvig*).
[3] saevientis ς: seuientem *P*.
[4] litteris senatus ς (*Madvig*): litteris s̄c̄. *P*.
[5] cum invicto ς: cumque inuicto *P*.

and then office. He had held the quaestorship and both aedileships—plebeian and curule—and finally even the praetorship. He now ventured to aspire to the consulship, and with considerable shrewdness sought to capture the favour of the populace by exploiting their animosity against the dictator, with the result that he alone reaped all the popularity growing out of the plebiscite. B.C. 217

Everyone, whether in Rome or with the army, whether friend or foe, looked on the passing of this bill as an insult to the dictator—everyone, that is, but the dictator himself, who with the same unruffled spirit with which he had borne the slanders uttered against him before the multitude by his adversaries now bore the injustice of the infuriated people. While still on the way he received a dispatch from the senate about the equal division of command, but fairly confident that though the authority of the commanders had been equalized, their abilities had not, he returned to the army with a spirit that neither fellow citizens nor enemies could daunt.

XXVII. As for Minucius, success and the favour of the crowd had already made him well-nigh insufferable. But now, at all events, he cast away all modesty and moderation and boasted of his triumph not only over Hannibal but over Quintus Fabius as well: that wonderful leader, to whom his countrymen had turned in their distress as a match for Hannibal, had by vote of the people been reduced to a level—the superior with his subordinate, the dictator with his master of the horse; and this action, to which history could afford no parallel, had been taken in that very state in which masters

A.U.C. 537 equitum virgas ac secures dictatoris tremere atque
4 horrere soliti sint: tantum suam felicitatem virtutemque enituisse. Ergo secuturum[1] se fortunam suam, si dictator in cunctatione[2] ac segnitie deorum
5 hominumque iudicio damnata perstaret. Itaque quo die primum congressus est cum Q. Fabio, statuendum omnium primum ait esse quem ad modum imperio
6 aequato utantur: se optimum ducere aut diebus alternis, aut, si maiora intervalla placerent, partitis temporibus alterius summum ius imperiumque esse,
7 ut par hosti non solum consilio[3] sed viribus etiam esset, si quam occasionem rei gerendae habuisset.
8 Q. Fabio haudquaquam id placere: omnia enim fortunam[4] eam habituram quaecumque temeritas collegae habuisset: sibi communicatum cum alio,[5]
9 non ademptum imperium esse: itaque se nunquam volentem parte qua posset rerum consilio gerendarum cessurum, nec se tempora aut dies imperii cum eo, exercitum divisurum, suisque consiliis, quoniam
10 omnia non liceret, quae posset servaturum. Ita obtinuit ut legiones, sicut consulibus mos esset, inter se dividerent. Prima et quarta Minucio,
11 secunda et tertia Fabio evenerunt. Item equites pari numero sociumque et Latini nominis auxilia

[1] secuturum *edd.*: secuturumque *P.*

[2] dictator in cunctatione (con-) *Gronovius*: dictatoris cunctationi *P.*

[3] non solum consilio ς (*Madvig*): solum non consilio *P*: non consilio solum *Alschefski.*

[4] enim fortunam ς: fortunam enim *P.*

[5] alio *P*: illo ς (*Madvig*): eo *Novák.*

---

[1] So in the campaign of Cannae (216 B.C.), Varro and Paulus commanded on alternate days. In the present instance, however, Polybius III. (ciii. 7) says that it was Fabius who proposed the alternation, and that Minucius preferred that the army be divided.

of the horse had been used to tremble and shudder B.C. 217 at the rods and axes of the dictator; so conspicuous had been his own success and courage. He would therefore follow up his good fortune, if the dictator persisted in that dilatory and inactive course which gods and men had united in condemning. Accordingly, on the day of his first meeting with Quintus Fabius, he said that the very first thing to be settled was the manner in which they should exercise the joint command: he himself thought that the best way would be for each to have supreme command and authority either every other day,[1] or, if longer periods seemed preferable, for equally apportioned times, to the end that he might be a match for the enemy not only in strategy but in numbers also, if he should meet with a favourable opportunity for fighting.

This proposal by no means suited Quintus Fabius, for he saw that everything which his rash colleague should have got control of would be controlled by Fortune: he had been made, he said, to share the supreme command with another, not deprived of it; he would therefore never voluntarily relinquish that share which he possessed of the power to guide the campaign prudently; he would not divide with Minucius the times or days of commanding, but would divide the army, and in accordance with his own plans would save what he could, since he was not permitted to save everything. In this way he brought about a division of the legions, such as was customary between consuls. The first and fourth fell to Minucius, the second and third to Fabius. In like manner they divided equally the cavalry and auxiliaries, both allies and Latins. The master of

A.U.C. 537 diviserunt. Castris quoque se separari magister equitum voluit.

XXVIII. Duplex inde Hannibali gaudium fuit—neque enim quicquam eorum quae apud hostes agerentur eum fallebat, et perfugis multa indicanti-
2 bus[1] et per suos explorantem;—nam et liberam Minuci temeritatem se suo modo captaturum et sollertiae Fabi dimidium virium decessisse.
3 Tumulus erat inter castra Minuci et Poenorum, quem qui occupasset haud dubie iniquiorem erat
4 hosti locum facturus. Eum non tam capere sine certamine volebat Hannibal, quamquam id operae pretium erat, quam causam certaminis cum Minucio, quem procursurum[2] ad obsistendum satis sciebat,
5 contrahere.[3] Ager omnis medius erat prima specie inutilis insidiatori, quia non modo silvestre quic-
6 quam, sed ne vepribus quidem vestitum habebat, re ipsa natus tegendis[4] insidiis, eo magis quod in nuda valle nulla talis fraus timeri poterat; et erant in anfractibus cavae rupes, ut quaedam earum ducenos
7 armatos possent capere. In has latebras, quot quemque locum apte insidere poterant, quinque milia
8 conduntur peditum equitumque. Necubi tamen aut motus alicuius temere egressi aut fulgor armorum fraudem in valle tam aperta detegeret, missis paucis prima luce ad capiendum quem ante diximus tumulum avertit oculos hostium.

[1] indicantibus ς: non indicantibus *P*: ultro indicantibus *Pluygers*.
[2] procursurum *Madvig*: per/occursurum *P*.
[3] contrahere ς: et contrahere *P*.
[4] tegendis ς: detegendis *P*.

the horse chose that their camps, too, should be separated. B.C. 217

XXVIII. All this caused Hannibal a twofold joy, for, fully acquainted as he was with whatever went on amongst his enemies both from much information brought in by deserters and from the discoveries of his own spies, he reckoned on entrapping the uncontrolled rashness of Minucius after his own fashion, while he saw that the sagacity of Fabius had been deprived of half its strength.

There was a hill between the camp of Minucius and that of the Phoenicians, and it was certain that he who occupied it would place his enemy in a rather bad position. This Hannibal was desirous not so much of capturing without a struggle—though this would have been worth while—as of using to bring on a battle with Minucius, who would sally forth, as he well knew, to oppose him. It appeared at first sight that none of the ground between could be used for an ambush, since it not only had nothing on it in the shape of trees, but was nowhere so much as screened with brambles. But in fact it was formed by nature for covering an ambuscade—all the more because in a bare valley no such trap could be suspected—for in its windings there were hollow cliffs, so large that some of them would hold two hundred soldiers. In these lurking-places Hannibal concealed five thousand foot and horse—as many in each as could readily lie in wait there. Lest, however, the movement of anyone who might carelessly step out or the glint of arms should betray the ruse, in a valley so bare and open, he dispatched a small party at dawn to seize the hill already mentioned and draw off the enemy's attention.

A.U.C. 537

9 Primo statim conspectu contempta paucitas, ac
sibi quisque deposcere pellendos inde hostes ac
locum[1] capiendum; dux ipse inter stolidissimos
ferocissimosque ad arma vocat et vanis minis[2]
10 increpat hostem. Principio levem armaturam di-
mittit; deinde conferto agmine mittit equites;
postremo, cum hostibus quoque subsidia mitti
11 videret, instructis legionibus procedit. Et Hannibal
laborantibus suis alia atque alia crescente[3] certamine
mittens auxilia peditum equitumque iam iustam
expleverat aciem, ac totis utrimque viribus certatur.
12 Prima levis armatura Romanorum, praeoccupatum
ex inferiore loco[4] succedens tumulum, pulsa de-
trusaque terrorem in succedentem intulit equitem
13 et ad signa legionum refugit. Peditum acies inter
perculsos impavida sola erat, videbaturque, si iusta
ac directa[5] pugna esset, haudquaquam impar
futura: tantum animorum fecerat prospere ante
14 paucos dies res gesta; sed exorti repente insidiatores
eum tumultum terroremque in latera utrimque
ab tergoque incursantes fecerunt ut nec animus[6]
ad pugnam neque ad fugam spes cuiquam superesset.

XXIX. Tum Fabius primo clamore paventium

[1] ac locum *Perizonius*: ad locum *P*.
[2] minis ς: animis et nimis *P*: animis et minis ς.
[3] crescente ς: aut crescente *P*.
[4] ex inferiore loco *Madvig*: inferiore loco *P*.
[5] directa *Madvig*: si recta *P*: recta ς.
[6] ut nec animus ς: nec ut animus *P*.

The Romans no sooner descried them than they laughed at their small numbers, and everybody asked to be assigned the duty of dislodging the Carthaginians and capturing the place. Their general himself, as fatuous and rash as anyone, called the men to arms and railed at the enemy with idle threats. First he ordered out the light infantry; then he sent the cavalry off in a solid column; finally, when he saw that the enemy too were bringing up supports, he set forth with his legions in battle array. Hannibal likewise, as the struggle waxed hotter and his men were sore bested, sent in reinforcement after reinforcement, horse and foot, till he now had a regular army in the field, and both sides were engaged with all their forces. The Roman light infantry, as they were advancing from the lower ground on to the height which the enemy had already occupied, was the first to suffer a repulse, and as they were driven downhill, caused a panic among the cavalry, which was coming up behind them, and fled to the standards of the legions. These alone maintained their line undaunted, when all the rest were in full flight, and it looked as if, had the battle been a regular front-to-front engagement, they would have proved fully equal to their enemy—so encouraged had they been by the successful action a few days before. But the men in ambush, suddenly springing out and charging them on both flanks and in the rear, worked such havoc and alarm that not one of them had any courage left for fighting or any hope in flight. B.C. 217

XXIX. "There it is," said Fabius, when first the cries of the frightened soldiers were heard, and

A.U.C. 537

audito, dein conspecta procul turbata acie, "Ita est" inquit; "non celerius[1] quam timui deprendit
2 fortuna temeritatem. Fabio aequatus imperio Hannibalem et virtute et fortuna superiorem videt. Sed aliud iurgandi suscensendique tempus erit: nunc signa extra vallum proferte; victoriam hosti[2] extorqueamus, confessionem erroris civibus."

3 Iam magna ex parte caesis aliis, aliis circumspectantibus fugam Fabiana se acies repente velut
4 caelo demissa ad auxilium ostendit. Itaque, priusquam ad coniectum teli veniret aut manum consereret, et suos a fuga effusa et ab nimis[3] feroci pugna hostes continuit. Qui solutis ordinibus vage dissipati erant undique confugerunt ad integram
5 aciem; qui plures simul terga dederant conversi in hostem volventesque orbem nunc sensim referre pedem, nunc conglobati restare. Ac iam prope una acies facta erat victi atque integri exercitus
6 inferebantque signa in hostem, cum Poenus receptui cecinit, palam ferente Hannibale ab se Minucium, se ab Fabio victum.

7 Ita per variam fortunam diei maiore parte exacta
8 cum in castra reditum esset, Minucius convocatis militibus, "Saepe ego" inquit "audivi, milites, eum primum esse virum qui ipse consulat quid in rem

[1] non celerius *P*: celerius *Lipsius* (Plut., *Fab.* 12).
[2] hosti ς: hostibus *Drakenborch*: hostis *P*.
[3] ab nimis *M*²: ab animis *PC*¹*M*¹: a nimis *C*².

then the confusion in the distant battle-line became discernible; "misfortune has not overtaken rashness more quickly than I feared. Though made equal to Fabius in authority, he finds Hannibal his superior, both in courage and in fortune. But another time will do for upbraiding and resentment; for the present, march out from your trenches, and let us wrest from the enemy his victory and from our fellow citizens a confession of their blunder." B.C. 217

By this time large numbers of the Romans had either been slain or were casting about for a way to escape, when suddenly Fabius and his army appeared, as though they had come down from heaven to help them; and before they got within a javelin's range or struck a blow, had checked both the headlong flight of the Romans and the reckless fury of the enemy's attack. Those who had quitted their ranks and dispersed this way and that came running up on every side to the unbroken line; those who had retreated in a body faced about to meet the enemy and, forming a circle, at first slowly retreated, but presently, being more compactly drawn together, stood their ground. And now the beaten army and the fresh one had pretty much united into a single line and were ready to advance against the enemy, when Hannibal sounded the recall, declaring openly that he had beaten Minucius, but that Fabius had beaten him.

When the troops had got back to their camps, towards the close of a day of such varied fortune, Minucius called his men together and thus addressed them: "Soldiers, I have often heard that the best man is he who can himself advise us what is profit-

A.U.C. 537 sit; secundum eum qui bene monenti oboediat; qui nec ipse consulere nec alteri parere sciat,[1] eum
9 extremi ingenii esse. Nobis quoniam prima animi ingeniique negata sors est, secundam ac mediam teneamus, et dum imperare discimus, parere pru-
10 denti in animum inducamus. Castra cum Fabio iungamus; ad praetorium eius signa cum tulerimus,[2] ubi ego eum parentem appellavero, quod beneficio
11 eius erga nos ac maiestate eius dignum est, vos, milites, eos quorum vos modo arma ac dexterae[3] texerunt patronos salutabitis, et si nihil aliud, gratorum certe nobis animorum gloriam dies hic dederit."

XXX. Signo dato conclamatur inde ut colligantur vasa. Profecti et agmine incedentes ad dictatoris[4] castra in admirationem et ipsum et omnes qui circa
2 erant converterunt. Ut constituta sunt ante tribunal signa, progressus ante alios magister equitum cum patrem Fabium appellasset circumfusosque militum eius totum agmen patronos consalutasset,
3 "Parentibus" inquit "meis, dictator, quibus te modo nomine, quod[5] fando possum, aequavi, vitam

[1] sciat *M*[2]: nesciat *PCM*[1].
[2] cum tulerimus ς: contulerimus *P*: cum detulerimus *Novák*.
[3] ac dexterae *Madvig*: dexterae *P*: dexteraeque ς.
[4] ad dictatoris ς: di///catoris *P*: per dictatoris *Madvig*.
[5] quod *Voss*: quo *P*.

---

[1] A sentiment borrowed from the *Works and Days* of Hesiod, who says (293 ff.): That man is altogether best who considers all things himself and marks what will be better afterwards and at the end; and he, again, is good who listens to a good adviser; but whoever neither thinks for

able; the next best he who listens to good advice; B.C. 217
but that he who can neither counsel well nor obey another has the meanest capacity of all.[1] Since to us the first rank of intelligence and capacity has been denied, let us hold fast to the second or middle state, and while we are learning to command, make up our minds to obey a man of wisdom. Let us join our camp to that of Fabius; and when we have brought our standards to his tent, and I have given him the name of 'Father'—as befits his goodness to us and his great position—you, soldiers, will salute as 'patrons'[2] those whose hands and swords just now protected you; and, if nothing else, this day shall at least have conferred on us the glory of possessing thankful hearts."

XXX. The moment the signal was given, the order to pack was shouted round.[3] Setting forth they marched in column to the dictator's camp, to the astonishment of Fabius himself and all who were about. When they had planted their ensigns before the tribunal,[4] the master of the horse advanced in front of the rest and called upon Fabius by the name of Father, and his entire army saluted the soldiers who had gathered round them as their patrons. Then Minucius said, "To my parents, Dictator, with whom I have just made you equal in name, which is all that speech can do, I owe only my life; to

himself nor keeps in mind what another tells him, he is an unprofitable man (Evelyn White's Trans. in *L.C.L.*).

[2] The soldiers of Fabius, by preventing the Carthaginians from capturing the soldiers of Minucius, have preserved their liberty, as the *patronus* guarded the liberty of his client.

[3] *vasa colligere* means literally "to collect one's traps," hence "to prepare to march."

[4] A platform in front of the general's tent.

A.U.C. 537 tantam debeo, tibi cum meam salutem tum omnium
4 horum. Itaque plebeiscitum, quo oneratus magis
quam honoratus sum,[1] primus antiquo abrogoque
et, quod tibi mihique exercitibusque[2] his tuis,
servato ac conservatori, sit felix, sub imperium
auspiciumque tuum redeo et signa haec legionesque
5 restituo. Tu, quaeso, placatus me magisterium
equitum, hos ordines suos[3] quemque tenere iubeas."
6 Tum dextrae interiunctae militesque contione dimissa
ab notis ignotisque benigne atque hospitaliter invitati,
laetusque dies ex admodum tristi paulo ante
ac prope exsecrabili factus.
7 Romae, ut est perlata fama rei gestae, dein
litteris non magis ipsorum imperatorum quam volgo
militum ex utroque exercitu adfirmata, pro se
8 quisque Maximum laudibus ad caelum ferre. Pari[4]
gloria apud Hannibalem hostesque Poenos erat; ac
tum demum sentire cum Romanis atque in Italia
9 bellum esse; nam biennio ante adeo et duces
Romanos et milites spreverant ut vix cum eadem
gente bellum esse crederent cuius terribilem[5] famam
10 a patribus accepissent; Hannibalemque[6] ex acie
redeuntem dixisse ferunt tandem eam nubem quae
sedere in iugis montium solita sit cum procella
imbrem dedisse.

[1] honoratus sum ς: oneratus *P*.
[2] mihique exercitibusque ς: mihique quod exercitusque *P*.
[3] magisterium equitum, hos ordines suos *Gronovius*: magisterium equitum hos ordinibus suis *P*.
[4] pari *Pavlikovski*: par *P* (*Madvig*).
[5] terribilem ς: terribilem eam *P*: tam terribilem *Perizonius*.
[6] Hannibalemque *Luchs*: hannibalem quoque *P*.

---

[1] The battle on the Ticinus had been fought in the autumn of 218 B.C., and it was now late in the year 217, but the war had already lasted through two *campaigns*.

you I owe not merely my own safety but the safety of all of these. Accordingly I am the first to reject and repeal that plebiscite which has been more onerous to me than honourable, and to place myself again under your command and auspices and restore to you these standards and these legions; and may good fortune come of it to you and to me and to these your armies, to the preserved and the preserver. Lay aside, I pray, your just resentment, and bid me retain my post of master of the horse and these their own proper companies and ranks." Then hands were clasped, and the assembly being dismissed, the soldiers were kindly and hospitably entertained, alike by friends and strangers, and a day which a little earlier had been very gloomy and almost accurst was turned into one of rejoicing. B.C. 217

In Rome, when the report of this affair came in, and was later confirmed by letters not only from both commanders, but from the soldiers generally in both armies, all men joined in lauding Maximus to the skies. With Hannibal and the hostile Phoenicians his renown was equally great; then for the first time they realized that they were fighting with Romans and in Italy. For during the past two years[1] they had so despised the Roman generals and soldiers that they could hardly believe that they were at war with the same nation as that of which they had heard such terrifying stories from their fathers. And Hannibal is said to have remarked, as he was returning from the field, that at last that cloud which had long been hovering about the mountain-tops had broken in a storm of rain.

A.U.C. 537

XXXI. Dum haec geruntur in Italia, Cn. Servilius Geminus consul cum classe centum viginti[1] navium circumvectus Sardiniae et Corsicae oram et obsidibus utrimque acceptis in Africam transmisit, et priusquam in continentem escensiones faceret,
2 Menige insula vastata et ab incolentibus Cercinam,[2] ne et ipsorum ureretur diripereturque ager, decem talentis argenti acceptis ad litora Africae accessit
3 copiasque exposuit. Inde ad populandum agrum ducti milites navalesque socii iuxta effusi, ac si in
4 insulis[3] cultorum egentibus praedarentur. Itaque in insidias temere inlati, cum a frequentibus palantes, ab locorum gnaris ignari,[4] circumvenirentur, cum multa caede ac foeda fuga retro ad naves compulsi
5 sunt. Ad mille hominum cum Ti.[5] Sempronio Blaeso quaestore amissum. Classis ab litoribus hostium plenis trepide soluta in Siciliam cursum tenuit
6 traditaque Lilybaei T. Otacilio praetori, ut ab legato
7 eius P. Cincio[6] Romam reduceretur; ipse per Siciliam pedibus profectus freto in Italiam traiecit, litteris Q. Fabi accitus et ipse et collega eius M. Atilius, ut exercitus ab se exacto iam prope semestri imperio acciperent.

[1] centum viginti (centum et viginti) navium *Lipsius*: nauium *P*.

[2] Cercinam *Sigonius*: circanam *P*[1]: circa eam *P*[2].

[3] in insulis *Weissenborn*: insulis *P*.

[4] ab locorum gnaris ignari *Gronovius*: ad locorum et ignari gnaris (gnaris *deleted by P*[2]) *P*.

[5] cum Ti. *Ruperti*: cum iis *P*: cum *Doujatius*: cum Tib. *H. J. Mueller* (XLI. xii. 4).

[6] Cincio *Hertz*: circi *P*[1]: circa *P*[2].

---

[1] Menix (or Meninx) and Cercina were in the Lesser Syrtis. The former was supposed to have been the land of the lotus-eaters. (The modern names are Djerba and Kerkenna.)

XXXI. While these things were happening in Italy, Gnaeus Servilius Geminus the consul, with a fleet of a hundred and twenty ships, sailed round Sardinia and Corsica, and after taking hostages from both, bore away for Africa. Before descending on the mainland, he plundered the island of Menix; and after accepting ten talents of silver, which the people of Cercina gave him,[1] to induce him not to burn and pillage their territory also, he sailed in to the coast of Africa and disembarked his troops.[2] Soldiers and naval allies went off to pillage the country-side and dispersed as freely as if they were plundering desert islands. And so they quickly fell into an ambush, and losing contact with each other, and knowing nothing of the country, were set upon by large bands of their enemies, who knew it well, and driven back to their ships in a bloody and disgraceful rout. Fully a thousand men were lost, including the quaestor, Tiberius Sempronius Blaesus. Moorings were cast off in a hurry, and the fleet, leaving the shore behind it lined with enemies, stood away for Sicily. At Lilybaeum it was handed over to the praetor Titus Otacilius, to be conducted by his lieutenant, Publius Cincius, back to Rome. The consul himself proceeded overland through Sicily to the straits, where he crossed into Italy, in obedience to a dispatch from Quintus Fabius. The dictator had sent for Servilius, and for Marcus Atilius his colleague, to take over his armies, for his six months' tenure of authority was drawing to a close. B.C. 217

[2] Polybius (III. xcvi. 13) mentions the ransom of Cercina, and speaks of the capture not of Menix but of Cossyrus (a little island to the E. of Carthage). He says nothing of the landing in Africa.

A.U.C. 537 8 Omnium prope annales Fabium dictatorem adversum Hannibalem rem gessisse tradunt; Coelius etiam eum primum a populo creatum dictatorem
9 scribit. Sed et Coelium et ceteros fugit uni consuli Cn. Servilio, qui tum procul in Gallia provincia
10 aberat, ius fuisse dicendi dictatoris; quam moram quia exspectare territa tanta[1] clade civitas non poterat, eo decursum esse ut a populo crearetur
11 qui pro dictatore esset; res inde gestas gloriamque insignem ducis et augentes titulum imaginis[2] posteros, ut, qui pro dictatore creatus erat fuisse dictator[3] crederetur[4] facile obtinuisse.

XXXII. Consules Atilius Fabiano, Geminus Servilius Minuciano exercitu accepto, hibernaculis mature communitis, quod reliquum[5] autumni erat Fabi artibus cum summa inter se concordia bellum
2 gesserunt. Frumentatum exeunti Hannibali diversis locis opportuni aderant carpentes agmen palatosque excipientes; in casum universae dimicationis, quam omnibus artibus petebat hostis, non
3 veniebant[6]; adeoque inopia est coactus Hannibal ut, nisi cum fugae specie abeundum timuisset,[7]

[1] tanta *H. J. Mueller*: iam *P*.

[2] augentes titulum imaginis *Gronovius*: augendis titulum imagines *P*.

[3] dictatore creatus erat fuisse dictator *H. J. Mueller*: dictatore *P*.

[4] crederetur ς: caederetur *P*.

[5] quod reliquum (-quom) *Madvig*: quom P^1: cum P^2.

[6] Consules (§ 1) . . . veniebant *P places after* gererent (§ 3): *the transposition was made by Froben* (*ed.* 1531).

[7] timuisset *P* (*Weissenborn*): si fuisset *Madvig*.

---

[1] *i.e.* in Northern Italy, in the neighbourhood of Ariminum.

[2] In this inscription the expression *II dictator* (as in the *Fasti*) or *bis dictator* (as in the *Elogium* of Fabius, *C. I. L.*,

Nearly all the annalists state that Fabius was dictator in his campaign against Hannibal; Coelius even writes that he was the first to be created dictator by the people. But Coelius and the rest forget that only the consul Gnaeus Servilius, who was then far away in his province of Gaul,[1] had the right of naming a dictator. It was because the nation, appalled by their great disaster, could not put up with so long a delay that resort was had to the popular election of an *acting* dictator. Thereafter the general's successes and his great renown, and the additions which his descendants made to the inscription which accompanies his portrait,[2] led easily to the belief that one who had in fact been made acting dictator had been dictator. B.C. 217

XXXII. The consuls—Atilius taking over the army of Fabius and Geminus Servilius that of Minucius—constructed a winter camp betimes, and carried on the war for the rest of the autumn with the greatest harmony, on the lines laid down by Fabius. As often as Hannibal went out to forage, they were sure to appear, at one place or another, harassing his march and cutting off the stragglers: a general engagement, which the enemy sought with all the arts at his command, they declined to risk; and Hannibal was driven to such extremity of want, that if he had not thought that his departure would

I. 228) very likely occurred, conveying the erroneous impression that Fabius was in 217 formally elected dictator, whereas he was in fact invested with the *powers* of a dictator but not with the actual *title*. Note that at chap. viii. § 6 Livy accepted, without citing his authority, the tradition which he now rejects and ascribes to Cœlius. This is a striking instance of the ancient custom of citing sources only in cases where the writer's suspicions are aroused.

A.U.C. 537 Galliam repetiturus fuerit nulla relicta spe alendi exercitus in eis locis, si insequentes consules eisdem artibus bellum gererent.

4 Cum ad Gereonium iam hieme impediente constitisset bellum, Neapolitani legati Romam venere. Ab iis quadraginta paterae aureae magni ponderis in curiam inlatae atque ita verba facta ut dicerent
5 scire sese populi Romani[1] aerarium bello exhauriri, et cum iuxta pro urbibus agrisque sociorum ac
6 pro capite atque arce Italiae, urbe Romana, atque imperio geratur, aequum censuisse Neapolitanos, quod auri sibi cum ad templorum ornatum, tum ad subsidium fortunae, a maioribus relictum foret,
7 eo iuvare populum Romanum; si quam opem in sese[2] crederent, eodem studio fuisse oblaturos. Gratum sibi patres Romanos populumque facturum,
8 si omnes res Neapolitanorum suas duxissent, dignosque iudicaverint ab quibus donum, animo ac voluntate eorum qui libentes darent quam re maius
9 ampliusque, acciperent. Legatis gratiae actae pro munificentia curaque; patera quae ponderis minimi fuit accepta.

XXXIII. Per eosdem dies speculator[3] Carthaginiensis qui per biennium fefellerat Romae de-
2 prensus praecisisque manibus dimissus, et servi quinque et viginti in crucem acti, quod in campo

[1] populi Romani ς: populi *P*.
[2] in sese *P*: in sese esse *Weissenborn*: in se esse *H. J. Mueller*.
[3] speculator ς: spectator *P*.

necessarily look like flight, he would have gone back B.C. 217
into Gaul. For he had given up all hope of supporting his army in those regions, if the next consuls should make use of the same strategy.

Winter had already brought the fighting about Gereonium to a standstill, when envoys from Neapolis arrived in Rome. Bringing forty massive golden bowls into the senate-house, they delivered themselves to this effect: that they knew that the treasury of the Roman People was becoming exhausted by the war, and since it was being waged no less in behalf of the cities and lands of the allies than for the capital and citadel of Italy—the City of Rome—and for its empire, the Neapolitans had deemed it right to employ the gold which their ancestors had bequeathed them, whether for the adornment of their temples or as a subsidy in time of need, to assist the Roman People; had they thought themselves capable of helping with their persons, they would have offered these with the same heartiness; it would gratify them if the Roman senators and people would look on all the possessions of the Neapolitans as their own, and consider that their gift deserved a willing acceptance, as being greater and of more account in respect of the friendliness and good-will of the givers than in actual value. The envoys received a vote of thanks for this generosity and thoughtfulness, and the bowl of least weight was accepted.

XXXIII. At about this time a Carthaginian spy who for two years had eluded capture was caught in Rome, and after his hands had been cut off, was allowed to go; and five and twenty slaves were crucified, on the charge of having conspired in the

A.U.C. 537 Martio coniurassent.[1] Indici data libertas et aeris
3 gravis viginti milia. Legati et ad Philippum Macedonum regem missi ad deposcendum Deme-
4 trium Pharium, qui bello victus ad eum fugisset, et alii in Ligures ad expostulandum, quod Poenum opibus auxiliisque suis iuvissent, simul ad visendum ex propinquo quae in Bois atque Insubribus gere-
5 rentur. Ad Pineum quoque regem in Illyrios legati missi ad stipendium, cuius dies exierat, poscendum, aut si diem proferri[2] vellet, obsides accipiendos.
6 Adeo, etsi bellum ingens in cervicibus erat, nullius usquam terrarum rei cura Romanos, ne longinqua[3]
7 quidem, effugiebat. In religionem etiam venit aedem Concordiae, quam per seditionem militarem biennio ante L. Manlius praetor in Gallia vovisset,
8 locatam ad id tempus non esse. Itaque duumviri ad eam rem creati a M. Aemilio praetore urbano C. Pupius et K. Quinctius Flamininus aedem in arce faciendam locaverunt.

[1] quod in campo Martio coniurassent *P*: in campo Martio quod coniurassent *V. Voss.*

[2] proferri *Madvig*: proferre *P.*

[3] longinqua *P*: longinque ς: longinquae *J. H. Voss.*

---

[1] Philip V., with whom the Romans were to fight the first two Macedonian wars of 216–205 B.C. and 200–197 B.C.

[2] Demetrius of Pharus (an island off the coast of Illyria) had (in 229 B.C.) treacherously surrendered to the Romans the island Corcyra, of which the Illyrian queen Teuta had made him governor. Rewarded for this service with the governorship of a number of islands, he was guilty of plundering Roman allies, and Aemilius Paulus led an expedition against him which resulted (in 219) in his defeat and exile.

[3] In view of the revolt recorded in XXI. XXV.

[4] Whom the Romans had placed on the Illyrian throne in 228 B.C. after their defeat of Teuta.

Campus Martius. The informer was rewarded with freedom and twenty thousand sesterces. Ambassadors were dispatched to Philip,[1] King of the Macedonians, to demand the person of Demetrius of Pharus,[2] who, beaten in war, had fled to him for refuge; and others to expostulate with the Ligurians, because they had aided the Phoenician with supplies and men, and at the same time to observe at close range what was going on amongst the Boi and the Insubres.[3] Ambassadors were likewise sent to King Pineus[4] in Illyria, to demand a tribute which was overdue, or, in case he wished the time extended, to take hostages. So far were the Romans, though bearing upon their shoulders the burden of a mighty war, from permitting any concern of theirs to escape them, in however remote a part of the world it lay. They were troubled, too, that the contract for the temple of Concord, which the praetor Lucius Manlius had vowed two years before in Gaul, during the mutiny of the soldiers,[5] had hitherto not been let. Accordingly the city praetor, Marcus Aemilius, appointed for the purpose two commissioners, Gaius Pupius and Caeso Quinctius Flamininus, who arranged to have the temple built on the Citadel.[6] B.C. 217

[5] Livy says nothing of this mutiny, which probably occurred (notwithstanding the phrase *biennio ante*) in connexion with the events related in XXI. XXV.

[6] One of the two summits of the Capitoline, the other being the Capitol, where stood the temple of Jupiter, Juno and Minerva. The temple of Concord, dedicated in 216 (XXIII. xxi. 7), must not be confounded with the temple of the same goddess situated at the N.W. corner of the Forum—the ruins of which may still be seen—which was first erected in 367 by Camillus on the passing of the Licinian Laws.

A.U.C. 537 9 Ab eodem praetore ex senatus consulto litterae ad consules missae, ut si iis videretur, alter eorum ad consules creandos Romam veniret: se in eam
10 diem quam iussissent comitia edicturum. Ad haec a consulibus rescriptum sine detrimento rei publicae abscedi non posse ab hoste; itaque per interregem comitia habenda esse potius quam consul alter a
11 bello avocaretur. Patribus rectius visum est dictatorem a consulibus[1] dici comitiorum habendorum causa. Dictus L. Veturius Philo M. Pomponium
12 Mathonem magistrum equitum dixit. Iis vitio creatis iussisque die quarto decimo se magistratu abdicare res ad interregnum rediit.

XXXIV. Consulibus prorogatum in annum imperium. Interrex proditus[2] a patribus C. Claudius[3] Appi filius Cento, inde P. Cornelius Asina. In eius interregno comitia habita magno certamine patrum ac plebis.

2 C. Terentio Varroni, quem sui generis hominem, plebi[4] insectatione principum popularibusque artibus conciliatum, ab Q. Fabi opibus et dictatorio imperio concusso[5] aliena invidia splendentem, volgus extrahere[6] ad consulatum nitebatur, patres summa ope obstabant, ne se insectando sibi aequari adsuescerent

[1] consulibus *Ruperti*: consul *P*.
[2] interrex proditus *Luchs*: interreges proditius *P*.
[3] C. Claudius *Sigonius*: cn̄. claudius *P*.
[4] plebi *Aldus*: plebis *P*.
[5] concusso ς concussū *P*.
[6] extrahere ς: et extrahere *P*.

The same praetor, acting on instructions from the senate, wrote to the consuls, requesting that, if it seemed good to them, one of them would come to Rome to hold an election of consuls, and promising to appoint the comitia for the day which they should designate. To this the consuls answered that they could not withdraw from the presence of the enemy without detriment to the republic; it would therefore be better that the election be conducted by an interrex than that one of the consuls be called away from the seat of war. To the senators it seemed preferable that the consuls should appoint a dictator to preside at the election. They appointed Lucius Veturius Philo, who named Marcus Pomponius Matho master of the horse. There was a flaw in their appointment and they were commanded on the fourteenth day to resign their magistracy, whereupon the state reverted to an interregnum. B.C. 217

XXXIV. The authority of the consuls was extended for a year. To be interrex the Fathers named Gaius Claudius Cento, the son of Appius, and after him Publius Cornelius Asina. The latter conducted an election, which was marked by a bitter struggle between patricians and plebeians.

Gaius Terentius Varro had endeared himself to the plebeians—the class to which he himself belonged—by invectives against the leading men and the usual tricks of the demagogue. The blow he had struck at the influence and dictatorial authority of Fabius brought him the glory which is won by defaming others, and the rabble was now striving to raise him to the consulship, while the patricians opposed the attempt with all their might, lest men should acquire the custom of assailing them

A.U.C. 537 homines. Q. Baebius Herennius tribunus plebis,
3 cognatus C. Terenti, criminando non senatum modo
sed etiam augures, quod dictatorem prohibuissent
comitia perficere, per invidiam eorum favorem
4 candidato suo conciliabat: ab hominibus nobilibus
per multos annos bellum quaerentibus Hannibalem
in Italiam adductum; ab iisdem, cum debellari
5 possit, fraude bellum trahi. Cum quattuor[1] legionibus universis pugnari prospere[2] posse apparuisset[3]
eo quod M. Minucius absente Fabio prospere
6 pugnasset, duas legiones hosti ad caedem obiectas,
deinde ex ipsa caede ereptas, ut pater patronusque
appellaretur qui prius vincere prohibuisset Romanos
7 quam vinci. Consules deinde Fabianis artibus, cum
debellare possent,[4] bellum traxisse. Id foedus
inter omnes nobiles ictum, nec finem ante belli
habituros quam consulem vere plebeium, id est
8 hominem novum, fecissent; nam plebeios nobiles
iam eisdem initiatos esse sacris et contemnere
plebem ex quo contemni a patribus desierint
9 coepisse. Cui non apparere[5] id actum et quaesitum
esse ut interregnum iniretur, ut in patrum potestate

[1] quattuor *Crévier*: quattuor milia *P*.
[2] pugnari prospere *Riemann*: pugnari *P*.
[3] posse apparuisset ς: posset apparuisse *P*.
[4] debellare possent ς: debellare posset *P*: debellari posset ς.
[5] non apparere id ς: non id apparere id *P*.

---

[1] The absurdity of this allegation is evident as soon as one recalls the bitter opposition to Fabius and his policy on the part of a large section of the senate (see Dimsdale's note).

[2] A *novus homo* was one who, like Cicero, attained, first of

as a means of rising to their level. Quintus Baebius Herennius, a tribune of the plebs and kinsman of Gaius Terentius, railed not only at the senate but at the augurs too, because they had forbidden the dictator to accomplish the election, and by placing them in an unfavourable light, strengthened the candidacy of his friend. The nobles, he said, had been seeking war for many years, and it was they who had brought Hannibal into Italy. It was their machinations, too, that were spinning out the war, when it might be brought to a victorious conclusion.[1] That four legions if united were able to hold their own in a general engagement had been shown in a successful battle fought by Marcus Minucius, when Fabius was absent. Notwithstanding this, two legions had just been exposed to be massacred by the enemy and subsequently rescued from the massacre, to the end that the names of Father and Patron might be conferred on one who had kept the Romans from conquering before keeping them from being conquered. After that the consuls had employed the arts of Fabius to prolong the war, when they were able to have ended it. The nobles had all made a compact to this effect; nor would his hearers see an end of the war until they had elected a true plebeian, a new man,[2] to the consulship; for the plebeian nobles had already been admitted to the same rites as the others and had begun to look down on the plebs from the moment when they themselves had ceased to be looked down on by the patricians. Who could fail to see that their end and purpose in resorting to an interregnum had been to keep the election in the hands of the B.C. 217

his family, to curule office. Such a man and his descendants were thereafter reckoned as nobles.

A.U.C. 537 10 comitia essent? Id consules ambos ad exercitum
morando quaesisse; id postea, quia invitis iis dictator
esset dictus comitiorum causa, expugnatum esse,
11 cum[1] vitiosus dictator per augures fieret. Habere[2]
igitur interregnum eos; consulatum unum certe
plebis Romanae esse,[3] et populum eum liberum
habiturum ac daturum ei qui mature[4] vincere quam
diu imperare malit.

XXXV. Cum his orationibus accensa plebs esset,
tribus patriciis petentibus, P. Cornelio Merenda
2 L. Manlio Volsone M. Aemilio Lepido, duobus
nobilium iam[5] familiarum plebeis,[6] C. Atilio Serrano
et Q. Aelio Paeto, quorum alter pontifex,
alter augur erat, Terentius consul unus creatur, ut
in manu eius essent comitia rogando collegae.
3 Tum experta nobilitas parum fuisse virium in
competitoribus eius L. Aemilium Paulum, qui cum
M. Livio consul fuerat, ex damnatione collegae,
ex qua[7] prope ambustus evaserat, infestum plebei,
diu ac multum recusantem ad petitionem compellit.

[1] esse cum *Luchs*: esse ut *P*.
[2] habere *P. Rubens*: haberet *P*.
[3] esse ς: esset *P*.
[4] mature *Kiehl*: magis uere *P*.
[5] nobilium iam *Freinsheimius*: nobilibus iam *P*: nobilium *Weissenborn*.
[6] familiarum plebeis ς: familiarium plebei *P*.
[7] ex damnatione collegae ex qua *Harant*: et damnatione collegae et sua *P*.

---

[1] The magistrate who presided at the elections was naturally in a position to influence the voters by his attitude towards the various candidates.

[2] L. Aemilius Paulus and M. Livius Salinator were consuls in 219 B.C. On the expiration of their term of office, Livius was tried and convicted by the people (XXVII. xxxiv. 3) for

patricians? To this end both consuls had remained B.C. 217
with their army in the field; to this end, later on, because a dictator had been named, against their wishes, for the purpose of holding an election, they had succeeded in having the augurs declare that there had been a flaw in his appointment. They had therefore the interregnum they desired. But at least one consulship belonged to the Roman plebs; and the people meant to keep it free, and bestow it on him who would rather win an early victory than remain long in command.

XXXV. When the plebs had been inflamed by these harangues, though there were three patrician candidates, Publius Cornelius Merenda, Lucius Manlius Volso, and Marcus Aemilius Lepidus, and two plebeians of families which had already been ennobled, namely, Gaius Atilius Serranus and Quintus Aelius Paetus, of whom one was a pontifex, the other an augur, Gaius Terentius was the only consul elected, and the assembly called to choose a colleague for him was therefore under his control.[1] The nobles, finding that Varro's competitors had not been able to command the necessary strength, thereupon obliged Lucius Aemilius Paulus to stand, though he held out long and earnestly against their importunity. He had been consul together with Marcus Livius, and the condemnation of his colleague—from which he had not himself escaped unscathed—had embittered him against the plebs.[2] On the next election day

peculation in connexion with the war against Demetrius of Pharus (*De viris illustr.* 50), or unfair division of the spoil (Frontinus, *Strategemata*, IV. i. 45). In 207 B.C. he and his colleague in the consulship, Gaius Nero, defeated Hasdrubal near Sena Gallica, at the river Metaurus (XXVII. xl.-xlix.).

A.U.C. 537
4 Is[1] proximo comitiali die concedentibus omnibus
qui cum Varrone certaverant, par magis in ad-
5 versando[2] quam collega datur consuli. Inde prae-
torúm comitia habita: creati M. Pomponius Matho
et P. Furius Philus. Philo[3] Romae iuri dicundo
urbana sors, Pomponio inter cives Romanos et
6 peregrinos evenit. Additi duo praetores, M.
Claudius Marcellus in Siciliam, L. Postumius[4]
7 Albinus in Galliam. Omnes absentes creati sunt,
nec cuiquam[5] eorum praeter Terentium consulem
mandatus honos quem non iam[6] antea gessisset,
praeteritis aliquot fortibus ac strenuis viris, quia in
tali tempore nulli novus magistratus videbatur
mandandus.

XXXVI. Exercitus quoque multiplicati sunt;
quantae autem copiae peditum equitumque additae
sint,[7] adeo et numero et genere copiarum variant
auctores ut vix quicquam satis certum adfirmare
2 ausus sim. Decem milia novorum militum alii
scripta in supplementum tradunt,[8] alii novas quattuor
3 legiones, ut[9] octo legionibus rem gererent. Numero
quoque peditum equitumque legiones auctas milibus[10]
peditum et centenis equitibus in singulas adiectis,
ut quina milia peditum, treceni equites essent,

[1] is ς: is ius *P*.
[2] adversando *Fuegner*: aduersandum *P* (*Madvig and Luchs*).
[3] Philus. Philo *Alschefski*: philo *P*: philus ς.
[4] L. Postumius ς: ā postumius *P*.
[5] nec cuiquam ς: ne cuiquam *P*.
[6] non iam *Madvig*: iam non *P*.
[7] sint ς: sunt *P*.
[8] in supplementum tradunt *Luterbacher*: in supplementum *P*.

all those who had been Varro's rivals withdrew their names, the consul was given Paulus, rather as a competent opponent than as a colleague. The election of praetors then took place, and Marcus Pomponius Matho and Publius Furius Philus were chosen. To Philus the lot assigned the urban praetorship, for administering justice in Rome;[1] to Pomponius the jurisdiction in suits between Roman citizens and foreigners. Two additional praetors were elected, Marcus Claudius Marcellus for Sicily, and Lucius Postumius Albinus for Gaul. These were all elected in their absence, and not one of them, except Terentius the consul, received a magistracy which he had not already filled before, a number of stout-hearted, active men being passed over because it seemed unwise at such a juncture to give any man an office to which he was new. B.C. 217

XXXVI. The armies also were augmented. But how large were the additions of infantry and cavalry I should hardly venture to declare with any certainty —so greatly do historians differ in regard to the numbers and kinds of troops. Some say that ten thousand new soldiers were enlisted as replacements; others that four new legions were enrolled, so that they took the field with eight. Some assert that the legions were also increased in the numbers of their infantry and cavalry, and that each received an additional thousand foot and a hundred horse, bringing up the total of every one to five thousand

[1] *Sc.* between litigants both of whom were citizens.

---

[9] ut ς: et *P*.
[10] milibus ς: militibus *P*.

A.U.C. 537 socii duplicem numerum equitum darent, peditis[1]
5 aequarent,[2] quidam[3] auctores sunt. Illud haudquaquam discrepat, maiore conatu atque impetu rem actam quam prioribus annis, quia spem posse vinci
A.U.C. 538 hostem dictator praebuerat.

6 Ceterum priusquam signa ab urbe novae legiones moverent, decemviri libros adire atque inspicere iussi propter territos volgo homines novis prodigiis.
7 Nam et Romae in Aventino et Ariciae nuntiatum erat sub idem tempus lapidibus pluvisse, et multo cruore signa in Sabinis, Caere[4] aquas fonte calido[5]
8 manasse—id quidem etiam, quod saepius acciderat, magis terrebat; et in via fornicata, quae ad campum erat, aliquot homines de caelo tacti exanimatique
9 fuerant. Ea prodigia ex libris procurata. Legati a Paesto pateras aureas Romam attulerunt. Iis sicut Neapolitanis gratiae actae, aurum non acceptum.

XXXVII. Per eosdem dies ab Hierone classis
2 Ostia cum magno commeatu accessit. Legati in senatum introducti nuntiarunt caedem C. Flamini consulis exercitusque allatam adeo aegre tulisse regem Hieronem ut nulla sua propria regnique sui
3 clade moveri magis potuerit. Itaque, quamquam probe sciat magnitudinem populi Romani admirabiliorem prope adversis rebus quam secundis esse,

[1] peditis *Drakenborch*: pediti *P*.
[2] aequarent *edd.*: aequarunt *P*.
[3] quidam *Weissenborn*: septem et octoginta milia armatorum et ducentos in castris Romanis cum pugnatum ad Cannas est quidam *P*.
[4] Caere *Luterbacher*: caedes *P*.
[5] calido ς: callidos *P*.

---

[1] Cf. chap. i. § 10. Aelian (*Varia Historia*, xii. 67) and Diodorus (XVII. 10) allude to the story that the fountain of Dirce ran with blood just before the destruction of Thebes by Alexander.

foot and three hundred horse; and that double the number of horse and an equal number of foot were furnished by the allies. One thing is not disputed —that they proceeded with more energy and enthusiasm than in former years, because the dictator had given them ground for hoping that they would be able to defeat the enemy. B.C. 217

Before, however, the new legions marched out from the City, the decemvirs were instructed to consult the Sacred Books, on account of a general alarm occasioned by strange portents. For a shower of stones had been reported as having fallen at Rome on the Aventine, and about the same time at Aricia; in the Sabine country the images of the gods, and at Caere the waters that flowed from the hot spring had been drenched with blood—a prodigy all the more alarming from its having occurred so often;[1] and in the arched way which used to lead to the Campus Martius some men had been struck by lightning and killed. These prodigies were expiated as the Books directed. Ambassadors came from Paestum, bringing golden bowls to Rome. They were thanked, as the Neapolitans had been, but the gold was not accepted. B.C. 216

XXXVII. About this time a fleet came in to Ostia from King Hiero with a great store of supplies. His envoys were introduced into the senate, where they told how the news of the destruction of Gaius Flaminius the consul and his army had so grieved the King that no disaster to himself or his own kingdom could have distressed him more. Accordingly, though well aware that the greatness of the Roman People was almost more astonishing in adversity than in prosperity, he had nevertheless sent

A.U.C. 538 4 tamen se[1] omnia quibus a bonis fidelibusque sociis
bella iuvari soleant misisse; quae ne accipere abnuant
5 magno opere se patres conscriptos orare. Iam
omnium primum ominis causa Victoriam auream
pondo ducentum ac viginti adferre sese: acciperent
eam tenerentque et haberent propriam et perpetuam.
6 Advexisse etiam trecenta milia modium tritici, du-
centa hordei, ne commeatus deessent, et quantum
praeterea opus esset, quo iussissent, subvecturos.
7 Milite atque equite scire nisi Romano Latinique
nominis non uti populum Romanum; levium armorum[2] auxilia etiam externa vidisse in castris
8 Romanis; itaque misisse mille sagittariorum ac
funditorum, aptam manum adversus Baliares ac
9 Mauros pugnacesque alias missili telo gentes. Ad
ea dona consilium[3] quoque addebant, ut praetor
cui provincia Sicilia evenisset classem[4] in Africam
traiceret, ut et hostes in terra sua bellum haberent
minusque laxamenti daretur iis ad auxilia Hannibali
summittenda.

10 Ab senatu ita responsum regiis[5] est, virum bonum
egregiumque socium Hieronem esse atque uno
tenore, ex quo in amicitiam populi Romani venerit,
fidem coluisse ac rem Romanam omni tempore ac
loco munifice adiuvisse. Id perinde ac deberet
11 gratum populo Romano esse. Aurum et a civita-

[1] tamen se *Gronovius*: mense P^1: missa a se P^2: tamen senatui (*or* tamen) *Luterbacher*.

[2] armorum *Gronovius*: armatorum *P*.

[3] consilium ϛ: consilio *P*.

[4] classem *P*: classe *C. Heraeus*.

[5] regiis *Bitschofsky*: regis *P*: regi ϛ: regis legatis *Luchs*.

---

[1] The *modius* was about equivalent to our peck.

them all those things with which good and faithful B.C. 216 allies were wont to assist their friends in time of war, and he earnestly besought the Conscript Fathers not to refuse them. In the first place, for the omen's sake, they were bringing a golden Victory, weighing two hundred and twenty pounds, which they begged the Romans to accept and keep, and to regard it as their own for ever. They had also brought three hundred thousand measures[1] of wheat and two hundred thousand of barley, that there might be no failure of provision; and whatever additional quantity were needed they stood ready to convey to any place which the senate might designate. For heavy foot and horse, the King knew that the Roman People employed none but Romans and Latins; but amongst the light-armed auxiliaries, he had seen in the camps of the Romans even foreigners; he had therefore sent a thousand archers and slingers, a force well adapted to cope with Moors and Baliares and other tribes that fought with missiles. To these gifts they added a piece of advice, that the praetor, namely, who might be assigned to Sicily should sail over with his fleet to Africa, so that the enemy, too, might have war on their own soil, whereby they would experience less freedom in dispatching aid to Hannibal.

The senate, in replying to the royal emissaries, said that Hiero was a good man and a rare ally, who from the time when he became a friend of the Roman People had maintained an unswerving loyalty, and always and in every place had given generous assistance to the Roman cause. For this the Romans were grateful, as in duty bound. As for the gold, other states as well had proffered it, but the Roman

A.U.C. 538 tibus quibusdam allatum gratia rei accepta non
12 accepisse populum Romanum; Victoriam omenque accipere sedemque ei divae[1] dare dicare Capitolium, templum Iovis optimi maximi. In ea arce urbis Romanae sacratam, volentem propitiamque, firmam ac stabilem fore populo Romano.

13 Funditores sagittariique et frumentum traditum consulibus. Quinqueremes ad quinquaginta navium[2] classem quae cum T. Otacilio[3] propraetore in Sicilia erat[4] quinque et viginti additae, permissumque est ut, si e re publica censeret esse, in Africam traiceret.

XXXVIII. Dilectu perfecto consules paucos morati dies, dum ab sociis ac[5] nomine Latino venirent
2 milites. Tum, quod nunquam antea factum erat,
3 iure iurando ab tribunis militum adacti milites; nam ad eam diem nihil praeter sacramentum fuerat, iussu consulum conventuros neque iniussu abituros,[6] et ubi convenissent,[7] sua voluntate ipsi inter sese de-
4 curiati equites, centuriati pedites coniurabant sese fugae atque formidinis ergo non abituros neque ex ordine recessuros nisi teli sumendi aut petendi et
5 aut hostis feriendi aut civis servandi causa. Id ex voluntario inter ipsos foedere ad tribunos ac[8] legitimam iuris iurandi adactionem translatum.

[1] ei divae *Novák*: ei se divae *P*.

[2] ad quinquaginta navium *Luterbacher* (XXI. li. 7): ad nauium *P*: ad centum viginti navium *Gronovius* (XXII. xxxi. 1): ad navium centum *Boettcher* (XXIV. xxvii. 5).

[3] T. Otacilio *Aldus*: m̄ otacilio *P*.

[4] erat ς: erant *P*.

[5] ab sociis ac *Madvig*: sociis ab *P*.

[6] *the words* iussu . . . iniussu abituros *were placed here by Crévier*: *in P they stand after* adacti milites.

[7] convenissent *C. F. Mueller*: ad decuriatum aut centuriatum conuenissent *P*.

People, though thankful for the kind intention, had B.C. 216 not accepted it; the Victory and her omen they did accept; and to that goddess they dedicated and assigned the Capitol, the temple of Jupiter Optimus Maximus, to be her seat. Established in that citadel of Rome she would be gracious and propitious, faithful and steadfast, to the Roman People.

The slingers and archers and the corn were turned over to the consuls. Twenty-five quinqueremes were added to the fleet of fifty ships that was under the command of Titus Otacilius in Sicily, and permission was given him, if he deemed it advantageous to the state, to sail across to Africa.

XXXVIII. When they had finished with the levy, the consuls waited a few days for the soldiers from the allies and the Latins to come in. An oath was then administered to the soldiers by their tribunes—which was a thing that they had never done before. For until that day there had only been the general oath[1] to assemble at the bidding of the consuls and not depart without their orders; then, after assembling, they would exchange a voluntary pledge amongst themselves—the cavalrymen in their decuries and the infantry in their centuries—that they would not abandon their ranks for flight or fear, but only to take up or seek a weapon, either to smite an enemy or to save a fellow citizen. This voluntary agreement amongst the men themselves was replaced by an oath administered formally by the tribunes.

[1] Like the one mentioned in chap. xi. § 8 of the year before, or in III. XX. 3, of 460 B.C.

---

[8] ac *Weissenborn*: ad *P*.

A.U.C. 538 6 Contiones, priusquam ab urbe signa moverentur,
consulis Varronis multae ac feroces fuere denuntiantis[1] bellum arcessitum in Italiam ab nobilibus
7 mansurumque in visceribus rei publicae, si plures
Fabios imperatores haberet, se quo die hostem
8 vidisset perfecturum. Collegae eius Pauli una,
pridie quam ab urbe[2] proficisceretur, contio fuit,
verior quam gratior populo, qua nihil inclementer
9 in Varronem dictum nisi id modo, mirari se, quidni,
qui[3] dux, priusquam aut suum aut hostium exercitum, locorum situm, naturam regionis nosset,
iam nunc togatus[4] in urbe sciret quae sibi agenda
10 armato forent, et diem[5] quoque praedicere posset
11 qua cum hoste signis collatis esset dimicaturus. Se,
quae consilia magis res dent hominibus quam homines
rebus, ea ante tempus immatura non praecepturum.
Optare ut quae caute ac[6] consulte gesta essent satis
12 prospere evenirent; temeritatem, praeterquam quod
stulta sit, infelicem etiam ad id locorum fuisse.
13 Sua[7] sponte apparebat tuta celeribus consiliis prae-
positurum; et, quo id constantius perseveraret, Q.
Fabius Maximus sic eum proficiscentem adlocutus
fertur:

XXXIX. "Si aut collegam, id quod mallem, tui
similem, L. Aemili, haberes aut tu collegae tui
2 esses similis, supervacanea esset oratio mea; nam
et duo boni consules etiam me indicente[8] omnia

[1] denuntiantis C^2: denuntiantes PC^1.
[2] ab urbe ς: ex urbe ς: in urbe *P*: urbi *Riemann*.
[3] quidni, qui *Zachariae*: quodnequi *P*: quinam *C. Heraeus*.
[4] togatus *Muretus*: locatus *P*.
[5] et diem (diem *Zachariae*) *Madvig*.
[6] ac ς: a P^1: et *H. J. Mueller*.
[7] sua *Luchs*: id sua *P*: et sua *Gronovius*.
[8] indicente ς (*Gronovius*): indigentes *P*.

Before the troops marched from the City, the consul Varro uttered many truculent harangues. He declared that the war had been brought into Italy by the nobles, and would not cease to prey upon the nation's vitals, if they had many generals like Fabius; but that he himself would put an end to it on the day when he came within sight of the enemy. His colleague Paulus spoke but once, on the day before he left the City. His words were more truthful than agreeable to the people; but he said nothing harsh against Varro, except this: that he marvelled—and indeed how should he not?—that a general, who before he knew either his own or the enemy's army or the lie of the land or the character of the country, was already certain, ere he had yet laid aside the dress of a civilian, what measures he must adopt when in the field—he marvelled that such a general should even be able to predict the very day on which he would be giving battle to the enemy! For himself, he would not anticipate, before they ripened, those plans with which circumstances provided men but which men could not well impose on circumstances. He hoped that what was done with care and caution would turn out for the best: rashness was not only foolish but had hitherto been unfortunate as well It was quite apparently his own intention to choose a safe course rather than a hasty one; and, to confirm him in this resolution, Quintus Fabius Maximus is said to have addressed him, on his setting out, to this effect:— B.C. 216

XXXIX. "If either, Lucius Aemilius, you had, as I should prefer, a colleague like yourself, or if you were like your colleague, my words would be superfluous. For, as two good consuls, even if I held my

A.U.C. 538 e re publica fideque[1] vestra faceretis, et mali[2] nec
mea verba auribus vestris nec consilia animis acci-
3 peretis. Nunc et collegam tuum et te talem virum
intuenti mihi tecum omnis oratio est, quem video
nequiquam et virum bonum et civem fore, si altera
parte claudente re publica[3] malis consiliis idem ac
4 bonis iuris et potestatis erit. Erras enim, L. Paule,
si tibi minus certaminis cum C. Terentio quam cum
Hannibale futurum censes; nescio an infestior hic
5 adversarius quam ille hostis maneat te, et[4] cum illo
in acie tantum cum hoc omnibus locis ac temporibus
sis certaturus, et[5] adversus Hannibalem legionesque
eius tuis equitibus ac peditibus pugnandum tibi sit,
Varro dux tuis militibus te sit oppugnaturus.
6 "Ominis etiam tibi causa absit C. Flamini memoria.
Tamen ille consul demum et in provincia et ad exercitum coepit furere: hic, priusquam peteret consulatum, deinde in petendo consulatu, nunc quoque
consul, priusquam castra videat aut hostem, insanit.
7 Et qui[6] tantas iam nunc procellas proelia atque acies
iactando inter togatos ciet, quid inter armatam iuventutem censes facturum et ubi extemplo res verba
8 sequitur? Atqui si,[7] quod facturum se denuntiat,
extemplo pugnaverit, aut ego rem militarem, belli

[1] fideque *Perizonius*: fide *P*: ac fide *H. J. Mueller*.
[2] mali ϛ: malem *P*.
[3] claudente re publica *Ussing*: claudet rei p̄ *P*.
[4] maneat te, et *Fabri*: maneat et *P*: maneat te *Madvig*.
[5] scis certaturus, et ϛ: si certaturus est P^1: certaturus est P^2.
[6] qui ϛ: quia *P*.
[7] si *Luchs*: sic *P*: si hic ϛ: si, id *Harant*.

peace, you would act in all respects in accordance with the public interest and your own loyalty; and, as bad ones, you would neither take my words into your ears nor my advice into your hearts. As it is, when I see what your colleague is like and what you are like, it is to you alone that I must address myself: though I perceive that you will be a good man and good citizen to little purpose, if the state is lame on the other side and evil counsels enjoy the same rights and the same authority as good. For you err, Lucius Paulus, if you suppose that your struggle will be less with Gaius Terentius than with Hannibal. I am not sure that you may not find the one more dangerous as an opponent than the other as an enemy, and that with your enemy you will have to contend only in battle; with your opponent, everywhere and at all times. Against Hannibal and his legions you will have your cavalry and infantry to fight for you: when Varro takes the field, it will be to attack you with your own soldiers. B.C. 216

"For the very omen's sake, I would not have you remember Gaius Flaminius! Yet Flaminius only began to rave when he had been made consul and was in his province and had joined his army; whereas Varro was mad before he sought the consulship, as he was thereafter during his canvass, and is now as consul, before he has ever beheld his camp or the enemy. And if a man can rouse such gusts of passion even now, by bragging of battles and of stricken fields among civilians, what think you he will do when surrounded by armed youths, where words are translated instantly into deeds? And yet, if he fights at once, as he declares that he intends to do, either I know nothing of military science, of the

A.U.C. 538 hoc genus, hostem hunc ignoro, aut nobilior alius
Trasumenno locus nostris cladibus erit.
9 "Nec[1] gloriandi tempus adversus unum est, et[2]
ego contemnendo potius quam adpetendo gloriam
modum excesserim; sed ita res se habet: una ratio
belli gerendi adversus Hannibalem est qua ego gessi.
10 Nec eventus modo hoc docet—stultorum iste magister
est—sed eadem ratio quae fuit futura,[3] donec res
11 eaedem manebunt, immutabilis est. In Italia bellum
gerimus, in sede ac solo nostro; omnia circa plena
civium ac sociorum sunt; armis viris equis com-
12 meatibus iuvant iuvabuntque—id iam fidei documentum in adversis rebus nostris dederunt; meliores,
prudentiores constantiores nos tempus diesque facit.
13 Hannibal contra in aliena, in hostili est terra, inter
omnia inimica infestaque, procul ab domo ac patria;[4]
neque illi terra neque mari est pax; nullae eum
urbes accipiunt, nulla moenia; nihil usquam sui
14 videt; in diem rapto[5] vivit; partem vix tertiam
exercitus eius habet quem Hiberum amnem traiecit;
plures fame quam ferro absumpti,[6] nec his paucis
15 iam victus suppeditat. Dubitas ergo quin sedendo
superaturi simus eum qui senescat in dies, non
commeatus, non supplementum, non pecuniam
16 habeat? Quam diu pro Gereoni, castelli Apuliae

[1] nec ς: ne *P*. [2] et ς: ut *P*.
[3] futura *J. Fischer*: futura quae *P*: futuraque ς.
[4] ac patria *H. J. Mueller*: ab patria *P*.
[5] rapto ς: capto *P*.
[6] absumpti *Heerwagen*: absumsit *P*.

---

[1] Mommsen, *History of Rome*, ii. p. 285 (cited by Dowdall), remarks that "it was not the Cunctator that saved Rome but the compact structure of its confederacy, and not less, perhaps, the national hatred with which the Phoenician hero was regarded on the part of the Occidentals."

nature of this war, and of our enemy, or another B.C. 216 place will be more notorious than Trasumennus for our overthrow.

"It is no time to boast, when I am speaking to one man, and for my part I had rather go too far in despising than in seeking reputation; but the simple truth is that the only way of conducting a war with Hannibal is the way in which I have conducted it; and not only the event—that schoolmaster of fools—teaches us this, but the same reasoning which held good then will hold unchanged, so long as circumstances remain the same. It is in Italy, our home-land, that we are fighting; everywhere about us are fellow citizens and friends; they are helping us with arms, men, horses, and supplies, and will continue helping us—such proof of loyalty have they already given us in our adversity;[1] each day that passes makes us better, wiser, more steadfast men. Hannibal, on the contrary, is in an alien and hostile country, where all his surroundings are inimical and threatening, far from home and native city; for him there is no peace, on either land or sea; no cities receive him, no walls protect him; nowhere does he see aught that he can call his own; he subsists on the plunder of each day; he has barely a third of that army which he led across the Ebro; more have perished by starvation than by the sword, and the few that are left have no longer any food. Can you doubt then that if we sit still we must gain the victory over one who is growing weaker every day and is destitute of provisions, of replacements, and of money? How long, before Gereonium,[2] a pitiful fort in Apulia, as if it had been

[2] See chap. xxiii. § 9. The sentence was to have ended with something like *sedet*? ("has he been sitting?").

A.U.C. 538 inopis, tamquam pro Carthaginis moenibus—sed ne
17 adversus te quidem de me[1] gloriabor; Servilius[2]
atque Atilius, proximi consules, vide quem ad modum
eum ludificati sint.

"Haec una salutis est via, L. Paule, quam difficilem
infestamque cives tibi[3] magis quam[4] hostes facient.
18 Idem enim tui quod hostium milites volent; idem
Varro consul Romanus quod Hannibal Poenus imperator cupiet. Duobus ducibus unus resistas oportet.
Resistes autem, si adversus[5] famam rumoresque
hominum satis firmus steteris, si te neque collegae
19 vana[6] gloria neque tua falsa infamia moverit. Veritatem[7] laborare nimis saepe aiunt, exstingui nun-
20 quam; vanam gloriam[8] qui spreverit veram habebit.
Sine timidum pro cauto, tardum pro considerato,
imbellem pro perito belli vocent. Malo te sapiens
hostis metuat quam stulti cives laudent. Omnia
audentem contemnet Hannibal, nihil temere agentem
21 metuet. Nec ego ut nihil agatur suadeo,[9] sed ut
agentem te ratio ducat, non fortuna; tuae potestatis
semper tu tuaque omnia sint; armatus intentusque
sis; neque occasioni tuae desis neque suam occa-
22 sionem hosti des. Omnia non properanti clara
certaque erunt; festinatio improvida est et caeca."

XL. Adversus ea oratio consulis haud sane laeta fuit magis fatentis[10] ea quae diceret vera quam facilia

[1] quidem de me *Alschefski*: quideme *P*.
[2] Servilius *Luchs*: p̄. seruilius *P*: cn. seruilius ς.
[3] tibi ς: sibi *P*. [4] magis quam ς: quam magis *P*.
[5] si adversus *Madvig*: aduersus *P*. [6] vana ς: una *P*.
[7] veritatem ς: ueritate *P*.
[8] vanam gloriam *H. J. Mueller* (gloriam vanam *Muretus*): gloriam *P*.
[9] agatur suadeo *Madvig*: agatur *P*.
[10] fatentis ς: patentis *P*[1]: petentis *P*[2].

the walls of Carthage, has he—but of myself I will B.C. 216
not boast, even to you. See how the consuls of last year, Servilius and Atilius, made a mock of him!

"This is the only way of safety, Lucius Paulus, and your fellow citizens will do more than your enemies to make it hard and dangerous for you. For your own soldiers will desire the same thing as the soldiers of the enemy; Varro, the Roman consul, will long for the same thing as Hannibal, the Phoenician commander-in-chief. Single-handed you will have to thwart two generals. But thwart them you will, if you stand out with sufficient firmness against rumours and men's idle talk, if neither the foolish applause bestowed upon your colleague nor your own unmerited disgrace shall move you. Truth, they say, is all too frequently eclipsed but never extinguished. He who scorns false glory shall possess the true. Let them call you timid, instead of cautious; slow, instead of circumspect; unwarlike, instead of experienced soldier. I had rather a wise enemy should fear you than foolish fellow citizens should praise you. He who dares all things will earn Hannibal's contempt; he who does nothing rashly will inspire him with fear. Yet I do not urge that you do nothing, but that reason and not fortune should be your guide. Be master always of yourself and all that is yours; be armed and watchful; be not wanting when opportunity presents itself to you, neither present an opportunity to your enemy. All things will be clear and definite to one who does not hurry. Haste is improvident and blind."

XL. In reply to this the consul spoke in no very cheerful strain, admitting rather that what Fabius said was true than that it was easy of accomplish-

A.U.C. 538 2 factu esse. Dictatori magistrum equitum intolera-
bilem fuisse: quid consuli[1] adversus collegam
seditiosum ac temerarium virium atque auctoritatis
3 fore? Se populare incendium priore consulatu
semustum effugisse; optare ut omnia prospere evenirent;[2] sed si[3] quid adversi caderet,[4] hostium se
telis potius quam suffragiis iratorum civium caput
4 obiecturum.

Ab hoc sermone profectum Paulum tradunt prose-
quentibus primoribus patrum; plebeium consulem
sua plebes prosecuta, turba conspectior, cum digni-
tates deessent.

5 Ut in castra venerunt, permixto novo exercitu ac
vetere, castris bifariam factis, ut nova minora essent
propius Hannibalem, in veteribus maior pars et omne
6 robur virium esset, consulum[5] anni prioris M. Atilium
aetatem excusantem Romam miserunt, Geminum
Servilium in minoribus castris legioni Romanae et
socium peditum equitumque duobus milibus praefici-
7 unt. Hannibal, quamquam parte dimidia auctas
hostium copias cernebat, tamen adventu consulum
mire gaudere. Non solum enim nihil ex raptis in
diem commeatibus superabat, sed ne unde raperet
quidem quicquam reliqui erat[6] omni undique frumento, postquam ager parum tutus erat, in urbes
8 munitas convecto, ut vix decem dierum, quod com-

[1] consuli ς (*Florebellus*): consilia *P*.

[2] prospere evenirent ς: prospe/reuenirent *P*: prospera euenirent ς.

[3] sed si *Heerwagen*: et si *P*: at si ς: si *H. J. Mueller*.

[4] caderet ς: caperet *P*.

[5] consulum *Crévier*: consultum *P*: consulum tum (*or* tum consulum) ς.

[6] reliqui erat ς: reliquerat *P*.

ment. The dictator had found his master of the horse intolerable: what power or influence then would a consul have over a turbulent and headstrong colleague? In his former consulship he had escaped badly burnt from the flames of popular resentment; he hoped that everything would turn out for the best; but if any misfortune should befall, he would sooner expose his life to the swords of the enemy than to the suffrages of his angry fellow citizens. B.C. 216

Immediately after this conference they say that Paulus set out, escorted by the foremost senators: the plebeian consul was escorted by his own friends, the plebeians—in point of numbers the more imposing throng, though it contained no persons of distinction.

When they got to the camp, the new forces were united with the old and the camp was divided into two, with the new and smaller one nearer Hannibal, while the greater part of the army and all the choicest troops were in the old one. Of the consuls of the year before, Marcus Atilius pleaded the excuse of age and was sent back to Rome; Geminus Servilius was put in command of the smaller camp, having under him a Roman legion and two thousand infantry and cavalry of the allies. Hannibal, though he perceived that the forces of his enemies were augmented by a half, was nevertheless greatly rejoiced at the coming of the consuls. For not only were the spoils exhausted on which his men had subsisted from day to day, but there was not even any district left for them to spoil; for when it appeared that the farms were no longer safe, the corn had everywhere been carried into the walled towns, and in consequence there was barely grain

A.U.C. 538 pertum postea est, frumentum superesset Hispanorumque ob inopiam transitio parata fuerit, si maturitas temporum exspectata foret.

XLI. Ceterum temeritati consulis ac praepropero[1] ingenio materiam etiam fortuna dedit, quod in prohibendis praedatoribus tumultuario proelio a procursu[2] magis militum quam ex praeparato aut iussu imperatorum orto haudquaquam par Poenis dimicatio
2 fuit. Ad mille et septingenti caesi, non plus centum Romanorum sociorumque occisis. Ceterum victoribus effuse sequentibus metu insidiarum obstitit Paulus
3 consul, cuius eo die—nam alternis imperitabant—imperium erat, Varrone indignante ac vociferante emissum hostem e manibus debellarique, ni cessatum foret, potuisse.

4 Hannibal id damnum haud aegerrime pati; quin potius gaudere[3] velut inescatam temeritatem ferocioris consulis ac novorum maxime militum esse.
5 Et omnia ei hostium haud secus quam sua nota erant: dissimiles discordesque imperitare, duas prope
6 partes tironum militum in exercitu esse. Itaque locum et tempus insidiis aptum se habere ratus nocte proxima nihil praeter arma ferente secum milite[4]
7 castra plena omnis fortunae publicae privataeque

[1] praepropero ς: prospero *P*.
[2] a procursu *Heraeas*: ac procursu *P*.
[3] gaudere *Pluygers*: credere *P*.
[4] ferente secum milite *Weissenborn*: ferentis secum milites *P*.

[1] Obviously Varro is meant, but it is rather odd that he should not be specified. Weissenborn thinks it likely that with this paragraph Livy began to draw from another source and did not notice the indefiniteness of the word *consulis* in the resulting context.

enough left—as was afterwards discovered—to last ten days, and the Spaniards, for want of food, had made ready to desert, if the Romans had only waited till the time was ripe. B.C. 216

XLI. But even Fortune furnished material to the recklessness and over-hasty temper of the consul.[1] The repulse of a foraging party had led to a general mellay, which came about from the soldiers rushing forward to attack the enemy, rather than from any plan or orders on the part of the generals; and in this the Phoenicians by no means held their own. About seventeen hundred of them were slain and not more than a hundred of Romans and allies. But the consul Paulus, who was in command that day—for they commanded on alternate days—was fearful of an ambuscade and checked the victors in their headlong pursuit, despite the angry remonstrances of Varro, who cried out that they had let the enemy slip through their hands and that they might have brought the war to a conclusion if they had not relaxed their efforts.

Hannibal was not greatly disconcerted by this reverse; indeed he rejoiced that the hook should have been baited, as it were, for the rashness of the more impetuous consul, and especially for that of the new soldiers. All the circumstances of his enemies were as familiar to him as his own: that their generals were unlike each other and were at loggerheads, and that nearly two-thirds of their army consisted of recruits. Believing, therefore, that place and time were favourable for a ruse, he left his camp full of every sort of public and of private riches, and putting himself at the head of his troops, who carried nothing but their weapons, marched over the nearest

A.U.C. 538 relinquit transque proximos montes laeva pedites instructos condit, dextra equites, impedimenta per
8 convallem[1] mediam[2] traducit, ut diripiendis velut desertis fuga dominorum castris occupatum impedi-
9 tumque hostem opprimeret. Crebri relicti in castris ignes, ut fides fieret, dum ipse longius spatium fuga praeciperet, falsa imagine castrorum, sicut Fabium priore anno frustratus esset, tenere in locis consules voluisse.

XLII. Ubi inluxit, subductae primo stationes, deinde propius adeuntibus insolitum silentium ad-
2 mirationem fecit. Tum satis comperta solitudine in castris concursus fit ad praetoria consulum nuntiantium fugam hostium adeo trepidam ut tabernaculis stantibus castra reliquerint, quoque fuga obscurior
3 esset crebros etiam relictos ignes. Clamor inde ortus ut signa proferri iuberent ducerentque ad persequendos hostes ac protinus castra diripienda, et
4 consul alter velut unus turbae militaris erat. Paulus etiam atque etiam dicere providendum praecavendumque esse; postremo, cum aliter neque seditionem neque ducem seditionis sustinere posset, Marium Statilium praefectum cum turma Lucana exploratum mittit.

5 Qui ubi adequitavit portis, subsistere extra munimenta ceteris iussis ipse cum duobus equitibus vallum

[1] convallem *Gronovius*: cornuallem P^1: cornua in P^2.
[2] mediam *Madvig*: medium amnem PC^1: medium agnem C^2: medium agmen *M*.

ridge, drew up the infantry in ambush on the left, and the cavalry on the right, and made the baggage-train pass through the valley between, intending to fall upon the enemy whilst they were preoccupied and encumbered with the pillage of the camp, which would seem to them to have been deserted by its owners. He left a large number of fires burning, as though he had sought by means of this illusory appearance of an encampment to hold the consuls to their positions—as he had cheated Fabius the year before—till he could gain as long a start as possible in his retreat. B.C. 216

XLII. When day came, first the fact that the outposts had been withdrawn, and afterwards—as they came nearer—the unwonted silence filled the Romans with amazement. Then, as it became quite evident that there was no one in the camp, there was a rush of men to the headquarters of the consuls, announcing that the enemy had retreated in such trepidation as to quit the camp without striking their tents, and had even left a great number of fires burning to conceal their flight. Next they began to clamour for the order to advance and to pursue the enemy and plunder the camp without delay, and one of the consuls behaved like a member of the mob of soldiers. Paulus kept insisting on the need for watchfulness and circumspection, and finally, when there was no other way in which he could withstand the mutiny and the leader of the mutiny, he sent the praefect Marius Statilius with a troop of Lucanian horse to reconnoitre.

Riding up to the gates, Statilius commanded the others to wait outside the trenches, and himself with two horsemen entered the camp. After making a

A.U.C. 538 intravit speculatusque omnia cum cura renuntiat
6 insidias profecto esse: ignes in parte castrorum quae vergat[1] in hostem[2] relictos, tabernacula aperta et omnia cara in promptu relicta; argentum quibusdam locis temere per vias velut obiectum ad praedam vidisse.

7 Quae ad deterrendos[3] a cupiditate animos nuntiata erant, ea accenderunt, et clamore orto a militibus, ni signum detur sine ducibus ituros, haudquaquam dux defuit: nam extemplo Varro signum dedit proficis-
8 cendi. Paulus, cum ei sua sponte cunctanti pulli quoque[4] non addixissent, nuntiari iam efferenti porta
9 signa collegae iussit. Quod quamquam Varro aegre est passus, Flamini tamen recens casus Claudique consulis primo Punico bello memorata navalis clades
10 religionem animo incussit. Di prope ipsi eo die magis distulere quam prohibuere imminentem pestem Romanis: nam forte ita evenit ut, cum referri signa
11 in castra iubenti consuli milites non parerent, servi duo, Formiani unus alter Sidicini equitis, qui Servilio atque Atilio consulibus inter pabulatores excepti a Numidis fuerant, profugerent eo die ad dominos deductique ad consules nuntiant omnem exercitum

[1] quae vergat ς: quae uergant *P*: qua vergant *Frigell.*
[2] in hostem ς: ad hostem MC^2 (*Madvig*): ad in hostem PC^1.
[3] deterrendos *Gronovius*: deterendos P^1: detenendos P^2.
[4] pulli quoque *Fuegner*: pulli quoque auspicio *P*.

---

[1] sc. between the rows of tents.
[2] A Roman general took with him on his campaign a *pullarius*—keeper of the sacred chickens—who reported favourable or unfavourable omens, according to the eagerness with which the fowls fed. See VI. xli. 8, VIII. xxx. 2.

thorough and careful examination he reported that there was undoubtedly some treachery afoot. The fires, he said, had been left on the side of the camp that faced the Romans; the tents were open and all kinds of valuables were left exposed to view; here and there he had seen silver carelessly flung down in the lanes,[1] as if to tempt a pillager. B.C. 216

The report, which had been made with the purpose of checking the soldiers' greed, only inflamed it, and they began to shout that if the signal were not given, they would go without any leaders. But there was no lack of a leader; for Varro at once gave the command to start. Paulus himself wished to delay; and when the sacred fowls had refused their sanction,[2] he gave orders to notify his colleague, who was just setting forth with the standards from the gate. Varro was greatly vexed at this, but the recent disaster of Flaminius and the memorable defeat at sea of the consul Claudius, in the first Punic War[3] made him fearful of offending the heavenly powers. On that day, it might almost be said, the very gods put off, but did not prevent, the calamity that impended over the Romans: for it chanced that when the consul ordered the standards back into the camp and the soldiers were refusing to obey him, two slaves appeared on the scene, one belonging to a Formian, the other to a Sidicinian knight. They had been captured by the Numidians, along with other foragers, in the consulship of Servilius and Atilius, and on that day had escaped back to their masters. Being conducted to the

[3] P. Claudius Pulcher disregarded the warning of the sacred fowls and was defeated off Drepanum in 249 B.C. (Summary of Book XIX.)

A.U.C. Hannibalis trans proximos montes sedere in insidiis.
538 12 Horum opportunus adventus consules imperii po-
tentes fecit, cum ambitio alterius suam primum apud
eos prava indulgentia maiestatem[1] solvisset.

XLIII. Hannibal, postquam motos magis incon-
sulte Romanos quam ad ultimum temere evectos
vidit, nequiquam detecta fraude in castra rediit.
2 Ibi plures dies propter inopiam frumenti manere
nequit, novaque consilia in dies non apud milites
solum mixtos ex conluvione omnium gentium, sed
3 etiam apud ducem ipsum oriebantur. Nam cum
initio fremitus, deinde aperta vociferatio fuisset
exposcentium stipendium debitum querentiumque
annonam primo, postremo famem; et mercennarios
4 milites, maxime Hispani generis, de transitione
cepisse consilium fama esset; ipse etiam interdum
Hannibal de fuga in Galliam dicitur agitasse, ita
ut relicto peditatu omni cum equitibus se proriperet.
5 Cum haec consilia atque hic habitus animorum esset
in castris, movere inde statuit in calidiora atque eo
maturiora messibus Apuliae loca, simul quod, quo[2]
longius ab hoste recessisset transfugia impeditiora

[1] apud eos prava indulgentia maiestatem *edd.*: apud eos prauam indulgentiam maiestate *P*: apud eos maiestatem *C. Heraeus*: deinde collegae maiestatem *Novák*.

[2] quod, quo *Weissenborn*: quod *P*: ut quo ς.

---

[1] According to Polybius (III. cvii. ff.), Servilius, consul in 217, was still in command of the army before Gereonium when Hannibal marched south and seized the citadel of Cannae, which the Romans had been using as a granary. On receiving the disquieting news of this serious loss, Servilius sent to Rome and asked for instructions. The senate decided to give battle, and sent the new consuls to the front to take command. The engagement at Cannae

consuls, they stated that Hannibal's entire army was lying in ambush just over the nearest hills. Their opportune arrival restored the authority of the consuls, when one of them, by running after popularity, and by unprincipled indulgence, had impaired their prestige—beginning with his own—amongst the soldiers. B.C. 216

XLIII. Hannibal, perceiving that the Romans, although they had acted ill-advisedly, had not proceeded to the extremity of rashness, returned to the camp, his stratagem having been detected and rendered idle. There, however, the scarcity of corn forbade his remaining many days, and new plans were daily forming, not only amongst the soldiers, the mingled offscourings of every race on earth, but even in the mind of the general himself. For when the men, with murmurs at first and afterwards with loud clamours, demanded their arrears of pay, and complained at first of the scarcity of corn, and finally of being starved; and when the report went round that the mercenaries—particularly those of Spanish blood—had resolved on going over to the enemy; they say that even Hannibal himself had thoughts of abandoning all his infantry and saving himself and his cavalry by escaping into Gaul. Such being the projects that were entertained in camp and such the temper of his soldiers, he decided to move from his present quarters to Apulia,[1] where the climate was warmer and in consequence of this the harvest earlier; at the same time it would be the more difficult, the greater their distance from the enemy, for those of his followers who

was fought seven days after the Romans had set out to follow Hannibal.

A.U.C. 538

6 levibus ingeniis essent. Profectus est nocte ignibus similiter factis tabernaculisque paucis in speciem relictis, ut insidiarum par priori metus contineret Romanos.

7 Sed per eundem Lucanum Statilium omnibus ultra castra transque montes exploratis cum relatum esset visum procul hostium agmen, tum de sequendo eo[1]
8 consilia agitari coepta. Cum utriusque consulis eadem quae ante semper fuisset[2] sententia, ceterum Varroni fere omnes, Paulo nemo praeter Servilium
9 prioris anni consulem adsentiretur, ex maioris[3] partis sententia ad nobilitandas clade Romana Cannas
10 urgente fato profecti sunt. Prope eum vicum Hannibal castra posuerat aversa a Volturno vento, qui
11 campis torridis siccitate nubes pulveris vehit. Id cum ipsis castris percommodum fuit, tum salutare praecipue futurum erat, cum aciem dirigerent, ipsi

[1] de sequendo eo *Novák*: die sequenti eo *P*: de insequendo eo *Lipsius*.
[2] fuisset *P*: esset *Doering*.
[3] ex maioris *Luchs*: maioris *P*.

---

[1] Weissenborn suggests the possibility that the repetition of this stratagem in Livy's narrative may be due to a combination of different versions occurring respectively in Coelius Antipater and in Valerius Antias. The whole passage (chap. xl.—chap. xliii.) is discussed by De Sanctis, III. 2, p. 59[90], who regards the story of the two camps at Gereonium as a repetition of the situation on the Aufidus (chap. xliv. § 1). The scarcity of provisions attributed to Hannibal was invented, he thinks, in order to make it appear the less excusable in the Romans to have accepted battle. The new skirmish at Gereonium is a repetition of the one to which Polybius refers as taking place fifty stades from Cannae. Finally, the stratagem of the abandoned camp

were fickle to desert. He set out in the night, B.C. 216 after making up some fires, as before, and leaving a few tents standing where they would be seen, so that the Romans might be withheld from following him through fear of an ambush, as before.[1]

But when the same Lucanian, Statilius, had made a thorough reconnaissance beyond the camp and on the other side of the mountains, and had reported seeing the enemy on the march a long way off, then the question of pursuing him began to be debated. The consuls were each of the same mind as they had always been; but Varro had the support of almost everybody, Paulus of none except Servilius, the consul of the year before. The will of the majority prevailed, and they set forward, under the urge of destiny, to make Cannae famous for the calamity which there befell the Romans. This was the village near which Hannibal had pitched his camp,[2] with his back to the Volturnus,[3] a wind that brings clouds of dust over the drought-parched plains. Such a disposition was very convenient for the camp itself and bound to be particularly salutary when the troops formed up for battle, facing in the opposite direction, with

is ridiculous and absurd, for the Romans had only to occupy it with a couple of legions and Hannibal would have found it very difficult to recover, and even if Aemilius had chosen to allow Hannibal to return to his camp, he would have deserved a court-martial if he had not first destroyed the tents and levelled the camp and filled the trenches. De Sanctis thinks that the whole episode is characteristic of Valerius Antias.

[2] Livy forgets to point out that Hannibal later crossed the river and encamped on the western side (Map 7).

[3] This was the Eurus of the Greeks (Seneca, *Nat. Quaest.* v. xvi. 4), now called Scirocco. The Latin name is from Mt. Voltur in Apulia, S.W. of Cannae.

A.U.C. 538

aversi, terga tantum adflante vento, in occaecatum pulvere offuso[1] hostem pugnaturi.

XLIV. Consules satis exploratis itineribus sequentes Poenum,[2] ut ventum ad Cannas est et in[3] conspectu Poenum habebant, bina castra communiunt eodem ferme intervallo quo ad Gereonium, sicut
2 ante copiis divisis. Aufidus[4] amnis utrisque[5] castris adfluens aditum aquatoribus ex sua cuiusque oppor-
3 tunitate haud sine certamine dabat; ex minoribus tamen castris, quae posita trans Aufidum erant, liberius aquabantur Romani, quia ripa ulterior nullum habebat hostium praesidium.

4 Hannibal spem nanctus locis natis ad equestrem pugnam, qua parte virium invictus erat, facturos copiam pugnandi consules, derigit aciem lacessitque
5 Numidarum procursatione hostes. Inde rursus sollicitari seditione militari ac discordia consulum Romana castra, cum Paulus Semproni que et Flamini temeritatem Varroni, Varro Paulo[6] speciosum timidis ac
6 segnibus ducibus exemplum Fabium obiceret, testareturque deos hominesque hic, nullam penes se culpam esse, quod Hannibal iam velut usu[7] cepisset

[1] offuso *Walch*: effuso *P*.
[2] sequentes Poenum *P*: sequentes *Schenkl*.
[3] et in *Gronovius*: ut in *P*.
[4] Aufidus P^2: aufidius (*and in* § 3 aufidium *corrected from* aufidum) P^1 (*cf. Plut., Fab.* 15 *and Ptol.* III. i. 15).
[5] utrisque *edd.*: utriusque *P*.
[6] Varro Paulo *Wesenberg*: uarro *P*.
[7] velut usu ς: uel usu *P*.

---

[1] At chap. xl. § 5 we were not told how far apart the camps were, but only that the smaller one was nearer Hannibal than the larger one.

[2] Neither Livy nor Polybius (III. cx.) states explicitly that the larger camp of the Romans was on the left, or western bank, but that such was the fact may fairly be inferred from

the wind blowing only on their backs, and ready to fight with enemies half-blinded by the dust driven into their faces. B.C. 216

XLIV. The consuls, after making a sufficient reconnaissance of the roads, followed the Phoenicians until they came to Cannae, where, having the enemy in view, they divided their forces, as they had done before, and fortified two camps, at about the same distance from one another as at Gereonium.[1] The river Aufidus, flowing past both their camps, was readily accessible to water-carriers at such spots as were convenient for each, though not without fighting; it was, however, from the smaller camp, which was situated across the Aufidus,[2] that the Romans could fetch water more freely, since the enemy had no troops posted on the further bank.

Hannibal had conceived a hope that the consuls would give him an opportunity of fighting in a place that was formed by nature for a cavalry action, in which arm he was invincible. He therefore drew out his men in battle array and ordered the Numidians to make a sally and provoke the enemy. This caused the camp of the Romans to be once more the scene of strife amongst the soldiers and dissension between the consuls. Paulus cast in Varro's teeth the recklessness of Sempronius and Flaminius; Varro retorted that Fabius was a specious example for timid and slothful generals, and called on gods and men to witness that it was through no fault of his that Hannibal had by now acquired as it were a

Livy's *trans Aufidum* (§ 3) and Polybius's πέραν, ἀπὸ διαβάσεως πρὸς τὰς ἀνατολάς (III. cx. 10), both of which phrases are used of the smaller camp, and such is the view of Professor Kromayer. (See map.)

A.U.C. 538 Italiam; se constrictum a collega teneri; ferrum
atque arma iratis et pugnare cupientibus adimi
7 militibus: ille, si quid proiectis ac proditis ad in-
consultam atque improvidam pugnam legionibus accideret, se omnis culpae exsortem, omnis eventus participem fore diceret; videret ut quibus lingua prompta [1]
ac temeraria aeque in pugna vigerent manus.

XLV. Dum altercationibus magis quam consiliis
tempus teritur, Hannibal ex acie, quam ad multum diei
tenuerat instructam, cum in castra ceteras reciperet
2 copias, Numidas ad invadendos ex minoribus castris
3 Romanorum aquatores trans flumen mittit. Quam
inconditam turbam cum vixdum in ripam egressi
clamore ac tumultu fugassent, in stationem [2] quoque
pro vallo locatam atque ad ipsas [3] prope portas evecti
4 sunt. Id vero adeo indignum [4] visum, ab tumultuario
auxilio [5] iam etiam castra Romana terreri, ut ea modo
una causa ne extemplo transirent flumen derigerent-
que aciem tenuerit Romanos, quod summa imperii
eo die penes Paulum fuerit.

5 Itaque postero die Varro,[6] cui sors eius diei imperii
erat, nihil consulto collega signum proposuit in-
structasque copias flumen traduxit sequente Paulo,
quia magis non probare quam non adiuvare consilium
6 poterat. Transgressi flumen eas quoque quas in

[1] lingua prompta *P*: lingua tam prompta *C* (*Madvig*).

[2] in stationem ς: stationem *P*.

[3] ad ipsas *Fügner*: ipsas *P*.

[4] adeo indignum ς: indignum *P*.

[5] auxilio *P*: vexillo *Hachtmann*.

[6] postero die Varro *Alschefski*: uarro postero die uarro *P*[1]: uarro postero die *P*[2]*C*.

prescriptive right to Italy, for he was kept in fetters by his colleague, and the soldiers, enraged as they were and eager to fight, were deprived of swords and arms. Paulus rejoined that if anything untoward should befall the legions, recklessly abandoned to an ill-advised and rash engagement, he would himself be guiltless of all blame, but would share in all the consequences; let Varro, he said, see to it, that where tongues were bold and ready, hands—when it came to fighting—were no less so. B.C. 216

XLV. While they wasted time, rather quarrelling than consulting, Hannibal withdrew the rest of his troops, whom he had kept in line till far on in the day, into his camp, and sent the Numidians across the river to attack the men from the smaller Roman camp who were fetching water. They had hardly come out upon the other bank when their shouts and tumult sent that unorganized rabble flying, and they rode on till they came to the party that was stationed in front of the rampart, and almost to the very gates. So wholly outrageous, however, did it seem that by now even a Roman camp should be terrorized by irregular auxiliaries, that only one thing kept the Romans from crossing the river forthwith and giving battle—the fact that Paulus happened then to be in command.

The next morning, therefore, Varro, whom the lot had made commander for that day, hung out the signal, without saying a word of the matter to his colleague, and, making his troops fall in, led them over the river. Paulus followed him, for he could more easily disapprove the plan than deprive it of his help. Once across, they joined to their own the

A.U.C. 538 castris minoribus habuerant copias suis adiungunt atque ita instruunt aciem:[1] in dextro cornu—id erat
7 flumini propius—Romanos equites locant, deinde pedites; laevum cornu extremi equites sociorum, intra pedites, ad medium iuncti legionibus Romanis, tenuerunt; iaculatores cum ceteris[2] levium armorum auxiliis prima acies facta. Consules cornua tenuere,[3]
8 Terentius laevum, Aemilius dextrum; Gemino Servilio media pugna tuenda data.

XLVI. Hannibal luce prima Baliaribus levique alia armatura praemissa transgressus flumen, ut
2 quosque traduxerat ita in acie locabat: Gallos Hispanosque equites prope ripam laevo in cornu
3 adversus Romanum equitatum; dextrum cornu Numidis equitibus datum; media acies[4] peditibus firmata, ita ut Afrorum utraque cornua essent, inter-
4 ponerentur his medii Galli atque Hispani. Afros[5] Romanam crederes[6] aciem: ita armati erant armis et ad Trebiam, ceterum magna ex parte ad Trasu-
5 mennum captis. Gallis Hispanisque scuta eiusdem formae fere erant, dispares ac dissimiles gladii, Gallis praelongi ac sine mucronibus, Hispano, punctim magis quam caesim adsueto petere hostem, brevitate habiles et cum mucronibus. Ante alios[7] habitus[8] gentium harum cum magnitudine corporum tum

[1] instruunt aciem *Weissenborn*: instructa acie *P*.
[2] cum ceteris *Doujatius and Drakenborch*: ex ceteris *P*.
[3] tenuere *Alschefski*: tenuerent P^1: tenerent P^2.
[4] acies ς: acie *P*.
[5] Afros ς: afro P^1: afri P^2: Afrorum *Alschefski*.
[6] crederes *Woelfflin*: magna ex parte crederes *P*.
[7] ante alios *Madvig*: antetalius *P*.
[8] habitus ς: hannibatus P^1: hanimatus P^2.

---

[1] The Romans adopted this sword for their legionaries. It was provided with two sharp edges for cutting as well

forces which they had kept in the smaller camp, B.C. 216 and marshalled their battle-line as follows: on the right wing—the one nearer the river—they placed the Roman cavalry, and next them the Roman foot; the left wing had on the outside the cavalry of the allies; and nearer the centre, in contact with the Roman legions, the infantry of the allies. The slingers and other light-armed auxiliaries were formed up in front. The consuls had charge of the wings, Terentius of the left, Aemilius of the right; and Geminus Servilius was entrusted with the centre.

XLVI. Hannibal crossed the river at break of day, after sending ahead of him the Baliares and the other light-armed troops, and posted each corps in line of battle, in the order in which he had brought it over. The Gallic and Spanish horse were next the river, on the left wing, facing the Roman cavalry; the right wing was assigned to the Numidian horse; the centre was composed of infantry, so arranged as to have the Africans at both ends, and between them Gauls and Spaniards. The Africans might have passed for an array of Romans, equipped as they were with arms captured partly at the Trebia but mostly at Lake Trasumennus. The Gauls and the Spaniards had shields of almost the same shape; their swords were different in use and in appearance, those of the Gauls being very long and pointless, whilst the Spaniards, who attacked as a rule more by thrusting than by striking, had pointed ones that were short and handy.[1] These tribes were more terrifying to look on than the others, because of the size of their bodies and the display they made of them. The Gauls

as with a point, and had a strong, firm blade (Polybius VI. xxiii. 7).

A.U.C. 538
6 specie terribilis erat. Galli super umbilicum erant
nudi: Hispani linteis praetextis purpura tunicis
candore miro fulgentibus constiterant. Numerus[1]
omnium peditum qui tum[2] stetere in[3] acie milium
7 fuit quadraginta, decem equitum. Duces cornibus
praeerant, sinistro Hasdrubal, dextro Maharbal; mediam aciem Hannibal ipse cum fratre Magone tenuit.
8 Sol, seu de industria ita locatis seu quod forte ita
stetere,[4] peropportune utrique parti obliquus erat,
Romanis in meridiem, Poenis in septemtrionem
9 versis; ventus—Volturnum regionis incolae vocant
—adversus Romanis coortus multo pulvere in ipsa
ora volvendo prospectum ademit.

XLVII. Clamore sublato procursum ab auxiliis[5]
et pugna levibus primum armis commissa; deinde
equitum Gallorum Hispanorumque laevum cornu
cum dextro Romano concurrit, minime equestris
2 more pugnae: frontibus enim adversis concurrendum
erat quia nullo circa ad evagandum relicto spatio
3 hinc amnis hinc peditum acies claudebant. In
derectum utrimque nitentes stantibus ac confertis[6]
postremo turba equis vir virum amplexus detrahebat
equo. Pedestre magna iam ex parte certamen
factum erat; acrius tamen quam diutius pugnatum
est, pulsique Romani equites terga vertunt.

4 Sub equestris finem certaminis coorta est peditum

[1] Numerus *Gronovius*: numerum *P*.
[2] qui tum *Gronovius*: equititum *P*.
[3] stetere in ς: steterentin P^1: terentina P^2.
[4] stetere *Gronovius*: statere P^1: stare P^2.
[5] ab auxiliis ς: auxiliis *P*.
[6] ac confertis ς: ad confertis *P*.

were naked from the navel up; the Spaniards had B.C. 216
formed up wearing crimson-bordered linen tunics that shone with a dazzling whiteness. The total number of the infantry who then took their place in line was forty thousand, of the cavalry ten thousand. The generals commanding on the wings were Hasdrubal on the left, Maharbal on the right; Hannibal himself, with his brother Mago, had the centre.

The sun—whether they had so placed themselves on purpose or stood as they did by accident—was, very conveniently for both sides, on their flanks, the Romans looking south, the Phoenicians north. A wind—which those who live in those parts call Volturnus—beginning to blow against the Romans carried clouds of dust right into their faces and prevented them from seeing anything.[1]

XLVII. With a shout the auxiliaries rushed forward and the battle began between the light-armed troops. Then the Gallic and Spanish horse which formed the left wing engaged with the Roman right in a combat very unlike a cavalry action. For they had to charge front to front, there being no room to move out round the flank, for the river shut them in on one side and the ranks of infantry on the other. Both parties pushed straight ahead, and as the horses came to a standstill, packed together in the throng, the riders began to grapple with their enemies and drag them from their seats. They were fighting on foot now, for the most part; but sharp though the struggle was, it was soon over, and the defeated Roman cavalry turned and fled.

Towards the end of the cavalry engagement the

[1] Note the repetition—apparently unconscious—of what was said at chap. xliii. § 10.

A.U.C. 538 pugna, primo et viribus et animis par, dum[1] consta-
5 bant ordines Gallis Hispanisque; tandem Romani,
diu ac saepe conisi, aequa[2] fronte acieque densa
impulere hostium cuneum nimis tenuem eoque parum
6 validum, a cetera prominentem acie. Impulsis
deinde ac trepide referentibus pedem institere[3] ac
tenore uno per praeceps pavore fugientium agmen[4]
in mediam primum aciem inlati, postremo nullo
7 resistente ad subsidia Afrorum pervenerunt, qui
utrimque reductis alis constiterant, media, qua
Galli[5] Hispanique steterant, aliquantum prominente
8 acie. Qui cuneus ut pulsus aequavit frontem primum,
dein cedendo[6] etiam sinum[7] in medio dedit, Afri
circa iam cornua fecerant irruentibusque incaute in
medium Romanis circumdedere alas, mox cornua
9 extendendo clausere et ab tergo hostes. Hinc
Romani, defuncti nequiquam proelio uno, omissis

[1] par, dum *Madvig*: parum *P*.
[2] conisi (connisi) aequa ς (*cf. Franz Miltner, Wiener Studien* 45 (1926–7) 251–253): consiliaequa P^1: consilio qua P^2: connisi obliqua *Lipsius*.
[3] institere *Gronovius*: insistere *P*.
[4] agmen ς: agmine *P*.
[5] qua Galli ς: quaefalli *P*.
[6] dein cedendo *Alschefski*: deindetendo P^1: deinde nitendo P^2: deinde cedendo *Ruperti*.
[7] sinum ς: in sinum *P*.

---

[1] Polybius says (III. cxv. 6) that "they had crowded up from the wings to the centre, where the fighting was going on." Consequently their line was much *deeper* than that of their adversaries.

[2] This is called by Polybius (III. cxiii. 8) μηνοειδὲς κύρτωμα, "a crescent-shaped convexity." Kromayer rightly insists that this expression must not be taken literally, and understands it of a formation in echelon (see Schlachten-Atlas I., columns 23 and 26, and his map reproduced as No. 7 in this volume.)

infantry got into action. At first they were evenly B.C. 216
matched in strength and courage, as long as the Gauls and Spaniards maintained their ranks; but at last the Romans, by prolonged and frequent efforts, pushing forward with an even front and a dense line,[1] drove in the wedge-like formation [2] which projected from the enemy's line, for it was too thin to be strong; and then, as the Gauls and Spaniards gave way and fell back in confusion, pressed forward and without once stopping forced their way through the crowd of fleeing, panic-stricken foes, till they reached first the centre [3] and ultimately—for they met with no resistance—the African supports. These had been used to form the two wings, which had been drawn back, while the centre, where the Gauls and Spaniards had been stationed, projected somewhat. When this wedge was first driven back so far as to straighten the front, and then, continuing to yield, even left a hollow in the centre, the Africans had already begun a flanking movement on either side, and as the Romans rushed incautiously in between, they enveloped them, and presently, extending their wings, crescent-wise, even closed in on their rear.[4] From this moment the Romans, who had gained one battle to no purpose, gave over the

[3] *in mediam aciem* is a puzzling phrase, as it ought to mean the same thing as the projecting wedge which constituted the Carthaginian centre. But the Romans had already driven in this wedge. Livy perhaps means that the Romans have now reached a point where they are level with the two flanks (consisting of Africans) and midway between them.

[4] Polybius (III. cxv. 9) gives a somewhat different account of this manœuvre. According to him the Africans—who must have been drawn up in a line so deep as to be more like a column—merely *faced* inward, as the Romans pursued the fleeing Gauls and Spaniards, and charged them on both flanks.

A.U.C. 538 Gallis Hispanisque, quorum terga ceciderant,[1] ad-
10 versus Afros integram pugnam ineunt, non tantum
eo[2] iniquam quod inclusi adversus circumfusos sed
etiam quod fessi cum recentibus ac vegetis pugnabant.

XLVIII. Iam et sinistro cornu Romano,[3] ubi
sociorum equites adversus Numidas steterant, con-
sertum proelium erat, segne primo et a Punica
2 coeptum fraude. Quingenti ferme Numidae, praeter
solita[4] arma telaque gladios occultos sub loricis
habentes, specie transfugarum cum ab suis parmas
3 post terga habentes adequitassent, repente ex equis
desiliunt parmisque et[5] iaculis ante pedes hostium
proiectis in mediam aciem accepti ductique ad
ultimos considere ab tergo iubentur. Ac dum
proelium ab omni parte conseritur, quieti manserunt;
4 postquam omnium animos oculosque occupaverat
certamen, tum arreptis scutis, quae passim inter
acervos caesorum corporum strata erant, aversam
adoriuntur Romanam aciem tergaque ferientes ac
poplites caedentes stragem ingentem ac maiorem
5 aliquanto pavorem ac tumultum fecerunt. Cum alibi
terror ac fuga, alibi pertinax in mala iam spe proelium esset, Hasdrubal, qui ea parte praeerat, sub-
ductos ex media acie Numidas, quia[6] segnis eorum
cum adversis pugna erat, ad persequendos passim

[1] ceciderant ς: caeciderat et *P*.
[2] eo ς: in eo *P*.
[3] Romano ς: romani *P*.
[4] praeter solita *N. Heinsius and J. Perizonius*: praeter consueta ς: praeterita *P*: praeter iusta *Gronovius*.
[5] et ς: etiam *P*.
[6] quia *C*: qui *P*.

---

[1] The "panic rout" was on the Roman left (the Roman right had already been annihilated), the "obstinate though hopeless struggle" at the centre.

pursuit and slaughter of the Gauls and Spaniards and began a new fight with the Africans. In this they were at a twofold disadvantage: they were shut in, while their enemies ranged on every side of them; they were tired, and faced troops that were fresh and strong. B.C. 216

XLVIII. By this time the Roman left, where the cavalry of the allies had taken position facing the Numidians, was also engaged, though the fighting was at first but sluggish. It began with a Punic ruse. About five hundred Numidians, who, in addition to their customary arms and missiles, carried swords concealed under their corslets, pretended to desert. Riding over from their own side, with their bucklers at their backs, they suddenly dismounted and threw down bucklers and javelins at the feet of their enemies. Being received into the midst of their ranks they were conducted to the rear and ordered to fall in behind. And while the battle was getting under way at every point, they kept quite still; but no sooner were the minds and eyes of all absorbed in the struggle, than they snatched up the shields which lay strewn about everywhere amongst the heaps of slain, and assailing the Romans from behind and striking at their backs and hamstrings, effected a great slaughter and a terror and confusion that were even greater. And now in one place there was a panic rout and in another an obstinate though hopeless struggle,[1] when Hasdrubal, who commanded in that part of the field, withdrew the Numidians from the centre—since they fought but half-heartedly against men who met them face to face—and dispatching them in pursuit of the scattered fugitives, sent in the Spanish and Gallic cavalry to help the

A.U.C. 538 6 fugientes mittit, Hispanos et Gallos equites[1] Afris prope iam fessis caede magis quam pugna adiungit.

XLIX. Parte altera pugnae Paulus, quamquam primo statim proelio funda graviter ictus fuerat,
2 tamen et occurrit saepe cum confertis Hannibali et aliquot locis proelium restituit, protegentibus eum equitibus Romanis, omissis postremo equis, quia consulem vel ad[2] regendum equum vires deficiebant.
3 Tum nuntianti[3] cuidam, iussisse consulem ad pedes descendere equites, dixisse Hannibalem ferunt:
4 "Quam mallem, vinctos mihi traderet!" Equitum pedestre proelium, quale iam haud dubia hostium victoria, fuit, cum victi mori in vestigio mallent quam fugere, victores morantibus victoriam irati
5 trucidarent, quos pellere non poterant. Pepulerunt tamen iam paucos superantes et labore ac volneribus fessos, inde dissipati omnes sunt equosque ad fugam qui poterant repetebant.

6 Cn. Lentulus tribunus militum, cum praetervehens equo sedentem in saxo cruore oppletum consulem

[1] equites *Gronovius*: pedites *P*: *deleted by Fabri.*
[2] vel ad *Heraeus*: et ad *P*: ad ς.
[3] nuntianti (nunc-) *Crévier*: denuntianti *P*: renuntianti *Gronovius.*

---

[1] The Numidians (both the five hundred and the main body of them) after routing the Roman left had presumably swung round to attack the Roman centre, when Hasdrubal withdrew them from the battle to use them as pursuit troops, replacing them with the cavalry originally posted on the Punic left, which after defeating the Roman cavalry (chap. xlvii. §§ 1-3) had presumably ridden round the Roman centre and joined the Numidians. The episode of the five hundred (not mentioned by Polybius) is perhaps derived from the account of Coelius Antipater. Appian (vii. iv. 22) describes the ruse as being executed by five hundred Celtiberians (foot-soldiers in the Punic centre).

Africans, who were now almost exhausted, though more with slaying than with fighting.[1] B.C. 216

XLIX. In the other part of the field[2] Paulus, although he had received a severe wound from a sling at the very outset of the battle, nevertheless repeatedly opposed himself to Hannibal,[3] with his men in close formation, and at several points restored the fight. He was guarded by Roman cavalry, who finally let their horses go, as the consul was growing too weak even to control his horse. At this Hannibal, being told by someone that the consul had ordered his troopers to dismount, is said to have exclaimed: "How much better if he had handed them over to me in fetters!"[4] The dismounted horsemen fought as men no longer doubting that the enemy must be victorious. They were beaten, but chose rather to die where they stood than to run away; and the victors, angry that their victory was thus delayed, cut them down, when they could not rout them. But they routed them at last, when only a few were left, exhausted with fighting and with wounds. The survivors were now all dispersed, and those who could attempted to regain their horses and escape.

Gnaeus Lentulus, a tribune of the soldiers, as he rode by on his horse, caught sight of the consul sitting on a stone and covered with blood. "Lucius

[2] In chap. xlviii. § 5 *ea parte* means the Punic right = Roman left. Here *Parte altera* is the centre—where Livy thinks of Paulus as having taken over the command from Servilius.

[3] That is, the Punic centre.

[4] An ironical intimation that, since the consul's order amounted to depriving his troopers of any hope of escape, he might as well have surrendered them at once and saved Hannibal all further trouble.

A.U.C. 538
7 vidisset, "L. Aemili," inquit, "quem unum insontem
culpae cladis hodiernae dei respicere debent, cape
hunc equum, dum et tibi virium aliquid superest et
8 comes[1] ego te tollere possum ac protegere. Ne
funestam hanc pugnam morte consulis feceris;
etiam sine hoc[2] lacrimarum satis luctusque est."
9 Ad ea consul: "Tu[3] quidem, Cn. Corneli, macte
virtute esto: sed cave frustra miserando exiguum
10 tempus e manibus hostium evadendi absumas. Abi,
nuntia publice patribus, urbem Romanam muniant
ac priusquam victor hostis advenit praesidiis firment;
privatim Q. Fabio, L. Aemilium[4] praeceptorum eius
11 memorem et vixisse adhuc et mori. Me[5] in hac
strage militum meorum patere exspirare, ne aut reus
iterum e consulatu sim aut accusator collegae exsistam,
ut[6] alieno crimine innocentiam meam protegam."
12 Haec eos[7] agentes prius turba fugientium civium
deinde hostes oppressere; consulem ignorantes quis
esset, obruere[8] telis, Lentulum inter tumultum[9]
abripuit equus. Tum undique[10] effuse fugiunt.
13 Septem milia hominum in minora castra, decem in
maiora, duo ferme in vicum ipsum Cannas perfugerunt; qui extemplo a Carthalone atque equitibus
nullo munimento tegente[11] vicum circumventi sunt.
14 Consul alter, seu forte seu consilio nulli fugientium

[1] et comes *Walch*: comes *P*.
[2] sine hoc ς: si hoc *P*: sine hac *Gronovius*.
[3] consul: "Tu ς: consulto *P*.
[4] L. Aemilium ς: aemilium *P*.
[5] me ς: me et *P*: memet *Weissenborn*.
[6] ut ς: aut *P*.
[7] haec eos *Madvig*: haec ex *P*: haec *Weissenborn*.
[8] obruere ς: obruerent *P*.
[9] inter tumultum *Gronovius*: in tumulum *P*: in tumultu ς.
[10] undique *Alschefski*: unde *P*.
[11] tegente ς: tegentes *P*.

Aemilius," he cried, "on whom the gods ought to look down in mercy, as the only man without guilt in this day's disaster, take this horse, while you have still a little strength remaining and I can attend you and raise you up and guard you. Make not this battle calamitous by a consul's death; even without that there are tears and grief enough." B.C. 216

To this the consul answered, "All honour, Cornelius, to your manhood! But waste not in unavailing pity the little time you have to escape the enemy. Go, and tell the senators in public session to fortify the City of Rome and garrison it strongly before the victorious enemy draws near: in private say to Quintus Fabius that Lucius Aemilius has lived till this hour and now dies remembering his precepts. As for me, let me breathe my last in the midst of my slaughtered soldiers, lest either for a second time I be brought to trial after being consul,[1] or else stand forth the accuser of my colleague, blaming another in defence of my own innocence." While they were speaking, there came up with them first a crowd of fleeing Romans, and then the enemy, who overwhelmed the consul, without knowing who he was, beneath a rain of missiles. Lentulus, thanks to his horse, escaped in the confusion. The rout was now everywhere complete. Seven thousand men escaped into the smaller camp, ten thousand into the larger, and about two thousand into the village of Cannae itself. These last were immediately cut off by Carthalo and his cavalry, for the village was not fortified. The other consul, whether by accident

[1] Chap. xxxv. § 3.

A.U.C. 538 insertus[1] agmini, cum quinquaginta fere equitibus Venusiam perfugit.

15 Quadraginta quinque milia quingenti pedites, duo milia septigenti equites et tantadem[2] prope civium
16 sociorumque pars caesi dicuntur; in his ambo consulum quaestores, L. Atilius et L. Furius Bibaculus, et undetriginta[3] tribuni militum, consulares quidam praetoriique et aedilicii—inter eos Cn. Servilium Geminum[4] et M. Minucium numerant, qui magister equitum priore anno, aliquot annis ante consul[5] fuerat,
17 —octoginta praeterea aut senatores aut qui eos magistratus gessissent unde in senatum legi deberent cum sua voluntate milites in legionibus facti essent.
18 Capta eo proelio tria milia peditum et equites mille et quingenti dicuntur.

L. Haec est[6] pugna Cannensis, Alliensi[7] cladi nobilitate par, ceterum uti eis[8] quae post pugnam
2 accidere levior, quia ab hoste est cessatum, sic strage
3 exercitus gravior foediorque. Fuga namque ad

[1] insertus *C. L. Bauer*: infestus *P*.
[2] et tantadem *Madvig*: etanta *P*.
[3] undetriginta (XXIX) *Gronovius*: uigintiunudice *P*.
[4] Geminum *Gronovius*: inimum *P*.
[5] aliquot annis ante consul *J. Gronovius*: consul aliquot ante annis *J. F. Gronovius*: aliquot annis ante *P*.
[6] est ς: et *P*.
[7] Cannensis, Alliensi (*the spelling* -ll- *is established by the Fasti Antiates, an inscr. of* A.D. 51) *Gronovius*: aliiensi (*and in* § 3 aliam) P^1: cannensi P^2.
[8] uti eis *Luchs*: utilis *P*: ut illis ς: ut iis *Novák*.

---

[1] The other ancient accounts give the numbers as follows: Eutropius (III. 10) 40,000 foot and 3500 horse; Appian (VII. iv. 25) and Livy himself in three speeches (chap. lix. § 5; chap. lx. § 14 and XXV. vi. 13) as well as Plutarch

or by design, had not joined any throng of fugitives, B.C. 216 but fled to Venusia with some fifty horsemen.

It is said that forty-five thousand five hundred foot and two thousand seven hundred horse were slain, in an almost equal proportion of citizens and allies.[1] In the number were the quaestors of both consuls, Lucius Atilius and Lucius Furius Bibaculus, and twenty-nine military tribunes,[2] some of consular rank, some of praetorian or aedilician—amongst others are mentioned Gnaeus Servilius Geminus and Marcus Minucius, who had been master of the horse in the preceding years and consul several years before[3]—and besides these, eighty senators or men who had held offices which would have given them the right to be elected to the senate,[4] but had volunteered to serve as soldiers in the legions. The prisoners taken in this battle are said to have numbered three thousand foot-soldiers and fifteen hundred horsemen.

L. Such was the battle of Cannae, a calamity as memorable as that suffered at the Allia, and though less grave in its results—because the enemy failed to follow up his victory—yet for the slaughter of the army even more grievous and disgraceful. For

(*Fab.* 16), 50,000 men; Quintilian (VIII. vi. 26), 60,000 men; Polybius (III. cxvii. 4), 70,000.

[2] There would have been forty-eight when the battle began (six for each legion), assuming that there were eight legions, as some of Livy's authorities held (chap. xxxvii. § 2).

[3] 221 B.C.

[4] The Ovinian Law (soon after 368 B.C.) had provided that the censors must enrol in the senate such as had held curule office (curule aedileship, praetorship, consulship) since the last censorship.

A.U.C. 538 Alliam sicut urbem prodidit ita exercitum servavit: ad Cannas fugientem consulem vix quinquaginta secuti sunt, alterius morientis prope totus[1] exercitus fuit.

4 Binis in castris cum multitudo semiermis sine ducibus esset, nuntium qui in maioribus erant mittunt, dum proelio deinde ex laetitia epulis fatigatos quies nocturna hostes premeret, ut ad se transirent: uno
5 agmine Canusium abituros esse. Eam sententiam alii totam aspernari; cur enim illos qui se arcessant ipsos non venire, cum aeque coniungi possent? Quia videlicet plena hostium omnia in medio essent et aliorum quam sua corpora tanto periculo mallent obicere.
6 Aliis non tam sententia[2] displicere quam animus deesse. Tum P. Sempronius[3] Tuditanus tribunus militum, "Capi ergo mavoltis," inquit, "ab avarissimo et crudelissimo hoste aestimarique capita vestra et exquiri pretia ab interrogantibus Romanus civis sis an Latinus socius, ut ex tua contumelia et miseria
7 alteri honos quaeratur? Non tu, si quidem L. Aemili consulis, qui se bene mori quam turpiter vivere maluit, et tot fortissimorum virorum qui circa
8 eum cumulati iacent cives estis. Sed antequam opprimit lux maioraque hostium agmina obsaepiunt iter, per hos qui inordinati atque incompositi obstre-
9 punt portis[4] erumpamus! Ferro atque audacia via fit

[1] totus ς: totius *P*.
[2] sententia ς: sententia est *P*.
[3] Tum P. Sempronius *Luchs*: p. sempronius *P*.
[4] portis ς: portas *P*.

---

[1] An allusion to the story told in chap. vii. § 5. Note how in the text the shift from plural (*mavoltis*) to singular (*tua . . . tu*) has all the effect of a personal appeal to each of the men Tuditanus is addressing.

the flight at the Allia, though it betrayed the City, B.C. 216
saved the army: at Cannae the consul who fled was accompanied by a scant fifty men; the other, dying, had well-nigh the entire army with him.

In the two Roman camps the crowd was half-armed and destitute of leaders. The men in the larger camp sent a messenger bidding those in the smaller one come over to them in the night, while the enemy, exhausted by the fighting and by the feasting that had followed on their triumph, were sunk in sleep: they would then set out in one body for Canusium. This plan some were for totally rejecting. Why, they asked, did not those who summoned them come themselves to the smaller camp, where they could just as well effect a junction? Clearly because the ground between was covered with enemies and they preferred to expose to such danger the persons of others rather than their own. Some were not so much displeased with the plan as wanting in resolution. Then said the military tribune Publius Sempronius Tuditanus: "So you had rather be captured by the greediest and most cruel of foes, and be appraised at so much a head by those who ask, 'Are you a Roman citizen or a Latin ally?' in order that from the insults and misery you suffer, the other may win distinction?[1] 'Not so!' each man will answer, if you are indeed fellow citizens of Lucius Aemilius the consul, who preferred an honourable death to life with ignominy, and of all those heroes who lie in heaps around him! But before daylight surprises us and the enemy blocks our way in greater force, let us break out through these men that are clamouring in disorder and confusion at our gates. With a

A.U.C. 538 quamvis per confertos hostes. Cuneo quidem hoc laxum atque solutum agmen, ut si nihil obstet, disicias.[1] Itaque ite mecum, qui et vosmet ipsos et
10 rem publicam salvam voltis!" Haec ubi dicta dedit, stringit gladium cuneoque facto per medios vadit
11 hostes; et cum in latus dextrum, quod patebat, Numidae iacularentur, translatis in dextrum scutis in maiora castra ad sescenti[2] evaserunt atque inde protinus alio magno agmine adiuncto Canusium in-
12 columes perveniunt. Haec apud victos magis impetu animorum, quos[3] ingenium suum cuique aut fors dabat, quam ex consilio ipsorum aut imperio cuiusquam agebantur.

LI. Hannibali victori cum ceteri circumfusi gratularentur suaderentque ut tanto perfunctus bello diei quod reliquum esset noctisque insequentis quietem et ipse sibi sumeret et fessis[4] daret militibus,
2 Maharbal praefectus equitum minime cessandum ratus, "Immo, ut quid hac pugna sit actum scias, die quinto" inquit "victor in Capitolio epulaberis.

[1] disicias (dissicias) *Gronovius*: uisscias *P*: dissicias *Ribbeck*.

[2] ad sescenti (sex-) *J. Gronovius*: ad dc *P*: ad sexcentos ς.

[3] quos *Bauer*: quod *P*: quem ς.

[4] et fessis ς: fessis *P*.

---

[1] *cuneus* (literally "wedge") is a technical term sometimes used to designate a body of men drawn up in fighting column, in order, as here, to force a way through the enemy's lines (Caesar, *B.G.* VI. xl. 2).

[2] In the original the words *Haec . . . medios* form a complete hexameter and half of another. We have here perhaps a bit appropriated from Ennius, either directly, or, more probably, at second hand, through Coelius (see next note).

[3] A detail which Livy may have owed to Coelius, from whom the grammarian Priscian (III. 22) cites the phrase:

sword and a stout heart a man may pass through enemies, be they never so thick. In close formation[1] you may scatter this loose and unorganized force as though there were nothing in your way. Follow me, then, as many of you as desire safety for yourselves and for the commonwealth!" Uttering these words he grasped his sword, and, forming a column, strode away through the midst of the enemy;[2] and when the Numidians hurled missiles at their right sides, which were unprotected, they shifted their shields to the right[3] and so got through, about six hundred[4] of them, to the larger camp; and thence, after being joined by the other great body of men, they made their way at once without loss to Canusium. These things the conquered did rather from the urge of such courage as each derived from his own nature or from chance than in consequence of their own deliberation or any man's authority. B.C. 216

LI. Hannibal's officers crowded round him with congratulations on his victory. The others all advised him, now that he had brought so great a war to a conclusion, to repose himself and to allow his weary soldiers to repose for the remainder of that day and the following night. But Maharbal, the commander of the cavalry, held that no time should be lost. "Nay," he cried, "that you may realize what has been accomplished by this battle, in five days you shall banquet in the Capitol!

dextimos in dextris scuta iubet habere ("he orders those on the right to carry their shields on the right arm").

[4] Pseudo-Frontinus (IV. v. 7) says that only twelve horsemen and fifty foot-soldiers followed Sempronius and another tribune, Cn. Octavius.

A.U.C. 538 Sequere; cum equite, ut prius venisse[1] quam ven-
3 turum sciant, praecedam." Hannibali nimis laeta res est visa[2] maiorque quam ut eam statim capere[3] animo posset. Itaque voluntatem se laudare Maharbalis ait; ad consilium pensandum temporis opus
4 esse. Tum Maharbal: "Non omnia nimirum eidem di[4] dedere: vincere scis, Hannibal, victoria uti nescis." Mora eius diei satis creditur saluti fuisse urbi atque imperio.

5 Postero die, ubi primum inluxit, ad spolia legenda foedamque etiam hostibus spectandam stragem
6 insistunt.[5] Iacebant tot Romanorum milia, pedites passim equitesque, ut quem cuique fors aut pugna iunxerat aut fuga. Adsurgentes quidam ex strage media cruenti, quos stricta matutino[6] frigore excita-
7 verant volnera, ab hoste oppressi sunt; quosdam et iacentes vivos succisis[7] feminibus poplitibusque invenerunt, nudantes cervicem iugulumque et re-
8 liquum sanguinem iubentes[8] haurire; inventi quidam sunt mersis in effossam terram capitibus, quos sibi[9] ipsos fecisse foveas obruentesque ora superiecta[10]
9 humo interclusisse spiritum apparebat. Praecipue convertit omnes subtractus[11] Numida mortuo super-

[1] venisse *P*: te uenisse ς.

[2] praecedam." Hannibali nimis laeta res est visa *Gronovius*: praecedant hannibalinimicis-l-aeturesetuisa *P*.

[3] capere ς: capite *P*.

[4] eidem di (dii) ς: eidemin *P*.

[5] spectandam stragem insistunt ς: spectandainstrage | insistunt *P*: spectandam stragem exeunt *Madvig*.

[6] quos stricta (-tā) matutino P^2: quęstracta | aututino P^1.

[7] succisis ς: succisos *P*.

[8] iubentes *Gronovius*: libentes *P*.

[9] quos sibi ς: quod si *P*.

[10] superiecta ς: subiecta super *P*.

[11] subtractus *P*: substratus ς.

Follow after; I will precede you with the cavalry, B.C. 216
that the Romans may know that you are there before they know that you are coming!" To Hannibal the idea was too joyous and too vast for his mind at once to grasp it. And so, while praising Maharbal's goodwill, he declared that he must have time to deliberate regarding his advice. Then said Maharbal, "In very truth the gods bestow not on the same man all their gifts; you know how to gain a victory, Hannibal: you know not how to use one." That day's delay is generally believed to have saved the City and the empire.

The morning after, as soon as it was light, they pressed forward to collect the spoil and to gaze on a carnage that was ghastly even to enemies. There lay those thousands upon thousands of Romans, foot and horse indiscriminately mingled, as chance had brought them together in the battle or the rout. Here and there amidst the slain there started up a gory figure whose wounds had begun to throb with the chill of dawn, and was cut down by his enemies; some were discovered lying there alive, with thighs and tendons slashed,[1] baring their necks and throats and bidding their conquerors drain the remnant of their blood. Others were found with their heads buried in holes dug in the ground. They had apparently made these pits for themselves, and heaping the dirt over their faces shut off their breath. But what most drew the attention of all beholders was a Numidian who was dragged out alive from under

[1] *i.e.* cut down from behind as they fled. Cf. Horace's *nec parcit imbellis iuventae poplitibus timidove tergo* (*Odes*, III. ii. 15 sq.)

A.U.C. 538 incubanti Romano vivus naso auribusque laceratis, cum ille,[1] manibus ad capiendum telum inutilibus, in rabiem ira versa laniando dentibus hostem exspirasset.

LII. Spoliis ad multum diei[2] lectis Hannibal ad minora ducit castra oppugnanda et omnium primum
2 bracchio obiecto a flumine[3] eos excludit. Ceterum ab omnibus labore vigiliis volneribus etiam fessis maturior
3 ipsius spe deditio est facta. Pacti ut arma atque equos traderent, in capita Romana trecenis nummis quadrigatis, in socios ducenis, in servos centenis, et ut eo pretio persoluto cum singulis abirent vestimentis, in castra hostes acceperunt, traditique in
4 custodiam omnes sunt, seorsum cives sociique. Dum ibi tempus teritur, interea, cum ex maioribus castris, quibus satis virium et animi[4] fuit, ad quattuor milia hominum et ducenti equites, alii agmine alii palati passim per agros, quod haud minus tutum erat, Canusium perfugissent, castra ipsa ab sauciis timidisque eadem condicione qua altera tradita hosti.
5 Praeda ingens parta[5] est, et praeter equos virosque

[1] cum ille *H. J. Mueller*: cum *P*.
[2] diei ς: de *P*: die *Alschefski*.
[3] obiecto a flumine *H. J. Mueller*: obiecto flumine ς: flumine obiecto *P*.
[4] et animi ς: ut nimis *P*.
[5] parta ς: parata *P*.

---

[1] cf. Dante's Ugolino, *Inferno*, xxxii.
[2] The chariot-pieces were silver *denarii* stamped with a Jupiter in a four-horse chariot. This money was used not only by the Romans, who coined it, but by their allies, who had been denied the right to coin silver since 268 B.C. The ransom of the citizen would be roughly equivalent in weight of silver to $50 or £10.

a dead Roman, but with mutilated nose and ears; for the Roman, unable to hold a weapon in his hands, had expired in a frenzy of rage, while rending the other with his teeth.[1] B.C. 216

LII. After spending a good part of the day in gathering spoils, Hannibal proceeded to attack the smaller camp. The first thing that he did was to throw up an entrenchment which cut them off from the river. But they were all so tired out from fighting and lack of sleep, as well as from wounds, that they surrendered even sooner than he had expected. The terms agreed upon were as follows: they were to give up their arms and horses; the ransom was fixed at three hundred chariot-pieces for every Roman, two hundred for every ally, and one hundred for every slave; on the payment of this price they were to go free, with a single garment each.[2] They then received their enemies into the camp and were all placed in custody, citizens being separated from allies. During the delay there, those in the larger camp who possessed sufficient strength and courage, amounting to four thousand foot and two hundred horse, had escaped, some in a body, others scattering—no less safely—over the country-side, and reached Canusium. The camp itself the wounded and timorous surrendered to the enemy on the same terms as the other.[3] It yielded enormous spoils, and except for

[3] Polybius (III. cxvii.) gives a very different story. According to him ten thousand Romans were left in camp when the battle was fought, with orders to attack the camp of Hannibal. Hannibal, however, had left a garrison in his own camp and they held the Romans at bay, till Hannibal, having now gained the battle, came up and rescued them, killing two thousand of the Romans and afterwards making the rest of them prisoners.

A.U.C. 538 et si quid argenti—quod plurimum in phaleris equorum erat, nam ad vescendum facto perexiguo, utique militantes, utebantur—omnis cetera praeda
6 diripienda data est. Tum sepeliendi causa conferri in unum corpora suorum iussit. Ad octo milia fuisse dicuntur fortissimorum virorum. Consulem quoque Romanum conquisitum[1] sepultumque quidam auctores sunt.

7 Eos qui Canusium perfugerant mulier Apula[2] nomine Busa, genere clara ac divitiis, moenibus tantum tectisque a Canusinis acceptos, frumento veste viatico etiam iuvit, pro qua ei munificentia postea, bello perfecto, ab senatu honores habiti sunt.

LIII. Ceterum cum ibi tribuni militum quattuor essent, Q. Fabius Maximus[3] de legione prima, cuius
2 pater priore anno dictator fuerat, et de legione secunda L. Publicius Bibulus et P. Cornelius Scipio et de legione tertia Ap. Claudius Pulcher, qui
3 proxime aedilis fuerat, omnium consensu ad P. Scipionem admodum adulescentem et ad[4] Ap.
4 Claudium summa imperii delata est. Quibus consultantibus inter paucos de summa rerum nuntiat P. Furius Philus, consularis viri filius, nequiquam eos perditam spem fovere; desperatam comploratamque
5 rem esse publicam; nobiles iuvenes quosdam, quorum

[1] conquisitum *P*: inquisitum *Fuegner*.
[2] Apula *Lipsius*: paula (*corrected from* apaula) *P*.
[3] Q. Fabius Maximus *Weissenborn*: Fabius Maximus *P*.
[4] admodum adulescentem et ad ς: atmodum *P*.

[1] For similar legends of Hannibal's generosity see XXV. xvii. 4, XXVII. xxviii. 1. and chap. vii. § 5 of this book.

[2] Valerius Maximus (IV. viii. 2) says that the woman supplied about ten thousand Romans with food without wrecking her fortune. The name Busa is Oscan.

the horses and men and such silver as there was—which was mostly on the harness of the horses, for they then used very little plate, especially when in the field—the rest of the booty was all given up to pillage. He then commanded the bodies of his dead to be brought into one place for burial. It is said that they numbered about eight thousand of his bravest men. Some historians state that the Roman consul, too, was sought out and given burial.[1] B.C. 216

Those who escaped to Canusium were aided by an Apulian woman of birth and fortune named Busa. The townspeople had merely afforded them the protection of the walls and shelter, but she provided them with corn, clothing, and money for the way, in return for which munificence she was afterwards, on the conclusion of the war, voted honours by the senate.[2]

LIII. Now though there were four tribunes of the soldiers on the ground—Quintus Fabius Maximus of the first legion, whose father had been dictator the year before, Lucius Publicius Bibulus and Publius Cornelius Scipio of the second legion, and Appius Claudius Pulcher, who had very recently been aedile, of the third legion—the supreme command was by unanimous consent made over to Publius Scipio, the merest youth,[3] and to Appius Claudius. These two were considering the general situation, in company with a few others, when Publius Furius Philus, the son of an ex-consul, came in and told them that they were idly entertaining a lost hope; the state was already given over and mourned as dead; some of the young

[3] He was about nineteen years old (XXI. xlvi. 7 and Polybius X. iii. 4).

A.U.C. 538 principem M. Caecilium Metellum,[1] mare ac naves
spectare, ut deserta Italia ad regum aliquem trans-
6 fugiant. Quod malum, praeterquam atrox, super tot
clades etiam novum, cum stupore ac miraculo tor-
pidos defixisset qui aderant et consilium advocandum
de eo censerent, negat consilii rem esse Scipio
7 iuvenis, fatalis dux huiusce belli. Audendum atque
agendum non consultandum ait in tanto malo esse;[2]
irent secum extemplo armati qui rem publicam
8 salvam vellent; nulla[3] verius quam ubi ea cogitentur
9 hostium castra esse. Pergit ire sequentibus paucis
in hospitium Metelli, et cum concilium ibi iuvenum
de quibus adlatum erat invenisset, stricto super
10 capita consultantium gladio "Ex mei animi sententia,"
inquit, "ut ego rem publicam populi Romani non
deseram neque alium civem Romanum deserere
11 patiar; si sciens fallo, tum me Iuppiter optimus
maximus[4] domum familiam remque meam pessimo
12 leto adficiat. In haec verba, M. Caecili, iures pos-
tulo ceterique qui adestis: qui non iuraverit, in se
13 hunc gladium strictum esse sciat." Haud secus
pavidi quam si victorem Hannibalem cernerent,
iurant omnes custodiendosque semet ipsos Scipioni
tradunt.

LIV. Eo tempore quo haec[5] Canusii agebantur Venusiam ad consulem ad quattuor milia et quingenti pedites equitesque, qui sparsi fuga per agros

[1] M. Caecilium Metellum *H. J. Mueller*: l. caecilium metellum (*so also* § 12) *P*.

[2] esse ς: esse scipio *P*.

[3] nulla *Bauer*: nullo *P*: nullo loco ς.

[4] optimus maximus *Drakenborch*: optime maxime *P*: optime maxime (*with* afficias) ς (*Madvig*).

[5] haec ς: et *P*.

nobles, of whom Marcus Caecilius Metellus was the chief, were looking to the sea and ships, proposing to abandon Italy and flee for refuge to some king. These evil tidings, dreadful in themselves and coming as a new distress on the top of so many disasters, stunned those who heard them with a dull amazement. But when they would have called a council to talk the matter over, young Scipio, the predestined leader in this war, declared that it was no matter for taking counsel: they must be bold and act, not deliberate, in the face of this great evil; let them take arms and go with him at once, as many as wished to save the state; no camp was so truly the camp of the enemy as one where such thoughts were rife. He proceeded, with only a few followers, to the quarters of Metellus, where he found a gathering of the young men of whom he had been informed. Raising his sword over their heads, as they sat in consultation, "I solemnly swear," he said, "that even as I myself shall not desert the republic of the Roman People, so likewise shall I suffer no other Roman citizen to do so; if I wittingly speak false, may Jupiter Optimus Maximus utterly destroy me, my house, my family, and my estate. Marcus Caecilius, I call on you and the others who are present to swear after these terms, and if any refuse to swear, let him know that against him this sword is drawn." Quaking as though they beheld the victorious Hannibal, all took the oath, and delivered themselves into the custody of Scipio. B.C. 216

LIV. While this was happening at Canusium, about four thousand five hundred horse and foot, who had scattered over the country-side in flight,

A.U.C. 538

2 fuerant, pervenere. Eos omnes Venusini per familias benigne accipiendos curandosque cum divisissent, in singulos equites togas et tunicas et quadrigatos nummos quinos vicenos et pediti denos et arma,
3 quibus deerant, dederunt; ceteraque publice ac privatim hospitaliter facta, certatumque ne a muliere Canusina populus Venusinus officiis vinceretur.

4 Sed gravius onus Busae multitudo faciebat—et iam
5 ad decem milia hominum erant—Appiusque et Scipio, postquam incolumem esse alterum consulem acceperunt, nuntium extemplo mittunt, quantae secum peditum equitumque copiae essent, sciscitatumque simul utrum[1] Venusiam adduci exercitum
6 an manere iuberet Canusi. Varro ipse Canusium copias traduxit; et iam aliqua species[2] consularis exercitus erat, moenibusque se certe, etsi non armis, ab hoste videbantur defensuri.

7 Romam ne has quidem reliquias superesse civium sociorumque, sed occidione occisum cum duobus consulibus[3] exercitum[4] deletasque omnes copias
8 allatum fuerat. Nunquam salva urbe tantum pavoris tumultusque intra moenia Romana fuit. Itaque succumbam oneri neque adgrediar narrare

[1] utrum *edd.*: utrumque *P.*

[2] species ς: specie *P.*

[3] duobus consulibus *Gronovius*: duobus *P*: ducibus *Luterbacher.*

[4] exercitum *Gronovius*: exercitibus *P.*

---

[1] From Polybius VI. xix. 12 we learn that the cavalryman received pay at the rate of a denarius *per diem*, and the infantryman one-third as much. It appears then that the present given to the soldiers—if the toga and tunic of the cavalryman be reckoned in—amounted to about one

made their way to Venusia, to the consul. All these the inhabitants distributed amongst various families where they might be kindly received and cared for, and bestowed on each horseman a toga and a tunic and twenty-five chariot-pieces, and on each foot-soldier ten pieces, together with arms, where they were needed.[1] In all other matters, too, they dealt hospitably by them, both as a town and as individuals, in their zeal that the People of Venusia should not lag behind a Canusian woman in friendly offices. B.C. 216

But the great multitude was beginning to be too heavy a burden upon Busa—and indeed there were now as many as ten thousand men[2]—and Appius and Scipio, when they learned that the other consul was alive, immediately dispatched a messenger to let him know what forces of infantry and cavalry they had with them, and at the same time to enquire whether he desired the army to be brought to Venusia or remain at Canusium. Varro transferred his own troops to Canusium; and they now had something resembling a consular army, and might look to defend themselves against the enemy, behind walls, at all events, if not in the field.

But at Rome it was reported that not even these pitiful remnants of citizens and allies survived, but that the army with its two consuls was clean destroyed and all their forces blotted out. Never, save when the City had been captured, was there such terror and confusion within the walls of Rome. I shall therefore confess myself unequal to the task,

month's pay. (The toga was then worn even by soldiers when in garrison or in winter quarters.)

[2] *i.e.* in both camps, see chap. lvi. § 2.

A.U.C. 538
9 quae edissertando minora vero faciam.[1] Consule
exercituque ad Trasumennum priore anno amisso
non volnus super volnus sed multiplex clades, cum
duobus consulibus duo[2] consulares exercitus amissi
nuntiabantur, nec ulla iam castra Romana nec ducem
10 nec militem esse; Hannibalis Apuliam, Samnium,
ac iam prope totam Italiam factam. Nulla profecto
11 alia gens tanta mole cladis non obruta esset. Compares[3] cladem ad Aegates insulas Carthaginiensium
proelio navali acceptam, qua fracti Sicilia ac Sardinia
cessere et[4] vectigales ac stipendiarios fieri se passi
sunt, aut pugnam adversam in Africa cui postea hic
ipse Hannibal succubuit? Nulla ex parte com-
parandae sunt, nisi quod minore animo latae sunt.

LV. P. Furius Philus et M. Pomponius praetores
senatum in curiam Hostiliam vocaverunt, ut de
2 urbis custodia consulerent; neque enim dubitabant
deletis exercitibus hostem ad oppugnandam Romam,
3 quod unum opus belli restaret, venturum. Cum in
malis[5] sicuti ingentibus ita ignotis ne consilium
quidem satis expedirent, obstreperetque clamor
lamentantium mulierum et nondum palam facto vivi
mortuique per omnes paene[6] domos promiscue
4 complorarentur, tum Q. Fabius Maximus censuit
equites expeditos et Appia et Latina via mittendos,

[1] faciam *J. H. Voss*: facie *P*.
[2] duo ς: cum *P*.
[3] compares *P*[1]: comparesset *P*.
[4] et *Madvig*: in *P*.
[5] in malis ς: in aliis *P*.
[6] per omnes paene ς: et paene omnes paene *P*.

nor attempt a narrative where the fullest description would fall short of the truth. The year before a consul and his army had been lost at Trasumennus, and now it was not merely one blow following another, but a calamity many times as great that was reported; two consuls and two consular armies had been lost, and there was no longer any Roman camp, or general, or soldier; Hannibal was master of Apulia, Samnium, and well-nigh the whole of Italy. Surely there was no other people that would not have been overwhelmed by a disaster of such vast proportions. Would you compare the disaster off the Aegatian islands, which the Carthaginians suffered in the sea-fight, by which their spirit was so broken that they relinquished Sicily and Sardinia and suffered themselves to become tax-payers and tributaries? or the defeat in Africa to which this very Hannibal afterwards succumbed? In no single aspect are they to be compared with this calamity, except that they were endured with less of fortitude. B.C. 216

LV. Publius Furius Philus and Marcus Pomponius, the praetors, called the senate together in the Curia Hostilia, to consult about the defence of Rome; for they made no doubt that the enemy, after wiping out their armies, would be advancing to besiege the City, which was all that remained to do to end the war. But when, amid dangers at once so immense and so incalculable, they failed to think of even any tolerable plan of action, and were deafened with the cries and lamentations of the women, both the living and the dead—in the lack as yet of any announcement—being indiscriminately mourned in almost every house, then Quintus Fabius Maximus urged that light-armed horsemen be sent out along the Appian

A.U.C. 538 qui obvios percunctando—aliquos profecto[1] ex fuga
passim dissipatos fore[2]—referant quae fortuna con-
5 sulum atque exercituum sit, et si quid di immortales,
miseriti imperii, reliquum Romani nominis fecerint,
ubi eae copiae sint; quo[3] se Hannibal post proelium
contulerit, quid paret, quid agat acturusque sit.
6 Haec exploranda noscendaque per impigros iuvenes
esse; illud per patres ipsos agendum, quoniam
magistratuum parum sit, ut tumultum ac trepidationem in urbe tollant, matronas publico arceant
continerique intra suum quamque limen cogant,
7 comploratus familiarum coerceant, silentium per
urbem faciant, nuntios rerum omnium ad praetores
deducendos curent—suae quisque fortunae domi
8 auctorem exspectent—custodesque praeterea ad portas ponant, qui prohibeant quemquam egredi urbe[4]
cogantque homines nullam nisi urbe ac moenibus
salvis salutem sperare. Ubi conticuerit tumultus,[5]
tum in curiam patres revocandos consulendumque
de urbis custodia esse.

LVI. Cum in hanc sententiam pedibus omnes
issent, summotaque foro per magistratus[6] turba
patres diversi ad sedandos tumultus discessissent,
tum demum litterae a C. Terentio consule allatae
2 sunt: L. Aemilium consulem exercitumque caesum;
sese Canusi esse reliquias tantae cladis velut ex
naufragio colligentem; ad decem milia militum

[1] profecto ς (*Jac. Gronovius*): profectos *P*.

[2] fore ς (*Jac. Gronovius*): forte *P*.

[3] quo ς; quae P^1: qua P^2.

[4] urbe *Madvig*: urbem *P*.

[5] tumultus *Ulrich*: recte tumultus *P*: certe tumultus *Frigell and Kiderlin*.

[6] summotaque . . . per magistratus ς: summotasque . . . magistratus *P*.

and Latin ways, and questioning those they met— B.C. 216 for some there would surely be who had dispersed and made off in the rout—bring back word of the fortunes of the consuls and the armies, and if the immortal gods, taking pity on the empire, had spared any remnant of the Roman name, where those forces were; whither Hannibal had gone after the battle, what his plans were, what he was doing and was likely to do. To discover and ascertain these facts was a task, he said, for active youths; what the Fathers themselves must do, since there were not magistrates enough, was this: quell the panic and confusion in the City; keep the matrons off the streets and compel them each to abide in her own home; restrain families from lamentation; procure silence throughout the City; see that bearers of any news were brought before the praetors—every man must wait at home for tidings that concerned himself;—and, besides this, post sentries at the gates, to keep anyone from leaving the City, and make the people rest all hope of safety on the safety of Rome and of its walls. When the tumult had died down, then the Fathers must be convened again and consider how to defend the City.

LVI. After they had all voted for this proposal without debate, and the throng had been cleared out of the Forum by the magistrates, and the Fathers had dispersed in various directions to still the uproar, then at last came a dispatch from Gaius Terentius the consul, announcing that the consul Lucius Aemilius and his army had been destroyed; that he himself was at Canusium, collecting—as though after a storm at sea—the wreckage of that great disaster; that he had about ten thousand men, not organised

A.U.C. 538 ferme esse incompositorum inordinatorumque;
3 Poenum[1] sedere ad Cannas in[2] captivorum pretiis
praedaque alia nec victoris animo nec magni ducis
more nundinantem.[3]

4 Tum privatae quoque per domos clades volgatae
sunt, adeoque totam urbem opplevit luctus ut
sacrum anniversarium Cereris intermissum sit, quia
nec lugentibus id facere est fas nec ulla in illa
5 tempestate matrona expers luctus fuerat. Itaque
ne ob eandem causam alia quoque sacra publica aut
privata desererentur, senatus consulto diebus triginta
luctus est finitus.

6 Ceterum cum sedato urbis tumultu revocati in
curiam patres essent, aliae insuper ex Sicilia litterae
allatae sunt ab T. Otacilio propraetore: regnum
7 Hieronis classe Punica vastari; cui cum opem
imploranti ferre vellet, nuntiatum sibi esse[4] aliam
classem ad Aegates insulas stare paratam instruc-
8 tamque, ut, ubi se versum ad[5] tuendam Syracusanam
oram Poeni sensissent, Lilybaeum extemplo provinciamque aliam Romanam adgrederentur; itaque
classe opus esse, si regem socium Siciliamque tueri
vellent.

[1] Poenum *Gronovius*: menum P^1: me nunc P^2.
[3] in ς: an *P*.
[2] nundinantem *Gronovius*: nuntiantem *P*.
[4] vellet, nuntiatum sibi esse ς: uellent nuntiatum his est *P*.
[5] versum ad ς: aduersum *P*.

or assigned to companies; that the Phoenician was sitting down at Cannae, haggling over the ransom of his prisoners and over the rest of the booty, exhibiting neither the spirit of a conqueror nor the behaviour of a great commander. B.C. 216

Announcement was then made from house to house of the losses they had each sustained, and the entire City was so filled with lamentation that the annual rite of Ceres was allowed to lapse, since it may not be performed by mourners, nor was there at that time a single matron who was not bereaved. Accordingly, lest for this same reason other public or private rites might be neglected, the senate decreed that mourning should be limited to thirty days.[1]

But when the confusion in the City had subsided and the Fathers had been summoned back to the senate-house, another dispatch was brought in from Sicily, from the propraetor Titus Otacilius. He reported that Hiero's kingdom was being laid waste by a Punic fleet, and that when he would have responded to Hiero's appeal for help, he had got news of another fleet, that was standing off the Aegatian islands, all ready and equipped, so that when the Phoenicians should perceive that he had turned his back on them to go to the rescue of the Syracusan coast, they might instantly descend on Lilybaeum and the rest of the Roman province. A fleet was therefore necessary if they desired to protect the king, their ally, and Sicily.[2]

[1] The Cerealia, the chief festival in honour of Ceres, took place on April 19th. The reference in the text must be to another, otherwise unknown, festival, as the battle of Cannae was fought on August 2nd.

[2] Otacilius already had a fleet, according to chap. xxxvii. § 13.

A.U.C. 538 LVII. Litteris consulis praetorisque recitatis censuerunt praetorem[1] M. Claudium,[2] qui classi ad Ostiam stanti praeesset, Canusium ad exercitum mittendum, scribendumque consuli, ut, cum praetori exercitum tradidisset, primo quoque tempore, quantum per commodum rei publicae fieri posset, Romam veniret.

2 Territi etiam super tantas clades cum ceteris prodigiis, tum quod duae Vestales eo anno, Opimia atque Floronia, stupri compertae et altera sub terra, uti mos est, ad portam Collinam necata fuerat, altera
3 sibimet ipsa mortem consciverat; L. Cantilius, scriba pontificius,[3] quos nunc[4] minores pontifices appellant, qui cum Floronia stuprum fecerat, a pontifice maximo eo usque virgis in comitio caesus erat ut
4 inter verbera exspiraret. Hoc nefas cum inter tot, ut fit, clades in prodigium versum esset, decemviri
5 libros adire iussi sunt, et Q. Fabius Pictor Delphos ad oraculum missus est sciscitatum quibus precibus suppliciisque deos possent placare et quaenam futura
6 finis tantis cladibus foret. Interim ex fatalibus libris sacrificia aliquot extraordinaria facta; inter

[1] recitatis censuerunt praetorem *added by Woelfflin* (censuerunt *had been added by ς and* praetorem *by Gronovius*).

[2] M. Claudium ς: m|arcium P^1: m appium P^2: Marcellum *Heusinger*.

[3] pontificius *Vaassen* (*Cassius Hemina ap. Priscian* VII. xi.): pontificis *P*.

[4] nunc ς: non *P*: *deleted by Vaassen*.

---

[1] M. Claudius Marcellus, one of the best of the Roman generals in the war, had won renown by his defeat of the Gauls at Clastidium in 222 B.C., where he killed the enemy's chief, Virdomarus, with his own hand and won the "spoils of honour" (I. x. 5, and IV. xx. tell of the only other instances recorded). He fell in a cavalry engagement in 208,

LVII. When the dispatches from the consul and the praetor had been read out, the senate voted to send Marcus Claudius,[1] the praetor commanding the fleet at Ostia, to Canusium, and to write to the consul to turn the army over to him and come to Rome at the earliest moment compatible with the welfare of the state. B.C. 216

They were terrified not only by the great disasters they had suffered, but also by a number of prodigies, and in particular because two Vestals, Opimia and Floronia, had in that year been convicted of unchastity. Of these one had been buried alive, as the custom is, near the Colline Gate, and the other had killed herself. Lucius Cantilius, a secretary to the pontiffs—one of those who are now called the lesser pontiffs—had been guilty with Floronia, and the Pontifex Maximus had him scourged in the Comitium so severely that he died under the blows. Since in the midst of so many misfortunes this pollution[2] was, as happens at such times, converted into a portent, the decemvirs were commanded to consult the Books, and Quintus Fabius Pictor[3] was dispatched to Delphi, to enquire of the oracle with what prayers and supplications they might propitiate the gods, and what would be the end of all their calamities. In the meantime, by the direction of the Books of Fate, some unusual sacrifices were offered; amongst others a Gaulish

when a detachment with which he was making a reconnaissance was overwhelmed by a greatly superior force of Carthaginians (XXVII. xxvi.-xxvii).

[2] Not the death of Cantilius, but the Vestals' violation of their vows.

[3] This was the annalist, who wrote a history of Rome in Greek.

A.U.C. 538 quae Gallus et Galla,[1] Graecus et Graeca in foro
bovario sub terram [2] vivi demissi sunt in locum saxo
consaeptum,[3] iam ante [4] hostiis humanis, minime
Romano sacro, imbutum.

7 Placatis satis, ut rebantur,[5] deis M. Claudius
Marcellus ab Ostia mille et quingentos milites, quos
in classem scriptos habebat, Romam, ut urbi prae-
8 sidio essent, mittit; ipse, legione classica—ea legio
tertia erat—cum tribunis militum Teanum Sidicinum
praemissa, classe tradita P. Furio Philo collegae,
paucos post dies Canusium magnis itineribus con-
9 tendit. Inde [6] dictator ex auctoritate patrum dictus
M.[7] Iunius et Ti. Sempronius [8] magister equitum
dilectu edicto iuniores ab annis septendecim et
10 quosdam praetextatos scribunt. Quattuor ex his
legiones et mille equites effecti. Item ad socios
Latinumque nomen ad milites ex formula accipiendos mittunt. Arma, tela, alia parari iubent et
vetera spolia hostium detrahunt templis portici-
11 busque. Et formam [9] novi dilectus inopia liberorum

[1] Gallus et Galla ς: callus et galia (*corrected from* callus e galia) P^1: callus et galina P^2.

[2] terram *Duker*: terra *P*.

[3] consaeptum ς: consectum *P*.

[4] iam ante *Gronovius*: uiam ante P^1: ubi ante P^2.

[5] ut rebantur ς: uerebantur *P*.

[6] inde *Crévier*: in P^1: *deleted by* P^2.

[7] dictus M. *Aldine ed.*: dictum (*corr. from* ductum) P^1: dictus P^2.

[8] Ti. Sempronius *Sigonius*: t. sempronius *P*.

[9] et formam *Luchs*: et alia formam *P*: et aliam formam ς (*Madvig*).

man and woman and a Greek man and woman were buried alive in the Cattle Market, in a place walled in with stone, which even before this time had been defiled with human victims, a sacrifice wholly alien to the Roman spirit.[1] B.C. 216

Deeming that the gods had now been sufficiently appeased, Marcus Claudius Marcellus sent fifteen hundred soldiers whom he had under him, enrolled for service with the fleet, from Ostia to Rome, to defend the City; and sending before him to Teanum Sidicinum the naval legion (to wit, the third[2]) under its tribunes, handed over the fleet to his colleague Publius Furius Philus and a few days later hastened by forced marches to Canusium. The senate then authorized the appointment of a dictator and Marcus Junius [Pera] was named to that office, with Tiberius Sempronius as master of the horse. Proclaiming a levy they enlisted the young men over seventeen and some who still wore the purple-bordered dress of boyhood. Of these they made up four legions and a thousand horse. They also sent men to the allies and the Latins to take over their soldiers, as by treaty provided. They gave orders that armour, weapons and other equipment should be made ready, and took down from the temples and porticoes the ancient spoils of enemies. The levy wore a strange appearance, for, owing to

[1] Livy means that the sacrifice, prescribed by the Greek Sibylline Books, was a Greek and not a Roman rite. The earlier instance referred to in the text was in 228 B.C. (Zonaras VIII. xix.).

[2] In chap. liii. § 2 the "third" legion is one of those which fought at Cannae. Possibly the naval legions were separately numbered, or (more probably) there had now been a new numbering of all the legions.

A.U.C. 538 capitum ac necessitas dedit: octo milia iuvenum
validorum ex servitiis prius sciscitantes singulos,
12 vellentne militare, empta publice armaverunt. Hic
miles magis placuit, cum pretio minore redimendi[1]
captivos copia fieret.

LVIII. Namque Hannibal secundum tam pros-
peram ad Cannas pugnam victoris magis quam
bellum gerentis intentus curis, cum captivis pro-
ductis segregatisque socios, sicut ante ad Trebiam
2 Trasumennumque lacum, benigne adlocutus sine
pretio dimisisset, Romanos quoque vocatos, quod
nunquam alias antea, satis miti sermone adloquitur:
3 non internecivum sibi esse cum Romanis bellum;
de dignitate atque imperio certare. Et patres
virtuti Romanae cessisse, et se id adniti, ut suae
4 in vicem simul felicitati et virtuti cedatur. Itaque
redimendi se captivis copiam facere; pretium fore
in capita equiti quingenos quadrigatos nummos,
trecenos pediti, servo centenos.[2]

5 Quamquam aliquantum adiciebatur equitibus ad
id pretium quo pepigerant dedentes se, laeti tamen
quamcumque condicionem paciscendi acceperunt.
6 Placuit suffragio ipsorum decem deligi qui Romam
ad senatum irent, nec pignus aliud fidei quam ut
7 iurarent se redituros acceptum. Missus cum his
Carthalo, nobilis Carthaginiensis, qui, si forte ad

[1] redimendi ς: redime P^1: redimi P^2.
[2] centenos ς: centum *P*.

the scarcity of free men and the need of the hour, B.C. 216
they bought, with money from the treasury, eight thousand young and stalwart slaves and armed them, first asking each if he were willing to serve. They preferred these slaves for soldiers, though they might have redeemed the prisoners of war at less expense.

LVIII. For Hannibal, after his great victory at Cannae, had been more concerned with the projects of a conqueror than with those of one who was still waging war. Mustering the prisoners and dividing them into two groups, he addressed a few kindly words to the allies and dismissed them without ransom, as he had done previously at the Trebia and Lake Trasumennus. He then called up the Romans also and spoke to them with a mildness he had never shown before. He was waging, he said, no war of extermination with them, but was contending for honour and dominion. His forerunners had yielded to the valour of the Romans, and he was striving to compel them in their turn to yield to his own good fortune and valour. He would therefore give them an opportunity to redeem the prisoners, and would fix their ransom at five hundred chariot-pieces for each horseman, three hundred for each foot-soldier, and a hundred for each slave.

Although this was a rather large addition to the ransom which the horsemen had agreed to on surrendering, they joyfully accepted any terms of treaty. It was resolved that the prisoners should themselves elect ten representatives to go to the senate in Rome; nor did Hannibal take any other pledge of their good faith than their oath that they would return. Carthalo, a Carthaginian noble, was sent with them, so that, if he should see that the

A.U.C. 538 pacem inclinare cerneret animos,[1] condiciones ferret.
8 Cum egressi castris essent, unus ex iis, minime Romani ingenii homo, veluti[2] aliquid oblitus, iuris iurandi solvendi causa cum in castra redisset, ante
9 noctem comites adsequitur. Ubi Romam venire eos nuntiatum est, Carthaloni obviam lictor missus qui dictatoris verbis denuntiaret[3] ut ante noctem excederet finibus Romanis.

LIX. Legatis captivorum senatus ab dictatore datus est. Quorum princeps "M. Iuni vosque,[4] patres conscripti," inquit, "nemo nostrum ignorat nulli unquam civitati viliores fuisse captivos quam
2 nostrae; ceterum, nisi nobis plus iusto nostra placet causa, non alii unquam minus neglegendi vobis quam
3 nos[5] in hostium potestatem venerunt. Non enim in acie per timorem arma tradidimus, sed cum prope ad noctem superstantes cumulis caesorum corporum proelium extraxissemus, in castra recepimus nos;
4 diei reliquum ac noctem insequentem fessi labore
5 ac volneribus vallum sumus tutati; postero die, cum circumsessi ab exercitu victore aqua arceremur nec ulla iam per confertos hostes erumpendi spes esset, nec esse nefas duceremus quinquaginta milibus hominum ex acie nostra trucidatis aliquem ex
6 Cannensi pugna Romanum militem restare, tunc demum pacti sumus pretium quo redempti dimitteremur; arma, in quibus nihil iam auxilii erat, hosti
7 tradidimus. Maiores quoque acceperamus se a Gallis

[1] inclinare cerneret animos *Koch*: inclinaret animos *P*.
[2] veluti *Alschefski*: uelutillut *P*: uelut *C*.
[3] denuntiaret *Luchs*: nuntiaret *P*.
[4] Iuni vosque *Harant*: iuniusque P^1: iunius P^2.
[5] nos ς; alios *P*.

Romans inclined to peace, he might offer terms. B.C. 216
The envoys had just left the camp when one of them, a fellow of thoroughly un-Roman character, returned to it—as if he had forgotten something—in order to free himself from his oath, and before dark had caught up with his companions. When the news reached Rome that they were coming, a lictor was sent to meet Carthalo on the way and warn him in the name of the Dictator to depart before nightfall out of Roman territory.

LIX. As for the envoys of the prisoners, the dictator admitted them into the senate, where their leader spoke as follows: "Marcus Junius and Conscript Fathers, none of us is unaware that no state ever held prisoners of war in less esteem than ours. But, unless we overrate our cause, there have never been men who came into the power of the enemy less deserving than ourselves of your neglect. For we did not yield up our swords through fear on the field of battle, but standing on the heaped bodies of the slain prolonged the combat almost until nightfall and then retired to our camp. The rest of the day and the succeeding night, though exhausted with fighting and with wounds, we defended the stockade. On the following day, surrounded by a victorious army and cut off from water, having no longer any hope of breaking through the throng of enemies, and thinking it no disgrace that when fifty thousand of our troops had been cut down, some few Roman soldiers should survive the battle of Cannae, we finally stipulated for a price at which we might be ransomed, and delivered to the enemy the arms in which there was no longer any help. Even our ancestors—so we had heard—redeemed

A.U.C. 538 auro redemisse, et patres vestros, asperrimos illos
ad condiciones[1] pacis, legatos tamen captivorum[2]
8 redimendorum gratia Tarentum misisse. Atqui et
ad Alliam[3] cum Gallis et ad Heracleam cum Pyrrho
utraque non tam clade infamis quam pavore et fuga
pugna fuit. Cannenses campos acervi Romanorum
corporum tegunt, nec supersumus pugnae, nisi in
quibus trucidandis et ferrum et vires hostem de-
9 fecerunt. Sunt etiam de nostris quidam qui ne in acie
quidem fuerunt,[4] sed praesidio castris relicti, cum
castra traderentur, in potestatem hostium venerunt.
10 Haud equidem ullius civis et commilitonis fortunae
aut condicioni invideo nec premendo alium me
extulisse velim;—ne illi quidem, nisi pernicitatis
pedum et cursus aliquod praemium est, qui plerique
inermes ex acie fugientes non prius quam Venusiae
aut Canusi constiterunt, se nobis merito praetulerint
gloriatique sint in se plus quam in nobis praesidii
11 rei publicae esse. Sed et illis[5] bonis ac fortibus
militibus utemini et nobis etiam promptioribus pro
patria, cum[6] beneficio vestro redempti atque in
12 patriam restituti fuerimus. Dilectum ex omni
aetate et fortuna habetis; octo milia servorum
audio armari. Non minor numerus noster est, nec
maiore pretio redimi possumus quam ii emuntur;
nam si conferam nos cum illis, iniuriam nomini

[1] condiciones *C*: condicione *P*.
[2] captivorum ς; ad captiuorum *P*.
[3] ad Alliam *Gronovius*: aliam *P*.
[4] fuerunt *Alschefski and Madvig*: refugerunt *P*.
[5] et illis *Crévier*: illis et *P*: illis et nobis *Heerwagen*.
[6] cum *Luchs*: quod *P*.

themselves from the Gauls with gold; and your fathers, despite their fierce opposition to terms of peace, sent envoys to Tarentum to ransom prisoners. And yet neither the battle with the Gauls at the Allia nor that with Pyrrhus at Heraclea owed its unhappy fame so much to carnage as to craven flight. At Cannae the plains are covered with heaps of Roman corpses, and if we survive, it is only because our enemies' swords were dulled and their strength spent with slaughtering. There are some of us, too, who were never even in the battle, but were left to guard the camp, and on its surrender passed into the enemy's hands. Think not that I envy the good luck or circumstances of any fellow citizen or fellow soldier,[1] nor would I raise myself by thrusting another down; but—unless there be a prize for fleetness of foot and running—it is not those who, without weapons for the most part and fleeing from the fight, never stopped until they reached Venusia or Canusium that can justly set themselves above us or boast that they are better defenders of the state than we. Both in them and in us you shall have good and valiant soldiers; but we shall be even more eager than they to defend our country, since we shall owe to your kindness our redemption and our restoration to that country. You are levying soldiers of every age and condition; I hear that eight thousand slaves are being armed. Our number is not less than that, and our ransom would be no more costly than their purchase; I make no comparison between our worth and theirs, for that would be to insult the name of B.C. 216

[1] *i.e.* in one of the contingents of allies—the distinction is not between civilian and soldier, but between citizen soldier and allied soldier.

A.U.C. 538 13 Romano faciam. Illud etiam in tali consilio animadvertendum vobis censeam, patres conscripti, si iam[1] duriores esse velitis—quod nullo nostro merito
14 faciatis—cui[2] nos hosti relicturi sitis. Pyrrho videlicet, qui hospitum[3] numero captivos habuit? An barbaro ac Poeno, qui utrum avarior an crudelior sit
15 vix existimari potest? Si videatis catenas squalorem deformitatem civium vestrorum, non minus profecto vos ea species moveat quam si ex altera parte cernatis stratas Cannensibus campis legiones
16 vestras. Intueri potestis sollicitudinem et lacrimas in vestibulo curiae stantium cognatorum nostrorum exspectantiumque responsum vestrum. Cum ii pro nobis proque iis qui absunt ita suspensi ac solliciti sint, quem censetis animum ipsorum esse quorum in
17 discrimine vita libertasque est?[4] Si, me dius fidius, ipse in nos mitis Hannibal contra naturam suam esse velit, nihil tamen nobis vita opus esse censeamus, cum indigni ut redimeremur vobis[5] visi
18 simus.[6] Rediere Romam quondam[7] remissi a Pyrrho sine pretio captivi,[8] sed rediere cum legatis, primoribus civitatis, ad redimendos sese missis; redeam ego in patriam trecentis nummis non aestimatus civis? Suum quisque habet animum,[9] patres
19 conscripti. Scio in discrimine esse vitam corpusque meum: magis me famae periculum movet, ne a vobis

[1] iam *Valla*: tam *P*: tamen ς: *deleted by Sigonius.*
[2] cui ς: quin *P*.
[3] hospitum *Bauer and Fabri*: uos hospitum *P*: velut hospitum *Meyerhoefer*.
[4] est? ς: estse///P^1: esset P^2: est? sed *Alschefski.*
[5] vobis *Madvig*: a uobis *P*.
[6] simus *Muretus*: sumus *P*.
[7] quondam ς: quam *P*.
[8] captivi *C. Heraeus*: captiti P^1: capti *P*.

Roman. One other point I would suggest, as meriting B.C. 216 consideration, when you deliberate about this matter, Conscript Fathers: if haply you should incline to deal harshly by us—which we do not in the least deserve—to what enemy would you be leaving us? To a Pyrrhus, pray, who treated his prisoners like guests? or to a barbarian and Phoenician, of whom it can hardly be determined whether his avarice or cruelty be greater? If you could behold the fetters, the squalor, the degradation of your fellow-citizens, assuredly the sight would move you no less profoundly than if, on the other hand, you saw your legions lying slaughtered on the fields of Cannae. One thing you can see—the distress and tears of our kinsmen who are standing at the entrance of the Curia awaiting your decision. When these people are in such suspense and agony for us and for those who are absent, what think you the men themselves must feel whose life and liberty are hanging in the balance? If Hannibal—Heaven help me!—should himself be pleased, against his nature, to show us mercy, we should nevertheless deem life a worthless boon, if we had seemed to you unworthy of being ransomed. There once came back to Rome some prisoners whom Pyrrhus had allowed to go scot-free; but they came back in company with envoys, the first men of the state, whom you had sent to ransom them. Am I to come back to my country as a citizen not reckoned to be worth three hundred pieces? Every man, Conscript Fathers, has his own way of thinking. I know that my life and person are in jeopardy; but I am troubled more by the danger to my honour—lest we depart under your

[a] habet animum ς: animum *P*.

A.U.C. 538 damnati ac repulsi abeamus; neque enim vos pretio pepercisse homines credent."

LX. Ubi is finem fecit, extemplo ab ea turba quae in comitio erat clamor flebilis est sublatus, manusque ad curiam tendebant orantes ut sibi
2 liberos fratres cognatos redderent. Feminas quoque metus ac necessitas in foro[1] turbae virorum immiscuerat. Senatus summotis arbitris consuli coep-
3 tus. Ibi cum sententiis variaretur, et alii redimendos de publico, alii nullam publice impensam faciendam,
4 nec prohibendos ex privato redimi; si quibus argentum in praesentia deesset, dandam ex aerario pecuniam mutuam praedibusque ac praediis caven-
5 dum populo censerent; tum T. Manlius Torquatus, priscae ac nimis durae, ut plerisque videbatur,[2] severitatis, interrogatus sententiam ita locutus fertur:
6 "Si tantummodo postulassent legati pro iis qui in hostium potestate sunt, ut redimerentur, sine ullius insectatione eorum brevi sententiam pere-
7 gissem; quid enim aliud quam admonendi essetis, ut morem traditum a patribus necessario ad rem militarem exemplo servaretis? Nunc autem, cum prope gloriati sint quod se hostibus dediderint, praeferrique non captis modo in acie ab hostibus, sed etiam iis[3] qui Venusiam Canusiumque pervene-

[1] in foro *Gronovius*: in foro ac *P*: foro ac *Koehler*: in foro ac comitio *M. Mueller*: *deleted by Voss.*
[2] videbatur ς (*Madvig*)· uideuatur P^2: uideatur P^1.
[3] iis ς: ab iis *P*.

[1] The Comitium was an open area next to the Curia. Here stood the male relatives of the prisoners, and on the outskirts of the crowd (in the Forum, which lay just beyond the Comitium and sometimes, as in this sentence, is thought of as including it) their wives and mothers. The children

condemnation and rebuff; for the world will never believe that you were niggardly about the cost." B.C. 216

LX. As soon as he had finished speaking, the throng in the Comitium began to utter doleful cries, and holding out their hands to the Curia besought the senators to give them back their sons, their brothers, and their kinsmen. Even the women had been driven by their fear and destitute condition to mingle in the Forum with the crowd of men.[1] The senate was cleared of strangers and the debate began. Opinions differed. Some were for ransoming the prisoners at the public cost; others would have no money disbursed by the state, but would not prohibit ransoming at the expense of individuals, and to such as might not have the money in hand proposed to grant loans from the treasury, guarding the people against loss by taking sureties and mortgages. Then Titus Manlius Torquatus, a man of an old-fashioned and, as it seemed to many, a too harsh austerity, was called upon for his opinion and spoke as follows:

"If, in pleading the cause of those who are in the hands of our enemies, their representatives had been content to ask that they be ransomed, I should have said my say in a few words, without reflecting upon any of them; for what else need I have done than warn you to hold fast to the tradition of our fathers and teach a lesson necessary for military discipline? But as it is, since they have almost boasted of having surrendered to the enemy, and have held that they are to be preferred not only to those who were captured by the enemy in battle, but also to those who made their way to Venusia and Canusium, and

were not admitted even to the Forum, as Livy implies when in the foregoing sentence in the text he omits the word *patres*.

A.U.C. 538 runt, atque ipsi C. Terentio consuli aequum cen-
suerint, nihil vos eorum, patres conscripti, quae illic
8 acta sunt ignorare patiar. Atque utinam haec
quae apud vos acturus sum Canusi apud ipsum
exercitum agerem, optimum testem ignaviae cuiusque
et virtutis, aut unus hic saltem adesset P. Sempronius, quem si isti ducem secuti essent, milites
hodie in castris Romanis, non captivi in hostium
9 potestate essent. Sed[1] cum, fessis pugnando
hostibus tum victoria laetis, et ipsis plerisque
regressis in castra sua, noctem ad erumpendum
liberam habuissent, et septem milia[2] armatorum
hominum erumpere etiam per confertos[3] hostes
possent, neque per se ipsi id facere conati sunt
10 neque alium sequi voluerunt. Nocte prope tota P.
Sempronius Tuditanus non destitit monere, adhortari eos, dum paucitas hostium circa castra, dum
quies ac silentium esset, dum nox inceptum tegere
posset, se ducem sequerentur: ante lucem pervenire
11 in tuta loca, in sociorum urbes posse. Si ut
avorum memoria P. Decius tribunus militum in
Samnio, si ut[4] nobis adulescentibus priore Punico
bello M. Calpurnius Flamma[5] trecentis voluntariis,
cum ad tumulum eos capiendum situm inter medios
duceret hostes, dixit: 'Moriamur, milites, et morte
nostra eripiamus ex obsidione circumventas legiones,'
12 —si hoc P. Sempronius diceret, nec viros equidem
nec Romanos vos ducerem,[6] si nemo tantae virtutis

[1] sed *Gronovius*: et *P*.

[2] septem millia ς: septem *P*.

[3] per confertos *Alschefski*: confertos *P*.

[4] si ut . . . si ut *Madvig*: sicut . . . sicut *P*.

[5] M. Calpurnius Flamma *H. J. Mueller*: calpurnius flamma *P*.

[6] equidem . . . ducerem *Koch*: quidem . . . duceret *P*.

even to the consul, Gaius Terentius himself, I will not permit you to be ignorant, Conscript Fathers, of any part of their conduct there. And I wish that what I am going to say to you I might say at Canusium in the presence of the army itself, the most competent witness to any man's cowardice or valour, or that Sempronius, at least, were with us here, whose leadership if yonder men had followed, they would to-day be soldiers in a Roman camp, not prisoners in the hands of our enemies. But when the enemy, worn out with fighting, and rejoicing in their victory, had themselves for the most part gone back to their own camp and left the night free for a sally; though seven thousand armed men could have forced their way even through a close array of foes, they neither attempted to do this of themselves, nor yet were willing to follow another. During almost all that night Publius Sempronius Tuditanus ceased not to admonish and exhort them to let him lead them, while only a few of their enemies were near the camp, while everything was hushed and still, while the darkness might afford a cover for their enterprise. Before daylight, he declared, they could reach a place of safety among the towns of the allies. If he had said what, within the recollection of our grandsires, Publius Decius, tribune of the soldiers, said in Samnium; or what Marcus Calpurnius Flamma said, when we ourselves were young men, in the former Punic war, to three hundred volunteers whom he was leading to take a hill that rose in the very midst of the enemy: 'Soldiers, let us die, and by our death set free the beleaguered legions'—if Publius Sempronius had said *this*, I should have deemed you no true men, to say nothing of Romans,

B.C. 216

A.U.C. 538 13 exstitisset comes. Viam non ad gloriam magis
quam ad salutem ferentem demonstrat; reduces[1] in
patriam ad parentes ad coniuges ac liberos facit.
14 Ut servemini deest vobis animus; quid, si moriendum
pro patria esset, faceretis? Quinquaginta milia
civium sociorumque circa vos eo ipso die caesa
iacent. Si tot exempla virtutis non movent, nihil
unquam movebit; si tanta clades vilem[2] vitam non
15 fecit, nulla faciet. Liberi atque incolumes desiderate
patriam; immo desiderate, dum patria est, dum
cives eius estis. Sero[3] nunc desideratis, deminuti
capite, abalienati iure civium, servi Carthaginiensium
16 facti. Pretio redituri estis eo unde ignavia ac
nequitia abistis? P. Sempronium, civem vestrum,
non audistis arma capere ac sequi se iubentem:[4]
Hannibalem post paulo audistis castra prodi et arma
17 tradi iubentem.[5] Quamquam[6] quid ego[7] ignaviam
istorum accuso, cum scelus possim accusare? Non
modo enim sequi recusarunt bene monentem, sed
obsistere ac retinere conati sunt, ni strictis gladiis
viri fortissimi inertes summovissent. Prius, inquam,
P. Sempronio per civium agmen quam per hostium
18 fuit erumpendum. Hos cives patria desideret?
Quorum si ceteri similes fuissent, neminem hodie ex
19 iis qui ad Cannas pugnaverunt, civem haberet. Ex

[1] demonstrat; reduces *Lipsius*: demonstraret duces *P*.
[2] uilem ς: uelem P^1: inuelem P^2.
[3] sero ς: desero *P*.
[4] iubentem ς: iuuentem P^2: iuuentutem P^1.
[5] iubentem ς: iuuentutem *P*.
[6] quamquam *Ussing*: quam *P*.
[7] quid ego *Weissenborn*: ego *P*.

if none had come forward to share so brave an exploit. B.C. 216 But instead he points out to you a road that leads to safety as surely as to fame. He proposes to restore you to your country, to your parents, to your wives and children. You lack even the spirit to be saved! What would you do then if your country called on you to die? Fifty thousand fellow Romans and allies lay slaughtered round you that very day. If so many brave examples could not move you, nothing ever will. If that dreadful carnage has not made life cheap, none ever will. Long for your country, whilst you are free and unattainted. Nay, rather, long for it whilst it *is* your country, whilst you are reckoned with its citizens. Too late now is your longing; you have forfeited your status, lost your civic rights, been made slaves of the Carthaginians. Do you think to return, for ransom, to that condition which you forfeited by cowardice and turpitude? You would not listen to Publius Sempronius, your fellow citizen, when he bade you arm and follow him; but you listened to Hannibal a little later, when he bade you betray the camp and surrender your arms. But why do I charge these men with cowardice when I could bring against them a charge of crime? For not only did they refuse to follow a man who gave them good advice, but they tried to thwart and hinder him; and those heroic men were forced to draw their swords and thrust the cowards from their path. Aye, Publius Sempronius must needs break through a band of Roman citizens before he could break through their enemies! Can their country wish to recover such citizens as these? If the others had resembled these, she would possess to-day no single citizen of all those who fought at Cannae. Out of

A.U.C. 538 milibus septem armatorum sescenti exstiterunt qui erumpere auderent, qui in patriam liberi atque armati redirent, neque his sescentis[1] hostes ob-
20 stitere: quam tutum iter duarum prope legionum agmini futurum censetis fuisse? Haberetis hodie viginti milia armatorum Canusi fortia fidelia, patres conscripti. Nunc autem quem ad modum hi boni fidelesque—nam fortes ne ipsi quidem dixerint—
21 cives esse possunt? Nisi quis credere potest adfuisse[2] erumpentibus, qui, ne erumperent, obsistere conati sunt; aut non invidere eos cum incolumitati, tum gloriae illorum per virtutem partae, cum sibi timorem ignaviamque servitutis ignominiosae causam
22 esse sciant. Maluerunt in tentoriis latentes simul lucem atque hostem exspectare, cum silentio noctis erumpendi occasio esset. At enim ad[3] erumpendum e castris defuit animus, ad tutanda fortiter castra
23 animum habuerunt; dies noctesque aliquot obsessi vallum armis,[4] se ipsi tutati vallo sunt; tandem ultima ausi passique, cum omnia subsidia vitae deessent[5] adfectisque fame viribus arma iam sustinere nequirent, necessitatibus magis humanis quam
24 armis victi sunt. Orto sole hostis ad vallum accessit;[6] ante secundam horam, nullam fortunam certaminis experti, tradiderunt arma ac se ipsos.

[1] sescentis (sex-) *Ingerslev* (*Madvig*): sexcentis milia ς: sescenta milia *P*.
[2] adfuisse *Luchs*: fuisse ut *P*: fuisse utiles *Koch*.
[3] at enim ad ς: ad *P*.
[4] armis *Gronovius*: arma *P*.
[5] deessent ς: abdesunt P^1: desunt P^2.
[6] hostis . . . accessit ς: ab hostibus . . . accessit *P*.

seven thousand soldiers, six hundred were sufficiently courageous to force their way through and return to their country, free and armed. Nor did these six hundred encounter any opposition from the enemy; how safe then, think you, would have been their march, if they had amounted almost to two legions? You would have to-day under arms at Canusium, Conscript Fathers, twenty thousand brave and loyal men. But how can these men now be good and loyal citizens—for they themselves would hardly claim to be brave? Unless we are to believe that they helped their comrades to sally out, when in fact they tried to prevent the sally; or that they grudge not those men both the safety and the renown their courage has earned them, knowing, as they do, that fear and cowardice are the cause of their own disgraceful servitude. They had a good chance of escaping in the silence of the night, but preferred to hide in their tents and await both the day and the enemy. But perhaps, though they lacked the courage to sally forth, they had courage enough for a valiant defence of the camp? Perhaps they were besieged for several days and nights, and protected the rampart with their swords, and themselves with the rampart? and finally, after suffering the last extremities, when every support of life gave out and their strength was so impaired with hunger that they could now no longer hold up their shields, they were overcome by the necessities of human nature and not by arms? Nay, the sun was up when the enemy approached the rampart, and the day was not two hours old when, without once putting their fortune to the test of battle, they surrendered both their arms and their persons. Such, mark you, were B.C. 216

A.U.C. 538 25 Haec vobis istorum[1] per biduum militia fuit. Cum
in acie[2] stare ac pugnare decuerat,[3] in castra[4] refugerunt; cum pro vallo pugnandum erat, castra
tradiderunt, neque in acie neque in castris utiles.
26 Et vos[5] redimamus? Cum erumpere e castris
oportet, cunctamini ac manetis; cum manere et[6]
castra tutari armis necesse est, et castra et arma
27 et vos ipsos traditis hosti. Ego non magis istos
redimendos, patres conscripti, censeo quam illos
dedendos Hannibali qui per medios hostes e castris
eruperunt ac per summam virtutem se patriae
restituerunt."

LXI. Postquam Manlius dixit, quamquam patrum
quoque plerosque captivi cognatione attingebant,
praeter exemplum civitatis minime in captivos iam
inde antiquitus indulgentis, pecuniae quoque summa
2 homines movit, quia[7] nec aerarium exhauriri,[8] magna
iam summa erogata in servos ad militiam emendos
armandosque, nec Hannibalem maxime huiusce rei,
3 ut fama erat, egentem locupletari volebant. Cum
triste responsum, non redimi captivos, redditum

[1] istorum *Weissenborn*: ipsorum *P*.
[2] in acie ς: acie *P*.
[3] decuerat ς: decuerit *P*.
[4] in castra *Luchs*: cum in castra *P*.
[5] et vos *Alschefski*: quos *P*: uos ς.
[6] manere et ς: manere *P*.
[7] quia ς: quam *P*: qua ς.
[8] exhauriri *C. Heraeus*: exaurire *P*.

---

[1] But the senate could not keep Hannibal from making money out of his prisoners. When the senate would not ransom them, he sold them into slavery, and Polybius (see Livy XXXIV. 1. 6) told how, in 194 B.C., at the request of Flamininus, the Greek states bought up and liberated a

the exploits these men performed during two days. B.C. 216
When they ought to have stood fast in the line and fought, they fled to their tents; when they ought to have fought for their stockade, they surrendered the camp, worthless alike in the field and behind entrenchments. And you would have us ransom you? When it is time to sally from your camp, you hesitate and stop there; when it is needful that you stop and defend it with your swords, you hand over camp and swords and your own bodies to the enemy! No, Conscript Fathers, I would no more vote for ransoming these men than I would for giving those others up to Hannibal, who forced their way from the camp through the midst of enemies, and, by exerting the utmost valour, gave themselves back to their country."

LXI. After the speech of Manlius, though most of the senators, too, had relatives amongst the prisoners, yet, besides the example of a state which had shown from of old the scantiest consideration for prisoners of war, they were also moved by the greatness of the sum required, not wishing either to exhaust the treasury, on which they had already made a heavy draft to purchase slaves and arm them for service, or to furnish Hannibal with money[1]—the one thing of which he was rumoured to stand most in need. When the stern reply, that the prisoners would not be ransomed, had gone forth,

great number of Roman prisoners who had been purchased from Hannibal. No less than twelve hundred were freed by the Achaeans alone, at a cost to their state of one hundred talents. Valerius Maximus (v. ii. 6), puts the whole number at two thousand, and doubtless thousands more had died in the course of twenty-two years.

A.U.C. 538 esset, novusque super veterem luctus tot iactura
civium adiectus esset, cum magnis fletibus questi-
4 busque legatos ad portam prosecuti sunt. Unus ex
iis domum abiit, quod fallaci reditu in castra iure
iurando se exsolvisset. Quod ubi innotuit relatum-
que ad senatum est, omnes censuerunt comprehen-
dendum et custodibus publice datis deducendum ad
Hannibalem esse.

5 Est et alia de captivis fama: decem primo legatos[1]
venisse; de eis cum dubitatum in senatu esset,
admitterentur in urbem necne, ita admissos esse ne
6 tamen iis senatus daretur; morantibus deinde longius
omnium spe alios tres insuper legatos venisse, L.
7 Scribonium et C. Calpurnium et L. Manlium; tum
demum ab cognato Scriboni tribuno plebis de redi-
mendis captivis relatum esse nec censuisse redimendos senatum; et novos legatos tres ad Hannibalem
8 revertisse, decem veteres remansisse, quod per
causam recognoscendi nomina captivorum ad Hannibalem ex itinere regressi religione sese exsolvissent;
de iis dedendis magna contentione actum in senatu
esse, victosque paucis sententiis qui dedendos cen-
9 suerint; ceterum proximis censoribus adeo omnibus
notis ignominiisque confectos esse ut quidam eorum

[1] primo legatos *Luchs*: primos *P*: primo *Woelfflin*.

---

[1] This seems to be a fusion of the account preserved by Appian (*Hann.* 28), where the number of envoys is given as three, with the commoner version of the story, which speaks of ten. The combination may have been made by the C. Acilius who wrote a history in Greek in which he told of the battle of Cannae (Cicero, *De Officiis* III. 115), and is perhaps the man whose name is given by the MSS. of the Summary of Book LIII. as c. iulius (cf. Schanz-Hosius, *Römische Literaturgeschichte*, I.^{4}, p. 177).

and fresh sorrow had been added to the old, at the loss of so many of their fellow-citizens, the crowd attended the envoys to the gate with many tears and lamentations. One of them departed to his home, pretending to have freed himself from his oath when he deceitfully returned to the enemy's camp. As soon as this became known and was reported to the senators, they voted unanimously to arrest him and appointed guards to conduct him back to Hannibal. B.C. 216

There is also another account[1] of the prisoners of war: that ten envoys came at first, and that the senate, after hesitating whether or no to admit them to the City, admitted them, with the proviso that they should have no hearing. Later, on their delaying longer than anybody had anticipated, three additional envoys came, namely Lucius Scribonius and Gaius Calpurnius and Lucius Manlius; then at last a motion was made in the senate by a kinsman of Scribonius, who was tribune of plebs,[2] that the prisoners be ransomed, but the motion was defeated; the three new envoys now returned to Hannibal, but the original ten remained in Rome, alleging that they had freed themselves of their obligation by going back to Hannibal's camp, after starting on their journey, under the pretext of reviewing the prisoners' names. A proposal to surrender them was hotly debated in the senate and was lost by only a few votes. However, under the next censors the ten were so overwhelmed with every species of reprobation and disgrace that some of them killed themselves forthwith, and the rest

[2] This was probably the L. Scribonius Libo mentioned at XXIII. xxi. 6.

A.U.C. 538 mortem sibi ipsi extemplo consciverint, ceteri non
foro solum omni deinde vita, sed prope luce ac
10 publico caruerint. Mirari magis adeo discrepare
inter auctores quam quid veri sit discernere queas.
Quanto autem maior ea clades superioribus cladibus fuerit, vel[1] ea res indicio est, quod fides sociorum,[2]
quae ad eam[3] diem firma steterat, tum labare[4]
coepit, nulla profecto alia de re quam quod despera-
11 verant de imperio. Defecere autem ad Poenos hi
populi: Campani, Atellani,[5] Calatini, Hirpini, Apu-
lorum pars, Samnites praeter Pentros, Bruttii omnes,
12 Lucani, praeter hos Uzentini et Graecorum omnis
ferme ora, Tarentini, Metapontini, Crotonienses
13 Locrique, et Cisalpini omnes Galli. Nec tamen eae
clades defectionesque sociorum moverunt ut pacis
usquam[6] mentio apud Romanos fieret, neque ante
consulis Romam adventum nec postquam is rediit
14 renovavitque memoriam acceptae cladis; quo in
tempore ipso adeo magno animo civitas fuit ut
consuli ex tanta clade, cuius ipse causa maxima
fuisset, redeunti et obviam itum frequenter ab omnibus ordinibus sit et gratiae actae quod de re publica
15 non desperasset; qui si Carthaginiensium ductor
fuisset, nihil recusandum supplicii foret.

[1] vel ς: uelde *P*.
[2] indicio est, quod fides sociorum *Alschefski*: indiciorum *P*.
[3] ad eam ς: eadem *P*.
[4] labare ς: laborare *P*: labrare ς.
[5] Campani, Atellani *Weissenborn*: atellani *P*.
[6] usquam *P*: umquam ς.

---

[1] This list includes all the peoples of Italy who revolted at one time or another during the war with Hannibal.

[2] An allusion to the alleged Carthaginian custom of

during all the remainder of their lives avoided not B.C. 216
only the Forum, but, one might almost say, the light of day and the public streets. It is more amazing that the authorities should be so divergent than easy to make out the truth.

For the rest, how greatly this disaster exceeded those that had gone before is plain from this: the loyalty of the allies, which had held firm until the day of Cannae, now began to waver, assuredly for no other reason than because they had lost all hope of the empire. Now these are the peoples that revolted: the Campanians, the Atellani, the Calatini, the Hirpini, a part of the Apulians, all the Samnites but the Pentri, all the Bruttii, the Lucanians, and besides these the Uzentini and almost all the Greeks on the coast, the Tarentines, the Metapontines, the Crotoniates and the Locri, together with all the Cisalpine Gauls.[1] Yet these disasters and the falling away of the allies could not induce the Romans anywhere to mention peace, either before the consul came to Rome or after his coming had turned men's thoughts anew to the calamity which they had suffered. In that very hour there was such courage in the hearts of the citizens that when the consul was returning from that defeat for which he himself had been chiefly responsible, a crowd of all sorts and conditions went out to meet him on the way, and gave him thanks because he had not despaired of the state; whereas, had he been the commander of the Carthaginians, there was no punishment he would not have been compelled to suffer.[2]

crucifying incompetent generals. See XXXVIII. xlviii. 13 and Valerius Maximus II. vii. *Ext.* 1.

LIBRI XXII PERIOCHA

Hannibal per continuas vigilias in paludibus oculo amisso in Etruriam venit; per quas paludes quadriduo et tribus noctibus sine ulla requie iter fecit. C. Flaminius consul, homo temerarius, contra auspicia profectus, signis militaribus effossis, quae tolli non poterant, et ab equo quem conscenderat per caput devolutus, insidiis ab Hannibale circumventus ad Thrasymennum lacum cum exercitu caesus est. Sex milia, quae eruperant, fide ab Atherbale[1] data perfidia Hannibalis vincta sunt. Cum ad nuntium cladis Romae luctus esset, duae matres ex insperato receptis filiis gaudio mortuae sunt. Ob hanc cladem ex Sibyllinis libris ver sacrum votum.

Cum deinde Q. Fabius Maximus dictator adversus Hannibalem missus nollet acie cum eo confligere, ne contra ferocem tot victoriis hostem territos[2] adversis proeliis milites pugnae[3] committeret, et opponendo se tantum conatus Hannibalis impediret, M. Minucius magister equitum, ferox et temerarius, criminando dictatorem tamquam segnem et timidum effecit ut populi iussu aequaretur ei cum dictatore imperium; divisoque exercitu cum iniquo loco conflixisset et in magno discrimine legiones eius essent, superveniente cum exercitu Fabio Maximo liberatus est. Quo beneficio victus castra

[1] ab atherbale (*or* attherbale) *MSS.*: a Maharbale *Cod. Leidensis and ed. prin.* (*to agree with Liv.* XXII. vi. 11).
[2] hostem territos *edd.* (*after* hostem territum . . . militem *of the Aldine ed.*): hostem *MSS.*
[3] pugnae *cod. Vossianus and ed. prin.*: pugnare *MSS.*

---

[1] See note on text.

SUMMARY OF BOOK XXII

Hannibal, losing sleep continuously in the marshes, went blind in one eye, and reached Etruria after marching through the swamps for four days and three nights without repose. Gaius Flaminius the consul, a headstrong man, set out, against the warning of the auspices, after digging out the military standards which they had been unable to pull up, and after the horse which he had mounted had thrown him over its head; and, entrapped by Hannibal in an ambush at Lake Thrasymennus, was slain and his army cut to pieces. Six thousand men who had broken through the enemy's lines were thrown into chains through Hannibal's perfidy, notwithstanding the pledge which Atherbal[1] had given them. While the Romans were mourning at the tidings which had come of this calamity, two mothers died of joy on recovering the sons whom they had given up for lost. Because of this defeat a Sacred Spring was vowed, by the direction of the Sibylline Books.

When, after that, Quintus Fabius Maximus, who had been sent out as dictator to oppose Hannibal, was loath to meet him in the open field, for he would not trust his soldiers, who had been cowed by these defeats, in a battle with an enemy emboldened by his victories; and was satisfied merely to thwart the efforts of Hannibal, by blocking his way; Marcus Minucius, the master of the horse, a rash and headstrong man, charging the dictator with sluggishness and timidity persuaded the people to decree that his own authority should be equal to that of the dictator. But, the army being divided between them, Minucius gave battle in an unfavourable position, and his legions were in great peril, when Fabius Maximus came up with his army and saved him. Won over by this generosity, he joined his camp to that of

cum eo iunxit et patrem eum salutavit idemque facere milites iussit.

Hannibal, vastata Campania inter Casilinum oppidum et Calliculam montem a Fabio clusus, sarmentis ad cornua boum alligatis et incensis praesidium Romanorum quod Calliculam insidebat fugavit et sic transgressus est saltum. Idemque Q. Fabi Maximi dictatoris, cum circumposita ureret, agro pepercit, ut illum tamquam proditorem suspectum faceret.

Aemilio deinde Paulo et Terentio Varrone consulibus ducibus[1] cum magna clade adversus Hannibalem ad Cannas pugnatum est, caesaque eo proelio Romanorum XLV cum Paulo consule et senatoribus XC et consularibus aut praetoriis aut aediliciis XXX. Post quae cum a nobilibus adulescentibus propter desperationem consilium de relinquenda Italia iniretur, P. Cornelius Scipio tribunus militum, qui Africanus postea vocatus est, stricto supra capita deliberantium ferro iuravit pro hoste se habiturum eum qui in verba sua non iurasset, effecitque ut omnes non relictum iri a se Italiam iure iurando adstringerentur.

Propter paucitatem militum VIII servorum armata sunt. Captivi, cum potestas esset redimendi, redempti non sunt.

Praeterea trepidationem urbis et luctum et res in Hispania meliore eventu gestas continet. Opimia et Florentia[2] virgines Vestales incesti damnatae sunt. Varroni obviam itum et gratiae actae, quod de re publica non desperasset.

[1] consulibus ducibus *Madvig*: consulibus et ducibus *MSS.*
[2] Florentia *MSS.* : Floronia *Liv.* XXII. lvii. 2.

Fabius, and, saluting him as his father, bade his army do the same.

Hannibal, after laying waste Campania, was penned in by Fabius between the town of Casilinum and Mount Callicula. Binding twigs about the horns of oxen and setting them on fire, he frightened off the detachment of Romans stationed on Callicula, and so marched over the pass. It was Hannibal, too, who spared the farm of Quintus Fabius Maximus the dictator, when burning all that country-side, in order to make him suspected of being a traitor.

Aemilius Paulus and Terentius Varro then became consuls and commanded the army which fought disastrously with Hannibal at Cannae. There were slain in that battle forty-five thousand Romans, including the consul Paulus, and ninety senators, and thirty others who had been consuls or praetors or aediles. After that some young nobles were plotting, in their despair, to abandon Italy, when Publius Cornelius Scipio, a tribune of the soldiers, who was later surnamed Africanus, held his drawn sword over the heads of the conspirators and vowing that he would treat as a public enemy whoever should not swear at his dictation, compelled them all to bind themselves with an oath not to abandon Italy.

There were so few soldiers that they armed eight thousand slaves. They were given an opportunity of ransoming the prisoners, but did not ransom them.

The book also describes the panic and grief in the City, and the operations, conducted more successfully, in Spain. The Vestals Opimia and Florentia were convicted of unchastity. The people went out to meet Varro, and thanked him because he had not despaired of the Republic.

INDEX OF NAMES

(*The References are to Pages.*)

INDEX OF NAMES

INDEX OF NAMES

Adapted from Kromayer–Veith, Schlachten–Atlas, published by H. Wagner & E. Debes, Leipzig